CHRYSLER, DODGE, PLYMOUTH
1972-1987 REAR WHEEL DRIVE
REPAIR AND TUNE-UP GUIDE

ALAN AHLSTRAND
Editor

CLYMER PUBLICATIONS

*World's largest publisher of books
devoted exclusively to automobiles and motorcycles*

A division of INTERTEC PUBLISHING CORPORATION
P.O. Box 12901, Overland Park, Kansas 66212

Copyright ©1987 Intertec Publishing Corp.

FIRST EDITION
First Printing December, 1983

SECOND EDITION
Updated to by Kalton C. Lahue to include 1984 models
First Printing August, 1984

THIRD EDITION
Updated to by Kalton C. Lahue to include 1985 models
First Printing September, 1985

FOURTH EDITION
Updated to by Kalton C. Lahue to include 1986 models
First Printing July, 1986

FIFTH EDITION
Updated to by Kalton C. Lahue to include 1987 models
First Printing August, 1987
Second Printing June, 1988

Printed in U.S.A.

ISBN: 0-89287-383-3

Production Coordinator, Lana J. Olson

Technical assistance from Chrysler Service and Training Group, Centerline, Michigan and Fullerton, California.
Technical illustrations courtesy of Chrysler Corporation.

COVER: Photographed by Michael Brown Photographic Productions, Los Angeles, California.

CONTENTS

QUICK REFERENCE DATA

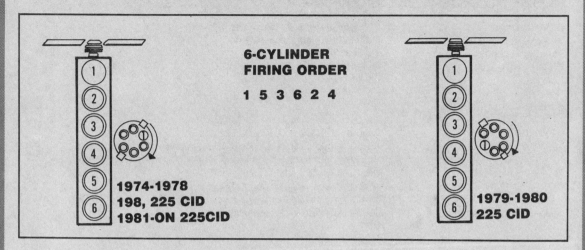

6-CYLINDER FIRING ORDER

1 5 3 6 2 4

1974-1978 198, 225 CID 1981-ON 225CID

1979-1980 225 CID

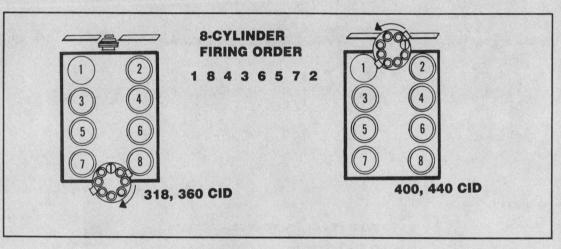

8-CYLINDER FIRING ORDER

1 8 4 3 6 5 7 2

318, 360 CID

400, 440 CID

RECOMMENDED OIL VISCOSITY

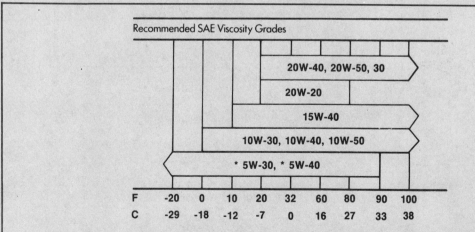

Recommended SAE Viscosity Grades

20W-40, 20W-50, 30

20W-20

15W-40

10W-30, 10W-40, 10W-50

* 5W-30, * 5W-40

F	-20	0	10	20	32	60	80	90	100
C	-29	-18	-12	-7	0	16	27	33	38

Temperature range anticipated before next oil change.

* SAE 5W-30 and 5W-40 are not recommended for vehicles equipped with a 318-4 Bbl. engine when operating at ambient temperatures above 60°F (16°C).

RECOMMENDED LUBRICANTS AND FLUIDS

Engine oil	API Designation SF
Coolant	Permanent ethylene glycol antifreeze
Power steering	Chrysler part No. 4318055 or equivalent
Front suspension and steering ball joints	Multi-mileage lubricant part No. 4318062 or equivalent
Clutch torque shaft bearing	Multi-mileage lubricant part No. 4318062 or equivalent
Rear axle, including Sure Grip	
1972	Hypoid lubricant part No. 2933565 or equivalent
1973-1976	Hypoid lubricant part No. 3744994 or equivalent
1977-on	Hypoid lubricant part No. 4318058 or equivalent
	Use friction modifier additive part No. 4318060 with Sure Grip axles
Manual transmission	DEXRON II automatic transmission fluid. Multi-purpose gear lubricant (SAE 90 or SAE 140) may be substituted to minimize gear rattle
Automatic transmission	DEXRON II automatic transmission fluid
Brake fluid	DOT 3
Front wheel bearings	High-temperature multi-purpose E.P. grease part No. 4318039 or equivalent
Manifold heat control valve	Manifold heat control solvent part No. 4318064 or equivalent
Choke, fast idle cam and throttle linkage	Chrysler combustion chamber conditioner part No. 4318001 or equivalent

FUEL PUMP PRESSURE SPECIFICATIONS

Engine Displacement	psi
198/225 cid	
1972-1980	3.5-5
1981-on	4-5.5
318 cid	
1972-1980	5-7
1981-on	5.75-7.25
340 cid	5-7
360 cid	5-7
400 cid	
1972-1974	3.5-5
1975	6-7.5[1]
1976-1978	5-7
440 cid	
1972-1974	3.5-5
1975	6-7.5[2]
1976-1978	5-7
440 cid HP	6.5-7
440 cid HP Police	5.5-6 .5

1. 2-bbl. Federal and 4-bbl. California only. For 4-bbl. Federal usage, 3.5-5 psi.
2. For California-sold vehicles only. For others, 4-5.5 psi.

CHRYSLER, DODGE, PLYMOUTH

1972-1987 REAR WHEEL DRIVE
REPAIR AND TUNE-UP GUIDE

CHAPTER ONE

GENERAL INFORMATION

This book provides lubrication, general maintenance and tune-up information for the following domestic Chrysler Corporation rear-wheel drive passenger cars manufactured between 1972-1987:
1. Chrysler.
    a. Cordoba.
    b. Fifth Avenue.
    c. Imperial.
    d. Imperial Le Baron.
    e. Le Baron.
    f. Newport.
    g. New Yorker.
    h. Town and Country.
2. Dodge.
    a. Aspen.
    b. Challenger.
    c. Coronet.
    d. Charger.
    e. Dart.
    f. Diplomat.
    g. Magnum.
    h. Mirada.
    i. Monaco.
    j. Polara.
    k. St. Regis.
3. Plymouth.
    a. Barracuda.
    b. Duster.
    c. Fury.
    d. Gran Fury.
    e. Road Runner.
    f. Satellite.
    g. Suburban.
    h. Valiant.
    i. Volare.

Due to the large number of vehicle/engine combinations used over this span of time, many of the maintenance procedures provided here are general in nature and may require some interpretation. Every effort has been made, however, to be as specific as possible.

Major mechanical procedures, such as rebuilding of the engine, transmission, differential, etc., are not provided. Many special tools and extensive experience are required for such work. Such service and repair should be entrusted to a dealer or automotive specialist.

Procedures requiring the use of special tools have been kept to a minimum. Where special tools are required, their designation is provided. Such tools may often be borrowed or rented or can be purchased directly from Miller Special Tools, 32615 Park Lane, Garden City, Michigan 48135. The resourceful mechanic can, in many cases, think of acceptable substitutes for special tools—there is always another way. However, using a substitute for a special tool is not recommended as it can be dangerous to you and may damage the part.

The terms NOTE, CAUTION and WARNING have specific meanings in this manual. A NOTE provides additional information to make a step or procedure easier or clearer. Disregarding a NOTE could cause inconvenience, but would not cause damage or personal injury.

A CAUTION emphasizes areas where equipment damage could result. Disregarding a CAUTION could cause permanent mechanical damage; however, personal injury is unlikely.

A WARNING emphasizes areas where personal injury or even death could result from negligence. Mechanical damage may also occur. WARNINGS *are to be taken seriously*. In some cases serious injury or death has resulted from disregarding such warnings.

MANUAL ORGANIZATION

This chapter describes the scope of this manual and provides some service hints and precautions to be observed. Recommended tools and test instruments necessary for proper tune-up and diagnostic work are also described.

Chapter Two provides procedures for isolating common automotive problems.

Chapter Three provides a plan for scheduled lubrication and preventive maintenance.

Chapter Four provides engine tune-up information and procedures.

Chapter Five covers engine and cylinder head removal/installation.

Carburetor adjustment and fuel pump testing is covered in Chapter Six.

Chapter Seven provides procedures for servicing the major electrical components such as the battery, alternator, starter motor and lighting systems.

Cooling system maintenance is discussed in Chapter Eight. Procedures are given for checking, cleaning and maintaining the system.

Instructions for bleeding, adjusting and relining brakes are provided in Chapter Nine.

Chapter Ten covers clutch adjustment procedures for all models equipped with a manual transmission.

Chapter Eleven provides replacement procedures for shock absorbers.

Chapter Twelve deals with minor body work and vinyl top repair.

Each chapter provides disassembly, repair and assembly procedures in easy-to-follow, step-by-step form. All procedures are given in the most practical sequence. Complex and lengthy operations are described in detail and are thoroughly illustrated. The exploded views show the correct sequence of parts; these can be of considerable help as a reference during disassembly and reassembly.

U.S. standards are used throughout and are accompanied by metric equivalents in parentheses where such reference might have practical value. Metric to inch conversion is given in **Table 1**.

IDENTIFICATION NUMBERS

Identification numbers are important when ordering replacement parts or identifying the automobile for registration purposes. The Vehicle Identification Number (VIN) is found at the top of the instrument panel at the left front edge and is visible through the windshield. See **Figure 1**. The engine serial number is stamped on a pad on the side of the engine block. Use these numbers when ordering replacement parts.

PARTS REPLACEMENT

Chrysler Corporation has made frequent internal component changes during the period covered by this book; some minor, some relatively major. When ordering replacement

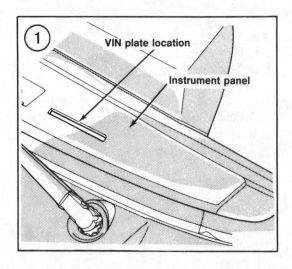

parts from a dealer or other parts distributor, always order by year, engine and chassis number. Write the numbers down and carry them with you. Compare new parts to old before purchasing them. If they are not alike, have the parts salesperson explain the difference.

SERVICE HINTS

Time, effort and frustration can be saved by following the practices suggested here.

1. "Front," as used in this manual, refers to the front of the vehicle; the front of any component is the end closest to the front of the vehicle. The left side of the vehicle is the driver's side; the right side of the vehicle is the passenger's side.

2. Never trust any jack, mechanical or hydraulic. Use jackstands to hold the car when working under it; always set the parking brake and block the wheels remaining on the ground.

3. Disconnect the negative battery cable when working on or near the electrical system and before disconnecting any wires. On most batteries, the negative terminal will be marked with a minus (-) sign and the positive terminal with a plus (+) sign. Never run the engine with the battery disconnected, as this can cause serious damage to the alternator.

4. When disassembling a part or component, a good practice is to tag the parts for location and mark all parts which mate together for location. Record the number and thickness of any shims as they are removed. Small parts, such as bolts, can be identified by placing them in plastic sandwich bags. Seal the bags and label them with masking tape and a marking pen. When reassembly will take place immediately, an accepted practice is to place small parts in a cupcake tin in the order of disassembly.

5. Finished surfaces should be protected from physical damage or corrosion. Keep gasoline and brake fluid off painted surfaces.

6. Use penetrating oil on frozen or tight bolts, then strike the bolt head a few times with a hammer and punch (use a screwdriver on screws). Avoid the use of heat where possible, as it can warp, melt or affect the temper of parts and also ruins finishes, especially paint.

7. Keep flames and sparks away from a charging battery or inflammable fluids and do not smoke in the area. It is a good idea to have a fire extinguisher handy in the work area.

8. No parts removed or installed in the procedures given in this book should require unusual force during disassembly or assembly. If a part is hard to remove or install, find out why before proceeding.

9. Cover all openings after removing parts or components to prevent dirt, small tools, etc. from falling in.

10. Read each procedure *completely* while looking at the actual parts before starting a job. Make sure you *thoroughly* understand what is to be done and then carefully follow the procedure, step-by-step.

11. Recommendations are occasionally made to refer service or maintenance to a dealer or a specialist in a particular field. In these cases, work will probably be done more quickly and economically than if you performed the job yourself.

12. In procedural steps, the term "replace" means to discard a defective part and replace it with a new or exchange unit. "Overhaul" means to remove, disassemble, inspect, measure, repair or replace defective parts, reassemble and install major systems and parts.

RECOMMENDED TOOLS

Some of the procedures in this manual specify special tools, which are generally expensive. Such tools can often be rented or bought, but it is usually more practical to have a dealer or repair shop perform the step which requires the special tool. Most of the procedures in this manual can be carried out with simple hand tools and test equipment familiar to the average home mechanic.

For proper servicing, you will need an assortment of ordinary hand tools. Recommended are:

   a. Combination wrenches.

   b. Sockets, socket extension(s) and a socket wrench.

c. Plastic mallet.

d. Small hammer.

e. Snap ring pliers.

f. Assorted pliers.

g. Phillips and flat-blade screwdrivers.

h. Feeler gauges (flat and round).

i. Tire pressure gauge.

j. Spark plug gauge.

k. Spark plug wrench.

Home mechanics intent on saving money and aggravation by doing their own repair and maintenance work should invest in the following test instruments.

Dwell Meter

A dwell meter (**Figure 2**) is useful for 1972 cars equipped with a breaker point ignition. It measures the distance of distributor cam rotation (in degrees) from the time the breaker points close until they open again while the engine is running. Since this angle is determined by the breaker point gap setting, dwell angle is an accurate indication of breaker point gap.

A dwell meter is not necessary for 1973 and later cars equipped with a breakerless ignition. Dwell is determined by an electronic control unit and cannot be changed.

Many tachometers intended for tuning and testing incorporate a dwell meter. Follow the manufacturer's instructions when using a combination instrument to measure dwell.

Tachometer

A tachometer is necessary for tune-up work, as ignition timing and carburetor adjustments must be made at specified engine speeds. The best instrument for this work is one with 2 ranges: a low range of 0-1,000 to 0-2,000 rpm for setting low or "curb" idle and a high range of 0-4,000 or more rpm for setting fast idle and checking ignition timing at different engine speeds. Tachometers with only one extended range (0-6,000 to 0-8,000 rpm) lack accuracy at lower speeds. The instrument should be capable of detecting changes of 25 rpm on the low range.

Timing Light

This instrument is required for accurate timing adjustment. The light is connected to

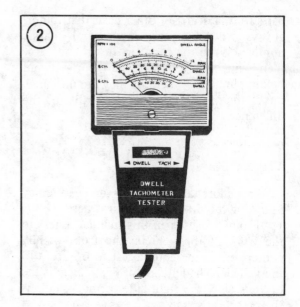

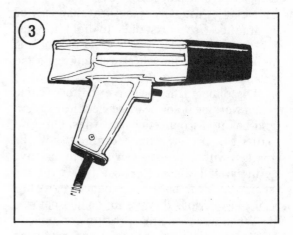

flash each time the No. 1 spark plug fires, making the position of the timing mark visible at that instant. When the engine is properly timed, the timing marks will be aligned.

Suitable timing lights range from inexpensive neon bulb types to powerful xenon strobe lights. See **Figure 3**. Neon timing lights are difficult to see and must be used in dimly lit areas. Xenon strobe timing lights can be used outside in bright sunlight. Xenon timing lights can be obtained for either AC or DC operation; the DC types can be operated from the car's battery. Timing lights with an inductive pickup are recommended for use with breakerless ignitions.

Compression Tester

The compression tester measures the pressure built up in each cylinder as the engine is turned over. The results, when properly interpreted, can indicate general cylinder and valve condition. Many compression testers have long flexible extensions as accessories (**Figure 4**).

Vacuum Gauge

The vacuum gauge (**Figure 5**) is one of the easiest instruments to use, but one of the hardest for the inexperienced mechanic to interpret. When interpreted with other findings, test results can give valuable clues to possible troubles and help isolate the cause of a problem.

Figure 6 shows a number of typical vacuum gauge readings with interpretations. Results should be compared with other test results, such as compression, before reaching conclusions.

Fuel Pressure Gauge

This instrument is needed for evaluating fuel pump performance. Usually a vacuum gauge and a fuel pressure gauge are combined.

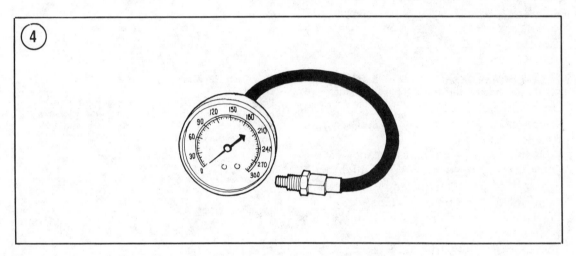

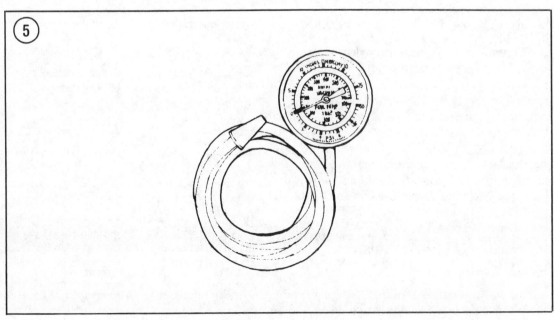

1. NORMAL READING
Reads 15 in. at idle.

2. LATE IGNITION TIMING
About 2 inches too low at idle.

3. LATE VALVE TIMING
About 4 to 8 inches low at idle.

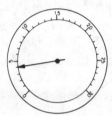

4. INTAKE LEAK
Low steady reading.

5. NORMAL READING
Drops to 2, then rises to 25 when accelerator is rapidly depressed and released.

6. WORN RINGS, DILUTED OIL
Drops to 0, then rises to 18 when accelerator is rapidly depressed and released.

7. STICKING VALVE(S)
Normally steady. Intermittently flicks downward about 4 in.

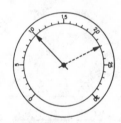

8. LEAKY VALVE
Regular drop about 2 inches.

9. BURNED OR WARPED VALVE
Regular, evenly spaced down-scale flick about 4 in.

10. WORN VALVE GUIDES
Oscillates about 4 in.

11. WEAK VALVE SPRINGS
Violent oscillation (about 10 in.) as rpm increases. Often steady at idle.

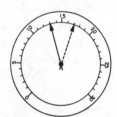

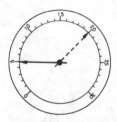

12. IMPROPER IDLE MIXTURE
Floats slowly between 13-17 in.

13. SMALL SPARK GAP or DEFECTIVE POINTS
Slight float between 14-16 in.

14. HEAD GASKET LEAK
Gauge floats between 5-19 in.

15. RESTRICTED EXHAUST SYSTEM
Normal when first started. Drops to 0 as rpm increases. May eventually rise to about 16.

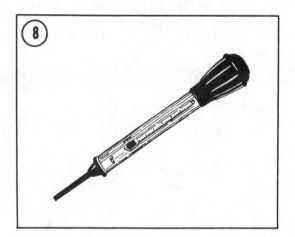

Voltmeter, Ammeter and Ohmmeter

A good voltmeter is required for testing ignition and other electrical systems. An instrument covering 0-20 volts is satisfactory. It should also have a 0-2 volt scale for testing relays, points or individual contacts where voltage drops are much smaller. Accuracy should be ±1/2 volt.

An ohmmeter measures electrical resistance. This instrument is useful in checking continuity (for open and short circuits) and testing fuses and lights.

The ammeter measures electrical current. Ammeters for automotive use should have scales covering 0-50 amperes and 0-250 amperes. These are useful for checking battery starting and charging currents.

Several inexpensive multimeters combine all 3 instruments (**Figure 7**) into one unit which fits into any toolbox. The ammeter ranges of such units are usually too low for automotive work. However, combination instruments designed especially for automotive diagnostic work are available at a reasonable price.

Hydrometer

Hydrometer testing is the best way to check the condition of unsealed batteries. The most efficient type is a temperature-compensated hydrometer with numbered gradations (**Figure 8**) from 1.100 to 1.300 rather than one with color-coded bands. Hydrometer use is described in Chapter Six.

Remote Starter Switch

An optional but convenient item of equipment is a remote starter switch. This is connected to the starter solenoid and permits cranking the engine from outside the car. It eliminates the need for an assistant during certain procedures, such as setting the breaker points.

Expendable Supplies

Certain expendable supplies are also required to correctly service your vehicle. These include greases, oil, gasket cement, RTV sealant, shop rags, cleaning solvent and distilled water. Special fastener locking compounds and silicone lubricants are available from a dealer or auto parts specialist to make maintenance simpler and easier. Solvent is available at auto parts stores and distilled water for the battery is available at most supermarkets.

SAFETY HINTS

A professional mechanic can work for years without sustaining a serious injury. If you observe a few rules of common sense and safety, you can safely service your own vehicle. You can also hurt yourself or damage your vehicle if you ignore these rules.
1. Never use gasoline as a cleaning solvent.
2. Never smoke or use a torch around flammable liquids such as cleaning solvents.
3. Never smoke or use a torch in areas where batteries are being charged. Highly explosive hydrogen gas is formed during the charging process.

4. Never arc the terminals of a battery to see if it is charged. The sparks can ignite the explosive hydrogen as easily as an open flame.

5. If welding or brazing is required on the vehicle, make sure that it is not in the area of the fuel tank or lines. In such case, the work should be entrusted to a specialist.

6. Always use the correct size wrench for loosening and tightening fasteners.

7. When replacing a fastener, make sure to use one with the same measurements and strength as the old one. Incorrect or mismatched fasteners can result in damage to the vehicle and possible personal injury.

8. Keep your work area clean and uncluttered.

9. Wear safety goggles in all operations involving drilling or grinding or the use of a chisel or an air hose.

10. Do not use worn tools or tools that are not appropriate to the job.

11. Keep a fire extinguisher handy. Be sure it is rated for gasoline and electrical fires.

12. When drying bearings or other rotating parts with compressed air, never allow the air jet to rotate the bearing or part; the jet is capable of rotating them at speeds far in excess of those for which they were designed. The bearing or rotating part is likely to disintegrate and cause serious injury and damage.

Table 1 METRIC CONVERSION CHART

mm	in.	mm	in.	mm	in.
0.01 = 0.0004		0.51 = 0.0201		1 = 0.0394	
0.02 = 0.0008		0.52 = 0.0205		2 = 0.0787	
0.03 = 0.0012		0.53 = 0.0209		3 = 0.1181	
0.04 = 0.0016		0.54 = 0.0213		4 = 0.1575	
0.05 = 0.0020		0.55 = 0.0217		5 = 0.1969	
0.06 = 0.0024		0.56 = 0.0221		6 = 0.2362	
0.07 = 0.0028		0.57 = 0.0224		7 = 0.2756	
0.08 = 0.0032		0.58 = 0.0228		8 = 0.3150	
0.09 = 0.0035		0.59 = 0.0232		9 = 0.3543	
0.10 = 0.0039		0.60 = 0.0236		10 = 0.3937	
0.11 = 0.0043		0.61 = 0.0240		11 = 0.4331	
0.12 = 0.0047		0.62 = 0.0244		12 = 0.4724	
0.13 = 0.0051		0.63 = 0.0246		13 = 0.5118	
0.14 = 0.0055		0.64 = 0.0252		14 = 0.5512	
0.15 = 0.0059		0.65 = 0.0256		15 = 0.5906	
0.16 = 0.0063		0.66 = 0.0260		16 = 0.6299	
0.17 = 0.0067		0.67 = 0.0264		17 = 0.6693	
0.18 = 0.0071		0.68 = 0.0268		18 = 0.7087	
0.19 = 0.0075		0.69 = 0.0272		19 = 0.7480	
0.20 = 0.0079		0.70 = 0.0276		20 = 0.7874	
0.21 = 0.0083		0.71 = 0.0280		21 = 0.8268	
0.22 = 0.0087		0.72 = 0.0284		22 = 0.8661	
0.23 = 0.0091		0.73 = 0.0287		23 = 0.9055	
0.24 = 0.0095		0.74 = 0.0291		24 = 0.9449	
0.25 = 0.0098		0.75 = 0.0295		25 = 0.9843	
0.26 = 0.0102		0.76 = 0.0299		26 = 1.0236	
0.27 = 0.0106		0.77 = 0.0303		27 = 1.0630	
0.28 = 0.0110		0.78 = 0.0307		28 = 1.1024	
0.29 = 0.0114		0.79 = 0.0311		29 = 1.1417	
0.30 = 0.0118		0.80 = 0.0315		30 = 1.1811	
0.31 = 0.0122		0.81 = 0.0320		31 = 1.2205	
0.32 = 0.0126		0.82 = 0.0323		32 = 1.2598	
0.33 = 0.0130		0.83 = 0.0327		33 = 1.2992	
0.34 = 0.0134		0.84 = 0.0331		34 = 1.3386	
0.35 = 0.0138		0.85 = 0.0335		35 = 1.3779	
0.36 = 0.0142		0.86 = 0.0339		36 = 1.4173	
0.37 = 0.0146		0.87 = 0.0343		37 = 1.4567	
0.38 = 0.0150		0.88 = 0.0347		38 = 1.4961	
0.39 = 0.0154		0.89 = 0.0350		39 = 1.5354	
0.40 = 0.0158		0.90 = 0.0354		40 = 1.5748	
0.41 = 0.0161		0.91 = 0.0358		41 = 1.6142	
0.42 = 0.0165		0.92 = 0.0362		42 = 1.6535	
0.43 = 0.0169		0.93 = 0.0366		43 = 1.6929	
0.44 = 0.0173		0.94 = 0.0370		44 = 1.7323	
0.45 = 0.0177		0.95 = 0.0374		45 = 1.7716	
0.46 = 0.0181		0.96 = 0.0378		46 = 1.8110	
0.47 = 0.0185		0.97 = 0.0382		47 = 1.8504	
0.48 = 0.0186		0.98 = 0.0386		48 = 1.8898	
0.49 = 0.0193		0.99 = 0.0390		49 = 1.9291	
0.50 = 0.0197				50 = 1.9685	

CHAPTER TWO

TROUBLESHOOTING

Troubleshooting mechanical problems can be relatively simple if you use orderly procedures and keep a few basic principles in mind.

The troubleshooting procedures in this chapter analyze typical symptoms and show logical methods of isolating causes. These are not the only methods. There may be several ways to solve a problem, but only a systematic, methodical approach can guarantee success.

Gather as many symptoms together as possible to aid in diagnosis. Note whether the engine lost power gradually or all at once, what color smoke (if any) came from the exhaust and so on. After the symptoms are defined, areas which could cause the problem are tested and analyzed. Guessing at the cause of a problem may eventually provide the solution, but it can also lead to frustration, wasted time and a series of expensive, unnecessary parts replacements.

You don't need exotic, complicated test equipment to determine whether repairs can be made at home. A few simple checks could save a large repair bill and time lost while the car sits in a dealer's service department. On the other hand, be realistic and don't attempt repairs beyond your abilities. Service departments tend to charge heavily to correct other people's mistakes.

During the years covered by this manual, Chrysler, Dodge and Plymouth Divisions used a large number of different displacement engines in their passenger car lines. These engines were used in an almost infinite number of combinations with various manual and automatic transmissions, carburetors and distributors. Because of these factors, it would be impossible to provide specific check-out procedures for all of the numerous combinations. Instead, the troubleshooting procedures given below have been purposely kept general in nature in order to cover the largest possible number of engine, transmission, carburetor and distributor combinations.

The following are commonly encountered problems.

STARTER

Starter system troubles are relatively easy to isolate. The following are common symptoms.

Engine Cranks Very Slowly or Not At All

Turn on the headlights. If the lights are very dim, the battery or connecting wires are most likely at fault. Check the battery with a hydrometer. Check wiring for breaks, shorts and dirty connections. If the battery and wires are all right, turn the headlights on and crank the engine. If the lights dim drastically, the starter is probably shorted to ground.

If the lights remain bright or dim slightly when cranking, the trouble may be in the starter, starter solenoid or wiring. If the starter spins, check the starter solenoid, relay and wiring to the ignition switch.

Connect a heavy jumper lead between the battery and solenoid terminals on the starter relay. If the engine cranks, the starter solenoid is good.

Place the transmission in NEUTRAL or PARK (automatic) or have an assistant depress and hold the clutch pedal (manual). Connect a heavy jumper lead between the battery and ignition terminals on the starter relay. If the engine cranks, the relay is good.

If it does not crank, connect a second jumper lead between the starter relay ground terminal and a good engine ground. If the engine cranks now, the starter relay is good but the neutral safety switch (automatic) or neutral start switch (manual) is defective or out of adjustment. If it still does not crank, replace the starter relay.

Some 1974-1975 models are equipped with seat belt/starter interlock systems. If the battery, cables and connections are satisfactory and no solenoid click is heard when the starter circuit is closed, the problem may be a malfunction in the interlock system.

If the starter still will not crank properly, refer the problem to a dealer or automotive electrical specialist.

Starter Turns, But Does Not Engage With Engine

This is usually caused by a defective pinion. The teeth on the pinion, flywheel ring gear or both may be worn too far to engage properly.

Starter Engages, But Does Not Crank Engine

This is usually caused by an open circuit in the solenoid armature or field coils or by a short or ground in the starter motor field coil or armature. Check out both systems to isolate the problem and then repair or replace the faulty component.

Starter Engages, But Will Not Disengage When Ignition Switch Is Released

Usually caused by a sticking starter solenoid or relay, but occasionally the pinion may jam on the flywheel. A sticking solenoid can sometimes be temporarily remedied by lightly tapping the solenoid with a piece of wood or a rubber mallet. The pinion can be temporarily freed on manual transmission cars by rocking the car in high gear.

Loud Grinding Noises When Starter Runs

The teeth on the pinion and/or flywheel are not meshing properly or the overrunning clutch mechanism is broken. Remove the starter and examine gear teeth and pinion drive assembly.

CHARGING SYSTEM

Charging system troubles may be in the alternator, voltage regulator or drive belt. When troubleshooting the charging system, observe the following precautions:

a. Do not polarize the alternator.

b. Do not short across or ground any of the charging system terminals unless specifically directed to do so in a procedure.

c. Never operate the alternator with the output terminal open circuited.

d. Make sure the alternator and battery are of the same ground polarity.

e. When connecting booster cables or a charger to the battery, connect negative terminal to negative terminal and positive terminal to positive terminal.

Instrument Panel Light
Shows Continuous Discharge

This usually means that battery charging is not taking place. Check drive belt tension. Check battery condition with hydrometer and electrical connections in the charging system. Finally, check the alternator and/or voltage regulator using procedures in Chapter Seven.

Instrument Panel Light
Shows Intermittent Discharge

Check drive belt tension and electrical connections. The trouble may be traced to worn alternator brushes or bad slip rings.

Battery Requires Frequent Addition of
Water or Lamps Require
Frequent Replacement

The alternator may be overcharging the battery or the voltage regulator is defective.

Noisy Alternator

Check for loose mountings and/or worn bearings.

ENGINE

These procedures assume the starter cranks the engine over normally. If not, refer to the *Starter* section.

Engine Won't Start

Could be caused by the ignition system or fuel system. First, determine if high voltage to spark plugs occurs. To do this, disconnect one spark plug wire and hold the exposed wire terminal about 1/4 to 1/2 in. from ground (any metal in the engine compartment) with insulated pliers. Crank the engine. If sparking does not occur or if the sparks are very weak, the trouble may be in the ignition system. If sparks occur properly, the trouble may be in the fuel system.

Engine Misses Steadily

Remove and ground each spark plug wire, one at a time. If engine miss increases, that cylinder is working properly. When a wire is disconnected and engine miss remains the same, that cylinder is not firing. Check spark

as described above. If no spark occurs for one cylinder only, check distributor cap, wire and spark plug. If spark occurs properly, check compression and intake manifold vacuum.

Engine Misses Erratically at All Speeds

Intermittent trouble can be difficult to find. It could be in the ignition system, intake system or fuel system. Follow troubleshooting procedures for these systems to isolate the trouble.

Engine Misses at Idle Only

Trouble could be in the ignition system or carburetor idle adjustment. Check idle mixture adjustment. Inspect for restrictions in the idle circuit. Check for inlet manifold and vacuum leaks.

Engine Misses at High Speed Only

Trouble is in the fuel system or ignition system. Check accelerator pump operation, fuel pump delivery, fuel line, etc. Check spark plugs and wires.

Low Performance at All
Speeds, Poor Acceleration

Trouble is usually in the ignition, fuel or exhaust system. Follow troubleshooting procedures for these systems to isolate trouble.

Excessive Fuel Consumption

Could be caused by a number of seemingly unrelated factors. Check for clutch slippage, brake drag, defective wheel bearings, poor front-end alignment, faulty ignition, leaky gas tank or lines and carburetor condition.

Low Oil Pressure Shown by
Oil Pressure Gauge or Light

If the oil pressure gauge shows a low pressure reading or if the indicator lamp lights with the engine running, stop the engine immediately. Coast to a stop with the clutch disengaged or the automatic transmission in NEUTRAL. The trouble may be caused by low oil level, blockage in the oil line, defective oil pump, overheated engine or a defective oil pressure gauge/light. Check the oil level and drive belt tension. Check for shorted oil pressure sender with an ohmmeter or other continuity tester. Do not restart the engine until you know why the low indication was given and you are sure the problem has been corrected.

Engine Overheats

Usually caused by trouble in the cooling system. Check the level of coolant in the radiator, condition of the drive belt and connecting hoses for leaks and loose connections. Check the operation of the fan fluid clutch, if so equipped. This problem can also be caused by late ignition or valve timing.

Engine Stalls As It Warms Up

The choke valve may be stuck closed, the manifold heat control valve may be stuck, the engine idling speed may be set too low or the emission control (PCV) valve may be faulty.

Engine Stalls After Idling or Slow-speed Driving

Can be caused by defective fuel pump, overheated engine, high carburetor float level, incorrect idle adjustment or a defective PCV valve.

Engine Stalls After High-speed Driving

Vapor lock within the fuel lines caused by an overheated engine is usually the cause of this trouble. Inspect and service the cooling system. If the trouble persists, changing to a different fuel or shielding the fuel line from engine heat may prove helpful.

Engine Backfires

Several causes can be suspected: ignition timing, overheating, excessive carbon in cylinders, wrong heat range spark plugs, hot or sticking valve, cracked distributor cap, a hole in the exhaust system, excessively rich fuel/air mixture or a defective air pump diverter valve.

Smoky Exhaust

Blue smoke indicates excessive oil consumption usually caused by worn rings or valve guides. Black smoke indicates an excessively rich fuel mixture.

Excessive Oil Consumption

Can be caused by external leaks through broken seals or gaskets or by burning oil in the combustion chamber. Check the oil pan and the front and rear of the engine for oil leaks. If the oil is not leaking externally, valve stem-to-guide clearances may be excessive, piston rings may be worn, cylinder walls may be scored or the PCV valve may be plugged.

Noisy Engine

1. *Regular clicking sound*—Valve and/or tappets out of adjustment.
2. *Ping or chatter on load or acceleration*—Spark knock due to low octane fuel, carbon buildup, overly advanced ignition timing and causes mentioned under *Engine Backfires*.
3. *Light knock or pound with engine not under load*—Indicates worn connecting rod bearings, worn camshaft bearings, misaligned crankpin and/or lack of engine oil.
4. *Light metallic double knock, usually heard during idle*—Worn or loose piston pin or bushing and/or lack of oil.
5. *Chattering or rattling during acceleration*—Worn rings, cylinder walls, low ring tension and/or broken rings.
6. *Hollow, bell-like muffled sound when engine is cold*—Piston slap due to worn pistons, cylinder walls, collapsed piston skirts, excessive clearances, misaligned connecting rods and/or lack of oil.
7. *Dull, heavy metallic knock under load or acceleration, especially when cold*—Regular noise: worn main bearings; irregular noise: worn thrust bearings.

BREAKER POINT IGNITION SYSTEM

The following procedures assume the battery is in good enough condition to crank the engine at a normal rate.

No Sparks to One Plug

The only causes are defective distributor cap or spark plug wire. Examine the distributor cap for moisture, dirt, carbon tracking caused by flashover and cracks. Check spark plug wire for breaks or loose connectors.

No Spark to Any Plug

This could indicate trouble in the primary or secondary ignition circuits. First, remove the coil wire from the center tower of the distributor cap. Hold the wire end about 1/4 in. from ground with insulated pliers. Crank the engine. If sparks are produced, the trouble is in the rotor or distributor cap. Remove the cap and check for burns, moisture, dirt, carbon tracking, cracks, etc. Check rotor for excessive burning, pitting and cracks. Check rotor continuity with a test light.

If the coil does not produce any spark, check the secondary wire for a break. If the wire is good, turn the engine over so the breaker points are open. Examine them for excessive gap, burning, pitting or loose connections. With the points open, check voltage from the coil to ground with a voltmeter or test lamp. If voltage is present, the coil is probably defective. Have it checked or substitute a coil known to be good.

If voltage is not present, check wire connections to coil and distributor. Disconnect the wire leading from the coil to the distributor and measure from the coil terminal to ground. If voltage is present, the distributor is shorted. Examine breaker points and connecting wires carefully. If voltage is still not present, measure the positive coil terminal. Voltage on the positive terminal, but not on the negative terminal, indicates a defective coil. No voltage indicates a broken wire between the coil and battery.

Weak Spark

If the spark is so small it cannot jump from the wire to ground, check the battery. Other causes are bad breaker points, condenser, incorrect point gap, dirty or loose connections in the primary circuit or a dirty or burned rotor/distributor cap. Check for worn cam lobes in breaker point distributors.

Missing

This is usually caused by fouled or damaged plugs, plugs of the wrong heat range, incorrect plug gap or defective plug wires.

IGNITION SYSTEM (BREAKERLESS)

The following procedures are for the diagnosis of basic problems in Chrysler Electronic Ignition system. For vehicles equipped with Lean Burn or Electronic Spark Control (engine control systems which incorporate the Electronic Ignition), refer testing to your dealer or qualified specialist, who has the necessary equipment to troubleshoot the system.

If there is no spark or a weak one from the coil wire on a breakerless ignition system, the problem is in the primary circuit. To isolate the exact cause, a series of electrical tests must be performed on the primary circuitry with a sensitive volt-ohmmeter. Refer this testing to your dealer or a qualified electrical shop.

Engine Cranks But Will Not Start

Turn the ignition off and place the transmission selector in PARK (automatic transmission) or NEUTRAL (manual transmission). Connect the leads of a voltmeter with a 20,000 ohm/volt rating across the battery terminal posts and note the battery voltage.

Disconnect the wiring harness multi-connector at the control unit. See **Figure 1** for typical system. Turn the ignition ON and connect a negative voltmeter lead to a good engine ground. Connect the positive voltmeter lead to the No. 1 cavity in the multi-connector. If the voltmeter reading exceeds battery voltage by more than one volt, the problem may be in the ballast resistor, ignition switch or connecting wiring.

Check cavity No. 2 of the multi-connector in the same manner. If the voltmeter reading exceeds battery voltage by more than one volt, the problem may be in the ignition coil,

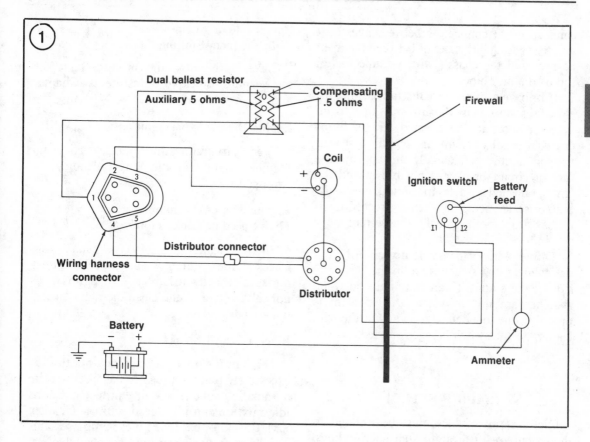

Dual ballast resistor — Auxiliary 5 ohms — Compensating .5 ohms — Firewall — Coil — Ignition switch — Battery feed — Distributor connector — Wiring harness connector — Distributor — Battery — Ammeter

ballast resistor, ignition switch or connecting wiring.

Check cavity No. 3 of the multi-connector. A voltmeter reading which exceeds battery voltage by more than one volt indictes a problem in the ballast resistor, ignition switch or connecting wiring.

If none of the 3 tests turn up the problem, turn the ignition OFF. Connect an ohmmeter between cavity No. 4 and cavity No. 5 of the multi-connector. A reading of 150-900 ohms indicates the distributor pickup coil is good. A reading outside this range indicates a defective pickup coil.

Engine Runs Rough or Cuts Out

Check the spark plugs and plug wires and repair or replace as needed. If engine still runs rough, have a dealer check the electronic control unit and replace if indicated. If this is not the problem, remove the distributor cap and inspect cap and distributor for signs of moisture, dust, cracks, burns, etc., and repair or replace as necessary.

BODY AND CHASSIS ELECTRICAL SYSTEMS

Circuit failures are usually caused by open or short circuits. Open circuits are generally caused by breaks in wiring, faulty connections or by failure of a switch, fuse or circuit breaker. Short circuits are usually caused by components of one circuit coming into contact with each other or by a wire or component grounding to the car body because of screws driven through wires, cut or abraded insulation, etc.

Finding electrical problems is usually a matter of painstakingly checking out the circuit involved to isolate the cause. Complete troubleshooting procedures covering all possible situations and corrective action for the complete electrical system are beyond the scope of this book. The following pointers, however, may be of help in locating and correcting body electrical wiring failures.
1. If all or the major portion of the electrical circuit fails at the same time, check for poor

connections at connectors between the front and rear wiring harnesses or between the front harness and the chassis wiring connector on top of the fuse block.

2. If only one of the circuits (all headlights, etc.) fails, the cause is probably due to an open or short in the affected circuit. Short circuits usually result in blown fuses or tripped circuit breakers. If the appropriate fuse or circuit breaker is not blown and the circuit affected is a lamp circuit, check the bulb or sealed beam unit before proceeding. If bulbs are good, check the circuit for continuity.

3. Dome and courtesy lamp circuits are designed so that switches are in the "ground" side of the circuit. If lamps remain on when switches are not activated, the problem is probably due to a defective switch or the wire leading to the switch being grounded.

FUEL SYSTEM (CARBURETTED)

Fuel system troubles must be isolated to the carburetor, fuel pump, fuel filter or lines. The following procedures assume the ignition system has been checked and is properly adjusted and that there is sufficient fuel in the fuel tank.

Engine Will Not Start

First, determine that fuel is being delivered to the carburetor. Remove the air cleaner and look into the carburetor throat while depressing the accelerator pump several times. There should be a stream of fuel from the accelerator pump discharge nozzle each time the accelerator is depressed. If not, check fuel pump delivery, float valve and float adjustment, fuel filter, fuel pump and lines. If fuel is present and the engine still will not start, check the automatic choke for sticking or damage. If necessary, rebuild or replace the carburetor.

Engine Runs at Fast Idle

Check for misadjustment of fast idle screw, defective carburetor, vacuum leak, intake manifold leak or carburetor gasket leak.

Rough Idle or Engine Miss With Frequent Stalling

Check carburetor idle mixture and idle screw and/or solenoid adjustments (Chapter Six).

Engine Diesels When Ignition is Shut OFF

Check carburetor adjustments, particularly the idle stop or "anti-dieseling" solenoid, if so equipped.

Engine Misses or Stumbles at High Speed or Lacks Power

This indicates possible fuel starvation. Check fuel filter and fuel pump pressure/capacity (Chapter Six). If this does not solve the problem, clean the main jet and float needle valve.

Black Exhaust Smoke

This means that the air-fuel mixture is excessively rich with fuel. Make sure that the automatic choke is working properly. Check idle mixture and idle speed settings (Chapter Six). Check for excessive fuel pump pressure, a leaky float or a worn float needle valve.

FUEL SYSTEM (FUEL INJECTED)

Troubleshooting the fuel injection system used on the 1981-1983 Imperial requires more thought, experience and know-how than any other part of the vehicle. A logical approach and proper test equipment are essential in order to successfully find and fix these troubles.

It is best to leave fuel injection troubles to your dealer. In order to isolate a problem to the injection system, make sure that the fuel pump is operating properly (Chapter Six). Also make sure that the fuel filter and air cleaner are not clogged.

EXHAUST EMISSION CONTROLS

Failure of the emission control systems to maintain exhaust output within acceptable limits is usually due to a defective carburetor, improper carburetor adjustment, incorrect engine timing, general engine condition or defective emission control devices.

CLUTCH

Several clutch troubles may be experienced. Usually, the trouble is quite obvious and will fall into one of the following categories:
1. Slipping, chattering or grabbing when engaging.
2. Spining or dragging when disengaged.
3. Clutch noises, clutch pedal pulsations and rapid clutch disc facing wear.

Clutch Slips While Engaged

Check for improper adjustment of clutch linkage, weak or broken pressure spring, worn friction disc facings and grease or oil on clutch disc.

Clutch Chatters or Grabs While Engaging

Usually caused by misadjustment of clutch linkage, dirt or grease on the friction disc facing, broken or worn clutch parts or a warped or burned flywheel.

Clutch Spins or Drags When Disengaged

The clutch friction disc normally spins briefly after disengagement and takes a moment to come to rest. This should not be confused with drag. Drag is caused by the friction disc not being fully released from the flywheel or pressure plate as the clutch pedal is depressed. The trouble can be caused by clutch linkage misadjustment, defective or worn clutch parts or a warped flywheel.

Clutch Noises

Clutch noises are usually most noticeable when the engine is idling. First, note whether the noise is heard when the clutch is engaged or disengaged. Clutch noises when engaged could be due to a loose friction disc hub, loose friction disc springs or a possible misalignment or looseness of engine or transmission mountings. When disengaged, noises can be due to a worn release bearing, defective pilot bearing or a misaligned release lever.

Clutch Pedal Pulsates

Usually noticed when slight pressure is applied to the clutch pedal with the engine running. As pedal pressure is increased, the pulsation ceases. Possible causes include misalignment of engine and transmission, bent crankshaft flange, distortion or shifting of the clutch housing, release lever misalignment, warped friction disc, damaged pressure plate or warped flywheel.

Rapid Friction Disc Facing Wear

This trouble is caused by any condition that permits slippage between facings and the flywheel or pressure plate. Probable causes are "riding" the clutch, slow releasing of the clutch after disengagement, weak or broken pressure springs, pedal linkage misadjustment or a warped clutch disc or pressure plate.

MANUAL TRANSMISSION

Hard Shifting Into Gear

Common causes are the clutch not releasing, misadjustment of linkage, linkage needing lubrication, detent ball stuck or gears tight on shaft splines.

Transmission Slips Out of FIRST or REVERSE Gear

Causes are gearshift linkage out of adjustment, gear loose on main shaft, gear teeth worn, excessive play, insufficient shift lever spring tension or worn bearings.

Transmission Slips Out of Gear

Gearshift linkage is out of adjustment, misalignment between engine and transmission, excessive main shaft end play, worn gear teeth, gear loose on main shaft, insufficient shift lever spring tension, worn bearings or a defective synchronizer.

No Power Through Transmission

May be caused by clutch slipping, stripped gear teeth, damaged shifter fork linkage, broken gear or shaft and stripped drive key.

Transmission Noisy in NEUTRAL

Transmission misaligned, bearings worn or dry, worn gears, worn or bent countershaft or excessive countershaft end play.

Transmission Noisy in Gear

Defective clutch disc, worn bearings, loose gears, worn gear teeth and faults listed above.

Gears Clash During Shifting

Caused by the clutch not releasing, defective synchronizer or gears sticking on main shaft.

Oil Leaks

Most common causes are foaming due to use of wrong lubricant, lubricant level too high, broken gaskets, damaged oil seals, loose drain plug and cracked transmission case.

AUTOMATIC TRANSMISSION

Many automatic transmission problems are caused by improper linkage adjustment or a low fluid level. If linkage adjustment and fluid level are satisfactory (Chapter Three), refer further troubleshooting to a dealer or qualified transmission specialist.

DIFFERENTIAL

Noise usually draws attention to trouble in the differential. It is not always easy to diagnose the trouble. Determine the source of noise and the operating conditions that produce the noise. Defective conditions in the universal joints, wheel bearings, muffler or tires may be wrongly diagnosed as trouble in the differential or axles.

Some clue as to the cause of trouble may be gained by noting whether the noise is a hum, growl or knock; whether it is produced when the car is accelerating under load or coasting; and whether it is heard when the car is going straight or making a turn.

1. *Noise during acceleration*—May be caused by shortage of lubricant, incorrect tooth contact between drive gear and drive pinion, damaged or misadjusted bearings in axles or side bearings or damaged gears.

2. *Noise during coasting*—May be caused by incorrect backlash between drive gear and drive pinion gear or incorrect adjustment of drive pinion bearing.

3. *Noise during turn*—This noise is usually caused by loose or worn axle shaft bearing, pinion gear too tight on shafts, side gear jammed in differential case or worn side gear thrust washer and pinion thrust washer.

4. *Broken differential parts*—Breaking of differential parts can be caused by insufficient lubricant, improper use of clutch, excessive loading, misadjusted bearings and gears, excessive backlash, damage to case or loose bolts. A humming noise in the differential is often caused by improper drive pinion or ring gear adjustment which prevents normal tooth contact between gears. If ignored, rapid tooth wear will take place and the noise will become more like a growl. Repair as soon as the humming is heard so that new gears will not be required.

Tire noise will vary considerably, depending upon the type of road surface. Radial tire noise at some road speeds is considered normal and may not even be cured by tire replacement. Differential noises will be the same regardless of road surface. If noises are heard, listen carefully to the noise over different road surfaces to help isolate the problem.

BRAKE SYSTEM

Brake Pedal Goes to Floor

Worn linings or pads, air in the hydraulic system, leaky brake lines, leaky wheel cylinders or leaky/worn master cylinder may be the cause. Check for leaks and worn brake linings or pads. Bleed and adjust the brakes. Rebuild wheel cylinders and/or master cylinder.

Spongy Pedal

Usually caused by air in the brake system. Bleed and adjust the brakes.

Brakes Pull

Check brake adjustment and wear on linings and disc pads. Check for contaminated linings, leaking wheel cylinders or loose calipers, lines or hoses. Check front-end alignment and suspension damage such as broken front or rear springs and shock absorbers. Tires also affect braking; check tire pressures and tire condition.

Brakes Squeal or Chatter

Check brake and pad lining thickness and brake drum/rotor condition. Ensure that shoes are not loose. Clean away all dirt on shoes, drums, rotors and pads.

Brakes Drag

Check brake adjustment, including handbrake. Check for broken or weak shoe return springs and swollen rubber parts due to improper or contaminated brake fluid. Check for defective master cylinder. Also check the brake pedal-to-master cylinder clearance.

Hard Pedal

Check brake linings for contamination. Check for brake line restrictions and frozen wheel cylinders and calipers.

High-Speed Fade

Check for distorted or out-of-round drums and rotors. Check linings or pads for contamination.

Pulsating Pedal

Check for distorted or out-of-round brake drums or rotors. Check for excessive disc runout.

COOLING SYSTEM

Engine Overheats

May be caused by insufficient coolant, loose or defective drive belt, defective thermostat, defective water pump, clogged coolant lines or passages, incorrect ignition timing, defective or loose hoses or a defective fan clutch. Inspect radiator and all parts for leaks.

Engine Does Not Warm Up

Usually caused by defective thermostat or extremely cold weather.

Coolant Loss

Radiator leaks, loose or defective hoses, defective water pump, leaks in cylinder head gasket, cracked cylinder head or engine block or defective radiator cap may be the cause.

Noisy Cooling System

Usually caused by defective water pump bearings, loose or bent fan blades or a defective drive belt.

STEERING AND SUSPENSION

Trouble in the suspension or steering is evident when any of the following occur:
a. Hard steering.
b. Car pulls to one side.
c. Car wanders or front wheels wobble.
d. Excessive play in steering.
e. Abnormal tire wear.
Unusual steering, pulling or wandering is usually caused by bent or misaligned suspension parts. If the trouble seems to be excessive play, check wheel bearing adjustment first. Next, check steering free play and kingpins or ball-joints. Finally, check tie rod ends by shaking each wheel.

Tire Wear Analysis

Abnormal tire wear should always be analyzed to determine the cause. The most common are incorrect tire pressure, improper driving, overloading and incorrect wheel alignment. **Figure 2** identifies wear patterns and their most probable causes.

Wheel Balancing

All 4 wheels and tires must be in balance along 2 axes. To be in static balance (**Figure 3**), weight must be evenly distributed around the axis of rotation. (A) shows a statically unbalanced wheel. (B) shows the result—wheel tramp or hopping. (C) shows proper static balance.

To be in dynamic balance (**Figure 4**), the centerline of the weight must coincide with the centerline of the wheel. (A) shows a dynamically unbalanced wheel. (B) shows the result—wheel wobble or shimmy. (C) shows proper dynamic balance.

(2)

Underinflation—Worn more on sides than in center.

Wheel Alignment—Worn more on one side than the other. Edges of tread feathered.

Road Abrasion—Rough wear on entire tire or in patches.

Overinflation—Worn more in center than on sides.

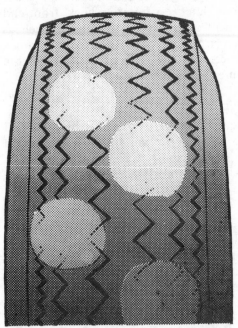

Wheel Balance — Scalloped edges indicate wheel wobble or tramp due to wheel unbalance.

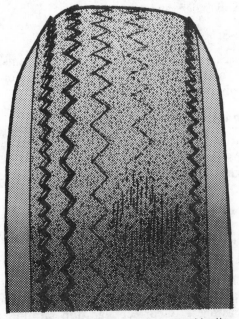

Combination—Most tires exhibit a combination of the above. This tire was overinflated (center worn) and the toe-in was incorrect (feathering). The driver cornered hard at high speed (feathering, rounded shoulders) and braked rapidly (worn spots). The scaly roughness indicates a rough road surface.

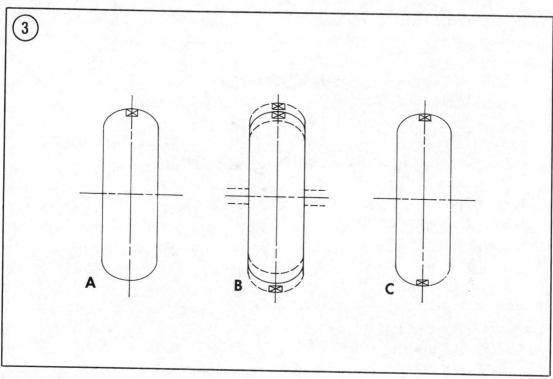

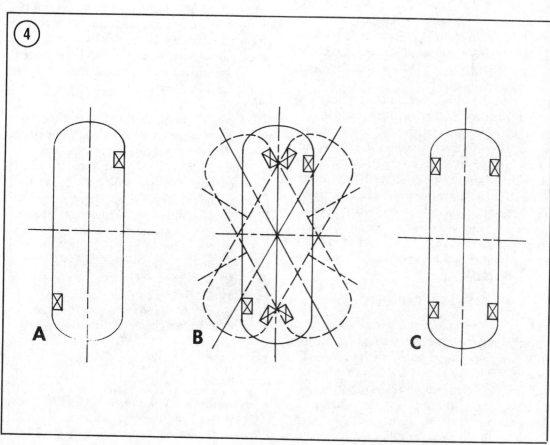

LUBRICATION AND PREVENTIVE MAINTENANCE

Following a careful program of lubrication and preventive maintenance will result in longer engine and vehicle life. It will also pay dividends in fewer and less expensive repair bills. Such a program is especially important if the car is used in remote areas or on heavily traveled freeways where breakdowns are not only inconvenient but dangerous. Such breakdowns or failures are much less likely to occur if the car has been well maintained.

Certain maintenance tasks and checks should be performed weekly. Others should be performed at certain time or mileage intervals. Still others should be done whenever certain symptoms appear.

Maintenance schedules are provided in **Tables 1-6**. Oil viscosity recommendations are provided in **Table 7** and recommended lubricants in **Table 8**. **Tables 1-9** are at the end of the chapter.

WEEKLY CHECKS

Many of the following checks were once routinely made by service station attendants when you stopped for gas. With the advent of the self-service station and the extra cost for "full service," you may want to perform the checks yourself. Although simple to perform, they are important, as such checks give an indication of the need for other maintenance.

Engine Oil Level

Engine oil should be checked before the car is started in the morning. At this time, all the oil is in the crankcase and the dipstick will give a true reading. If you find it necessary to check the oil after the engine has been started, let the car sit for an hour to allow oil in the upper part of the engine to drain back into the crankcase.

To check engine oil level, remove the dipstick and wipe clean with a cloth or paper towel. Reinsert the dipstick in the tube until it seats firmly. Wait a moment, then remove it again and read the oil level on the lower end. Reinsert the dipstick after taking the reading. **Figure 1** (6-cylinder) and **Figure 2** (V8) show typical dipstick locations.

The oil level should be maintained between the "ADD OIL" and "FULL" marks on the dipstick. Oil should be added whenever the level drops below the "ADD OIL" mark. Do not overfill the engine. Too much oil can be as harmful to the engine as too little.

Coolant Level

WARNING
Do not remove the radiator cap when the engine is warm or hot, especially if an air conditioner has been in use. You may be seriously scalded or burned.

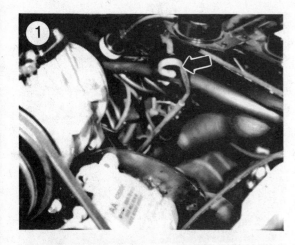

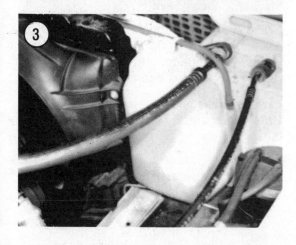

3

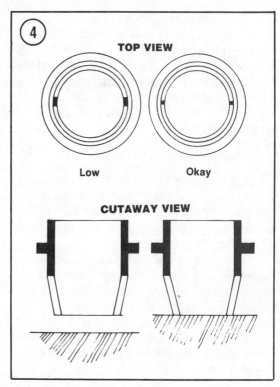

at the "MAX" or upper mark with the engine at operating temperature.

Coolant level on cars without a recovery system should be maintained 1 1/4 inches below the bottom of the filler neck when the cooling system is cold.

NOTE
The coolant level cannot be checked with the engine running if the cooling system is equipped with a recovery system. Check the level when the engine is cold.

Any significant loss of coolant could mean a leak in the cooling system or a system blockage. If the system consistently loses coolant, see Chapter Eight.

Battery Electrolyte Level

Unsealed batteries have individual cell vent caps or a bar with vented plugs which fits across 3 cells. To check electrolyte level with this type of battery, remove the vent caps or vent bars and observe the liquid level. It should touch the bottom of the vent well (**Figure 4**). If it does not, add distilled water

On vehicles equipped with coolant recovery systems, check coolant level by observing the liquid level in the reservoir (**Figure 3**, typical). The radiator cap should not be removed. Coolant should be at the "MIN" or lower mark on the reservoir with the engine coolant at ambient temperature or

until the level is satisfactory. Do not overfill, as this will result in loss of electrolyte and shorten the battery life. Carefully wipe any spilled water from the battery top before installing the vent caps or bars.

Periodic electrolyte level checks are not required on sealed maintenance-free batteries.

Windshield Wipers and Washers

Check the wiper blades for breaks or cracks in the rubber. Blade replacement intervals will vary with age, the weather, amount of use and the degree of chemical reaction from road salts or tar.

Operate the windshield washer and wiper blades. At the same time, check the amount and direction of the sprayed fluid. If the blades do not clean the windshield satisfactorily, wash the windshield and the blades with a mild undiluted detergent. Rinse with water while rubbing with a clean cloth or paper towels.

If the wiper pattern is uneven and streaks over clean glass, replace the blades.

Fill the fluid reservoir with a mixture of water and windshield washer fluid. A mixture of ammonia and water works equally well. **Figure 5** shows a typical reservoir on 1972-1977 models; **Figure 6** shows the 1978-on reservoir housed in the battery heat shield.

In cold weather areas, do not fill the reservoir more than 3/4 full to allow for expansion in freezing weather.

> *CAUTION*
> *Never use radiator antifreeze in the windshield washer reservoir, as it can damage painted surfaces.*

OWNER SAFETY CHECKS

The following simple checks should be performed on a daily basis during normal operation of the car. Some are driveway checks. The others can be performed while driving. If any result in unsatisfactory operation, see your dealer to have the condition corrected.

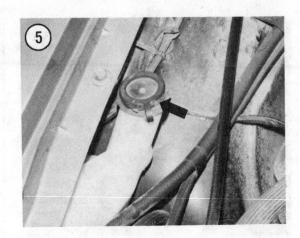

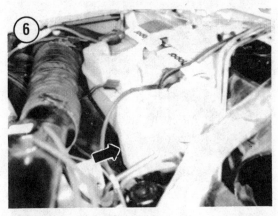

Steering Column Lock

The ignition key should turn to the LOCK position only when the transmission selector is in PARK (automatic transmission) or REVERSE (manual transmission).

Parking Brake and Transmission PARK Mechanism

Check holding ability by setting the parking brake with the car on a fairly steep hill. Check automatic transmission PARK mechanism by placing the transmission selector in PARK and releasing all brakes.

> *WARNING*
> *You should not expect the PARK mechanism to hold the car by itself even on a level surface. **Always** set the parking brake after placing the transmission selector in PARK. When parking on an incline, you should also turn the wheels to the curb before shutting off the engine.*

Transmission Shift Indicator

Make sure the automatic shift indicator accurately indicates the shift position selected.

Starter Safety Switch

The starter should operate only in PARK or NEUTRAL positions (automatic transmission) or in NEUTRAL with the clutch fully depressed (manual transmission, if equipped with starter safety switch).

Steering

Check the steering mechanism to make sure it operates freely and does not have excessive play or make harsh sounds when turning or parking.

Wheel Alignment and Balance

Visually check tires for abnormal wear. If the car pulls either to the right or left on a straight, level road, have the wheel alignment checked. Excessive vibration of the steering wheel or front of the car while driving at normal highway speeds usually indicates the need for wheel balancing.

Brakes

Observe brake warning light (if so equipped) during braking action. Also check for changes in braking action, such as pulling to one side, unusual sounds or increased brake pedal travel. If the brake pedal feels spongy, there is probably air in the hydraulic system. Bleed the brakes (Chapter Nine).

Exhaust System

Be alert to any smell of fumes in the car or to any change in the sound of the exhaust system that might indicate leakage.

Defroster

Turn on the heater, then move the control to defrost (DEF) and check the amount of air directed to the windshield.

Rear View Mirrors and Sun Visors

Make sure that the friction mounts are adjusted so that mirrors and visors stay in selected positions.

Horn

Check the horn to make sure that it works properly.

Lap and Shoulder Belts

Check all components for proper operation. Make sure that the anchor bolts are tight. Check the belts for fraying.

Head Restraints

If the seats are equipped with head restraints, check to see that they will adjust up and down properly and that no components are missing, loose or damaged.

Seat Back Latches

If the car is equipped with automatic seat back latches, pull forward on the seat backs with the doors closed to make sure the latches hold properly.

Lights and Buzzers

Verify that all interior lights and buzzers are working. These include seat belt reminder light and buzzer, ignition key buzzer, interior lights, instrument panel illumination and warning lights.

Check all exterior lights for proper operation. These include the headlights, license plate lights, side marker lights, parking lights, turn or directional signals, backup lights and hazard warning lights.

Glass

Check for any condition that could obscure vision or be a safety hazard. Correct as required.

Door Latches

Verify positive closing, latching and locking action.

3

Hood Latches

Verify that the hood closes firmly by lifting up on the hood after closing it. Check for missing, broken or damaged parts.

Fluid Leaks

Check under the vehicle after it has been parked for awhile for evidence of fuel, water or oil leaks. Water dripping from the air conditioner drain tube after use is normal. Immediately determine and correct the cause of any leaking gasoline fumes or liquids to avoid possible fire or explosion.

Tires and Wheels

Visually check tire condition. Look for nails, cuts, excessive wear or other damage. Remove all stones or other objects wedged in the tread. Check tire side walls for cuts or other damage. Check tire valve for air leaks; replace valve if necessary. Replace any valve caps that are missing. Check tire pressure with a reliable pressure gauge and adjust air pressure to agree with that specified for the tires. If the tread wear indicators are visible, replace the tire. See **Figure 7**.

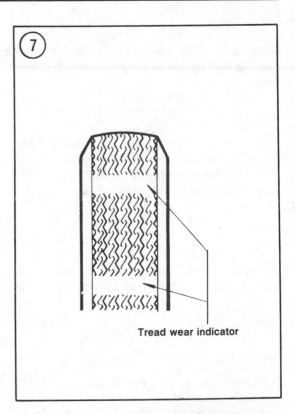

Tread wear indicator

SCHEDULED MAINTENANCE

Maintenance intervals differ with model years. These services are required to assure that the emission control system standards are maintained at the levels required by law. If your car is subjected to conditions such as heavy dust, continuous short trips or pulling trailers, more frequent servicing is necessary.

Following is a brief explanation of each of the services required by cars covered in this book. Use only those which apply to your vehicle.

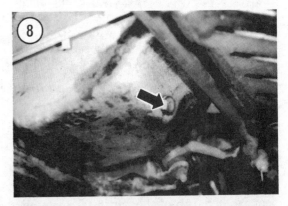

Engine Oil and Filter

Engine oil should be selected to meet the demands of the temperatures and driving conditions anticipated. Refer to **Table 7** to select a viscosity that is appropriate for the temperatures you expect to encounter for the next maintenance interval. The rating and viscosity range are usually printed on top of the can.

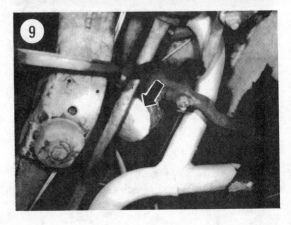

Chrysler Corporation recommends the use of a high grade motor oil with an API classification of SE or SF for all vehicles in this manual. SF is preferred.

Change the engine oil at the intervals stated in **Tables 1-6**. The oil filter should be changed at alternate oil changes.

The recommended oil and filter change interval should be cut in half under any of the following conditions:

a. Driving in dusty areas.
b. Trailer towing.
c. Extensive engine idling.
d. Short trip operation in sub-freezing weather.

Operation in a dust storm may require an immediate oil change.

CAUTION
Non-detergent, low quality oil should never be used. The regular use of oil additives is not recommended.

To drain the oil and change the filter, proceed as follows:

1. Drive the car until the engine warms up thoroughly. Place a suitable container under the oil pan.
2. Set the parking brake and block the rear wheels.
3. Maise the front of the car with a jack and place it on jackstands.
4. Remove the drain plug. **Figure 8** shows a typical drain plug location.
5. Clean the drain plug and check its gasket. Replace the gasket if damaged.
6. Allow the oil to drain completely (10-15 minutes), then reinstall the plug.
7. Move the drain pan beneath the oil filter. **Figure 9** shows a typical oil filter location on V8 engines; **Figure 10** shows the 6-cylinder filter location.
8. Loosen the filter with a filter wrench (**Figure 11**). Remove and discard the filter.

3

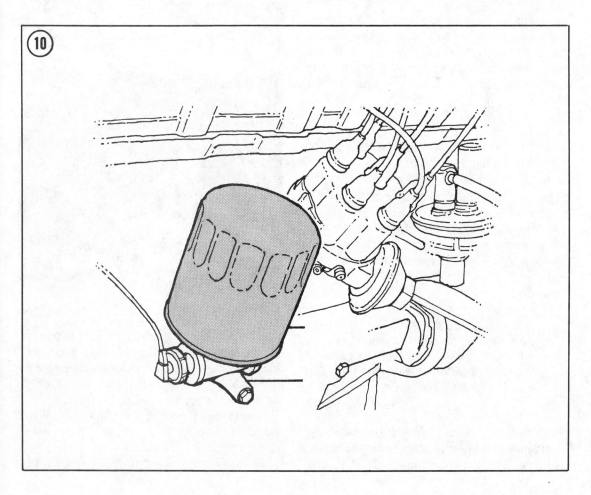

Wipe the filter mounting pad on the engine clean with a lint-free cloth or paper towel.

9. Coat the neoprene gasket on the new filter with a thin film of clean engine oil. Screw the filter in place *by hand* until it contacts the mounting pad surface. Tighten 1/2-2/3 turn further by hand. Do not overtighten as this can cause an oil leak.

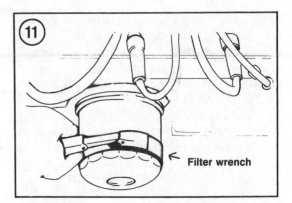

← **Filter wrench**

NOTE
Chrysler engines are equipped at the factory with short oil filters (MOPAR part No. 3549957 or equivalent). This filter must be used on 1973-1976 Valiant/Dart models with 318, 340 and 360 cu. in. engines and on all 400 or 440 cu. in. engines with an air pump or power steering. Either a short or a long filter (MOPAR part No. 1851658 or equivalent) may be used on all other engines.

10. Remove the filler cap on the valve cover. **Figure 12** shows the 6-cylinder engine; **Figure 13** shows a typical V8 engine. Fill the crankcase; subtract one quart from the the following specifications if the filter is not changed:

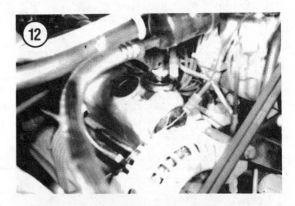

    a. The 1972 440 cu. in. HP engine requires 7 quarts of oil.

    b. The 1975-1976 400 and 440 cu. in. HP engines require 6 quarts.

    c. All other engines require 4 quarts.

Wipe up any spills on the valve cover with a clean cloth and reinstall the filler cap.

11. Start the engine. The engine warning or oil pressure light will stay on for several seconds. Allow the engine to idle for several minutes.

CAUTION
Do not operate the engine at more than idle speed until the oil has a chance to circulate thoroughly through the engine or damage could result.

12. Check the area under and around the drain plug and filter for leaks while the engine is idling. Shut the engine off.

Air Cleaner

A disposable paper element filter is used in all air cleaners. Service to a paper element filter consists only of replacement. Elements must not be cleaned with an air hose, tapped, washed or oiled. To change the filter:

1. Remove the wing nut at the center of the air cleaner cover (**Figure 14**). Remove the cover.

2. Remove and discard the filter (**Figure 15**).

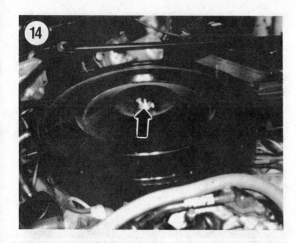

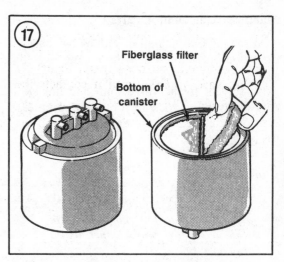

Fiberglass filter

Bottom of
canister

3

Crankcase Inlet Air Cleaner

At the interval stated in **Tables 1-6**, remove
the crankcase inlet air cleaner (**Figure 16**)
from the valve cover and air cleaner hose.
Wash thoroughly in kerosene or other solvent
housing. Drain thoroughly and invert, then
fill with clean engine oil. Place air cleaner to
permit excess oil to drain through the vent
nipple. Reinstall inlet air cleaner to valve
cover and attach air cleaner hose.

> *NOTE*
> *The crankcase inlet air cleaner used on*
> *1972-1982 engines has a tendency to*
> *leak oil at its seam. On 6-cylinder*
> *engines, this leakage may puddle on the*
> *block as if the head gasket is leaking*
> *oil. In other cases, an incorrect vent*
> *hose length may cause the cap to cock*
> *in the valve cover grommet, causing it*
> *to leak oil. If such leakage is noted and*
> *the hose length is satisfactory, replace*
> *the inlet air cleaner with Chrysler part*
> *No. 4273322.*

3. Wipe the inside of the air cleaner housing
with a damp rag to remove any dust, dirt or
debris. Do not let such material fall into the
carburetor.

4. Install a new filter element. Install the
cover and tighten the wing nut snugly.

Check hoses and ducts on the air cleaner
every 12,000 miles. Replace any hose or
ducting that is damaged. Check to make sure
the air control valve in the air cleaner snorkel
operates freely. Locate and correct any cause
of valve binding or sticking.

Vapor Canister Filter (1972-1980)

At the intervals stated in **Tables 1-6**,
remove the vapor canister from the engine
compartment. Invert the canister and replace
the element in the canister base. See **Figure
17**.

> *NOTE*
> *The canister used on 1981 and later*
> *models does not require a periodic filter*
> *change.*

Manifold Heat Control Valve

At the intervals stated in **Tables 1-6**, check the valve operation when the engine is cold and apply MOPAR manifold heat control valve solvent to the valve shaft and linkage. Allow solvent to soak in for a few minutes, then operate the shaft to make sure it moves freely.

Choke Shaft

> *CAUTION*
> *When cleaning the choke shaft, be careful not to spray cleaner in the heating element.*

Apply MOPAR combustion chamber conditioner (part No. 2933500) or equivalent to both ends of the choke shaft where it passes through the air horn to remove gum and varnish deposits. See **Figure 18**. Lubricate with WD-40 or equivalent.

Fast Idle Cam and Pivot Pin

Apply MOPAR combustion chamber conditioner (part No. 2933500) or equivalent to the fast idle cam and pivot pin to remove dirt, oil and other deposits. See **Figure 19**. Lubricate with WD-40 or equivalent.

Throttle Linkage

At the intervals stated, apply MOPAR combustion chamber conditioner (part No. 2933500) or carburetor cleaner to the throttle linkage (**Figure 20**, typical) to remove all gum and varnish desposits, then lubricate with WD-40 or equivalent.

Fuel Filter and Lines

An inline fuel filter is used in all Chrysler Corporation fuel systems. The filter canister is installed in the fuel pump-to-carburetor line. See **Figure 21**.

A clogged fuel filter can cause stumbling or cutting out at high speed and will eventually lead to complete fuel starvation. Change the filter at the intervals stated in **Tables 1-5**. No

interval is stated for 1981-1983 models but periodic changes at 30,000 miles intervals will prevent the filter from gradually clogging up and interrupting fuel flow. To change the filter:

1. Slide the clamp on each hose back with a pair of pliers.
2. Disconnect the old filter from the hoses.
3. Attach the hoses to the new filter fittings. Make sure the arrow stamped on the filter

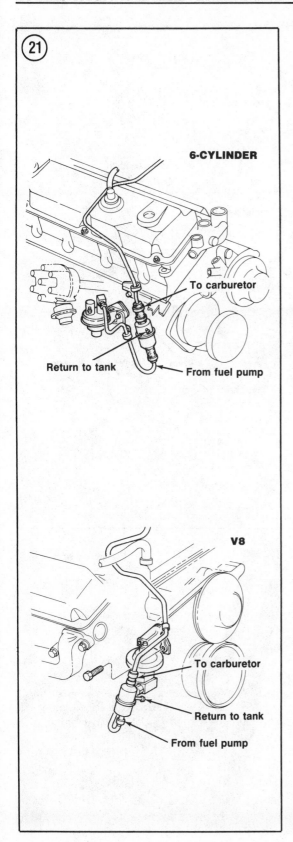

㉑

6-CYLINDER

To carburetor

Return to tank

From fuel pump

V8

To carburetor

Return to tank

From fuel pump

3

canister points in the direction of the carburetor.

4. Slide the clamp on each hose to within 1/4 in. of the filter canister.

NOTE
It is a good idea to replace the fuel line-to-fuel pump and filter return line hoses every 30,000 miles. Their close placement to the exhaust manifold on both 6-cylinder and V8 engines make them especially prone to premature failure.

Control Arm Bushing Inspection

At the intervals stated in **Tables 1-6**, raise the car, remove the front wheels and inspect the lower and upper control arm bushings. Check to make sure the inner and outer metal portions are not off-center in relation to each other. Total failure is indicated by excessive movement within the bushing and by a metal-to-metal contact noise. Small cracks in the outer visible (non-confined) rubber portion of the bushings is not necessarily an indication of failure. If failure exists, have the bushings replaced by a dealer or front-end shop.

Brake Lines and Hoses

Check the brake lines for damage or kinking. Check the hose connections and physical condition. Replace any hose that leaks or is damaged. Hardness, brittleness, cracking, checking, tears, cuts, abrasion and swelling are all signs of deterioration. If any of these conditions exist, replace the hose.

Drive Belts

At the intervals stated in **Tables 1-6**, check all drive belts for fraying, cracking or other defects. See Chapter Eight for belt adjustment and replacement procedures.

Clutch Torque Shaft Bearing

Inspect and lubricate clutch torque shaft bearing (**Figure 22**). After disassembly, clean in solvent and inspect bearings for wear. Replace damaged bearings and/or ball studs. When reassembling, coat inside surfaces at

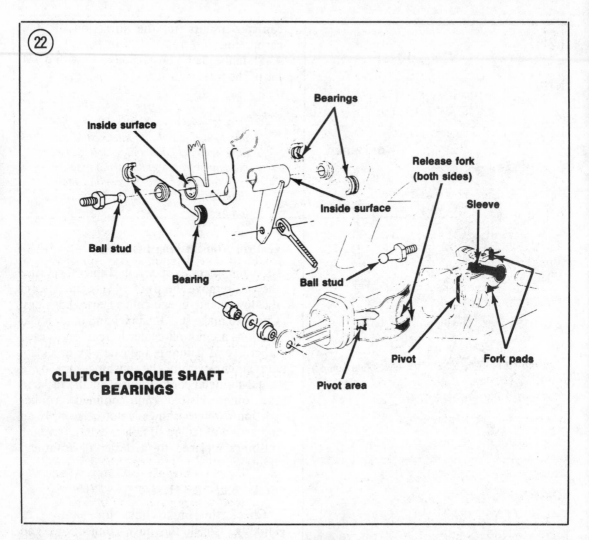

**CLUTCH TORQUE SHAFT
BEARINGS**

ends of shaft, inside and outside bearing surfaces and ball studs with multimileage lubricant (Chrysler part No. 2525035 or equivalent).

Transmission Shifter
(Floor-mounted)

Lubricate gear shift linkage with multipurpose grease. If there is no grease fitting, apply grease as shown in **Figure 23**.

Orifice Spark Advance Control

Inspect the valve for deposits which could cause plugging or sticking and replace if necessary. See Chapter Six.

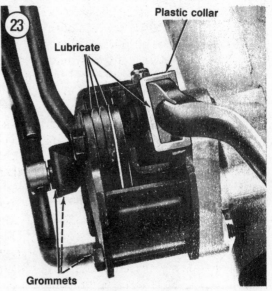

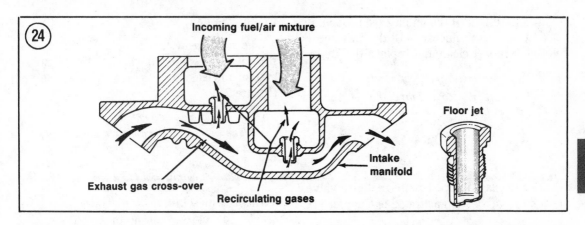

(24)

Incoming fuel/air mixture

Floor jet

Intake manifold

Exhaust gas cross-over

Recirculating gases

3

Catalytic Overtemperature Protection System

On models so equipped, inspect the system for proper operation. See Chapter Six.

Emission Hose Inspection

Check all vacuum lines and other emission control hoses for deterioration and tightness of connections. Tighten, clean or replace hoses and lines as required.

Oxygen Sensor Replacement

At the intervals stated in **Table 5**, replace the oxygen sensor and reset the mileage counter. See Chapter Six.

Unsealed Battery

Water is the only component of the battery which is lost as the result of charging and discharging. It must be replaced before the electrolyte level falls to the tops of the battery plates. If the plates become exposed they may become sulphated, which would reduce performance and eventually ruin the battery. Also, the plates cannot take part in the battery action unless they are completely covered by the electrolyte. Add distilled water as often as necessary to keep the fluid level approximately 1/2 in. above the top of the battery plates or at the bottom of the filler vent wells. Do not overfill.

The charging action of a battery creates heat. A battery that requires frequent addition of water may be subject to overcharging. This is a signal to have the charging system checked to see if the alternator and voltage regulator are doing their job properly.

When working with batteries, use extreme care to avoid spilling or splashing the electrolyte. Battery electrolyte is sulphuric acid, which can destroy clothing and cause serious chemical burns. If any electrolyte is spilled or splashed on clothing or body, immediately neutralize it with a solution of baking soda and water, then flush the affected area with plenty of clean water.

WARNING
Electrolyte splashed into the eyes is extremely dangerous. Always wear safety glasses when working with batteries. If electrolyte is splashed into the eyes, call a physician immediately, then force the eyes open and flood with cool, clean water for about 5 minutes.

If electrolyte is spilled or splashed onto painted or unpainted surfaces, neutralize it immediately with a baking soda and water solution and then rinse with clean water.

Keep the battery clean. Electrolyte which escapes through the vents will create a surface charge on the top of the battery which lowers battery performance. It also attacks metal surfaces such as the battery cable clamps. Periodically remove the battery from the engine compartment and clean it as described in Chapter Seven.

Exhaust Gas Recirculation (EGR) System

Inspect the floor jet on 1972 and later models so equipped for deposit buildup (**Figure 24**). With the engine off and the air cleaner removed, hold the choke and throttle valve open. Inspect the floor jets visually, using a flashlight. If the jet passage is open, its condition is satisfactory. If the passage is closed, remove, clean and replace the jet.

> *NOTE*
> *Use care not to damage the jet or enlarge the orifice. Install a new jet if necessary. Tighten to 25 ft.-lb. (35 N•m).*

On models equipped with an EGR valve, check the valve stem action. See Chapter Six.

Positive Crankcase Ventilation (PCV) System

At the intervals stated in **Tables 1-6**, check the PCV system operation. See Chapter Six.

Brake Master Cylinder

Clean all dirt and grime from the edge of the cover so it will not fall into the reservoir. To check fluid level on 1972-1977 and some 1978 master cylinders (**Figure 25**), insert a wide-blade screwdriver under the wire bail and pry it off the cover. Remove the cover. With some 1978 and all 1979-on master cylinders (**Figure 26**), rotate each of the caps counterclockwise and remove from the reservoir. If the fluid level is more than 1/4 in. below the top of the reservoir(s), add brake fluid marked DOT 3. Reinstall the cover or reservoir caps.

Inspect brake lines and fittings for abrasion, kinks, leakage and other damage.

Power Steering

Check the power steering fluid in the power steering pump reservoir (**Figure 27**, typical) at each oil change period. Add Chrysler power steering fluid (part No. 2084329) as required to bring the level to the proper range on the filler cap dipstick.

Some 1972-1973 pumps may not be equipped with a dipstick. If so, the level when hot should be kept 1/2-1 in. below the top of the filler neck (1 1/2-2 in. when cold).

Check all power steering hoses and lines for proper connections, leaks and deterioration. If abrasion or undue wear is evident, locate and correct the cause immediately.

Cooling System

The cooling system should be serviced at the intervals stated in **Tables 1-6**. Test the system for leaks and tighten the hose clamps (**Figure 28**).

> *NOTE*
> *The wire clamps installed at the factory cannot be tightened. These should be replaced by a worm drive or nut and bolt type clamp to prevent leakage.*

Inspect all cooling and heater hoses for cracks, checks, swelling or other signs of

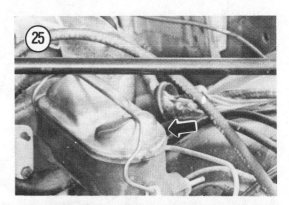

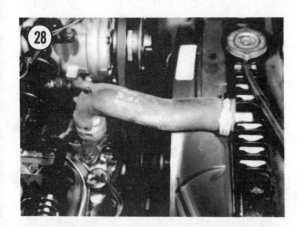

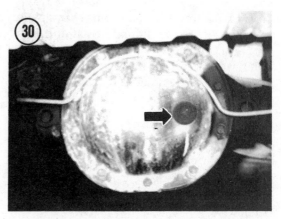

3

typical) to check the lubricant level at the intervals stated in **Tables 1-6**.

A threaded metal filler plug is used on 1972-1976 rear axles. A rubber "press-in" filler plug (**Figure 30**) was substituted as a running change on late production 1976 vehicles with a 7 1/4 or 9 1/4 rear axle. The rubber plug is used on all 1977 and later models. This change relocated the fill hole for 8 1/4 in. axles from the right side of the differential housing to the rear cover. Rubber plugs are not interchangeable with metal plugs.

The transmission fluid level should be at the bottom of the filler hole. Refer to **Table 9** for rear axle lubricant level according to axle size. If level is not correct, top up as required with the proper lubricant. Sure Grip rear axles require the use of a special hypoid lubricant. See **Table 8**.

Rear axle and manual transmission lubricants normally do not require changing during the life of the vehicle. However, if the vehicle is used consistently for trailer pulling, refer to the *Severe Service* recommendations in **Tables 1-6**.

To change rear axle or manaul transmission lubricant:

1. Raise the car with a jack and place it on jackstands.

2. Place a drain pan under the rear axle or transmission.

3a. Rear axle—remove the cover bolts and cover. Let the fluid drain. Install the cover with a new gasket. Remove the fill plug and fill to the correct level (**Table 9**) with the proper lubricant (**Table 8**).

deterioration. Replace hoses at every coolant change.

Clean exterior of radiator and air conditioning compressor with compressed air from the reverse side. Do not use a screwdriver, ice pick or other metal tool, as this can damage the radiator.

Drain, flush and refill the cooling system with a 50/50 solution of water and ethylene glycol antifreeze (MOPAR part No. 4106784, Prestone II or equivalent) at the intervals stated in **Tables 1-6** or whenever the coolant appears dirty, rusty or full of sediment.

Manual Transmission and Rear Axle

Remove the transmission filler plug (**Figure 29**, typical) and rear axle filler plug (**Figure 30**,

3b. Manual transmission—remove drain and fill plugs. Let the fluid drain. Install the drain plug. Fill to the correct level (bottom or filler hole) with the proper lubricant (**Table 8**).

4. Remove the jackstands and lower the car to the ground.

Automatic Transmission

Check the fluid level at each engine oil change. If the vehicle is used consistently for trailer towing or other severe service, refer to the *Severe Service* recommendations in **Tables 1-6**.

Checking the fluid level is basically the same for all models:

1. Check fluid level with the transmission at operating temperature, engine running, car parked on level ground, parking brake set and transmission selector in PARK.

2. Clean all dirt from the transmission dipstick cap (**Figure 31**, typical). Pull the dipstick from the tube, wipe clean and reinsert until cap fully seats. Remove dipstick and note reading. See **Figure 32**.

3. If the fluid level is low, add sufficient automatic transmission fluid of the recommended type (**Table 8**) to bring it to the proper level on the dipstick. Reinsert dipstick and make sure it is fully seated in the tube.

> *CAUTION*
> *Do not overfill the transmission. Too much fluid can cause damage to the transmission.*

If the car has been driven under severe service conditions such as those described in **Tables 1-6**, drain and refill the fluid at the appropriate intervals as follows:

1. Raise the front of the car with a jack and place it on jackstands.

2. Place a drain pan under the transmission.

3. Loosen all pan attaching bolts a few turns. Tap one corner of the pan with a rubber hammer to break it loose and let the fluid drain.

4. When the fluid has drained to the level of the pan flange, remove the pan bolts at the rear and along both sides of the pan. This will let the pan drop at one end and drain slowly.

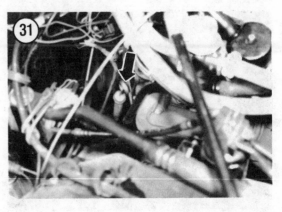

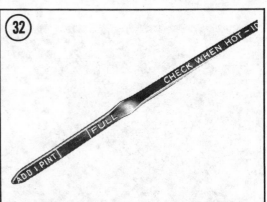

5. When all fluid has drained, remove the pan and let the strainer or filter drain.

6. Discard the pan gasket and clean pan thoroughly with solvent and lint-free cloths or paper towels.

7. Remove the strainer/filter-to-valve body bolts. Remove the strainer or filter.

8. On 1972-1979 models, remove the access plate in front of the converter. Remove converter drain plug and let converter drain. Install drain plug and tighten to 110 in.-lb., then install access plate.

9. Clean strainer assembly thoroughly in solvent and dry with compressed air. Replace paper filters.

10. Install the strainer or filter to the valve body and tighten attaching bolts to 35 in.-lb. (3.9 N•m).

11. Install the pan with a new gasket and tighten the attaching bolts in an alternating pattern to 150 in.-lb. (17 N•m).

12. Lower the vehicle and fill the transmission through the dipstick tube with approximately 2 quarts of the recommended

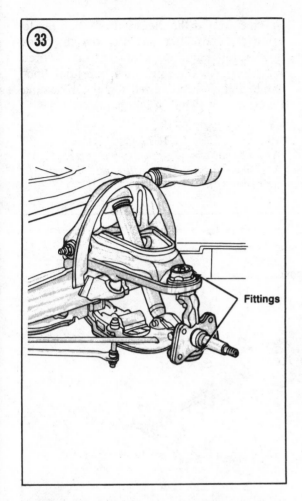

Fittings

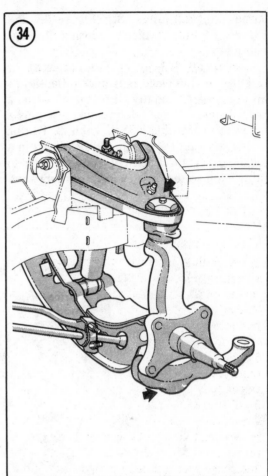

3

automatic transmission fluid (**Table 8**). Use a clean funnel inserted in the tube and a clean pouring spout installed in the fluid container to help prevent spillage.

13. Start the engine and let it idle for 2 minutes. Add enough fluid to bring the level to the "ADD ONE PINT" mark on the dipstick (**Figure 32**).

14. Set the parking brake, block the wheels and move the transmission selector lever through each gear range, pausing long enough for the transmission to engage. Return to NEUTRAL.

15. Remove the dipstick (**Figure 31**) and wipe it clean. Reinsert the dipstick in the filler tube until it seats completely.

16. Remove the dipstick and check the fluid level. Add sufficient automatic transmission fluid to bring to the "ADD ONE PINT" level on the dipstick (**Figure 32**). When the transmission reaches normal operating temperature, the fluid level will be at or close to the "FULL" mark.

Transmission Shift Linkage

Lubricate all pivot points in the shift linkage with engine oil.

Clutch Adjustment

Adjust the clutch as required. See Chapter Ten for this procedure.

Steering Linkage and Front Suspension

All models have 2 upper and 2 lower suspension ball-joints, 4 tie rod end ball-joints and a steering gear arm ball-joint. **Figure 33** and **Figure 34** show typical suspension ball-joints. See **Figure 35** and **Figure 36** for typical steering linkage ball-joints.

Inspect all ball-joints for damaged or leaking seals. Replace as required. Ball-joints are semi-permanently lubricated with a special grease. When relubricating, use only a long-life chassis grease. See **Table 8**. During winter weather, the car should be placed in a heated garage for at least 30 minutes prior to lubrication so the joints will accept lubricant.

Wipe around the plugs with a clean rag to remove accumulated dirt. Remove the plugs and install standard grease fittings. Force lubricant into the joint until the joint boot can be felt or seen to swell slightly, indicating that the boot is full of lubricant.

CAUTION
Do not overfill until lubricant escapes from boot. This will destroy the weathertight seal.

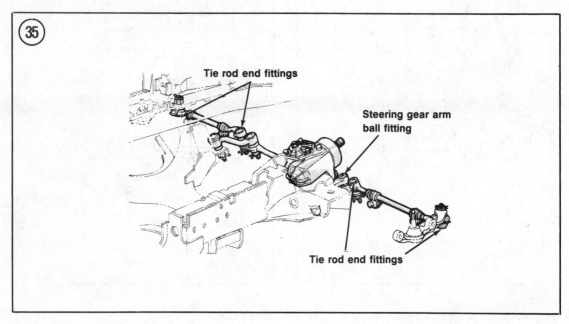

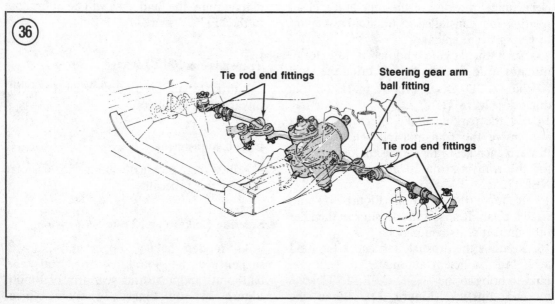

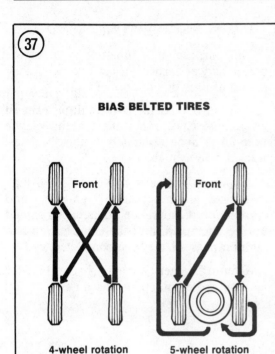

BIAS BELTED TIRES

4-wheel rotation   5-wheel rotation

RADIAL BELTED TIRES

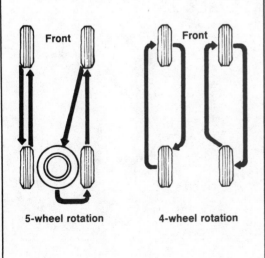

5-wheel rotation   4-wheel rotation

3

Universal Joints

At the intervals stated in **Tables 1-6**, inspect the universal joints for external leakage or damaged seals. Repair or replace as required.

Front Wheel Bearings

Inspect front wheel bearings at the intervals stated in **Tables 1-6**. Clean, repack and adjust wheel bearings whenever the brakes are serviced. See Chapter Nine for procedure. Use a high melting point, water resistant, front wheel bearing lubricant (**Table 8**).

Disc Brakes

Check brake pad and rotor condition when wheels are removed for tire rotation. See *Tire Rotation* in this chapter. Brake pads should be replaced if their thickness is less than 0.03 in. Replace pads in sets of 4.

Drum Brakes and Parking Brake

Inspect the brakes at the intervals stated in **Tables 1-6**. Remove the drums and check for cracked drums, shoe or lining wear, wheel cylinder leakage and other possible defects. See Chapter Nine for procedure.

Lubricate the parking brake cable and lever mechanism with chassis lubricant.

Exhaust System

Check the entire exhaust system from exhaust manifold to tailpipe(s). Look for broken, damaged, missing, corroded or misaligned components, open seams, holes, loose connections or any other defect that could allow exhaust gases to enter the car. Replace as necessary.

Inspect the catalytic converter heat shields (if so equipped) for looseness or damage. Tighten or replace as required. Make sure there is adequate clearance between the exhaust system components and nearby body areas.

Tire Rotation

Rotate tires every 10,000 miles. Refer to **Figure 37** for the recommended rotation patterns. Tires should be inflated to the pressures shown on the decal located on the body pillar at the rear of the left front door opening.

Hood Hinges and Latches

At each oil change interval, lubricate the hood hinge and latch assemblies as follows:
1. Wipe hinge and latch areas of accumulated dirt or contamination.
2. Apply lubricant to latch pilot bolts and locking plate.
3. Apply engine oil to all pivot points in hood release mechanism and primary/secondary latch mechanism.
4. Lubricate hinges with engine oil.
5. Check that all parts of the hinge and latch assemblies are functioning properly.

ENGINE TUNE-UP

The purpose of a tune-up is to restore power and performance lost over a gradual period of time due to normal wear.

Because of Federal laws limiting exhaust emissions, it is important that an engine tune-up is done accurately, using the latest information available.

A tune-up generally consists of 3 distinct categories: compression, ignition and carburetion. Carburetion adjustments should not be attempted until the compression and ignition phases have been completed.

Refer to Chapter Four and Chapter Five for ignition and carburetion procedures.

Table 1 MAINTENANCE SCHEDULE (1972)

First 1,000 miles	• Adjust engine idle
Every 4,000 miles or 3 months	• Change engine oil* • Check power steering fluid level • Clean air filter element
Every 8,000 miles or 6 months	• Change oil filter* • Rotate tires
Every 6 months	• Lubricate carburetor choke shaft • Lubricate manifold heat control valve • Check transmission and rear axle fluid level* • Check manual steering gear lubricant level* • Inspect steering linkage and suspension ball-joints* • Inspect universal joints* • Check master cylinder fluid level • Check brake lines and hoses* • Clean and lubricate hood latch • Check headlight aiming
Every 12 months	• Replace air cleaner filter element • Drain, flush and refill cooling system • Check PCV operation • Clean and lubricate crankcase inlet air cleaner • Lubricate throttle linkage
Every 12,000 miles or 12 months	• Check brakes • Clean, repack and adjust wheel bearings • Replace vapor canister filter
Every 18,000 miles	• Replace spark plugs
Every 24,000 miles	• Clean exhaust gas floor jets
Every 24,000 miles or 24 months	• Replace PCV valve • Replace breaker points • Replace fuel filter
Every 36,000 miles or 36 months	• Lubricate suspension ball-joints* • Lubricate steering tie rod ends* • Lubricate clutch torque shaft bearings

* SEVERE SERVICE OPERATION: If the vehicle is operated under any of the following conditions, change engine oil @ 2,000 miles or 2 months and oil filter @ alternate oil changes. Change automatic transmission fluid and service filter every 24,000 miles. Check manual transmission and rear axle fluid levels every 4,000 miles or 3 months and change fluid every 36,000 miles. Inspect brake lines and hoses and universal joints every 4,000 miles or 3 months.

  a. Extended idle or low-speed operation (short trips, stop-and-go driving).
  b. Trailer towing.
  c. Operation @ temperatures below 10° F for 60 days or more, with most trips under 10 miles.
  d. Sustained high-speed driving in hot weather.
  e. Very dusty conditions.

3

Table 2 MAINTENANCE SCHEDULE (1973-1974)

Every 4,000 miles or 3 months	• Change engine oil* • Check power steering fluid level • Inspect tires for wear
Every 8,000 miles or 6 months	• Change oil filter* • Rotate tires • Check brake lines and hoses • Lubricate floor-mounted manual transmission shift mechanism
Every 6 months	• Check master cylinder fluid level • Lubricate manifold heat control valve (6-cyl.) • Clean choke shaft, fast idle cam and pivot pin • Check transmission and rear axle fluid level* • Check exhaust system • Check cooling system operation and coolant condition • Clean and lubricate hood latch • Check headlight aiming
Every 12,000 miles or 12 months	• Clean air cleaner filter element • Drain, flush and refill cooling system • Inspect PCV system operation • Clean and lubricate crankcase inlet air cleaner • Check drive belt tension and condition • Check EGR system operation • Replace vapor canister filter • Check engine idle speed • Check ignition timing • Check and adjust valve lash (6-cyl.) • Inspect brake linings
Every 18,000 miles	• Replace spark plugs • Inspect ignition cables
Every 24,000 miles or 24 months	• Clean, repack and adjust wheel bearings • Inspect orifice spark advance control • Replace fuel filter • Check and adjust automatic choke
Every 36,000 miles or 36 months	• Lubricate suspension ball-joints* • Lubricate steering tie rod ends*

* SEVERE SERVICE OPERATION: If the vehicle is operated under any of the following conditions, change engine oil @ 2,000 miles or 2 months and oil filter @ alternate oil changes. Change automatic transmission fluid and service filter every 24,000 miles. Check manual transmission and rear axle fluid levels every 4,000 miles or 3 months and change fluid every 36,000 miles. Inspect brake lines and hoses and universal joints every 4,000 miles or 3 months.

　a. Extended idle or low-speed operation (short trips, stop-and-go driving).
　b. Trailer towing.
　c. Operation @ temperatures below 10° F for 60 days or more, with most trips under 10 miles.
　d. Sustained high-speed driving in hot weather.
　e. Very dusty conditions.

Table 3 MAINTENANCE SCHEDULE (1975-1976)

At first 5,000 miles	• Check and adjust idle speed and fast idle speed[1]
Every 5,000 miles or 6 months	• Change engine oil[2]
	• Inspect emission hoses
	• Check power steering fluid level
	• Check exhaust system
	• Check drive belt tension and condition
	• Inspect upper/lower control arm bushings
Every 6 months	• Check cooling system operation and coolant condition
	• Clean choke shaft, fast idle cam and pivot pin
	• Check master cylinder fluid level
	• Check transmission and rear axle lubricant level[2]
	• Check brake lines and hoses[2]
	• Inspect ball-joint and steering linkage seals
	• Inspect universal joint seals[2]
Every 10,000 miles or 12 months	• Change oil filter[2]
	• Tighten radiator hose clamps
Every 10,000 miles	• Rotate tires
	• Inspect brake linings
Every 15,000 miles or 12 months	• Clean air cleaner filter element
	• Drain, flush and refill cooling system
	• Service manifold heat control valve[1]
	• Clean and lubricate crankcase inlet air cleaner[1]
	• Check air pump drive belt tension and condition
	• Check EGR system operation
	• Replace vapor canister filter
	• Check engine idle speed
	• Check ignition timing
	• Check and adjust valve lash (6-cyl.)
	• Check PCV system operation
	• Replace spark plugs (leaded gas)
	• Check distributor cap, rotor and cables
	• Check orifice spark advance control operation[1]
	• Check and adjust automatic choke[1]
	• Replace fuel filter[1]
	• Service catalyst protection system[1]
Every 25,000 miles	• Inspect wheel bearings[3]
Every 30,000 miles	• Replace spark plugs (unleaded gas)
	• Replace air cleaner filter element
	• Replace PCV valve
	• Check and adjust automatic choke
	• Clean and lubricate crankcase inlet air cleaner[4]
	• Replace fuel filter[4]
	• Service manifold heat control valve[4]
Every 36,000 miles or 36 months	• Lubricate suspension ball-joints
	• Lubricate steering tie rod ends

1. 1975 only.
2. SEVERE SERVICE OPERATION: If the vehicle is operated under any of the following conditions, change engine oil and filter @ 2,500 miles or 3 months. Change automatic transmission fluid and service filter every 25,000 miles. Check manual transmission and rear axle fluid levels every 5,000 miles or 3 months and change fluid every 35,000 miles. Inspect brake lines and hoses and universal joints every 5,000 miles.
  a. Extended idle or low-speed operation (short trips, stop-and-go driving).
  b. Trailer towing.
  c. Operation @ temperatures below 10° F for 60 days or more, with most trips under 10 miles.
  d. Sustained high-speed driving in hot weather.
  e. Very dusty conditions.
3. Clean, repack and adjust whenever brakes are serviced.
4. 1976 only.

3

Table 4 MAINTENANCE SCHEDULE (1977-1979)

Every 7,500 miles or 6 months	• Change engine oil[1] • Inspect emission hoses • Check power steering fluid level • Check drive belt tension and condition • Inspect upper/lower control arm bushings • Check clutch pedal free play (1979) • Clean choke shaft, fast idle cam and pivot pin
Every 6 months	• Check exhaust system • Check master cylinder fluid level • Check transmission and rear axle lubricant level[1] • Check brake and power steering lines and hoses • Inspect ball-joint and steering linkage seals • Inspect universal joint seals[1]
Every 10,000 miles	• Rotate tires
Every 15,000 miles or 12 months	• Change oil filter[1] • Check cooling system operation and condition • Check and adjust idle speed • Check PCV system operation • Replace spark plugs (leaded gas) • Adjust valve lash (6-cyl.) • Inspect brake linings (1977-1978)
Every 22,500 miles	• Inspect wheel bearings (1977-1978) (see notes 1 & 2)
First 24 months or 30,000 miles, then every 12 months or 15,000 miles	• Drain, flush and refill cooling system
Every 30,000 miles or 24 months	• Replace spark plugs (unleaded gas) • Check and adjust automatic choke • Replace air cleaner filter element • Clean, repack and adjust wheel bearings (see notes 1 & 2) • Clean and lubricate crankcase inlet air cleaner • Replace fuel filter • Service manifold heat control valve • Replace PCV valve • Check brake linings (1979 only) • Replace vapor canister filter
Every 36,000 miles or 36 months	• Lubricate suspension ball-joints[1] • Lubricate steering tie rod ends[1]

1. SEVERE SERVICE OPERATION: If the vehicle is operated under any of the following conditions, change engine oil and filter @ 3,000 miles or 3 months. Change automatic transmission fluid and service filter every 24,000 miles (1977), 30,000 miles (1978) or 15,000 miles (1979). Check manual transmission level every 5,000 miles or 3 months and change fluid every 30,000 miles. Change rear axle lubricant every 36,000 miles. Inspect brake lines and hoses and universal joints every 7,500 miles. Lubricate steering and suspension ball-joints every 15,000 miles (1978-1979). Clean, repack and adjust wheel bearings every 9,000 miles (1978-1979).
   a. Extended idle or low-speed operation (short trips, stop-and-go driving).
   b. Trailer towing.
   c. Operation @ temperatures below 10° F for 60 days or more, with most trips under 10 miles.
   d. Sustained high-speed driving in hot weather.
   e. Very dusty conditions.
2. Clean, repack and adjust whenever brakes are serviced.

Table 5 MAINTENANCE SCHEDULE (1980)[1]

Every 7,500 miles or 12 months	• Change engine oil[2] • Clean choke shaft, fast idle cam and pivot pin (Schedule B)
Every 10,000 miles	• Rotate tires
Every 15,000 miles or 12 months	• Change oil filter[2] • Check drive belt tension and condition • Check and adjust idle speed (Schedule B) • Check ignition cables (Schedule B) • Check PCV system operation (Schedule B) • Replace spark plugs (leaded gas) • Adjust valve lash (6-cyl.) • Check all fuel system and emission system hoses
First 24 months or 30,000 miles, and every 12 months or 15,000 miles	• Drain, flush and refill cooling system
Every 30,000 miles or 24 months	• Replace spark plugs (unleaded gas) • Check and adjust automatic choke (Schedule B) • Replace oxygen sensor and reset mileage counter (Schedule A) • Replace air cleaner filter element • Clean, repack and adjust wheel bearings[3] • Clean and lubricate crankcase inlet air cleaner (Schedule B) • Clean fast idle cam and pivot pin (Schedule A) • Replace fuel filter (Schedule B) • Service manifold heat control valve (Schedule B) • Replace PCV valve (Schedule B) • Check brake linings and drum • Replace vapor canister filter (Schedule B) • Lubricate suspension ball-joints[2] • Lubricate steering tie rod ends[2]

1. Frequency and type of service varies according to model. Two schedules are used for 1980 models, Schedule A and Schedule B. The designation is found on the Vehicle Emission Control Information (VECI) label in the engine compartment. If not otherwise specified, perform the service on both A and B models.
2. SEVERE SERVICE OPERATION: If the vehicle is operated under any of the following conditions, change engine oil and filter @ 3,000 miles or 3 months. Change automatic transmission fluid and service filter every 15,000 miles. Change rear axle lubricant every 36,000 miles. Inspect brake linings every 9,000 miles. Lubricate steering and suspension ball-joints every 15,000 miles or 18 months. Clean, repack and adjust wheel bearings every 9,000 miles (1978-1979). Inspect universal joints @ every oil change.
  a. Extended idle or low-speed operation (short trips, stop-and-go driving).
  b. Trailer towing.
  c. Operation @ temperatures below 10° F for 60 days or more, with most trips under 10 miles.
  d. Sustained high-speed driving in hot weather.
  e. Very dusty conditions.
3. Clean, repack and adjust whenever brakes are serviced.

Table 6 MAINTENANCE SCHEDULE (1981-ON)

Every 7,500 miles or 12 months	• Change engine oil[1] • Check brake hoses • Check fluid levels
Every 10,000 miles	• Rotate tires
Every 15,000 miles	• Change oil filter[1] • Check drive belt tension and condition • Replace spark plugs (leaded gas)
Every 30,000 miles	• Replace spark plugs (unleaded gas) • Replace air cleaner filter element • Clean, repack and adjust wheel bearings[2] • Clean choke shaft, fast idle cam and pivot pin • Check front and rear brake linings, rotors and drums • Lubricate suspension ball-joints[1] • Lubricate steering tie rod ends[1] • Replace air cleaner filter[3]
Every 52,500 miles	• Clean and lubricate crankcase inlet air cleaner • Replace air cleaner filter[4]

1. SEVERE SERVICE OPERATION: If the vehicle is operated under any of the following conditions, change engine oil @ 3,000 miles or 3 months and filter @ alternate oil changes. Change automatic transmission fluid and service filter every 15,000 miles. Change rear axle lubricant every 36,000 miles. Inspect brake linings every 9,000 miles. Lubricate steering and suspension ball-joints every 15,000 miles or 18 months. Clean, repack and adjust wheel bearings every 9,000 miles. Inspect universal joints @ every oil change.
   a. Extended idle or low-speed operation (short trips, stop-and-go driving).
   b. Trailer towing.
   c. Operation @ temperatures below 10° F for 60 days or more, with most trips under 10 miles.
   d. Sustained high-speed driving in hot weather.
   e. Very dusty conditions.
2. Clean, repack and adjust whenever brakes are serviced.
3. Non-California 6-cylinder.
4. All except Non-California 6-cylinder.

Table 7 RECOMMENDED OIL VISCOSITY

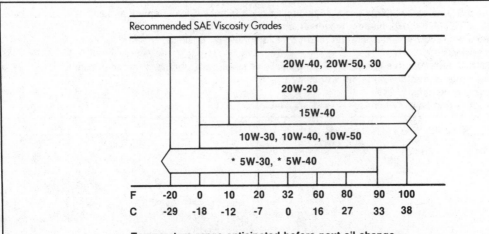

Temperature range anticipated before next oil change.

* SAE 5W-30 and 5W-40 are not recommended for vehicles equipped with a 318-4 Bbl. engine when operating at ambient temperatures above 60°F (16°C).

Table 8 RECOMMENDED LUBRICANTS AND FLUIDS

Engine oil	API Designation SF
Coolant	Permanent ethylene glycol antifreeze
Power steering	Chrysler part No. 4318055 or equivalent
Front suspension and steering ball joints	Multi-mileage lubricant part No. 4318062 or equivalent
Clutch torque shaft bearing	Multi-mileage lubricant part No. 4318062 or equivalent
Rear axle, including Sure Grip	
1972	Hypoid lubricant part No. 2933565 or equivalent
1973-1976	Hypoid lubricant part No. 3744994 or equivalent
1977-on	Hypoid lubricant part No. 4318058 or equivalent
	Use friction modifier additive part No. 4318060 with Sure Grip axles
Manual transmission	DEXRON II automatic transmission fluid. Multi-purpose gear lubricant (SAE 90 or SAE 140) may be substituted to minimize gear rattle
Automatic transmission	DEXRON II automatic transmission fluid
Brake fluid	DOT 3
Front wheel bearings	High-temperature multi-purpose E.P. grease part No. 4318039 or equivalent
Manifold heat control valve	Manifold heat control solvent part No. 4318064 or equivalent
Choke, fast idle cam and throttle linkage	Chrysler combustion chamber conditioner part No. 4318001 or equivalent

Table 9 REAR AXLE LUBRICANT LEVEL

Axle size	Filler Location	No. of Bolts	Capacity (Pints)	Lubricant Level
		1972-1976		
7 1/4	Cover	9	2.0	Bottom of filler hole to 5/8 in. below
8 1/4	Right side	10	4.4	1/8-1/4 in. below filler hole
8 3/4	Right	*	4.4	Bottom of filler hole
9 1/4	Cover	12	4.5	3/8-1/2 in. below filler hole
9 3/4	Cover	10	5.5	Bottom of filler hole to 1/2 in. below
		1977-on		
7 1/4	Cover	9	2.1	Bottom of filler hole to 3/8 in. below
7 1/4	Cover	10	2.5	Bottom of filler hole to 1/4 in. below
8 1/4	Cover	10	4.4	Bottom of filler hole to 1/4 in. below
9 1/4	Cover	12	4.5	Bottom of filler hole to 1/2 in. below

* Welded.

CHAPTER FOUR

TUNE-UP

A tune-up consists of a series of inspections, adjustments and parts replacements to compensate for normal wear and deterioration of engine components. Regular tune-ups are important for proper emission control and fuel economy.

Since proper engine operation depends upon a number of interrelated system functions, a tune-up consisting of only one or two corrections will seldom give lasting results. For improved power, performance and operating economy, a thorough and systematic procedure of analysis and correction is necessary.

Always refer to the Vehicle Emission Control Information (VECI) decal on the valve cover or elsewhere in the engine compartment for the correct tune-up specifications for your car. If the decal has been lost or damaged, refer to **Table 1** for tune-up specifications. These specifications are provided by Chrysler Corp. but, due to changes in emission calibrations during a model year, should be used only as a general guide.

If the VECI decal is missing and you do not know the displacement of your engine, check the vehicle identification number (VIN) against the information given in **Table 2**:

a. On 1972-1980 models, check the fifth digit of the VIN.
b. On 1981-on models, check the eighth digit of the VIN.

TUNE-UP SEQUENCE

Because different systems in an engine interact, the tune-up should be carried out in the following order.

1. Adjust valve lash (1972-1980 6-cylinder only).
2. Check engine compression.
3. Service ignition system:
   a. Replace spark plugs.
   b. Check ignition cable resistance.
   c. Replace or adjust breaker points.
   d. Replace condenser.
   e. Inspect or replace distributor cap and rotor.
   f. Check and adjust ignition timing.
4. Adjust carburetor.

VALVE LASH ADJUSTMENT (1972-1980 6-CYLINDER ONLY)

NOTE
This procedure may be messy due to oil splatter with the valve cover off and the engine running. Wear old clothes. You

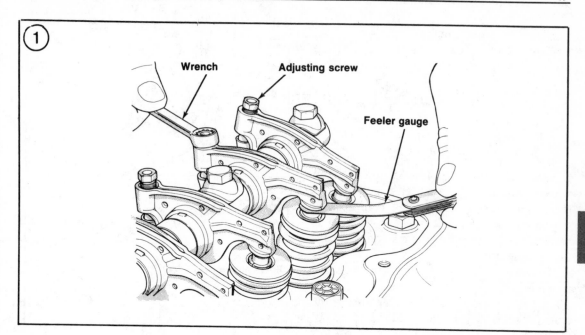

Wrench   Adjusting screw   Feeler gauge

4

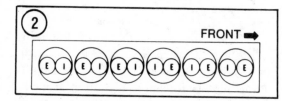

FRONT ➡

E I E I E I I E I E I E

can make a splash shield by cutting the top off an old valve cover; be sure there are no sharp edges which may cause personal injury.

1. Warm engine to normal operating temperature. Allow engine to idle at curb idle speed for 5 minutes.
2. Disconnect all vacuum hoses and wires which interfere with valve cover removal.
3. Disconnect the fender support bracket.
4. Remove the valve cover fasteners. Remove the valve cover.
5. Place an appropriate size box wrench on the adjusting screw, insert a feeler gauge and adjust intake tappets to 0.010 in. or exhaust tappets to 0.020 in. See **Figure 1** for adjustment procedure and **Figure 2** for valve location.
6. Install valve cover on cylinder head with a new gasket. Tighten fasteners to 40 in.-lb. (4 N•m).
7. Reconnect the fender support bracket. Reconnect all vacuum hoses and wires.

8. Check for oil leaks around the valve cover gasket (with engine running). If leaks are present, remove the valve cover. Clean the gasket surfaces on the head and cover. Reinstall the cover and gasket, using a suitable gasket cement on the gasket surfaces. Do not attempt to remedy leaks by applying additional torque.

COMPRESSION TEST

An engine with low or uneven compression cannot be properly tuned. A compression test measures the compression pressure built up in each cylinder. Its results can be used to assess general cylinder and valve condition. In addition, it can warn of developing problems inside the engine.
1. Warm the engine to normal operating temperature (upper radiator hose hot). Shut the engine off.
2. Remove the air cleaner from the carburetor and block the throttle and choke valves in a wide-open position.
3. Remove the distributor primary lead from the negative post of the ignition coil.
4. Connect a remote starter to the starter relay according to manufacturer's instructions. If a remote starter is not available, have an assistant crank the engine from the driver's seat as required.

5. Remove all spark plugs.

6. Firmly insert a compression gauge in the No. 1 cylinder spark plug hole (**Figure 3**).

> *NOTE*
> *The No. 1 cylinder is the one nearest the front of the vehicle. On V8 engines, note that one bank of cylinders is offset closer to the front than the other.*

7. Crank the engine at least 5 compression strokes with the remote starter switch or until there is no further increase in compression shown on the gauge.

8. Remove the compression tester and record the reading. Relieve the tester pressure valve.

9. Test the remaining cylinders in the same manner.

10. Check the readings against the specifications given in **Table 1** (end of chapter). If one or more cylinders are below the minimum limit, the engine needs repairs. If there is more than the allowable variation between the lowest and highest reading cylinders, corrective maintenance is beyond the scope of this book and the engine cannot be properly tuned until the necessary repairs have been made.

If the compression test indicates a problem (excessive variation in readings), isolate the cause with a wet compression test. This is done in the same way as the dry compression test above, except that about 1 tablespoon of oil is poured down the spark plug hole before checking each cylinder. If the wet compression readings are much greater the dry readings, the trouble is probably caused by worn or broken piston rings. If there is little difference between the wet and dry readings, the problem is probably due to leaky or sticking valves. When 2 adjacent cylinders read low in the dry test and do not increase in the wet test, the problem may be a defective head gasket.

SPARK PLUG REPLACEMENT

> *CAUTION*
> *Whenever the spark plugs are removed, dirt from around them can fall into the spark plug holes. This can cause expensive engine damage.*

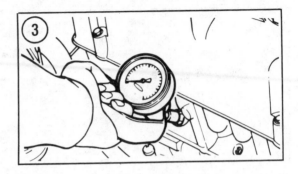

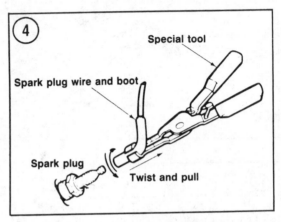

1. Blow out any foreign matter from around the spark plug with compressed air. Use a compressor if you have one or a can of compressed inert gas, available from photo stores.

> *NOTE*
> *It is a good idea to identify each spark plug wire with a piece of masking tape and a felt-tip pen before removing the wires in Step 2. Another way of identifying the wires is to write the wire location on a wooden clothes pin which is then clipped to the wire.*

2. Disconnect the spark plug wires by twisting the wire boot back and forth on the plug insulator while pulling upward. Pulling on the wire instead of the boot may cause internal damage to the wire. Use of a spark plug cable remover (**Figure 4**) is recommended.

3. Remove the spark plugs with a 13/16 in. spark plug socket. Keep the plugs in order so you know which cylinder they came from.

4. Examine each spark plug. Compare its condition with **Figure 5**. Spark plug condition

(5) **SPARK PLUG CONDITION**

NORMAL
- Identified by light tan or gray deposits on the firing tip.
- Can be cleaned.

GAP BRIDGED
- Identified by deposit buildup closing gap between electrodes.
- Caused by oil or carbon fouling. If deposits are not excessive, the plug can be cleaned.

OIL FOULED
- Identified by wet black deposits on the insulator shell bore electrodes.
- Caused by excessive oil entering combustion chamber through worn rings and pistons, excessive clearance between valve guides and stems, or worn or loose bearings. Can be cleaned. If engine is not repaired, use a hotter plug.

CARBON FOULED
- Identified by black, dry fluffy carbon deposits on insulator tips, exposed shell surfaces and electrodes.
- Caused by too cold a plug, weak ignition, dirty air cleaner, defective fuel pump, too rich a fuel mixture, improperly operating heat riser, or excessive idling. Can be cleaned.

LEAD FOULED
- Identified by dark gray, black, yellow, or tan deposits or a fused glazed coating on the insulator tip.
- Caused by highly leaded gasoline. Can be cleaned.

WORN
- Identified by severely eroded or worn electrodes.
- Caused by normal wear. Should be replaced.

FUSED SPOT DEPOSIT
- Identified by melted or spotty deposits resembling bubbles or blisters.
- Caused by sudden acceleration. Can be cleaned.

OVERHEATING
- Identified by a white or light gray insulator with small black or gray brown spots and with bluish-burnt appearance of electrodes.
- Caused by engine overheating, wrong type of fuel, loose spark plugs, too hot a plug, low fuel pump pressure, or incorrect ignition timing. Replace the plug.

PREIGNITION
- Identified by melted electrodes and possibly blistered insulator. Metallic deposits on insulator indicate engine damage.
- Caused by wrong type of fuel, incorrect ignition timing or advance, too hot a plug, burned valves, or engine overheating. Replace the plug.

indicates engine condition and can warn of developing trouble.

5. Discard the plugs. Although they could be cleaned, regapped and reused if in good condition, they seldom last very long. New plugs are inexpensive and far more reliable.

6. Remove the plugs from the box. All 1972-1974 6-cylinder engines use gasket-type spark plugs which are installed in tube sleeves without the gaskets. All other Chrysler engines require the use of gasket-type plugs *with* the gaskets. Some plug brands may have small end pieces that must be screwed on (**Figure 6**) before the plugs can be used.

7. Determine the correct gap setting from the VECI label. Use a spark plug gapping tool to check the gap. **Figure 7** shows one common type in use. Insert the appropriate size wire gauge between the electrodes. If the gap is correct, there will be a slight drag as the wire is pulled through. If there is no drag or if the wire will not pull through, bend the side electrode with the gapping tool (**Figure 8**) to change the gap and then remeasure with the wire gauge.

CAUTION
Never try to close the electrode gap by tapping the spark plug on a solid surface. This can damage the plug internally. Always use the special tool to open or close the gap.

8. Check spark plug hole threads and clean if necessary with a 14 mm thread chaser before installing plugs. This will remove any corrosion, carbon build-up or minor flaws from the threads. Coat the chaser with grease to catch chips or foreign matter. Use care to avoid cross threading.

9. Apply a thin film of oil to the spark plug threads and screw each plug in by hand until it seats. Very little effort is required. If force is necessary, the plug is cross threaded. Unscrew it and try it again.

10. Tighten the spark plugs by hand. If you have a torque wrench, tighten the plugs to 30 ft.-lb. (40 N•m). If a torque wrench is not available, tighten an additional 1/4-3/8 turn with the spark plug wrench. Do not overtighten, as excessive torque may change the gap setting.

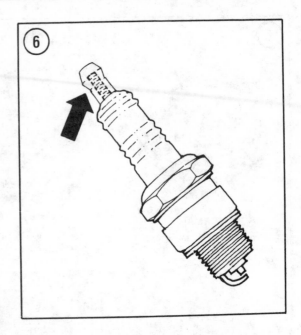

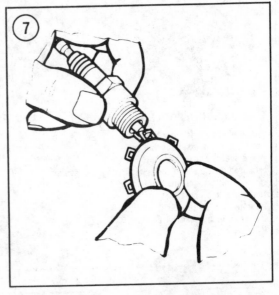

11. Inspect the spark plug wires before reinstalling them. See **Figure 9**. If the insulation is oil soaked, brittle, torn or otherwise damaged, replace the wire.

BREAKER POINT IGNITION SYSTEM

Inspection

1. Disconnect secondary wire between coil and distributor at the coil. See **Figure 10**.

2. Insert a screwdriver blade between the distributor body and spring clip. Twist

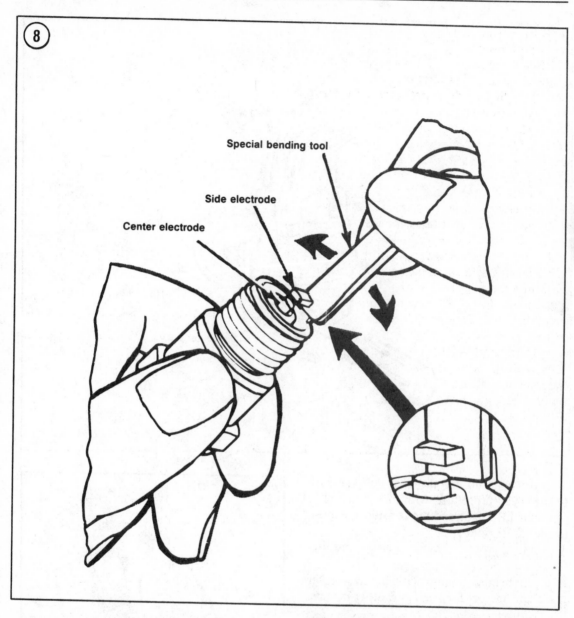

Center electrode

Side electrode

Special bending tool

4

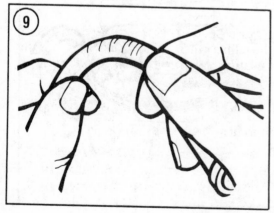

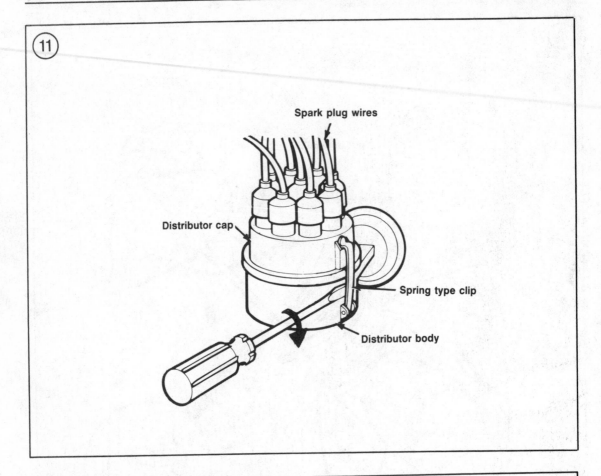

Spark plug wires

Distributor cap

Spring type clip

Distributor body

screwdriver to unsnap the spring clip (**Figure 11**). Repeat procedure with the other clip. Carefully lift cap off and move aside to expose inside of distributor.

3. Remove rotor (**Figure 12**) by pulling straight up.

4. Open breaker points with a screwdriver blade and inspect for pitting or other defects.

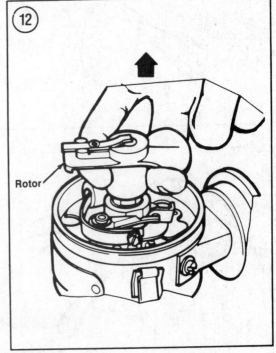

Rotor

> *CAUTION*
> *Do not touch breaker points with your fingers. The oil from your skin will stick to the points. The breaker point surfaces must remain dry and clean at all times.*

5. Wipe inside of distributor cap with a clean cloth. Check the cap electrodes for cracks and carbon tracks or burned, worn or corroded terminals (**Figure 13**). Replace if any of these defects are found.

6. Remove each cap wire with a twisting motion while pulling on the wire boot. Check

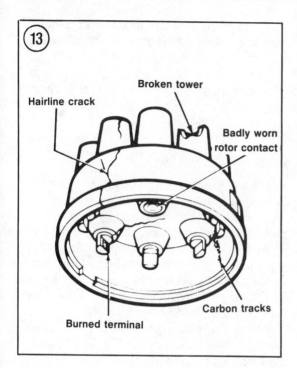

(13)

Hairline crack

Broken tower

Badly worn rotor contact

Burned terminal

Carbon tracks

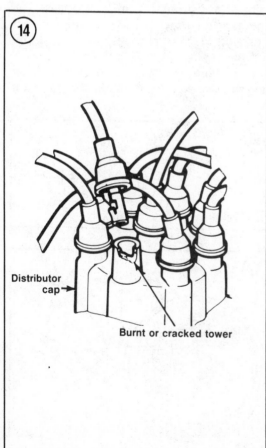

(14)

Distributor cap

Burnt or cracked tower

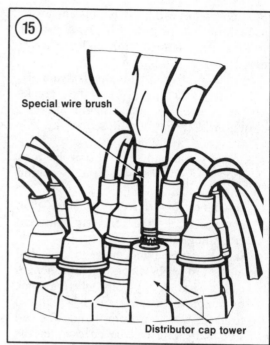

(15)

Special wire brush

Distributor cap tower

4

for damaged or corroded cap towers (**Figure 14**). If the towers are corroded, clean with a wire brush (**Figure 15**).

7. Clean and inspect rotor for damage or deterioration. Replace if necessary.

8. Check spark plug wiring for signs of wear or deterioration. Look for abrasion or heat damage on wires routed near exhaust manifolds.

9. Make sure all spark plug wires are installed to the correct plugs. Wires should be positioned properly in their supports to avoid contact with the engine and prevent crossfiring.

10. Tighten all ignition system connections and replace any loose, frayed or damaged wires.

Cable Resistance Check

1. Make sure that the coil and all spark plug wires are firmly seated in their proper distributor cap towers and that the nipples are in place.

NOTE
Do not remove wire or nipples from the towers unless testing indicates excessive resistance or broken insulation or the nipples are damaged.

2. Clean all wires with a cloth moistened with non-flammable solvent. Check wires for brittle or cracked insulation and replace if present.

3. If an automotive oscilloscope is available, check wires for punctures and cracks following the scope manufacturer's instructions. If an oscilloscope is not available, check as follows:

    a. Connect one end of a test probe to a good ground in the engine compartment.

    b. Disconnect a wire from one spark plug and insulate the end to prevent grounding.

    c. Start the engine and move the free end of the test probe along the entire length of the wire. At any point where a crack or puncture exists, a spark will jump from the wire to the probe end. The coil secondary wire can be checked in the same manner by operating the starter. Replace any damaged wires.

> *CAUTION*
> *On 1975 and later models with catalytic converters, complete this test as rapidly as possible to avoid heat buildup which could damage the converter. Total test time must not exceed 10 minutes.*

4. Check the resistance of each wire as follows:

    a. Disconnect the spark plug wires at the spark plugs.

    b. Remove the distributor cap from the distributor with the wires intact. *Do not* remove the wires from the cap.

    c. Connect an ohmmeter between one spark plug end terminal and its corresponding electrode inside the distributor cap. If the resistance exceeds 50,000 ohms, remove the wire from the cap tower and recheck the resistance. If still above 50,000 ohms, replace the wire. If wire is okay, clean or replace distributor cap. Repeat the test for all remaining spark plug wires.

    d. Connect the ohmmeter between the center contact inside the distributor cap

and either primary terminal at the coil. If combined resistance of coil and cable exceeds 25,000 ohms, remove the coil wire at the coil tower and recheck wire resistance. If greater than 15,000 ohms, check for a loose connection at the coil or a faulty coil.

Breaker Point Service

1. Check breaker point contact surfaces. Points with an even, overall gray color and only slight roughness or pitting need not be replaced. They can be dressed with a clean point file. Do not use sandpaper or emery cloth for dressing points, and do not attempt to remove all irregularities—just scale or dirt.

2. Check the alignment of the points and correct as necessary. See **Figure 16**.

3. Check the point gap with a feeler gauge placed between the points (**Figure 17**) while the breaker arm rubbing block is on the high point of a distributor cam lobe (**Figure 18**). The gap is correct when the gauge passes through the contact point gap with a slight bit of friction.

4. If the point gap needs adjustment, loosen the retaining screw. Insert a screwdriver tip

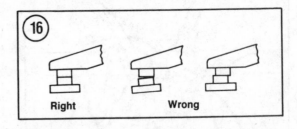

16

Right   Wrong

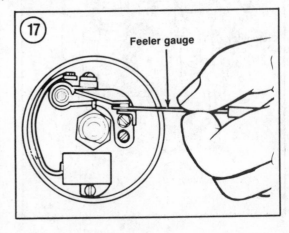

17

Feeler gauge

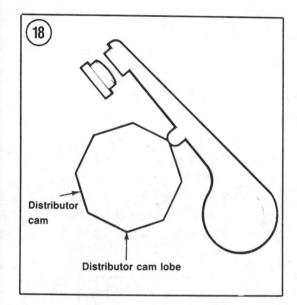

Distributor cam

Distributor cam lobe

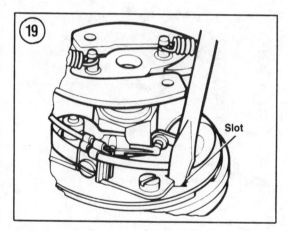

Slot

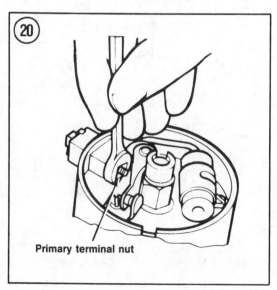

Primary terminal nut

into the notch beside the points (**Figure 19**) and twist to open or close the point gap. When adjustment is correct, tighten the retaining screw. Recheck gap to make sure it did not change when the screw was tightened.

5. If points need replacing, proceed as follows:

    a. Loosen fastener at center of point assembly and slide distributor and condenser leads away from terminal. Remove 2 breaker point attaching screws and lift point set from breaker plate. See **Figure 20**.

    b. Remove the condenser attaching screw and condenser.

    c. Wipe distributor breaker plate, cam and inside of housing with a lint-free cloth to remove all dirt and grease.

    d. Use the cam lubricant supplied with the new point set and lightly lubricate the cam surfaces (**Figure 21**).

    e. Position the new breaker point set on the breaker plate and install the attaching screws. Position a new condenser on the breaker plate and install attaching screw.

    f. Slide breaker point and condenser electrical leads under terminal attaching nut. Tighten nut securely.

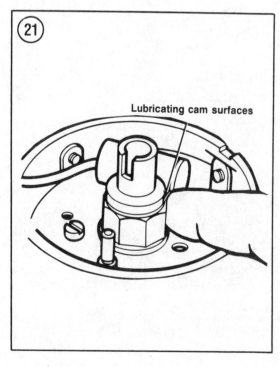

Lubricating cam surfaces

4

g. If distributor has a felt wick in the center of the shaft, lubricate with 1-2 drops of engine oil. See **Figure 22**.

h. Align points and adjust gap as described in Steps 2-4.

6. Align lug on inside of rotor body with distributor shaft cutout and install rotor by pressing downward until it is firmly seated in place. See **Figure 23**.

7. Install distributor cap on distributor housing with the locating tab in correct position. Snap retaining clips into place.

8. Make sure all ignition wires are firmly connected to the distributor cap towers. Install the secondary coil wire to the coil.

Dwell Angle Adjustment

1. Set the parking brake and block the front wheels.

2. Connect a dwell meter according to the manufacturer's instructions.

NOTE
Dwell meters have an adjustment switch for 4-, 6- and 8-cylinder readings. Be sure the switch is set properly for your engine or the reading will be incorrect.

3. Start the engine and let it idle. Read the dwell angle on the meter and compare with specifications (**Table 1**). Shut engine off.

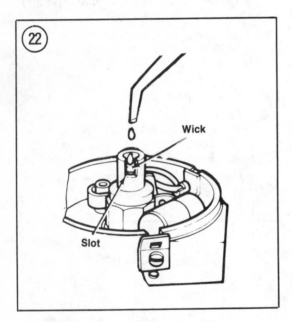

Wick

Slot

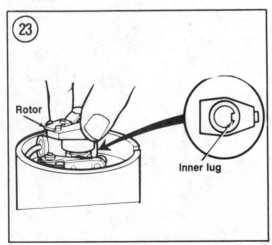

Rotor

Inner lug

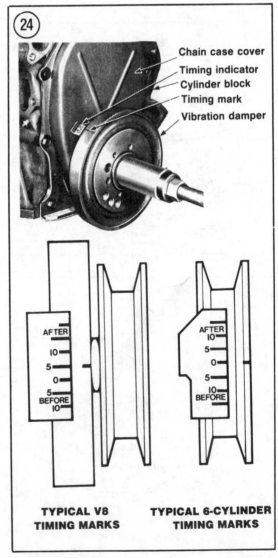

Chain case cover
Timing indicator
Cylinder block
Timing mark
Vibration damper

AFTER
10
5
0
5
BEFORE
10

AFTER
10
5
0
5
10
BEFORE

**TYPICAL V8
TIMING MARKS**

**TYPICAL 6-CYLINDER
TIMING MARKS**

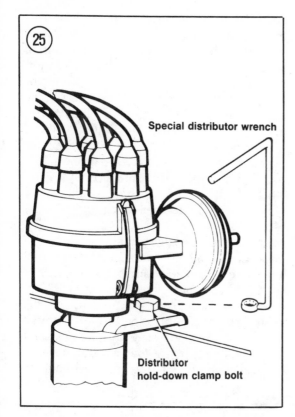

Special distributor wrench

Distributor
hold-down clamp bolt

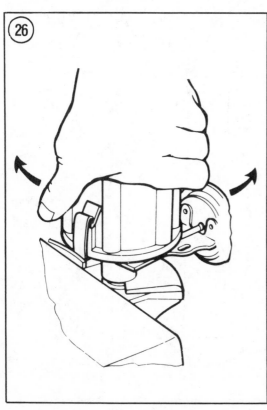

4. If the dwell angle was below the specified amount, the breaker point gap is too large; if angle was above specified amont, breaker point gap is too small. Adjust gap according to Step 3 and Step 4, *Breaker Point Service.*

5. Start engine again and take another dwell reading. Adjust points again if necessary. When dwell meets specifications, shut engine off and disconnect dwell meter.

Ignition Timing Adjustment

Ignition timing should be checked and adjusted (if required) after point replacement and dwell angle adjustment have been completed.

1. Locate the timing marks on your engine. They are found on the timing chain cover and the vibration damper at the front of the engine. See **Figure 24** (typical).

2. Clean the timing marks with a stiff brush. Mark the timing mark and pointer with white paint or chalk for better visibility.

3. Disconnect and plug the distributor vacuum line with a pencil or golf tee.

4. Connect a timing light and tachometer according to manufacturer's instructions.

5. Start the engine and run at idle. Check the idle speed and compare to specifications on the VECI decal. If necessary, adjust engine speed to idle specifications (see Chapter Six for procedure).

6. Aim the timing light at the timing marks. If the ignition is properly timed, the marks will appear to stand still exactly opposite each other under the flashing light. If the marks are not correctly aligned, shut the engine off and loosen the distributor hold-down clamp bolt one full turn. In some installations, the use of a special distributor wrench is necessary. See **Figure 25**.

7. Restart the engine and turn the distributor body slightly to the right or left (**Figure 26**). As you do this, the timing will change according to which direction and how much you turn the distributor.

NOTE
The 400 and 440 cu. in. V8 distributor rotates in a counterclockwise direction. To advance timing, rotate distributor clockwise. All other 6-cylinder and V8

distributors rotate clockwise. To advance timing, rotate distributor counterclockwise.

8. When the timing marks are properly aligned, shut the engine off and tighten the distributor clamp bolt. Restart the engine and recheck timing.

9. When timing is correct, turn off the engine, disconnect the timing light and make sure the distributor clamp bolt is tight. Reconnect the tachometer and start the engine.

10. Check carburetor idle speed and reset to specifications on VECI decal if necessary. Refer to Chapter Six for procedure. Shut engine off.

11. Disconnect the tachometer. Unplug and reconnect the distributor vacuum line.

BREAKERLESS IGNITION SYSTEM

Chrysler Electronic Ignition

The Chrysler Electronic Ignition system initially appeared on certain 1972 models. It is used on all 1973 and later models. This breakerless ignition uses a reluctor and magnetic pickup coil assembly instead of breaker points and a cam in the distributor. The number of teeth on the reluctor corresponds to the number of cylinders in the engine. **Figure 27** shows a breakerless distributor for an 8-cylinder engine; 6-cylinder distributors are the same except for the number of reluctor teeth. An electronic control unit mounted on the firewall (**Figure 28**) turns the ignition current on and off. A typical electronic ignition system is shown in **Figure 29**.

Routine maintenance should be limited to inspection of the distributor cap, rotor, wiring and the changing of spark plugs at intervals specified in Chapter Three. If these check out good and the trouble is still present, take the vehicle to a dealer. Testing of the electronic ignition requires special test equipment and skills and an otherwise good electronic circuit can be damaged by an incorrect test hookup.

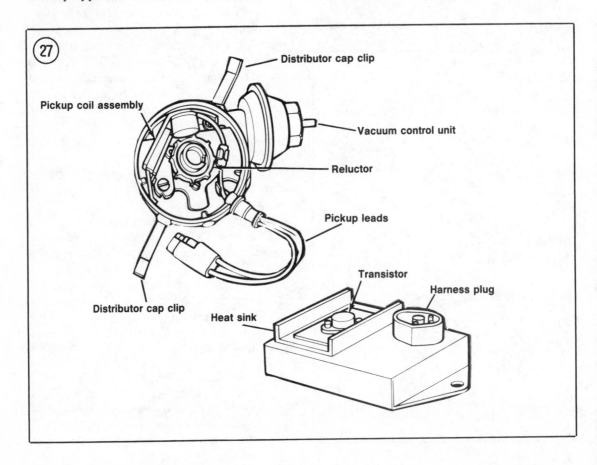

(27)

Distributor cap clip

Pickup coil assembly

Vacuum control unit

Reluctor

Pickup leads

Transistor

Harness plug

Distributor cap clip

Heat sink

It is possible to partially check out the system with a voltmeter and ohmmeter, but the procedure calls for the substitution of parts known to be good. Since parts dealers do not permit the return of electrical parts, this method can be very expensive and is not recommended.

Electronic Lean Burn (ELB) and Electronic Spark Control (ESC) Systems

Some 1976 and most later models use an ELB or ESC system which incorporates the Chrysler Electronic Ignition. These systems consist of a computer and vacuum transducer mounted on the air cleaner housing (**Figure 30**), several sensors located at various positions on the engine and a specially calibrated carburetor. Some applications use a breakerless distributor with one pickup coil; others use 2 pickup coils. The function of the electronic control unit is performed by the computer. Exact system configuration depends upon model year, engine application and point of sale. **Figure 31** shows a typical system.

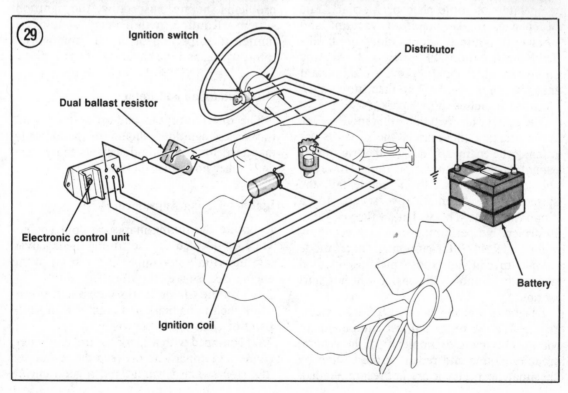

Ignition switch

Distributor

Dual ballast resistor

Electronic control unit

Ignition coil

Battery

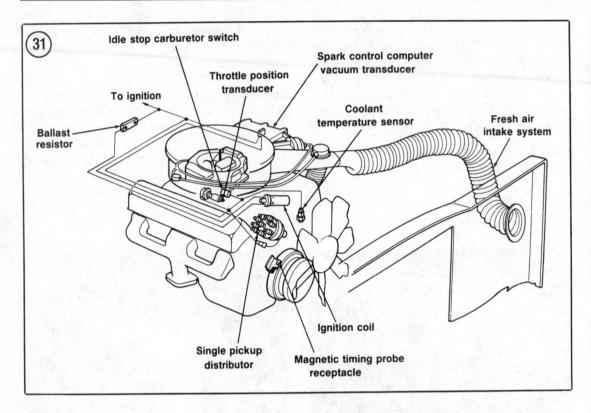

③① Idle stop carburetor switch

Throttle position transducer

Spark control computer vacuum transducer

To ignition

Coolant temperature sensor

Fresh air intake system

Ballast resistor

Single pickup distributor

Ignition coil

Magnetic timing probe receptacle

The sensors supply information concerning engine speed, ignition timing, coolant temperature, throttle plate position and rate of change, intake manifold vacuum and whether or not the engine is idling or off idle. This information is processed by the computer, which determines the exact instant that ignition is required and then supplies the electrical impulses to the spark plugs.

The system has two operating modes. One is for starting the engine; the other is for running the engine. By design, the two modes cannot operate at the same time. However, should the computer "run" mode fail, the system will automatically revert to a "limp-in" mode. This will allow the vehicle to be driven, but performance and gas economy will be affected. If the computer "start" mode or pickup coil fails (both pickups on dual pickup distributors), the engine will not start or run.

Diagnosis and repair of ELB/ESC systems require the use of special test equipment. In view of this and the complexity of the system, troubleshooting and repair of the system by the amateur mechanic are not recommended.

As with the electronic ignition system, eliminate all other possible causes of problems before suspecting the ignition system. Routine maintenance should be limited to inspection of the distributor cap, rotor, wiring and the changing of spark plugs.

Distributor Cap and Rotor

The distributor cap and rotor used with breakerless ignitions should be periodically inspected for the same defects as those seen on breaker point distributors.

Ignition Timing Adjustment

1. Locate the timing marks on your engine. They are located on the timing chain cover and the vibration damper at the front of the engine. See **Figure 24** (typical).
2. Clean the timing marks with a stiff brush. Mark the timing mark and pointer with white paint or chalk for better visibility.
3. If equipped with a spark control computer, connect a jumper wire between the carburetor idle stop switch terminal and a good engine

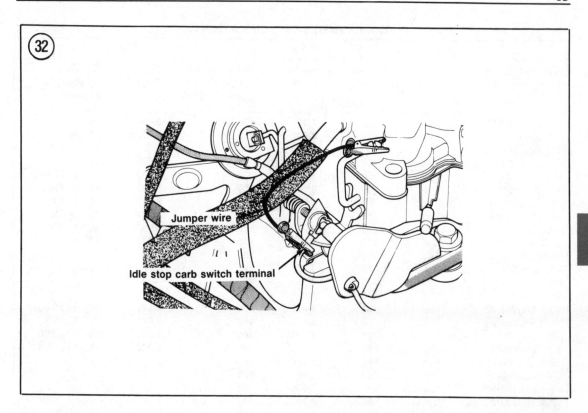

ground (**Figure 32**). On other engines, disconnect and plug the distributor vacuum advance line with a pencil or golf tee.

> *NOTE*
> *Use only a clamp-on or inductive timing light with breakerless ignitions.*

4. Connect an inductive timing light and tachometer according to manufacturer's instructions.
5. Start engine and set the parking brake. Place the transmission in NEUTRAL and let the engine warm to normal operating temperature (upper radiator hose hot).
6. Adjust the curb idle speed to specifications, if necessary. See VECI label on engine for specifications and procedure.
7. Aim timing light at timing marks. If timing is within ±2° of specifications, it is satisfactory.
8. If timing marks are not aligned within ±2°, shut the engine off and loosen the distributor hold-down clamp bolt one full turn. In some installations, the use of a special distributor wrench is necessary. See **Figure 25**.

9. Restart the engine and rotate the distributor body slightly to the right or left (**Figure 26**). As you do this, the timing will change according to which direction and how much you rotate the distributor. When the marks are properly aligned, tighten hold-down clamp bolt.

> *NOTE*
> *The 400 and 440 cu. in. V8 distributor rotates in a counterclockwise direction. To advance timing, rotate distributor clockwise. All other 6-cylinder and V8 distributors rotate clockwise. To advance timing, rotate distributor counterclockwise.*

9. Recheck timing and shut engine off.
10. Disconnect equipment. Unplug and reconnect vacuum line to distributor or remove carburetor switch jumper lead, as appropriate.

CARBURETOR ADJUSTMENTS

Refer to Chapter Six for procedures.

Table 1 TUNE-UP SPECIFICATIONS

Cyl./Carb./CID/ Transmission	Usage[1]	Idle Speed Curb	Fast	Compression (psi, minimum)[2]	Point Gap[3]	Dwell Angle @ rpm[4]
6/1 bbl/198/M	Fed.	800	2,000	100	0.020	44° @ 800
6/1 bbl/198/A	Fed.	800	1,900	100	0.020	44° @ 800
6/1 bbl/198/M,A	Cal.	700	2,000	100	0.020	44° @ 700
6/1 bbl/225/M	Fed.	750	2,000	100	0.020	44° @ 750
6/1 bbl/225/A	Fed.	750	1,900	100	0.020	44° @ 750
6/1 bbl/225/M,A	Cal.	700	2,000	100	0.020	44° @ 700
V8/2 bbl/318/M	Fed.	750	1,900	100	0.017	32° @ 750
V8/2 bbl/318/A	Fed.	750	1,700	100	0.017	32° @ 750
V8/2 bbl/318/M	Cal.	750	2,000	100	0.017	32° @ 750
V8/2 bbl/318/A	Cal.	700	1,800	100	0.017	32° @ 700
V8/4 bbl/340/M	Fed.	900	1,900	100		
V8/4 bbl/340/A	Fed.	750	1,900	100		
V8/4 bbl 340/M	Cal.	850	1,900	100		
V8/4 bbl 340/A	Cal.	750	1,900	100		
V8/2 bbl/360/A	Fed.	750	1,900	100	0.017	32° @ 750
V8/2 bbl/360/A	Fed.	750	2,000	100	0.017	32° @ 750
V8/2 bbl/400/A	Fed.	700	1,900	100	0.018	30.5° @ 700
V8/2 bbl/400/A	Cal.	700	2,000	100	0.018	30.5° @ 700
V8/4 bbl/400/M	Fed.	900	1,900	100		
V8/4 bbl/400/A	Fed.	750	1,900	100		
V8/4 bbl/400/M	Cal.	800	2,000	100		
V8/4 bbl/400/A	Cal.	750	2,100	100		
V8/4 bbl/440/A	Fed.	700	1,600	100	0.017	32° @ 750
V8/4 bbl/440/A	Cal.	700	1,500	100	0.018	30.5° @ 700
V8/4 bbl/440/M	Fed.	900	1,800	110		
V8/4 bbl/440/A	Fed.	900	1,600	110		
V8/4 bbl/440/M	Cal.	800	2,000	110		
V8/4 bbl/440/A	Cal.	700	1,500	110		
V8/3-2 bbl/440/A	Fed.	900	1,800	110		

Cyl./Carb./CID/ Transmission	Usage[1]	Spark Plugs Type (Champion)	Gap (in.)	Timing (degrees BTC)[5]	Air-fuel Ratio
6/1 bbl/198/M	Fed.	N14Y	0.035	2.5	14.2:1
6/1 bbl/198/A	Fed.	N14Y	0.035	2.5	14.2:1
6/1 bbl/198/M,A	Cal.	N14Y	0.035	2.5	14.3:1
6/1 bbl/225/M	Fed.	N14Y	0.035	TDC	14.2:1
6/1 bbl/225/A	Fed.	N14Y	0.035	TDC	14.2:1
6/1 bbl/225/M,A	Cal.	N14Y	0.035	2.5	14.3:1
V8/2 bbl/318/M	Fed.	N13Y	0.035	TDC	14.2:1
V8/2 bbl/318/A	Fed.	N13Y	0.035	TDC	14.2:1
V8/2 bbl/318/M	Cal.	N13Y	0.035	TDC	14.3:1
V8/2 bbl/318/A	Cal.	N13Y	0.035	TDC	14.3:1
V8/4 bbl/340/M	Fed.	N9Y	0.035	TDC	14.2:1
V8/4 bbl/340/A	Fed.	N9Y	0.035	2.5	14.2:1
V8/4 bbl 340/M	Cal.	N9Y	0.035	2.5	14.3:1

(continued)

Table 1 TUNE-UP SPECIFICATIONS (continued)

Cyl./Carb./CID/ Transmission	Usage[1]	Spark Plugs Type (Champion)	Gap (in.)	Timing (degrees BTC)[5]	Air-fuel Ratio
1972 (cont.)					
V8/4 bbl 340/A	Cal.	N9Y	0.035	2.5	14.3:1
V8/2 bbl/360/A	Fed.	N13Y	0.035	TDC	14.2:1
V8/2 bbl/360/A	Fed.	N13Y	0.035	TDC	14.3:1
V8/2 bbl/400/A	Fed.	J13Y	0.035	5	14.2:1
V8/2 bbl/400/A	Cal.	J13Y	0.035	5	14.3:1
V8/4 bbl/400/M	Fed.	J11Y	0.035	TDC	14.2:1
V8/4 bbl/400/A	Fed.	J11Y	0.035	10	14.2:1
V8/4 bbl/400/M	Cal.	J11Y	0.035	2.5	14.3:1
V8/4 bbl/400/A	Cal.	J11Y	0.035	5	14.3:1
V8/4 bbl/440/A	Fed.	J11Y	0.035	10	14.2:1
V8/4 bbl/440/A	Cal.	J11Y	0.035	5	14.3:1
V8/4 bbl/440/M	Fed.	J11Y	0.035	2.5	14.2:1
V8/4 bbl/440/A	Fed.	J11Y	0.035	10	14.2:1
V8/4 bbl/440/M	Cal.	J11Y	0.035	2.5	14.3:1
V8/4 bbl/440/A	Cal.	J11Y	0.035	5	14.3:1
V8/3-2 bbl/440/A	Fed.	J11Y	0.035	2.5	14.2:1

1. "Usage" indicates original point of sale; Cal. = California, Fed. = all others.
2. Maximum variation between cylinders: 6-cyl., 25 psi; V8, 40 psi.
3. ±0.003 in.; not required on engines with electronic ignition.
4. ±2°; not required on engines with electronic ignition.
5. ±2.5°.

Cyl./Carb./CID/ Transmission	Usage[1]	Idle Speed Curb	Fast	Compression (psi, minimum)[2]
1973				
6/1 bbl/198/M	All	800	2,000	100
6/1 bbl/198/A	All	750	1,700	100
6/1 bbl/225/M	Fed.	750	2,000	100
6/1 bbl/225/A	Fed.	750	1,700	100
V8/2 bbl/318/M	All	750	1,700	100
V8/2 bbl/318/A	Fed.	750	1,700	100
V8/2 bbl/318/A	Cal.	700	1,700	100
V8/4 bbl/340/M	All	900	1,300	100
V8/4 bbl/340/A	All	750	1,800	100
V8/2 bbl/360/A	All	750	1,900	100
V8/2 bbl/360/A	All	750	1,900	100
V8/2 bbl/400/A	All	700	1,800	100
V8/4 bbl/400/M	Fed.	800	1,700	100
V8/4 bbl/400/A	Fed.	750	1,800	100
V8/4 bbl/400/M	Cal.	900	1,700	100
V8/4 bbl/400/A	Cal.	750	1,800	100
V8/4 bbl/440/A	All	700	1,700	100
V8/4 bbl/440/A	All	800	1,700	100

4

(continued)

Table 1 TUNE-UP SPECIFICATIONS (continued)

1973 (cont.)					
Cyl./Carb./CID Transmission	Usage[1]	Spark Plugs Type (Champion)	Gap (in.)	Timing (degrees BTC)[3]	Air-fuel Ratio
6/1 bbl/198/M	All	N14Y	0.035	TDC	14.2:1
6/1 bbl/198/A	All	N14Y	0.035	TDC	14.2:1
6/1 bbl/225/M	Fed.	N14Y	0.035	2.5	14.2:1
6/1 bbl/225/A	Fed.	N14Y	0.035	2.5	14.2:1
V8/2 bbl/318/M	All	N13Y	0.035	TDC	14.2:1
V8/2 bbl/318/A	Fed.	N13Y	0.035	TDC	14.2:1
V8/2 bbl/318/A	Cal.	N13Y	0.035	TDC	14.3:1
V8/4 bbl/340/M	All	N12Y	0.035	5	14.2:1
V8/4 bbl/340/A	All	N12Y	0.035	2.5[4]	14.2:1
V8/2 bbl/360/A	All	N13Y	0.035	TDC	14.2:1
V8/2 bbl/360/A	All	N13Y	0.035	5	14.2:1
V8/2 bbl/400/A	All	J13Y	0.035	10	14.2:1
V8/4 bbl/400/M	Fed.	J11Y	0.035	2.5	14.2:1
V8/4 bbl/400/A	Fed.	J11Y	0.035	7.5	14.2:1
V8/4 bbl/400/M	Cal.	J11Y	0.035	2.5	14.2:1
V8/4 bbl/400/A	Cal.	J11Y	0.035	7.5	14.3:1
V8/4 bbl/440/A	All	J11Y	0.035	10	14.2:1
V8/4 bbl/440/A	All	J11Y	0.035	10	14.2:1

1. "Usage" indicates original point of sale; Cal. = California, Fed. = all others.
2. Maximum variation between cylinders: 6-cyl., 25 psi; V8, 40 psi.
3. ±2.5°.
4. Late California models, TDC.

1974				
Cyl./Carb./CID/ Transmission	Usage[1]	Idle Speed		Compression (psi, minimum)[2]
		Curb	Fast	
6/1 bbl/198/M	Fed.	800	1,600	100
6/1 bbl/198/A	Fed.	750	1,800	100
6/1 bbl/225/M	All	800	1,600	100
6/1 bbl/225/A	All	750	1,800	100
V8/2 bbl/318/M	All	750	1,700	100
V8/2 bbl/318/A	All	750	1,500	100
V8/2 bbl/360/A	Fed.	750	1,800	100
V8/4 bbl/360/A	Cal.	750	1,800	100
V8/4 bbl/360 HP/M	All	850	1,900	100
V8/4 bbl/360 HP/A	Fed.	850	1,900	100
V8/4 bbl/360 HP/A	Cal.	850	1,900	100
V8/2 bbl/400/A	Fed.	750	1,600	100
V8/4 bbl/400/A	All	900	2,000	100
V8/4 bbl/400 HP/M	Fed.	900	1,700	100
V8/4 bbl/400 HP/A	Cal.	900	1,800	100
V8/4 bbl/440/A	All	750	1,700	100
V8/4 bbl/440 HP/A	Fed.	800	1.700	100
V8/4 bbl/440 HP/A	Cal.	800	1,700	100

(continued)

Table 1 TUNE-UP SPECIFICATIONS (continued)

1974 (cont.)					
Cyl./Carb./CID/ Transmission	Usage[1]	Spark Plugs		Timing (degrees BTC)[3]	Air-fuel Ratio
		Type (Champion)	Gap		
6/1 bbl/198/M	Fed.	N14Y	0.035	2.5	14.3:1
6/1 bbl/198/A	Fed.	N14Y	0.035	2.5	14.3:1
6/1 bbl/225/M	All	N14Y	0.035	TDC	14.3:1
6/1 bbl/225/A	All	N14Y	0.035	TDC	14.3:1
V8/2 bbl/318/M	All	N13Y	0.035	TDC	14.3:1
V8/2 bbl/318/A	All	N13Y	0.035	TDC	14.3:1
V8/2 bbl/360/A	Fed.	N12Y	0.035	5	14.3:1
V8/4 bbl/360/A	Cal.	N12Y	0.035	5[4]	14.1:1
V8/4 bbl/360 HP/M	All	N12Y	0.035	5	14.3:1
V8/4 bbl/360 HP/A	Fed.	N12Y	0.035	5	14.3:1
V8/4 bbl/360 HP/A	Cal.	N12Y	0.035	5	14.1:1
V8/2 bbl/400/A	Fed.	J13Y	0.035	7.5[5]	14.3:1
V8/4 bbl/400/A	All	J13Y	0.035	5	14.3:1
V8/4 bbl/400 HP/M	Fed.	J11Y	0.035	5	14.3:1
V8/4 bbl/400 HP/A	Cal.	J11Y	0.035	2.5	14.1:1
V8/4 bbl/440/A	All	J11Y	0.035	10	14.3:1
V8/4 bbl/440 HP/A	Fed.	J11Y	0.035	10	14.3:1
V8/4 bbl/440 HP/A	Cal.	J11Y	0.035	5	14.1:1

1. "Usage" indicates original point of sale; Cal. = California, Fed. = all others.
2. Maximum variation between cylinders: 6-cyl., 25 psi; V8, 40 psi.
3. ±2°.
4. Late models and station wagons, 2.5° BTDC.
5. Station wagons, 5° BTDC.

1975				
Cyl./Carb./CID/ Transmission	Usage[1]	Idle Speed		Compres- sion (psi, minimum)[2]
		Curb	Fast	
6/1 bbl/225/M	All	800	1,600	100
6/1 bbl/225/A	Fed.	750	1,700	100
6/1 bbl/225/A	Cal.	750	1,700	100
V8/2 bbl/318/M	Fed.	750	1,500	100
V8/2 bbl/318/A	Fed.	750	1,500	100
V8/2 bbl/318/A	Cal.	750	1,500	100
V8/2 bbl/318/A	Fed.	900	1,500	100
V8/2 bbl/360/A	Fed.	750	1,600	100
V8/4 bbl/360/A	Cal.	750	1,600	100
V8/4 bbl/360 HP/M	Fed.	850	1,600	100
V8/2 bbl/400/A	Fed.	750	1,600	100
V8/4 bbl/400/A	Fed.	750	1,800	100
V8/4 bbl/400/A	Cal.	750	1,800	100
V8/4 bbl/400/A	Fed.	750	1,800	100
V8/4 bbl/400 HP/A	Cal.	850	1,800	100
V8/4 bbl/440/A	Fed.	750	1,600	100
V8/4 bbl/440 HP/A	Fed.	750	1,600	100
V8/4 bbl/440 HP/A	Cal.	750	1,600	100

(continued)

Table 1 TUNE-UP SPECIFICATIONS (continued)

1975 (cont.)					
Cyl./Carb./CID/ Transmission	Usage[1]	Spark Plugs Type (Champion)	Gap	Timing (Degrees BTDC)[3]	Idle CO %
6/1 bbl/225/M	All	BL13Y	0.035	TDC	0.3
6/1 bbl/225/A	Fed.	BL13Y	0.035	TDC	0.3
6/1 bbl/225/A	Cal.	BL13Y	0.035	TDC	1.5
V8/2 bbl/318/M	Fed.	N13Y	0.035	2	0.3
V8/2 bbl/318/A	Fed.	N13Y	0.035	2[4]	0.3
V8/2 bbl/318/A	Cal.	N13Y	0.035	TDC	0.5
V8/2 bbl/318/A	Fed.	N13Y	0.035	2° ATDC[5]	0.5
V8/2 bbl/360/A	Fed.	N12Y	0.035	6	0.3
V8/4 bbl/360/A	Cal.	N12Y	0.035	6	0.5
V8/4 bbl/360 HP/M	Fed.	N12Y	0.035	2	0.5
V8/2 bbl/400/A	Fed.	J13Y	0.035	10	0.3
V8/4 bbl/400/A	Fed.	J13Y	0.035	8	0.3
V8/4 bbl/400/A	Cal.	J13Y	0.035	8	0.5
V8/4 bbl/400/A	Fed.	RJ87P	0.035	8	0.3
V8/4 bbl/400 HP/A	Cal.	RJ87P	0.035	6	0.5
V8/4 bbl/440/A	Fed.	J13Y	0.035	8	0.3
V8/4 bbl/440 HP/A	Fed.	J11Y	0.035	10	0.3
V8/4 bbl/440 HP/A	Cal.	J11Y	0.035	10	0.5

1. "Usage" indicates original point of sale; Cal. = California, Fed. = all others.
2. Maximum variation between cylinders: 6-cyl., 25 psi; V8, 40 psi.
3. ±2°.
4. With catalytic converter.
5. Without catalytic converter.

1976				
Cyl./Carb./CID/ Transmission	Usage[1]	Idle Speed Curb	Fast	Compression (psi, minimum)[2]
6/2 bbl/225/M	Fed.	750	1,600	100
6/1 bbl/225/M	Cal.	800	1,600	100
6/1 bbl/225/A	Fed.	750	1,700	100
6/1 bbl/225/A	Cal.	750	1,700	100
V8/2 bbl/318/M	Fed.	750	1,500	100
V8/2 bbl/318/A	Fed.	750	1,200	100
V8/2 bbl/318/A	Cal.	750	1,500	100
V8/2 bbl/318/A	Fed.	900	1,500	100
V8/2 bbl/360/A	Fed.	700	1,600	100
V8/4 bbl/360/A	Cal.	750	1,700	100
V8/4 bbl/360 HP/M	Fed.	850	1,700	100
V8/2 bbl/400/A	Fed.	700	1,600	100
V8/4 bbl/400/A	Fed.	850	1,800	100
V8/4 bbl/400/A	Cal.	750	1,800	100
V8/4 bbl/400 ELB/A	Fed.	700	1,600	100
V8/4 bbl/440/A	All	750	1,600	100
V8/4 bbl/440 HP/A	Fed.	750	1,600	100
V8/4 bbl/440 HP/A	Fed.	750	1,600	100

(continued)

Table 1 TUNE-UP SPECIFICATIONS (continued)

1976 (cont.)

Cyl./Carb./CID/ Transmission	Usage[1]	Spark Plugs Type (Champion)	Gap	Timing (degrees BTC)	Idle CO %
6/2 bbl/225/M	Fed.	RBL13Y	0.035	6	0.3
6/1 bbl/225/M	Cal.	RBL13Y	0.035	4	1.0
6/1 bbl/225/A	Fed.	RBL13Y	0.035	2	0.3
6/1 bbl/225/A	Cal.	RBL13Y	0.035	2	1.0
V8/2 bbl/318/M	Fed.	RN12Y	0.035	2	0.3
V8/2 bbl/318/A	Fed.	RN12Y	0.035	2[4]	0.3
V8/2 bbl/318/A	Cal.	RN12Y	0.035	2	1.0
V8/2 bbl/318/A	Fed.	RN12Y	0.035	2° ATDC[5]	0.5
V8/2 bbl/360/A	Fed.	RN12Y	0.035	6	0.3
V8/4 bbl/360/A	Cal.	RN12Y	0.035	6	2.0
V8/4 bbl/360 HP/M	Fed.	RN12Y	0.035	2	0.5
V8/2 bbl/400/A	Fed.	RJ13Y	0.035	10	0.3
V8/4 bbl/400/A	Fed.	RJ13Y	0.035	6	0.5
V8/4 bbl/400/A	Cal.	RJ13Y	0.035	8	0.5
V8/4 bbl/400 ELB/A	Fed.	RJ87P/RJ13Y	0.035	8	0.1
V8/4 bbl/440/A	All	RJ13Y	0.035	8	0.3
V8/4 bbl/440 HP/A	Fed.	RJ11Y	0.035	10	0.3
V8/4 bbl/440 HP/A	Fed.	RJ11Y	0.035	8	0.5

1. "Usage" indicates original point of sale; Cal. = California, Fed. = all others.
2. Maximum variation between cylinders: 6-cyl., 25 psi; V8, 40 psi.
3. ±2°.
4. With catalytic converter.
5. Without catalytic converter.

1977[1]

Cyl./Carb./CID/ Transmission	Basic Timing (degrees BTDC)	Idle Speeds Curb	Propane Enriched	Idle CO %	Spark Plugs (Champion)
Federal and Canadian models with Electronic Ignition					
6/1 bbl/225/M	12	700	835	–	RBL15Y
6/1 bbl/225/A	12	700	790	–	RBL15Y
6/1 bbl/225/M	6	700	805	–	RBL15Y
6/1 bbl/225/A	12	700	830	–	RBL15Y
6/1 bbl/225/M	12	750	930	–	RBL15Y
6/1 bbl/225/A	12	750	900	–	RBL15Y
8/2 bbl/318/M	8	700	810	–	RN12Y
8/2 bbl/318/A	8	700	780	–	RN12Y
8/2 bbl/360/A	10	700	810	–	RN12Y
California models with Electronic Ignition					
6/1 bbl/225/M/A	8	750	–	0.3	RBL15Y
6/2 bbl/225/M/A	4	850	–	0.5	RBL15Y
8/2 bbl/318/M	TDC	850	–	0.5	RN12Y
8/4 bbl/360/A	6	750	–	0.2	RN12Y
8/4 bbl/440/A	8	750	–	1.0	RJ13Y
High altitude models with Electronic Ignition					
6/1 bbl/225/A	8	750	820[2]	–	RBL15Y
6/2 bbl/318/A	TDC	850	900[3]	–	RN12Y
8/4 bbl/360/A	6	750	830[4]	–	RN12Y
Federal and Canadian models with Lean Burn Ignition					
8/4 bbl/360/A	10	750	860	–	RN12Y
8/4 bbl/400/A	10	750	880	–	RJ13Y
8/4 bbl/440/A	12	750	850	–	RJ13Y

(continued)

Table 1 TUNE-UP SPECIFICATIONS (continued)

1977[1] (cont.)					
Cyl./Carb./CID/ Transmission	Basic Timing (degrees BTDC)	Idle Speeds		Idle CO %	Spark Plugs (Champion)
		Curb	Propane Enriched		
California models with Lean Burn Ignition					
8/4 bbl/440/A	8	750	–	0.3	RJ13Y
High altitude models with Lean Burn Ignition					
8/4 bbl/440/A	8	750	850[5]	–	RJ13Y

1. Compression pressure 100 psi, minimum. Maximum variation between cylinders: 6-cyl., 25 psi; V8, 40 psi.
2. Above 4,000 ft., adjust to 850 rpm.
3. Above 4,000 ft., adjust to 930 rpm.
4. Above 4,000 ft., adjust to 850 rpm.
5. Above 4,000 ft., adjust to 870 rpm.

1978[1]					
Cyl./Carb./CID/ Transmission	Basic Timing (degrees BTDC)	Idle Speeds		Idle CO %	Spark Plugs (Champion)
		Curb	Propane Enriched		
Federal and Canadian models with Electronic Ignition					
6/1 bbl/225/M	12	700	835	–	RBL16Y
6/1 bbl/225/A	12	700	790	–	RBL16Y
6/1 bbl/225/M	2° ATDC	750	880	–	RBL16Y
6/1 bbl/225/A	12	700	790	–	RBL16Y
6/2 bbl/225/M	12	750	930	–	RBL16Y
6/2 bbl/225/A	12	750	900	–	RBL16Y
California models with Electronic Ignition					
6/1 bbl/225/M,A	8	750	850	0.3	RBL16Y
6/1 bbl/225/A	8	750	880	0.3	RBL16Y
6/1 bbl/225/A	8	750	820	0.3	RBL16Y
8/4 bbl/360/A	6	750	830	0.5	RN12Y
8/4 bbl/360/A	8	750	830	0.5	RN12Y
8/4 bbl/440/A	8	750	860	1.0	OJ13Y
High altitude models with Electronic Ignition					
6/1 bbl/225/A	8	750	880[2]	–	RBL16Y
8/4 bbl/360/A	6	750	830[3]	–	RN12Y
8/4 bbl/360/A	8	750	750[4]	–	RN12Y
Federal and Canadian models with Lean Burn Ignition					
8/2 bbl/318/M	16	700	810	–	RN12Y
8/2 bbl/318/A	16	750	850	–	RN12Y
8/4 bbl/318/A	16	750	825	–	RN12Y
8/2 bbl/360/A	20[4]	750	890	–	RN12Y
8/4 bbl/360/A	16	750	900	–	RN12Y
8/4 bbl/400/A	24	750	840[5]	–	OJ13Y
8/4 bbl/400/A	20	750	840	–	OJ13Y
8/4 bbl/440/A	16	750	825	–	OJ13Y
California models with Lean Burn Ignition					
8/4 bbl/318/A	10	750	825	0.5	RN12Y
High altitude models with Lean Burn Ignition					
8/2 bbl/318/A	16	750	830[6]	–	RN12Y

1. Compression pressure 100 psi, minimum. Maximum variation between cylinders: 6-cyl., 25 psi; V8, 40 psi.
2. Above 4,000 ft., adjust to 910 rpm.
3. Above 4,000 ft., adjust to 850 rpm.
4. 12° BTDC on Canadian 4,000/4,500 GVW cars.
5. On Canadian vehicles, 20° BTDC and adjust propane enriched idle speed to 825 rpm.
6. Above 4,000 ft., adjust to 880 rpm.

Table 1 TUNE-UP SPECIFICATIONS (continued)

1979[1]					
Cyl./Carb./CID	Vehicle Weight (lbs.)	Basic Timing (degrees BTDC)	Idle Speeds		Spark Plugs (Mopar)
			Curb	Propane Enriched	
Federal and Canadian models with Electronic Ignition					
6/1 bbl/225	3500	12	675	830[2]	560 PR
6/1 bbl/225	4000	12	675	845	560 PR
6/1 bbl/225	3500-4000	12	830	830	560 PR
6/2 bbl/225	All	12	725[3]	890	560 PR
Federal and Canadian models with Electronic Spark Control					
8/2 bbl/318	4000	16	730	850	65 PR
8/4 bbl/318	4000	16	750	850	65 PR
8/2 bbl/360	4000/5000	12	750	850	65 PR
8/4 bbl/360	4000/5000	16[4]	750	870	65 PR
California models with Electronic Spark Control					
6/1 bbl/225	All	8	750	925[5]	560 PR
8/4 bbl/318	4000/5000	16	750	850[6]	65 PR
8/4 bbl/360	All	16	750	870[6]	65 PR

1. Compression pressure 100 psi, minimum. Maximum variation between cylinders: 6-cyl., 25 psi; V8, 40 psi.
2. 845 with manual transmission.
3. Late models, 750 rpm.
4. Canada, 10°.
5. Idle CO% 0.3.
6. Idle CO% 0.5.

4

1980[1]					
Cyl./Carb./CID	Vehicle Weight (lbs.)	Basic Timing (degrees BTDC)	Idle Speeds		Spark Plugs (Mopar)
			Curb	Propane Enriched	
Federal and Canadian models with Electronic Ignition					
6/1 bbl/225	All	12	725	880[2]	560 PR
6/2 bbl/225	3750/4000	12	750	885	560 PR
6/2 bbl/225	4000	12	700[3]	800[4]	560 PR
Federal and Canadian models with Electronic Spark Control					
8/4 bbl/318	4000/4250	10	750	800	65 PR
8/2 bbl/360	4250	12	700	800	65 PR
8/4 bbl/360	4000	10	750	870[5]	65 PR
8/4 bbl/360	4250	16	750	870[5]	65 PR
California models with Electronic Spark Control					
6/1 bbl/225	All	12	750	–	560 PR

1. Compression pressure 100 psi, minimum. Maximum variation between cylinders: 6-cyl., 25 psi; V8, 40 psi.
2. Canada, 860 rpm.
3. Canada, 730 rpm.
4. Canada, 760 rpm.
5. Canada, 830 rpm.

Table 1 TUNE-UP SPECIFICATIONS

1981[1]					
Cyl./Carb./CID	Vehicle Weight (lbs.)	Basic Timing (degrees BTDC)	Idle Speeds		Spark Plugs Mopar)
			Curb	Propane Enriched	
Federal and Canadian models with Electronic Ignition					
6/1 bbl/225	All	12	650	750	560 PR4
6/2 bbl/225	3500	12	750	885	560 PR4
Federal models with Electronic Spark Control					
8/2 bbl/318	4000	16	700	760	65 PR4
8/4 bbl/318	4000	16	700	775	65 PR4
8/EFI/318	All	12	580	–	68 ER
Canadian models with Electronic Spark Control					
8/2 bbl/318	4000	16	730	885	4091713
8/4 bbl/318	4000	16	750	800	4091713
8/EFI/318	All	12	580	–	68 ER
California models with Electronic Spark Control					
6/1 bbl/225	3750	16	750	870	560 PR4
8/2 bbl/318	4000	16	700	775	65 PR4
8/4 bbl/318	4250	16	700	775	65 PR4
8/EFI/318	All	12	580	–	68 ER

1. Compression pressure 100 psi, minimum. Maximum variation between cylinders: 6-cyl., 25 psi; V8, 40 psi.

1982[1]				
Cyl./Carb./CID/ Transmission	Basic Timing (degrees BTDC)	Idle Speeds		Spark Plugs (Mopar)
		Curb	Propane Enriched	
Federal and Canadian models with Electronic Ignition				
6/1 bbl/225/A	12	625	725	560 PR
6/2 bbl/225/A	12	750	885	560 PR
Federal models with Electronic Spark Control				
8/2 bbl/318/A	16	600	760	65 PR
8/4 bbl/318/A	16	650	775	65 PR4
8/EFI/318/A	12	580	–	68 ER
Canadian models with Electronic Spark Control				
8/2 bbl/318/A	16	730	830	65 PR
8/4 bbl/318/A	16	710	775	65 PR4
8/EFI/318/A	12	580	–	68 ER
California models with Electronic Spark Control				
6/1 bbl/225/A	12	725	870	560 PR
8/4 bbl/318/A	16	650	775	65 PR4
8/EFI/318/A	12	580	–	68 ER

1. Compression pressure 100 psi, minimum. Maximum variation between cylinders: 6-cyl., 25 psi; V8, 40 psi.

Table 1 TUNE-UP SPECIFICATIONS (continued)

Cyl./Carb./CID/ Transmission	Basic Timing (degrees BTDC)	Idle Speeds Curb	Propane Enriched	Spark Plugs (Mopar)
1983[1]				
Canadian models with Electronic Ignition				
6/2 bbl/225/A	12	750	885	560 PR
Federal models with Electronic Spark Control				
6/1 bbl/225/A	16	750	835	65 PR
8/2 bbl/318/A	16	700	760	65 PR
8/4 bbl/318/A	16	700	775	65 PR4
8/EFI/318/A	12	580	–	68 ER
Canadian models with Electronic Spark Control				
8/2 bbl/318/A	16	730	830	65 PR
8/4 bbl/318/A	16	730	775	65 PR4
8/EFI/318/A	12	580	–	68 ER
California models with Electronic Spark Control				
6/1 bbl/225/A	16	750	835	560 PR
8/2 bbl/318/A	16	700	760	65 PR
8/4 bbl/318/A	16	700	775	65 PR4
8/EFI/318/A	12	580	–	68 ER

1. Compression pressure 100 psi, minimum. Maximum variation between cylinders: 6-cyl., 25 psi; V8, 40 psi.

Cyl./Carb./CID/ Transmission	Basic Timing (degrees BTDC)	Idle Speeds Curb	Propane Enriched	Spark Plugs (Mopar)
1984[1]				
Federal models with Electronic Spark Control				
8/2 bbl/318/A	16	700	775	65PR
8/4 bbl/318/A	16	700	800	65PR
Canadian models with Electronic Spark Control				
8/2 bbl/318/A	16	700	775	65PR
8/4 bbl/318/A	16	700	800	65PR
California models with Electronic Spark Control				
8/2 bbl/318/A	16	730	830	65PR
8/4 bbl/318/A	16	700	800	65PR

1. Compression pressure 100 psi, minimum. Maximum variation between cylinders, 40 psi.

Cyl./Carb./CID/ Transmission	Basic Timing (° BTDC)	Idle Speeds Curb	Propane Enriched	Spark Plugs (Mopar)
1985[1]				
Federal and California Models with Electronic Spark Control				
8/2 bbl/318/A	7	680	740	65PR
8/4 bbl/318/A	16	750	700	65PR
Canadian Models with Electronic Spark Control				
8/2 bbl/318/A	7	730	740	65PR
8/4 bbl/318/A	16	750	740	65PR

1. Compression pressure 100 psi, minimum. Maximum variation between cylinders, 40 psi.

(continued)

Table 1 TUNE-UP SPECIFICATIONS (continued)

1986[1]

Cyl./Carb/CID/ Transmission	Basic Timing (° BTDC)	Idle Speeds		Spark Plugs (Champion)
		Curb	Propane Enriched	
Federal and California Models with Electronic Spark Control				
8/2 bbl/318/A	7	See note 2	See note 2	RN12Y
8/4/bbl/318/A	16	See note 2	See note 2	RN12Y
Canadian Models with Electronic Spark Control				
8/2 bbl/318/A	7[3]	See note 2	See note 2	RN12Y
8/4/bbl/318/A	16	See note 2	See note 2	RN12Y

1987

Cyl./Carb/CID Transmission	Basic Timing (° BTDC)	Idle Speeds		Spark Plugs (Champion)
		Curb	Propane Enriched	
50-State Models with Electronic Spark Control				
8/2 bbl/318/A	7	680	See note 2	RN12YC
8/4 bbl/318/A	16	750	See note 2	RN12YC
Canadian Models with Electronic Spark Control				
8/2 bbl/318/A	12	730	See note 2	RN12YC
8/4 bbl/318/A	16	750	See note 2	RN12YC

1. Compression pressure 100 psi, minimum. Maximum variation between cylinders, 25 psi.
2. See VECI label.
3. With computer part No. 4289881, 12° BTDC.

Table 2 ENGINE DISPLACEMENT CODE

Engine Code	Cubic Inch Displacement by Model Year
B	198 (1972-1974)
C	All 1972-1976 225, 1977-1980 225 1V
D	1977-1980 225 2V
E	1981-1982 225 1V
F	1982 225 HD
G	All 1972-1976 318, 1977-1980 318 2V, 1982 225 2V
H	1972-1973 340, 1978-1980 318 4V, 1982 225 HD*, 1983 225 1V
J	1974-1979 360 4V, 1981-1982 318 EFI, 1983 225 HD
K	All 1972-1973 360, 1974-1980 360 2V, 1981-1982 318 2V, 1983 225 2V
L	1974-1975 360 HP, 1979-1980 360 HP, 1982 318 HD, 1983 225 HD*
M	1972-1976 400 2V, 1981-1982 318 4V
N	1974-1978 400 4V
P	1972-1973 400 4V, 1974 400 HP, 1983-on 318 2V
R	1983-on 318 4V
S	1983-on 318 HD
T	1972-1978 440
U	1972-1976 440 HP
V	1972 440 3-2

* Canada only.

ENGINE

This chapter contains engine and cylinder head removal/installation procedures for all vehicles covered in this manual. While complete engine overhaul is beyond the scope of this manual, these procedures will allow you to install a professionally rebuilt engine or remove the cylinder head for gasket replacement or valve repair. **Tables 1-3** are at the end of the chapter.

IDENTIFICATION

All engines have an identification number (EIN). This number is stamped on a pad located below the No. 6 spark plug (6-cylinder, **Figure 1**) or on the right side of the block at the rear of the engine mount (V8, **Figure 2**).

In addition to the EIN, each engine has a serial number which must be used when ordering replacement parts. The 6-cylinder serial number is stamped on the right corner joint face next to the No. 1 cylinder bore. The serial number on all 318, 340 and 360 cid V8 engines is stamped on the left front corner of the block below the cylinder head. See **Figure 3**. The 400 cid V8 engine serial number is stamped on the right bank joint face at the front of the No. 2 cylinder bore. The 440 cid V8 engine serial number is stamped on the left bank pad next to the front tappet rail.

The Vehicle Identification Number (VIN) is the official identification for title and vehicle registration. The VIN is stamped on a metal plate attached to the upper left-hand corner of the instrument panel close to the windshield on the driver's side (**Figure 4**). It can be read from outside the car.

The engine code is the 5th digit/letter of the VIN on 1972-1980 models and the 8th digit/letter of the VIN on 1981 and later models. Engine codes are provided in Chapter Four.

REMOVAL/INSTALLATION

6-cylinder Models

If the car is equipped with air conditioning, have the system discharged by a dealer or air conditioning shop before starting this procedure.

1. Mark the location of the hinges and remove the hood.
2. Disconnect the negative battery cable at the battery and engine.
3. Drain the cooling system. See Chapter Eight.
4. Remove the air cleaner. See Chapter Six.
5. Disconnect the radiator and heater hoses. See Chapter Eight.
6. If equipped with an automatic transmission, disconnect the oil cooler lines

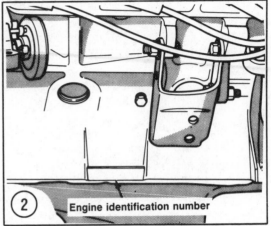

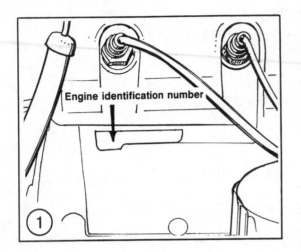

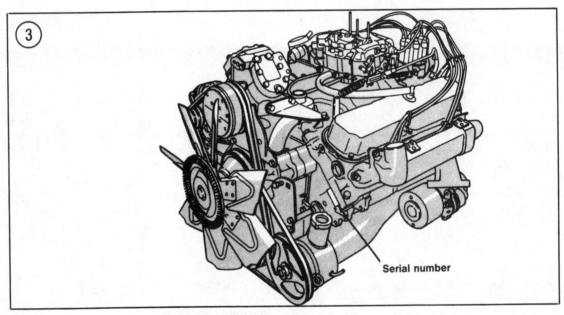

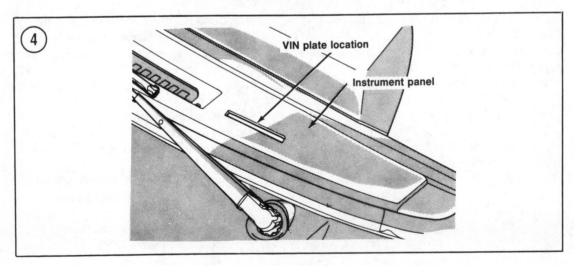

at the radiator tank. Plug the lines and cap the fittings to prevent leakage and contamination.

7. Remove the screws holding the fan shroud in place. Slide the fan shroud back on the fan assembly.

8. Remove the screws holding the radiator. Lift the radiator up and remove it from the engine compartment.

9. If equipped with air conditioning, remove the compressor and place it to one side.

10. If equipped with power steering:

   a. Disconnect the hydraulic fluid lines at the power steering pump. Plug the lines and cap the fittings to prevent leakage.

   b. Remove the power steering pump and place it to one side.

11. Label and disconnect all electrical and vacuum connections at the alternator, carburetor and engine.

12. Disconnect the fuel line at the fuel pump. Plug the line and cap the fitting to prevent leakage.

13. Remove the carburetor. See Chapter Six.

14. Disconnect the spark plug leads and remove the distributor cap. See Chapter Four.

15. Remove the starter motor and alternator. See Chapter Seven.

16. Disconnect and remove the charcoal canister(s).

17. Disconnect and remove the horn(s).

18. Disconnect the exhaust pipe at the exhaust manifold flange.

19. With the vehicle positioned on jackstands, support the transmission with a transmission jack.

20. If equipped with an automatic transmission:

   a. Remove the drive plate inspection cover and scribe a mark on the converter and drive plate for reinstallation reference.

   b. Remove the converter-to-drive plate bolts.

   c. Install a C-clamp at the bottom front of the converter housing to keep the torque converter properly positioned in the transmission.

21. Install engine support fixture part No. C-3487-A and leg part No. C-3806 (or equivalent) to support the rear of the engine.

22. Remove the engine-to-transmission bolts.

NOTE
At this point, there should be no hoses, wires or linkage connecting the engine to the vehicle. Recheck this to be sure nothing will hamper engine removal.

23. Attach an engine support bracket or hoist sling to the engine. Attach the bracket or sling to an engine hoist.

24. Disconnect the engine mounts. See **Figures 5-8**.

25. Pull forward on the engine until it disengages from the transmission. Remove the engine from the vehicle.

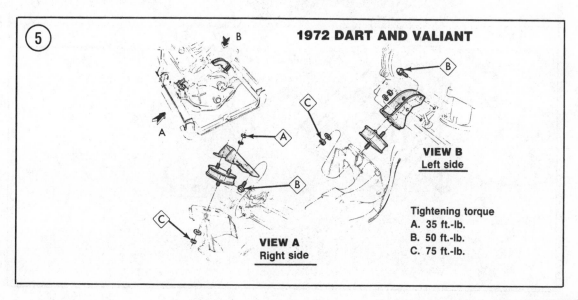

1972 DART AND VALIANT

VIEW B
Left side

VIEW A
Right side

Tightening torque
A. 35 ft.-lb.
B. 50 ft.-lb.
C. 75 ft.-lb.

⑥

ALL OTHER 1972 MODELS

Strut used with air conditioned models only

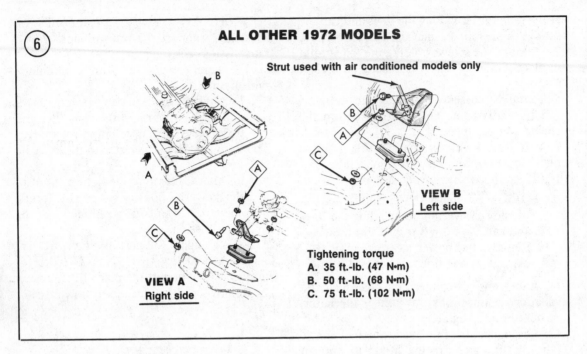

VIEW B
Left side

VIEW A
Right side

Tightening torque
A. 35 ft.-lb. (47 N•m)
B. 50 ft.-lb. (68 N•m)
C. 75 ft.-lb. (102 N•m)

⑦

ALL 1973-1978 MODELS

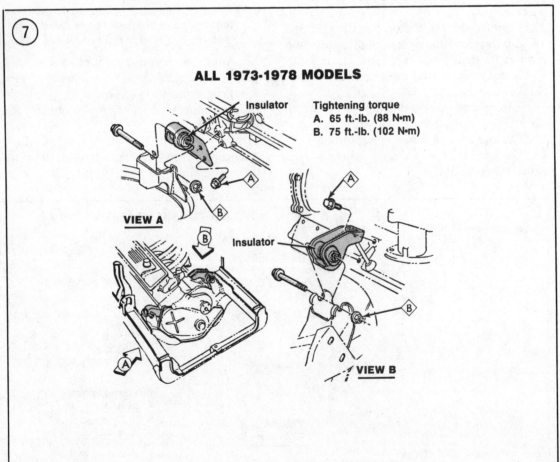

Insulator

Tightening torque
A. 65 ft.-lb. (88 N•m)
B. 75 ft.-lb. (102 N•m)

VIEW A

Insulator

VIEW B

ALL 1979 AND LATER MODELS

Insulator

Bolt

Bolt (A)

Nut (B)

VIEW A
Right side

FORWARD

Tightening torque
A. 65 ft.-lb. (88 N•m)
B. 75 ft.-lb. (102 N•m)
C. 30 ft.-lb. (41 N•m)

FORWARD

Bolt

Washer E and T

Bolt

Insulator

Screw

Strap

Crossmember

Nut

Strap

Screw

VIEW B
Left side

26. Installation is the reverse of removal, plus the following:

    a. Lower the engine into the vehicle. Leave the hoist attached and supporting the engine weight until all mounts have been installed and tightened to specifications (**Table 1**).

    b. Fill the engine with an oil recommended in Chapter Three.

    c. Fill the cooling system. See Chapter Eight.

    d. Adjust the drive belts. See Chapter Eight.

    e. Warm the engine to normal operating temperature and adjust the carburetor and ignition timing as required. See Chapter Four.

318, 340 and 360 cid Models

If the car is equipped with air conditioning, have the system discharged by a dealer or air conditioning shop before starting this procedure.

1. Mark the location of the hinges and remove the hood.

2. Disconnect the negative battery cable at the battery and engine. Disconnect the positive battery cable. Remove the battery.

3. Drain the cooling system. See Chapter Eight.

4. Remove the air cleaner. See Chapter Six.

5. Disconnect the radiator and heater hoses. See Chapter Eight.

6. If equipped with an automatic transmission, disconnect the oil cooler lines at the radiator tank. Plug the lines and cap the fittings to prevent leakage and contamination.

7. Remove the screws holding the fan shroud in place. Slide the fan shroud back on the fan assembly.

8. Remove the screws holding the radiator. Lift the radiator up and remove it from the engine compartment.

9. If equipped with air conditioning, remove the compressor and place it to one side.

10. If equipped with power steering:

    a. Disconnect the hydraulic fluid lines at the power steering pump. Plug the lines and cap the fittings to prevent leakage.

5

8

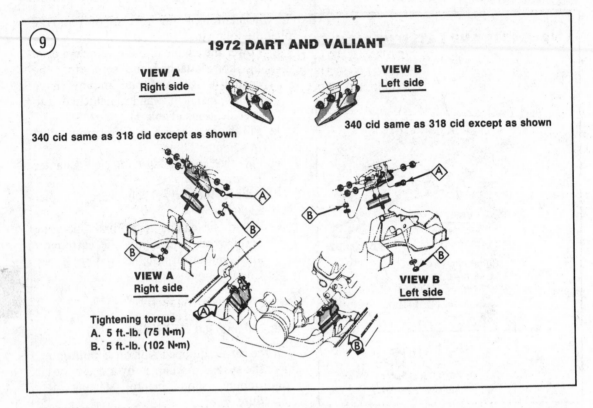

1972 DART AND VALIANT

VIEW A
Right side

VIEW B
Left side

340 cid same as 318 cid except as shown

340 cid same as 318 cid except as shown

VIEW A
Right side

VIEW B
Left side

Tightening torque
A. 5 ft.-lb. (75 N•m)
B. 5 ft.-lb. (102 N•m)

b. Remove the power steering pump and place it to one side.

11. Label and disconnect all electrical and vacuum connections at the alternator, carburetor and engine.

12. Disconnect the fuel line at the fuel pump. Plug the line and cap the fitting to prevent leakage.

13. Remove the carburetor. See Chapter Six.

14. Disconnect the spark plug leads and remove the distributor cap. See Chapter Four.

15. Remove the starter motor and alternator. See Chapter Seven.

16. Disconnect and remove the charcoal canister(s).

17. Disconnect and remove the horn(s).

18. Disconnect the exhaust pipe(s) at the exhaust manifold(s).

19. With the vehicle positioned on jackstands, support the transmission with a transmission jack.

20. If equipped with an automatic transmission:

    a. Remove the drive plate inspection cover and scribe a mark on the converter and drive plate for reinstallation reference.

    b. Remove the converter-to-drive plate bolts.

    c. Install a C-clamp at the bottom front of the converter housing to keep the torque converter properly positioned in the transmission.

21. Install engine support fixture part No. C-3487-A or equivalent) to support the rear of the engine.

22. Remove the engine-to-transmission bolts.

NOTE
At this point, there should be no hoses, wires or linkage connecting the engine to the vehicle. Recheck this to be sure nothing will hamper engine removal.

23. Attach an engine lifting fixture to the carburetor flange studs on the intake manifold. Attach an engine hoist to the lifting fixture eyebolt.

24. Disconnect the engine mounts. See **Figures 9-13**.

25. Pull forward on the engine until it disengages from the transmission. Remove the engine from the vehicle.

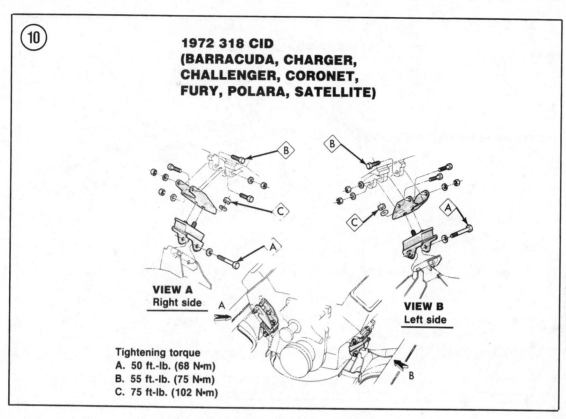

(10)

**1972 318 CID
(BARRACUDA, CHARGER,
CHALLENGER, CORONET,
FURY, POLARA, SATELLITE)**

VIEW A
Right side

VIEW B
Left side

Tightening torque
A. 50 ft.-lb. (68 N•m)
B. 55 ft.-lb. (75 N•m)
C. 75 ft.-lb. (102 N•m)

5

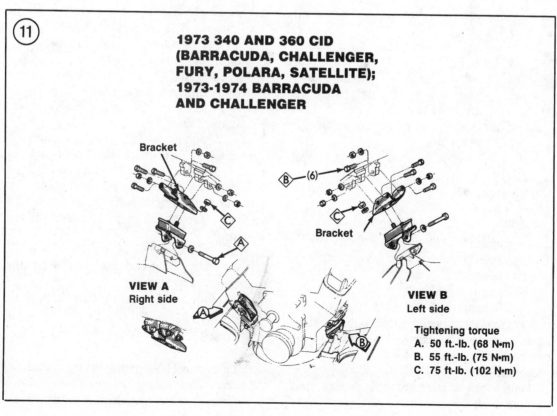

(11)

**1973 340 AND 360 CID
(BARRACUDA, CHALLENGER,
FURY, POLARA, SATELLITE);
1973-1974 BARRACUDA
AND CHALLENGER**

Bracket

Bracket

VIEW A
Right side

VIEW B
Left side

Tightening torque
A. 50 ft.-lb. (68 N•m)
B. 55 ft.-lb. (75 N•m)
C. 75 ft.-lb. (102 N•m)

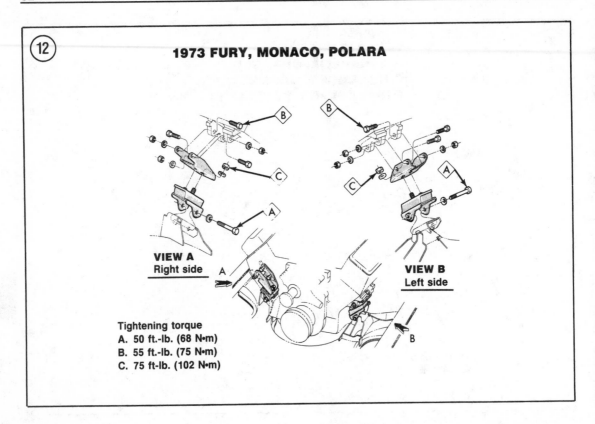

⑫ **1973 FURY, MONACO, POLARA**

VIEW A
Right side

VIEW B
Left side

Tightening torque
A. 50 ft.-lb. (68 N•m)
B. 55 ft.-lb. (75 N•m)
C. 75 ft-lb. (102 N•m)

26. Installation is the reverse of removal, plus the following:
   a. Lower the engine into the vehicle. Leave the hoist attached and supporting the engine weight until all mounts have been installed and tightened to specifications (**Table 2**).
   b. Fill the engine with an oil recommended in Chapter Three.
   c. Fill the cooling system. See Chapter Eight.
   d. Adjust the drive belts. See Chapter Eight.
   e. Warm the engine to normal operating temperature and adjust the carburetor and ignition timing as required. See Chapter Four.

400 and 440 cid Models

If the car is equipped with air conditioning, have the system discharged by a dealer or air conditioning shop before starting this procedure.
1. Mark the location of the hinges and remove the hood.

2. Disconnect the negative battery cable at the battery and engine. Disconnect the positive battery cable. Remove the battery.
3. Drain the cooling system. See Chapter Eight.
4. Remove the air cleaner. See Chapter Six.
5. Disconnect the radiator and heater hoses. See Chapter Eight.
6. If equipped with an automatic transmission, disconnect the oil cooler lines at the radiator tank. Plug the lines and cap the fittings to prevent leakage and contamination.
7. Remove the screws holding the fan shroud in place. Slide the fan shroud back on the fan assembly.
8. Remove the screws holding the radiator. Lift the radiator up and remove it from the engine compartment.
9. If equipped with air conditioning, remove the compressor and place it to one side.
10. If equipped with power steering:

   a. Disconnect the hydraulic fluid lines at the power steering pump. Plug the lines and cap the fittings to prevent leakage.

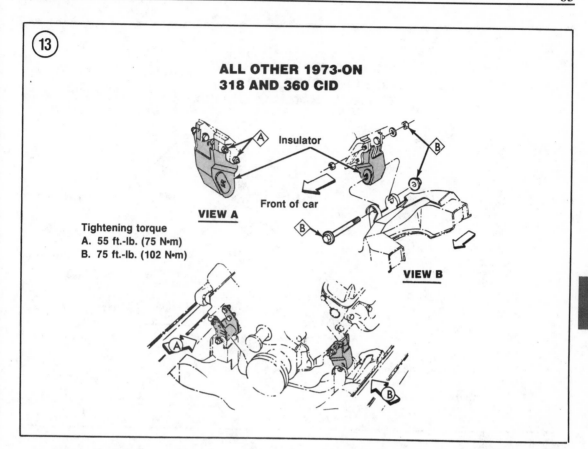

**ALL OTHER 1973-ON
318 AND 360 CID**

Insulator

Front of car

VIEW A

**Tightening torque
A.** 55 ft.-lb. (75 N•m)
B. 75 ft.-lb. (102 N•m)

VIEW B

5

b. Remove the power steering pump and place it to one side.

11. Label and disconnect all electrical and vacuum connections at the alternator, carburetor and engine.

12. Disconnect the fuel line at the fuel pump. Plug the line and cap the fitting to prevent leakage.

13. Remove the carburetor. See Chapter Six.

14. Disconnect the spark plug leads and remove the distributor cap. See Chapter Four.

15. Remove the starter motor and alternator. See Chapter Seven.

16. Disconnect and remove the charcoal canister(s).

17. Disconnect and remove the horn(s).

18. Disconnect the exhaust pipe(s) at the exhaust manifold(s).

19. With the vehicle positioned on jackstands, support the transmission with a transmission jack.

20. If equipped with an automatic transmission:

a. Remove the drive plate inspection cover and scribe a mark on the converter and drive plate for reinstallation reference.

b. Remove the converter-to-drive plate bolts.

c. Install a C-clamp at the bottom front of the converter housing to keep the torque converter properly positioned in the transmission.

21. Install engine support fixture part No. C-3487-A (or equivalent) to support the rear of the engine.

22. Remove the engine-to-transmission bolts.

NOTE
At this point, there should be no hoses, wires or linkage connecting the engine to the vehicle. Recheck this to be sure nothing will hamper engine removal.

23. Attach an engine lifting fixture to the carburetor flange studs on the intake manifold. Attach an engine hoist to the lifting fixture eyebolt.

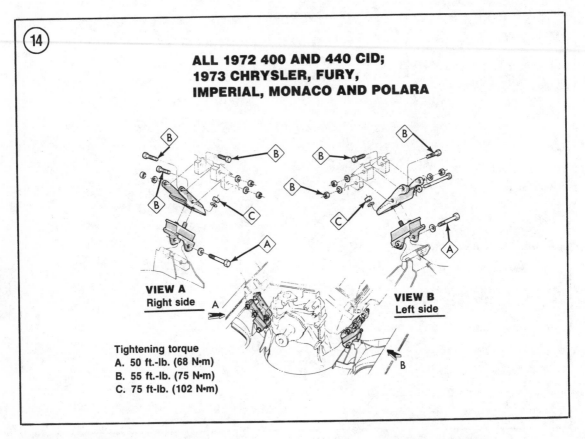

(14)

**ALL 1972 400 AND 440 CID;
1973 CHRYSLER, FURY,
IMPERIAL, MONACO AND POLARA**

VIEW A
Right side

VIEW B
Left side

Tightening torque
A. 50 ft.-lb. (68 N•m)
B. 55 ft.-lb. (75 N•m)
C. 75 ft.-lb. (102 N•m)

24. Disconnect the engine mounts. See **Figure 14** or **Figure 15**.

25. Pull forward on the engine until it disengages from the transmission. Remove the engine from the vehicle.

26. Installation is the reverse of removal, plus the following:

    a. Lower the engine into the vehicle. Leave the hoist attached and supporting the engine weight until all mounts have been installed and tightened to specifications (**Table 3**).

    b. Fill the engine with an oil recommended in Chapter Three.

    c. Fill the cooling system. See Chapter Eight.

    d. Adjust the drive belts. See Chapter Eight.

    e. Warm the engine to normal operating temperature and adjust the carburetor and ignition timing as required. See Chapter Four.

CYLINDER HEAD REMOVAL/INSTALLATION

6-cylinder

1. Disconnect the negative battery cable.

2. Drain the cooling system. See Chapter Eight.

3. Remove the air cleaner. See Chapter Six.

4. Disconnect the fuel line at the carburetor and fuel pump. Remove the line. Cap the carburetor and fuel pump fittings to prevent leakage.

5. Disconnect the throttle linkage at the carburetor.

6. Remove the carburetor-to-distributor vacuum line.

7. Disconnect the spark plug wires and remove the spark plugs. See Chapter Four.

8. Disconnect the heater hose at the intake manifold. Disconnect the bypass hose.

9. Disconnect the electrical connector at the temperature sending unit.

10. Disconnect the exhaust pipe at the exhaust manifold flange.

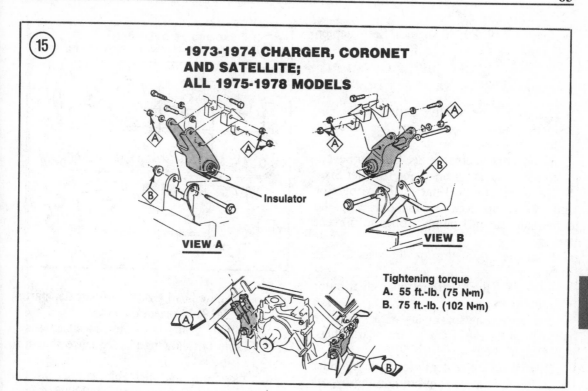

(15)

1973-1974 CHARGER, CORONET AND SATELLITE; ALL 1975-1978 MODELS

Insulator

VIEW A

VIEW B

Tightening torque
A. 55 ft.-lb. (75 N•m)
B. 75 ft.-lb. (102 N•m)

5

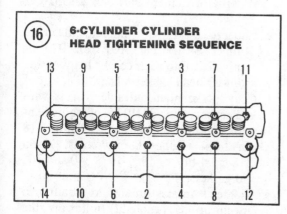

(16) **6-CYLINDER CYLINDER HEAD TIGHTENING SEQUENCE**

11. Disconnect the diverter valve vacuum line at the intake manifold.

12. Remove the air tube assembly from the cylinder head, if so equipped.

13. Disconnect the fender support bracket, if so equipped.

NOTE
If equipped with air conditioning, have an assistant hold the lines up and out of the way while performing Step 14.

14. Remove any remaining electrical or vacuum lines from the rocker arm cover clips. Remove the rocker arm cover.

15. Remove the rocker shaft bolts and retainers.

16. Remove the rocker arms and shaft assembly.

17. Remove the pushrods and place in order of removal for reinstallation in their original location.

18. Loosen all head bolts 1/2 turn. Repeat this until all bolts have been loosened a few turns, then remove all the bolts.

19. With the help of an assistant, remove the cylinder head and manifolds as an assembly.

20. Place the cylinder head/manifold assembly on a clean workbench. Unbolt and remove the manifold assembly from the cylinder head.

21. Installation is the reverse of removal, plus the following:

   a. Lightly coat a new head gasket with sealer part No. 3419115 or equivalent.

   b. Tighten head bolts to specifications (**Table 1**) following the sequence shown in **Figure 16**.

   c. Tighten all other fasteners to specifications (**Table 1**).

   d. Start the engine and warm to normal operating temperature. Adjust the valve lash on 1972-1980 engines. See Chapter Four.

318, 340 and 360 cid V8

1. Disconnect the negative battery cable.
2. Drain the cooling system. See Chapter Eight.
3. Remove the alternator. See Chapter Seven.
4. Remove the air cleaner. See Chapter Six.
5. Disconnect the fuel line at the carburetor and fuel pump. Remove the line. Cap the carburetor and fuel pump fittings to prevent leakage.
6. Disconnect the throttle linkage at the carburetor.
7. Remove the carburetor-to-distributor vacuum line.
8. Disconnect the spark plug wires. Remove the distributor cap. Remove the spark plugs. See Chapter Four.
9. Disconnect the heater hoses at the cylinder head. Remove the clamp holding the bypass hose.
10. Disconnect the electrical connector at the temperature sending unit.
11. Disconnect the ignition coil wires.
12. Remove any remaining electrical or vacuum lines from the valve cover clips. Remove the valve cover(s).
13. Loosen and remove the intake manifold bolts. Remove the intake manifold, carburetor and ignition coil as an assembly.
14. Remove the exhaust manifolds.
15. Remove the rocker shaft bolts and retainers.
16. Remove the rocker arms and shaft assembly.
17. Remove the pushrods and place in order of removal for reinstallation in their original location.
18. Loosen all head bolts 1/2 turn. Repeat this until all bolts have been loosened a few turns, then remove all the head bolts. Remove the cylinder head(s).
19. Installation is the reverse of removal, plus the following:
  a. Clean all pipe sealant residue from bolt threads and holes. Coat bolt threads with Mopar Lock N' Seal part No. 4057989 or equivalent.

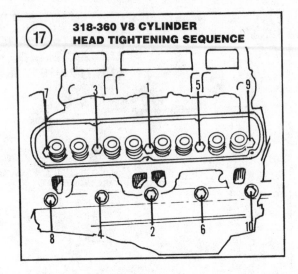

17 **318-360 V8 CYLINDER HEAD TIGHTENING SEQUENCE**

  b. Coat new head gaskets with sealer part No. 3419114 or equivalent.
  c. Tighten head bolts to specifications (**Table 2**) following the sequence shown in **Figure 17**.
  d. Coat front and rear block rails with Alternator Cement part No. 2299314 or equivalent.
  e. Squeeze a 1/4 in. diameter drop of Rubber Sealer part No. 4026070 or equivalent into each corner between the cylinder head gasket tabs.
  f. Coat intake manifold side gaskets with sealer part No. 3419115 or equivalent on 1972-1977 318 cid and 1978-on 318 cid 2-bbl. engines. Do *not* coat 1978-on 318 cid 4-bbl. or 1972-1977 340 and 360 cid gaskets.
  g. Tighten intake manifold bolts to specifications (**Table 2**) following the sequence shown in **Figure 18**.
  h. Tighten all other fasteners to specifications (**Table 2**).

400 and 440 cid V8

1. Disconnect the negative battery cable.
2. Drain the cooling system. See Chapter Eight.
3. Remove the air cleaner. See Chapter Six.
4. If equipped with an air pump:
  a. Disconnect the diverter valve vacuum line at the intake manifold.
  b. Disconnect the air pump line at the exhaust manifolds.

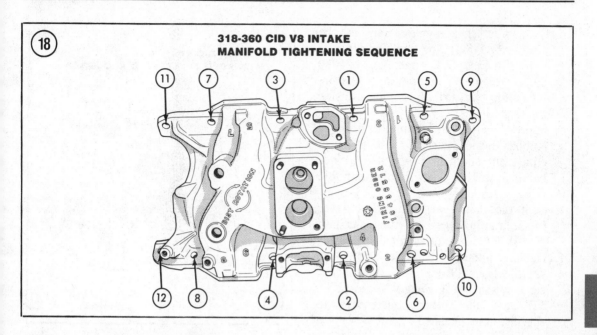

18

**318-360 CID V8 INTAKE
MANIFOLD TIGHTENING SEQUENCE**

5

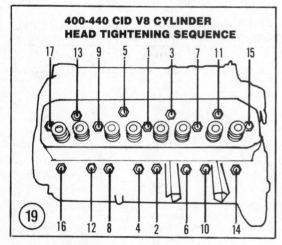

**400-440 CID V8 CYLINDER
HEAD TIGHTENING SEQUENCE**

19

c. Disconnect the diverter valve on high-mount air pumps and remove the air pump.

5. Remove the alternator. See Chapter Seven.

6. Disconnect the fuel line at the carburetor and fuel pump. Remove the line. Cap the carburetor and fuel pump fittings to prevent leakage.

7. Disconnect the throttle linkage at the carburetor.

8. Remove the carburetor-to-distributor vacuum line.

9. Disconnect the spark plug wires. Remove the distributor cap. Remove the spark plugs. See Chapter Four.

10. Disconnect the heater hoses at the intake manifold. Disconnect the bypass hose.

11. Disconnect the electrical connector at the temperature sending unit.

12. Disconnect the ignition coil wires.

13. Remove any remaining electrical or vacuum lines from the valve cover clips. Remove the valve cover(s).

14. Loosen all head bolts 1/2 turn. Repeat this until all bots have been loosened a few turns, then remove the head bolts. Remove the intake manifold, carburetor and ignition coil as an assembly.

15. Remove the tappet chamber cover.

16. Remove the exhaust manifolds.

17. Remove the rocker shaft bolts and retainers.

18. Remove the rocker arms and shaft assembly.

19. Remove the pushrods and place in order of removal for reinstallation in their original location.

20. Loosen and remove the head bolts. Remove the cylinder head(s).

21. Installation is the reverse of removal, plus the following:

a. Coat new head gaskets with sealer part No. 3419114 or equivalent.

b. Tighten head bolts to specifications (**Table 3**) following the sequence shown in **Figure 19**.

c. If cylinder head cover rail is the non-beaded (flat) type, run a continuous bead of Rubber Sealer part No. 4026070 or equivalent 1/8 in. wide and 1/16 in. high along the surface, looping it inside the screw holes.

d. Squeeze a 1/4 in. diameter drop of Rubber Sealer part No. 4026070 or equivalent on each corner of the block before installing a new intake manifold gasket.

e. Coat the beads on both sides of the intake manifold gasket with sealer part No. 3837795 or equivalent.

f. Tighten intake manifold bolts to specifications (**Table 3**) following the sequence shown in **Figure 20**.

g. Tighten all other fasteners to specifications (**Table 3**).

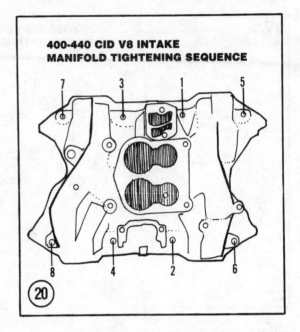

400-440 CID V8 INTAKE MANIFOLD TIGHTENING SEQUENCE

Table 1 6-CYLINDER ENGINE TORQUE SPECIFICATIONS

Fastener	ft.-lb.	N•m
Air conditioning compressor		
Bracket-to-water pump bolt	30	41
To bracket bolt	50	68
Support bolt	30	41
Air tube-to-cylinder head	8	11
Alternator		
Adjusting strap bolt	15	23
Bracket bolt		
5/16-18	15	23
3/8-16	30	41
Mounting bolt	30	41
Pivot nut	30	41
Carburetor flange nut	16	23
Cylinder head bolt		
First stage		
1972-1976	50	68
1977-on	35	47
Second stage		
1972	65	88
1973-on	70	95
Engine-to-transmission bolt		
3/8-16	30	41
7/16-14	50	68
Exhaust manifold nut	10	14
Exhaust pipe flange nut	35	47
Front mount		
To frame nut		
1972	85	116
1973-1976	75	102
1977-on	65	88

(continued)

Table 1 6-CYLINDER ENGINE TORQUE SPECIFICATIONS (continued)

Fastener	ft.-lb.	N·m
To block nut		
1972	45	63
1973-1976	50	68
To bracket nut	75	102
Intake-to-exhaust manifold		
Bolt		
1972-1976	20	27
1977-on	16	23
Nut		
1972-1976	30	41
1977-on	20	27
Rocker arm cover bolt	3	4
Rocker shaft bracket bolt		
1972-1976	25	34
1977-on	24	33
Starter mounting bolt	50	68

Table 2 318, 340 AND 360 CID V8 ENGINE TORQUE SPECIFICATIONS

Fastener	ft.-lb.	N·m
Air conditioning compressor		
Bracket-to-water pump bolt	30	41
To bracket bolt	50	68
Support bolt	30	41
Alternator		
Adjusting strap bolt	15	23
Bracket bolt	30	41
Mounting bolt	30	41
Pivot nut	30	41
Carburetor flange nut	16	23
Cylinder head bolt		
First stage	50	68
Second stage		
1972-1977	95	129
1978-on	105	142
Engine-to-transmission bolt		
3/8-16	30	41
7/16-14	50	68
Exhaust manifold		
Nut	15	20
Screw	20	27
Exhaust pipe flange nut		
318, 360	24	33
340	50	68
Flex plate-to-converter	23	31
Front engine mount		
To frame nut		
1972	50	68
1973-on	75	102
To block nut		
1972-1976	55	75
1977-on	65	88
To bracket nut	75	102

(continued)

5

Table 2 318, 340 AND 360 CID V8 ENGINE TORQUE SPECIFICATIONS (continued)

Fastener	ft.-lb.	N·m
Intake manifold		
1972, 1975-1976	40	54
1973-1974	35	47
1977-on	45	61
Rocker shaft bracket bolt	16	23
Starter mounting bolt	50	68
Valve cover bolt		
With gasket	3	4
With sealant	8	11

Table 3 400 AND 440 CID V8 ENGINE TORQUE SPECIFICATIONS

Fastener	ft.-lb.	N·m
Air conditioning compressor		
To engine bolt	15	20
Bracket-to-water pump bolt	30	41
To bracket bolt	50	68
Support bolt	30	41
Alternator		
Adjusting strap bolt	15	23
Bracket bolt	30	41
Mounting bolt	30	41
Pivot bolt	30	41
Carburetor flange nut	16	23
Cylinder head bolt		
First stage	40	54
Second stage	70	95
Engine-to-transmission bolt		
3/8-16	30	41
7/16-14	50	68
Exhaust manifold stud nut		
1972-1976, 1978	30	41
1977	40	54
Exhaust pipe flange nut		
1972-1976	50	68
1977-1978	24	32
Flex plate-to-converter	23	31
Front engine mount		
Bracket nut	75	102
To frame nut		
1972	50	68
1973-1978	75	102
To block nut		
1972-1977	55	75
1978	75	102
Intake manifold		
1972-1974	40	54
1975-1978	45	61
Rocker shaft bracket bolt	25	34
Starter mounting bolt	50	68
Valve cover nut		
With gasket	3	4
With sealant	8	11

CHAPTER SIX

FUEL AND EMISSION
CONTROL SYSTEMS

This chapter contains procedures for air cleaner service, carburetor adjustment and replacement, fuel pump testing and replacement and emission control system service.

The Electronic Fuel Injection (EFI) system used on 1981 and later Imperials is not covered. This fuel injection system requires special tools and test equipment for service procedures. All fuel injection problems should be referred to a dealer or qualified specialist.

Illustrations and procedures in this chapter are general in nature. During the years covered, the various Chrysler, Dodge and Plymouth models used many types of carburetors. Most of the carburetor types were produced in a number of variations to fit the individual requirements of the various engine-transmission-vehicle combinations and emission control laws. For this reason, 2 carburetors which look alike may not be interchangeable.

AIR CLEANER

Removal/Installation

1. Disconnect the crankcase ventilation hose at the air cleaner housing (**Figure 1**).
2. Disconnect the cold air intake tube at the flexible duct (if so equipped) and the heat riser tube at the heat shroud (**Figure 2**).

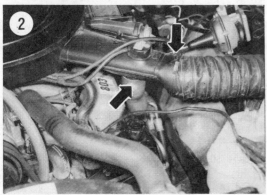

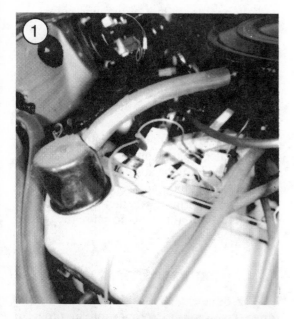

3. Remove the wing nut in the center of the air cleaner cover.

4. Lift the air cleaner housing from the carburetor and disconnect the vacuum line from the plastic tee underneath the housing.

NOTE
*The vacuum lines on some 1980 and later air cleaners may connect directly to the air cleaner instead of to a plastic tee (**Figure 3**). Tag or otherwise mark each line for proper reconnection, then disconnect from the air cleaner housing.*

5. If equipped with Electronic Lean Burn (ELB) or Electronic Spark Control (ESC), disconnect the connector underneath the spark control computer housing (**Figure 4**). Unclip the connector cable from the channel on the rear of the air cleaner housing.

6. Remove the air cleaner housing from the engine compartment.

7. Check the air cleaner-to-carburetor air horn mounting gasket. Replace the gasket if worn, damaged or missing.

8. Wipe the air cleaner housing and cover with a cloth moistened in solvent. Wipe the housing and cover dry, then inspect for damage or distortion at the gasket mating surfaces.

9. Installation is the reverse of removal.

FUEL QUALITY

Gasoline blended with alcohol is widely available, although it is not legally required to be labeled as such in many states. Fuels with an alcohol content tend to absorb moisture from the air. When the moisture content of the fuel reaches approximately one percent, it combines with the alcohol and separates from the fuel. This water-alcohol mixture settles at the bottom of the fuel tank where the fuel pickup carries it into the fuel line to the carburetor.

Gasoline mixed with alcohol can cause numerous and serious problems with an automotive fuel system, including:

  a. Corrosion formation on the inside of fuel tanks, steel fuel lines and carburetors.

  b. Deterioration of the plastic liner used in some fuel tanks, resulting in eventual plugging of the in-tank filter.

  c. Deterioration and failure of synthetic rubber or plastic materials such as O-ring seals, diaphragms, accelerator pump cups and gaskets.

  d. Premature failure of fuel line hoses.

The problem of gasoline blended with alcohol has become so prevalent around the United States that Miller Tools (32615 Park Lane, Garden City, MI 48135) now offers an Alcohol Detection Kit (part No. C-4846) so owners can determine the quality of fuel being used.

The procedure cannot differentiate between types of alcohol (ethanol, methanol, etc.) nor is it considered to be absolutely accurate from a scientific standpoint, but it is accurate enough to determine whether or not there is enough alcohol in the fuel to cause the user to take precautions.

CARBURETOR OPERATION

A gasoline engine must receive fuel and air mixed in a precise proportion in order to operate efficiently at various speeds. At sea level, under normal conditions, the ratio is 14.7:1 at high speed and 12:1 at low speeds. Carburetors are designed to maintain these ratios while providing for sudden acceleration or increased loads.

A mixture with an excess of fuel is said to be "rich." One with a deficiency of fuel is said to be "lean."

The choke valve in a carburetor produces a richer than normal mixture of fuel and air until the engine warms up.

The throat of a carburetor is often called a "barrel." A single-barrel carburetor has only one throat. Two-barrel carburetors have 2 throats and 2 complete sets of metering devices, but only one float bowl and float. A 4-barrel carburetor has 4 throats, 4 complete sets of metering devices and 2 floats.

WARNING
The use of gasohol is not recommended with Carter Thermo-Quad carburetors. It can dissolve the epoxy holding 2 casting plugs in the plastic fuel bowl. If this happens, the plugs will fall out and raw fuel will pour onto the hot intake manifold.

CARBURETOR ADJUSTMENTS

All carburetors manufactured for use on Chrysler Corp. passenger cars covered in this manual are equipped with plastic idle fuel mixture adjustment limiters. The limiters control the maximum idle richness and help prevent overly rich idle adjustments.

The plastic limiter cap is installed on the head of the idle fuel mixture adjusting screw. **Figure 5** shows a typical installation. Any adjustment must be within the range of the limiter. If the carburetor cannot be adjusted to run properly within this range, it should be overhauled or replaced.

The idle mixture screw has been made "tamperproof" on 1981 and later carburetors in accordance with Federal law to prevent unauthorized adjustment. The idle mixture screw is encased inside a locking plug cast in the carburetor throttle body and is covered by a hardened steel plug. This plug is to be removed only if the carburetor cannot be made to run correctly after an overhaul. All necessary adjustments are preset at the factory and should not be changed during a normal tune-up.

The only carburetor service required on 1972-1980 engines is an idle speed adjustment. Curb idle speed is set by adjusting the air-fuel mixture to the proper ratio and then adjusting the idle speed screw to obtain the specified rpm.

Carburetor adjustment on 1972-1976 models and those 1977 models produced for initial sale in California requires the use of special exhaust analyzers. Procedures for using this equipment are given in this chapter, even though the home mechanic is unlikely to have an accurate analyzer. While it is not economical to purchase one, they can often be obtained from equipment rental dealers for a small fee. A procedure is also provided for adjusting the air-fuel ratio without an analyzer but this should only be used in emergencies on 1975-1976 models equipped with catalytic converters. If the emergency procedure is used, have the air-fuel ratio set by your dealer or a competent shop equipped with an analyzer as soon as possible to prevent overheating of the converter.

All 1977 and later models, except 1977 models produced for initial sale in California, require the use of a propane-assisted idle speed/mixture adjustment procedure. This procedure requires the use of a propane metering tool (Chrysler tool part No. C-4464 or equivalent) and a container of propane. You may be able to obtain the propane tool through your dealer or an equivalent tool may be available through an auto parts dealer. The propane tool is not excessively expensive and

6

should be purchased if you plan to do all of your own service work.

Carburetor adjustment is critical, especially on engines equipped with Electronic Lean Burn (ELB) or Electronic Spark Control (ESC). In these systems, signals from a number of sensors are fed into a computer to determine the exact instant of ignition of the lean air-fuel mixture produced by the carburetor under varying operating conditions.

Carburetor adjustments should not be made to 1981 and later engines equipped with an Electronic Feedback (EFB) carburetor system. In this system, the computer controls air-fuel ratio according to signals provided by an exhaust gas oxygen sensor. In normal service, the idle speed and mixture should not require adjustment.

Correct adjustment is necessary on *all* models to ensure proper operation of other emission control systems. For these reasons, carburetor adjustments by methods other than those described in this chapter are not recommended.

Because of the complexity of the carburetors, service by the amateur mechanic should be limited to the procedures given in this chapter.

The following carburetors have been used:
1. Holley:
   a. Model 1920 1-bbl. (**Figure 6**).
   b. Model 1945 1-bbl. (**Figure 7**).
   c. Model 6145 1-bbl. (**Figure 8**).
   d. Model 2210 2-bbl. (**Figure 9**).
   e. Model 2245 2-bbl. (**Figure 10**).
   f. Model 2280/6280 2-bbl. (**Figure 11**).
   g. Model 2300 2-bbl. (**Figure 12**).
   h. Model 4160 4-bbl. (**Figure 13**).
2. Carter:
   a. Model BBD 2-bbl. (**Figure 14**).
   b. Thermo-Quad (Model TQ) 4-bbl. (**Figure 15**).
3. Rochester:
   a. Quadrajet 4-bbl. (**Figure 16**).

Curb Idle Adjustment
(1972-1974)

This procedure requires the use of an accurate ignition tachometer and a Sun

Electric Combustion-Vacuum Unit, Model 80, Exhaust Condenser, Model EC and Hose 669-14 or equivalent. Do not remove the air cleaner. Refer to the Vehicle Emission Control Information (VECI) decal in the engine compartment for specifications.
1. Set the parking brake and block the rear wheels.
2. Warm engine to normal operating temperature (upper radiator hose hot). Check ignition timing and adjust to specifications, if necessary. See Chapter Three.
3. Place automatic transmission (if so equipped) in NEUTRAL position—not PARK.
4. Turn on headlights and air conditioner on 1972 6-cylinder models. Make sure headlights and air conditioning are on all others.
5. Disconnect and plug appropriate vacuum lines as specified on the VECI decal.
6. Connect the tachometer according to the manufacturer's instructions.
7. Increase engine speed to approximately 2,000 rpm for at least 10 seconds, then return to curb idle.
8. Insert the analyzer probe into the tailpipe at least 2 ft. Use the left tailpipe on cars equipped with a dual exhaust.

NOTE
The probe and connecting tube must be free of leaks to obtain correct readings.

9. Connect the analyzer, allow it to warm up and calibrate it, using manufacturer's instructions.
10. If the engine is equipped with an air pump, disconnect the pump outlet hose and plug air injection tube to exhaust manifold.
11. Set the idle speed to specifications (VECI decal or Table 1, Chapter 4) as follows:

NOTE
The analyzer is very sensitive. To obtain true reading, make adjustments to idle mixture screws in 1/16 turn increments.

a. Turn each idle mixture screw 1/16 turn counterclockwise. Wait at least 30 seconds to let the reading stabilize. Note analyzer reading.

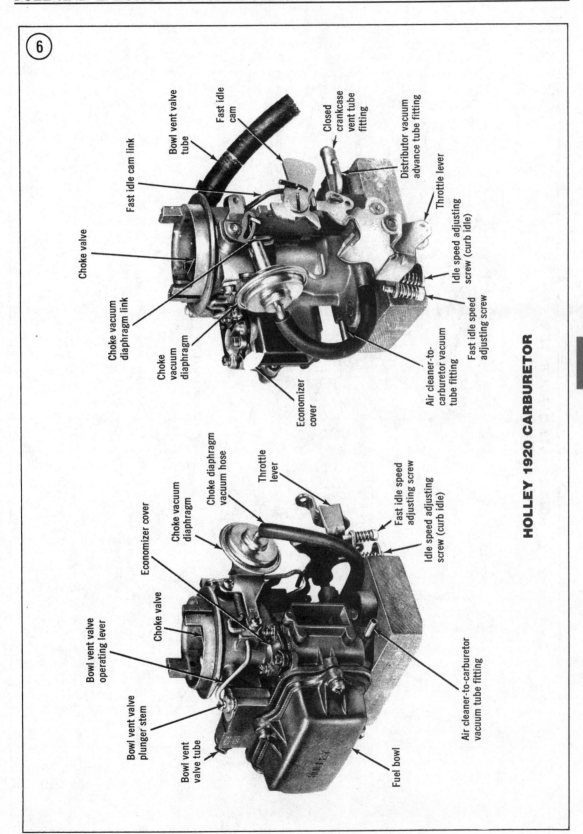

HOLLEY 1920 CARBURETOR

6

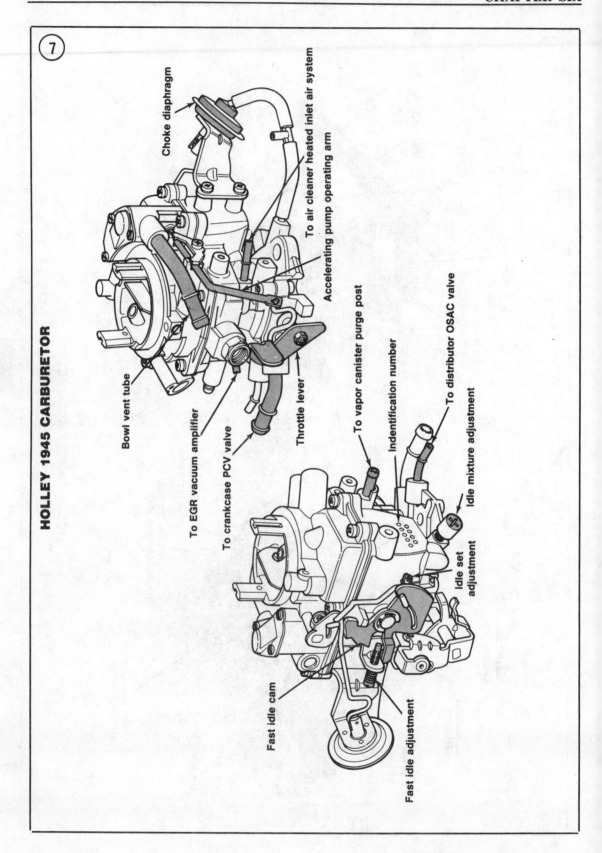

⑦

HOLLEY 1945 CARBURETOR

Choke diaphragm

To air cleaner heated inlet air system

Accelerating pump operating arm

Bowl vent tube

To EGR vacuum amplifier

To crankcase PCV valve

Throttle lever

To vapor canister purge post

Indentification number

To distributor OSAC valve

Idle mixture adjustment

Idle set adjustment

Fast idle cam

Fast idle adjustment

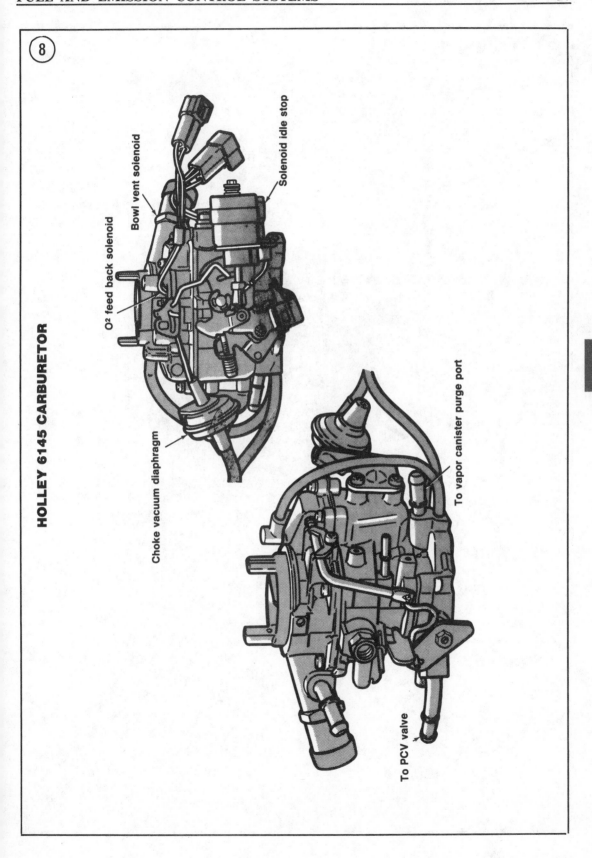

HOLLEY 6145 CARBURETOR

Bowl vent solenoid

Solenoid idle stop

O² feed back solenoid

Choke vacuum diaphragm

To vapor canister purge port

To PCV valve

6

⑨

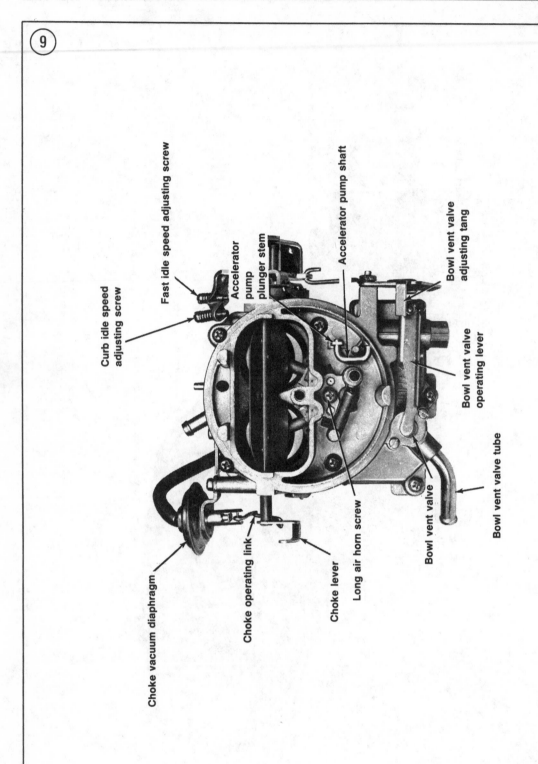

Curb idle speed adjusting screw

Fast idle speed adjusting screw

Accelerator pump plunger stem

Accelerator pump shaft

Bowl vent valve adjusting tang

Bowl vent valve operating lever

Bowl vent valve tube

Bowl vent valve

Long air horn screw

Choke lever

Choke operating link

Choke vacuum diaphragm

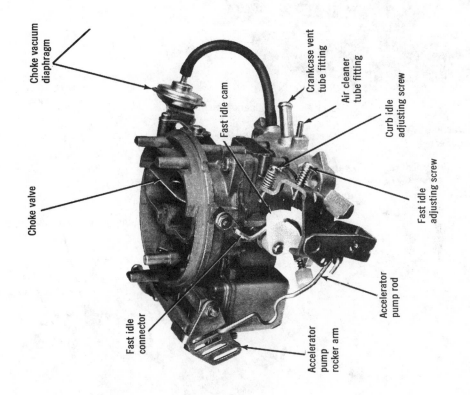

Choke vacuum diaphragm

Choke valve

Fast idle connector

Accelerator pump rocker arm

Fast idle cam

Crankcase vent tube fitting

Air cleaner tube fitting

Curb idle adjusting screw

Fast idle adjusting screw

Accelerator pump rod

HOLLEY 2210 CARBURETOR

6

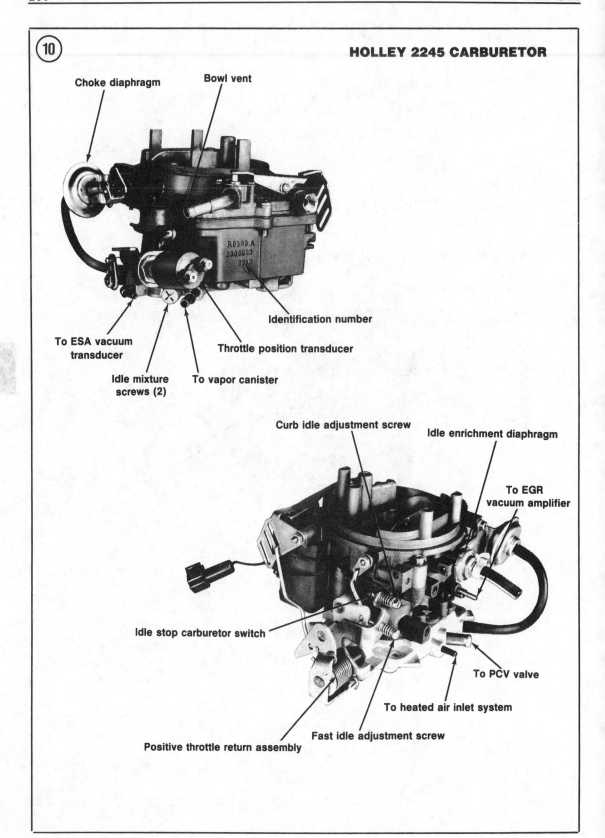

HOLLEY 2245 CARBURETOR

Choke diaphragm

Bowl vent

To ESA vacuum transducer

Idle mixture screws (2)

To vapor canister

Throttle position transducer

Identification number

Curb idle adjustment screw

Idle enrichment diaphragm

To EGR vacuum amplifier

Idle stop carburetor switch

To PCV valve

To heated air inlet system

Fast idle adjustment screw

Positive throttle return assembly

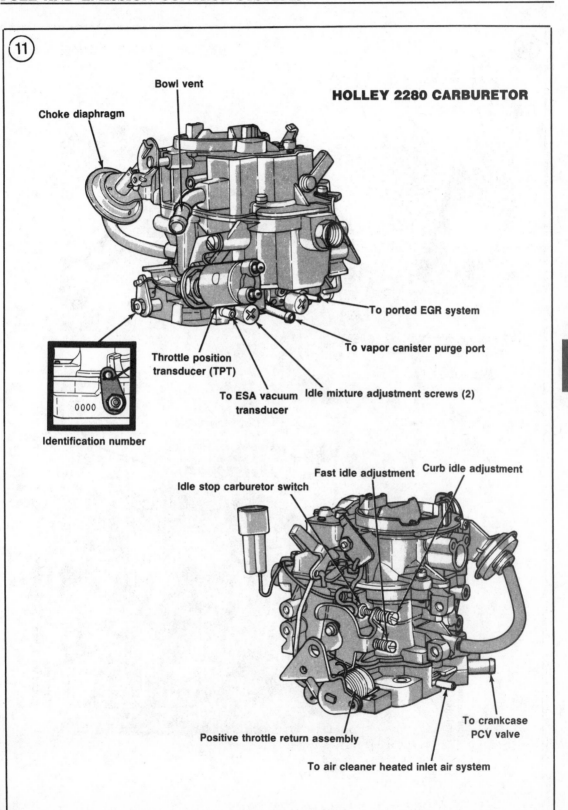

HOLLEY 2280 CARBURETOR

Bowl vent

Choke diaphragm

To ported EGR system

To vapor canister purge port

Throttle position transducer (TPT)

To ESA vacuum transducer

Idle mixture adjustment screws (2)

Identification number

0000

Fast idle adjustment

Curb idle adjustment

Idle stop carburetor switch

Positive throttle return assembly

To air cleaner heated inlet air system

To crankcase PCV valve

6

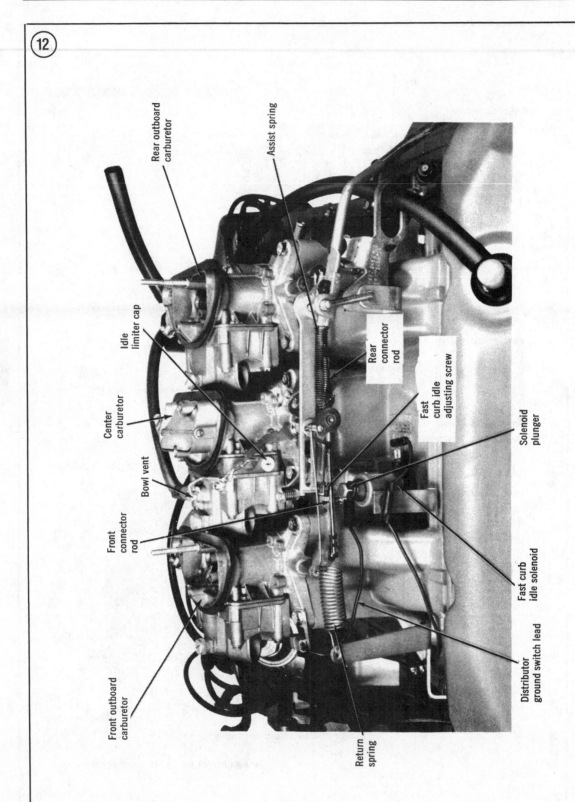

⑫

Rear outboard carburetor

Assist spring

Idle limiter cap

Center carburetor

Bowl vent

Front connector rod

Front outboard carburetor

Return spring

Rear connector rod

Fast curb idle adjusting screw

Solenoid plunger

Fast curb idle solenoid

Distributor ground switch lead

HOLLEY 2300 CARBURETOR

Throttle control vacuum diaphragm

Distributor vacuum advance tube

Front outboard carburetor

Vacuum diaphragm supply tube

Center carburetor

Bowl vent tube

Vacuum diaphragm supply tube

Crankcase vent tube

Rear outboard carburetor

Throttle control vacuum diaphragm

6

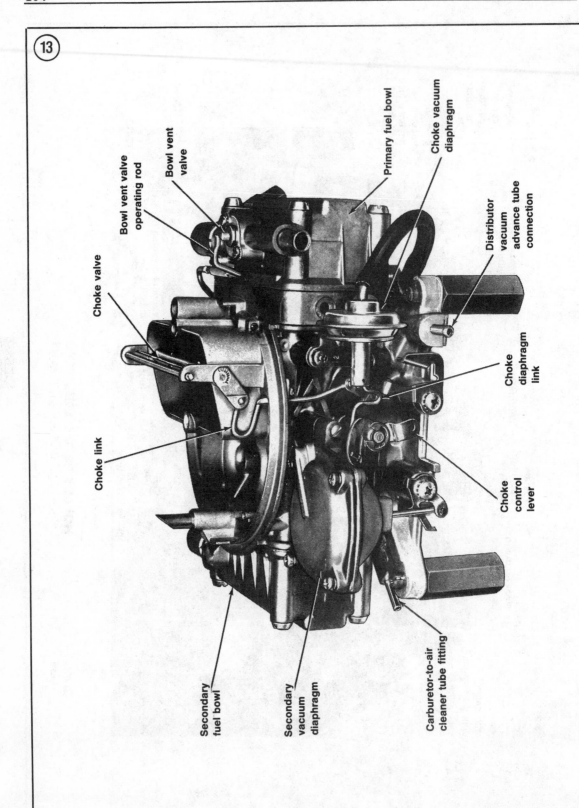

(13)

Choke valve

Bowl vent valve
operating rod

Bowl vent
valve

Primary fuel bowl

Choke vacuum
diaphragm

Distributor
vacuum
advance tube
connection

Choke link

Choke
diaphragm
link

Secondary
fuel bowl

Choke
control
lever

Secondary
vacuum
diaphragm

Carburetor-to-air
cleaner tube fitting

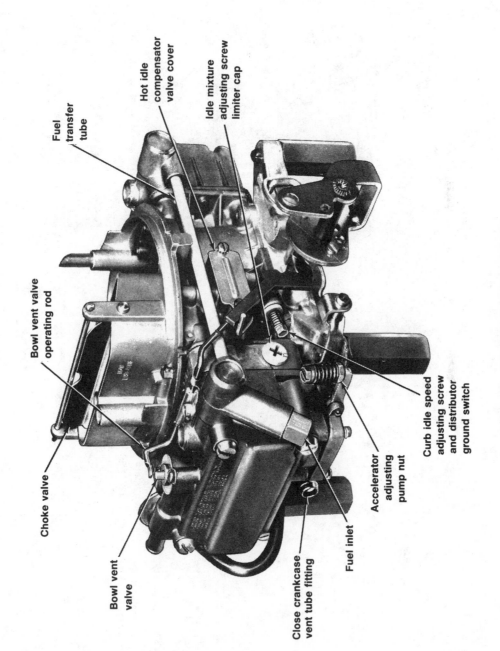

Fuel transfer tube

Hot idle compensator valve cover

Idle mixture adjusting screw limiter cap

Bowl vent valve operating rod

Choke valve

Bowl vent valve

Close crankcase vent tube fitting

Fuel inlet

Accelerator adjusting pump nut

Curb idle speed adjusting screw and distributor ground switch

HOLLEY 4160 CARBURETOR

6

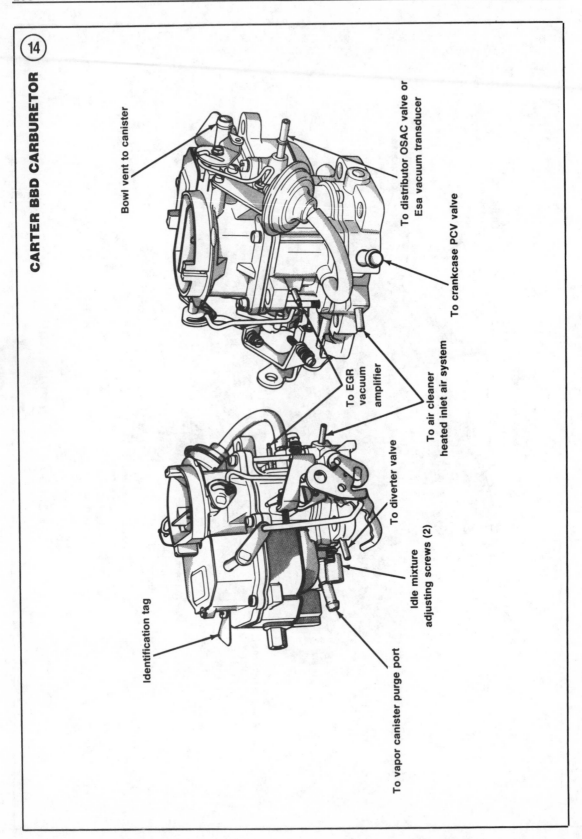

CARTER BBD CARBURETOR

14

Bowl vent to canister

To distributor OSAC valve or Esa vacuum transducer

To crankcase PCV valve

To EGR vacuum amplifier

To air cleaner heated inlet air system

To diverter valve

Idle mixture adjusting screws (2)

Identification tag

To vapor canister purge port

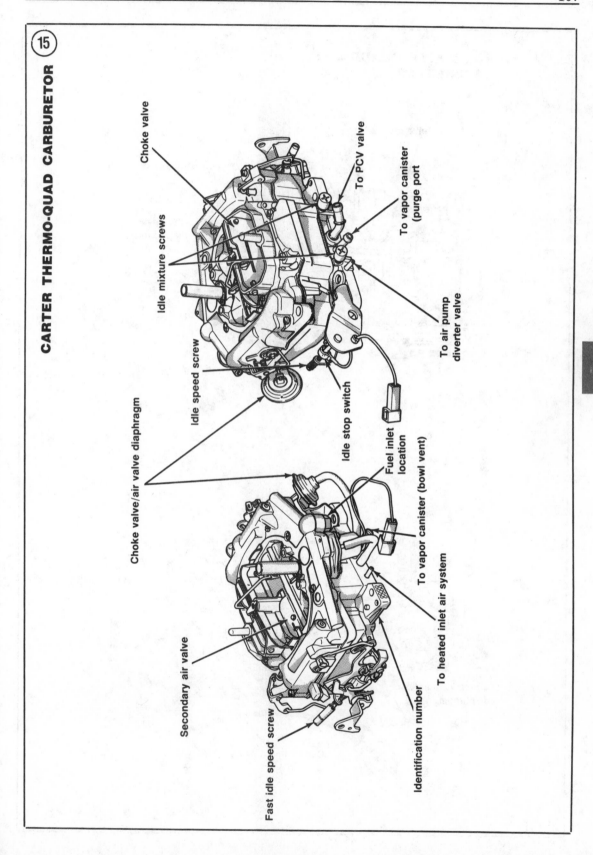

CARTER THERMO-QUAD CARBURETOR

15

Choke valve

To PCV valve

To vapor canister (purge port

Idle mixture screws

To air pump diverter valve

Idle speed screw

Idle stop switch

Fuel inlet location

Choke valve/air valve diaphragm

To vapor canister (bowl vent)

To heated inlet air system

Secondary air valve

Identification number

Fast idle speed screw

6

16

ROCHESTER QUADRAJET
CARBURETOR

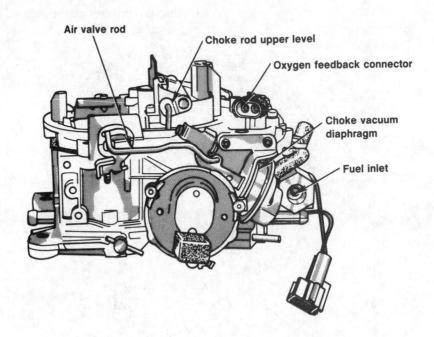

Air valve rod

Choke rod upper level

Oxygen feedback connector

Choke vacuum diaphragm

Fuel inlet

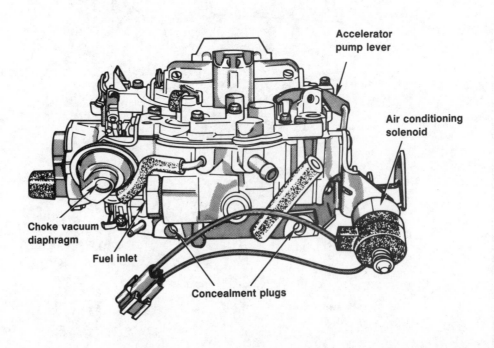

Accelerator pump lever

Air conditioning solenoid

Choke vacuum diaphragm

Fuel inlet

Concealment plugs

NOTE
Step b is critical. If the carburetor is set too lean, the analyzer will reverse itself and indicate a richer mixture.

b. Repeat Step a until meter indicates a definitely lower (richer) reading. A higher reading indicates a leaner mixture; a lower reading indicates a richer mixture.

c. Adjust carburetor to give the specified air-fuel ratio reading on the analyzer. Turn idle mixture screws counterclockwise to lower and clockwise to increase meter reading.

NOTE
Do not remove limiter caps from idle mixture screws to achieve an over-rich mixture.

d. When the air-fuel ratio has been set, use the curb idle adjustment screw to obtain the specified engine idle speed.

Curb Idle Adjustment
(All 1975-1976, 1977 California Models)

A Chrysler Huntsville Exhaust Emission Analyzer or equivalent unit reading in hydrocarbons (HC) and carbon monoxide (CO) is required for this procedure. Connect the analyzer according to the manufacturer's instructions. Refer to the Vehicle Emission Control Information (VECI) decal in the engine compartment for specifications and to determine whether the analyzer probe should be inserted in front of the catalytic converter or in the tailpipe.

NOTE
If your car has dual exhaust pipes, use the left pipe if the sample is to be taken from the tailpipe.

1. Let the engine sit without running for at least one hour.
2. Set the parking brake and block the rear wheels.
3. Disconnect and plug the appropriate vacuum lines as specified on the VECI decal.
4. If engine is equipped with an air pump, disconnect the pump outlet hose and plug the engine side of the air supply tube at the diverter valve.
5. Start engine and warm to normal operating temperature (upper radiator hose hot). Choke must be fully open and throttle at curb idle speed.
6. Place transmission in PARK (automatic) or NEUTRAL (manual).
7. On ELB engines, connect a jumper wire between the carburetor idle stop switch and a good engine ground (**Figure 17**).

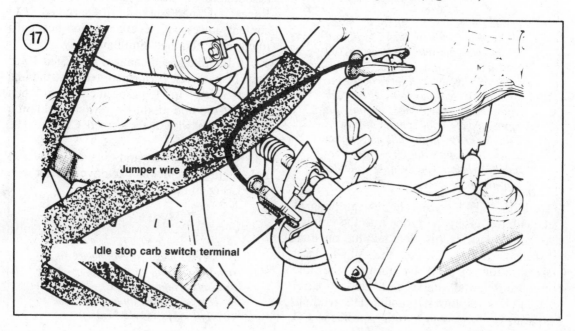
Jumper wire

Idle stop carb switch terminal

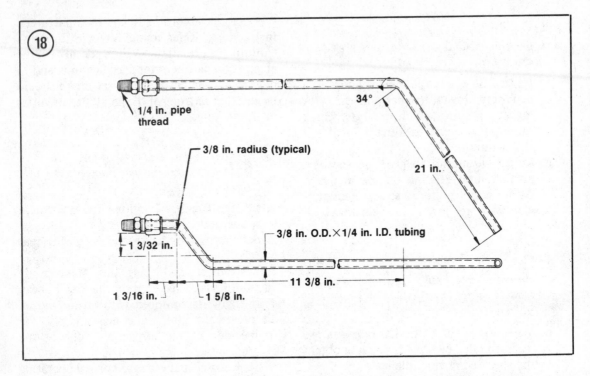

8. Connect the exhaust analyzer according to manufacturer's instructions and allow it to warm up.

9. Check ignition timing (Chapter Three). It should be within ±2° of the specifications given on the VECI decal. If not, adjust to specifications.

NOTE
Turning the idle mixture screw clockwise in Step 10 or Step 11 will lean the air-fuel mixture, decreasing CO content. Turning the screw counterclockwise will richen the mixture, increasing CO. After each adjustment, run the engine at approximately 2,000 rpm for at least 10 seconds, then return to idle and wait at least 30 seconds for the meters to stabilize before performing another adjustment.

10. If the VECI decal requires sampling at the tailpipe, insert the probe into the tailpipe as far as possible (use left tailpipe on dual exhaust). Adjust CO to the VECI decal specifications ±0.3% by turning the idle mixture screw(s). Balance 2- and 4-barrel carburetors for lowest possible HC reading. Repeat, if necessary, until specified CO content, lowest HC level and smoothest curb idle are all obtained simultaneously.

11. If the VECI decal requires sampling in front of the catalytic converter, remove access hole plug and insert adapter (**Figure 18**). Adjust idle CO to sticker specification -0.1% to +0.2% and balance 2- and 4-barrel carburetors for lowest possible HC reading. Repeat if necessary until specified CO content, lowest HC level and smoothest curb idle are all obtained simultaneously.

12. If the idle speed changes after Step 10 or Step 11 has been performed, readjust the idle speed screw to the specified rpm, then readjust the idle mixture screw(s) to obtain a smooth idle with the specified CO and HC levels.

13. Remove probe and install converter access plug, if removed. Remove jumper wire on ELB engines.

NOTE
If access plug is damaged during removal, install a new plug using anti-seize compound (FEL-PRO-C100 or equivalent) on threads. Torque to 100-140 in.-lb. (11-15 N•m).

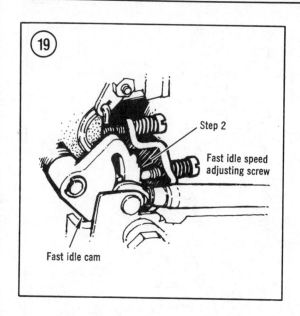

Step 2

Fast idle speed adjusting screw

Fast idle cam

Emergency Curb Idle Adjustment (1972-1976)

CAUTION
Use this procedure only in an emergency. If the idle mixture setting is altered, especially on 1975-1976 engines equipped with a catalytic converter, have the setting properly adjusted by a dealer as soon as possible to prevent converter overheating and possible damage.

1. Set the parking brake and block the rear wheels.
2. Start the engine and warm to normal operating temperature (upper radiator hose hot). Do not remove the air cleaner.
3. Make sure the air conditioning is off.
4. Place the transmission in PARK (automatic) or NEUTRAL (manual).
5. Disconnect and plug vacuum advance line at the distributor. Check ignition timing (Chapter Three). Adjust to specifications on VECI decal, if necessary. Reconnect vacuum advance line.
6. Turn idle speed screw to obtain idle rpm specified on VECI decal.
7. Turn idle mixture screw (either screw on 2- or 4-barrel carburetors) inward to obtain a drop of 20 rpm.
8. Turn idle mixture screw out 1/4 turn.
9. On 2- and 4-barrel carburetors, repeat Step 7 and Step 8 for second idle mixture screw.

10. Readjust idle speed screw to specified rpm, if necessary.

Idle Speed and Mixture Adjustment (1977 Federal, All 1978-1980)
Vehicle preparation (1977-1979)

Make all adjustments with engine fully warmed up, headlights and air conditioner off and transmission in NEUTRAL. Ground the carburetor idle stop switch on ELB engines with a jumper wire between the switch terminals and a good engine ground (**Figure 17**). The vacuum hoses at the exhaust gas recirculation (EGR) valve and the distributor or spark control unit must be disconnected and plugged.

Vehicle preparation (1980)

Make all adjustments with the engine fully warmed up and headlights and all other accessories off. Set parking brake and place transmission in NEUTRAL. If engine is equipped with Electronic Spark Control (ESC), disconnect and plug the vacuum line at the spark control computer and the EGR line at the EGR valve. Connect a jumper wire between the carburetor idle stop switch and a good engine ground (**Figure 17**). If not equipped with ESC, disconnect and plug the vacuum lines at the distributor and EGR valve. On all models, remove the PCV valve from the valve cover grommet and disconnect the canister purge hose at the carburetor. Do not cap or plug either line.

Curb idle and mixture adjustment

1. With transmission in NEUTRAL and parking brake set, start engine and allow it to warm up with the fast idle screw resting on the 2nd step of the fast idle cam (**Figure 19**, typical). When engine reaches normal operating temperature, kick off the fast idle cam.
2. Connect a tachometer according to manufacturer's instructions. Remove the air cleaner vacuum supply hose (if so equipped) or the choke vacuum diaphragm hose from the carburetor nipple. See **Figure 20** (typical).

6

3. Connect the propane supply hose (**Figure 21**) to the carburetor nipple. Open the propane ON-OFF valve. Slowly open the propane metering valve until maximum engine speed is reached (too much propane will reduce engine speed). Leave propane flowing at this rate and do not touch metering valve until throttle is adjusted.

NOTE
Start test with an adequate supply of propane. If engine speed begins to drop off for no obvious reason, check the propane supply.

4. With propane flowing, adjust curb idle screw until engine speed reaches the "Enriched rpm" shown in the VECI decal. If the decal is defaced or missing, use the "Propane Enriched Idle" speed given in Table 1, Chapter Four. If necessary, adjust the propane flow to maximum engine speed.

NOTE
When the specified "Enriched rpm" is obtained, do not readjust the curb idle speed.

5A. For 1977-1978 models, turn off propane and adjust idle mixture screw (**Figure 22,** typical) to obtain the smoothest idle within ± 100 rpm of the specified curb idle speed.

NOTE
On 1977 318 cid engines with high altitude package, adjust for the smoothest idle at 100 rpm below the specified curb idle speed.

5B. For 1979-1980 models, turn off propane and adjust idle mixture screw (**Figure 22,** typical) to obtain the smoothest idle at the specified "Idle Set rpm" on the VECI decal. Pause between adjustments to allow engine rpm to stabilize.

6. Turn on propane again and check maximum speed to make sure the idle setting was not disturbed. If the maximum speed varies more than 25 rpm from the specified enriched rpm, repeat Steps 4 through 6.

7. Turn off propane and remove the propane enrichment tool.

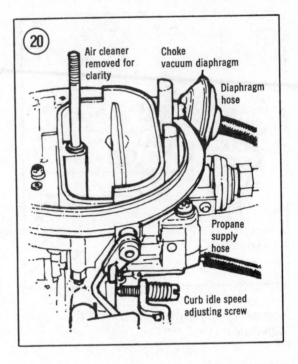

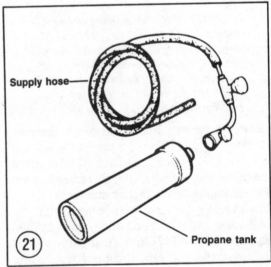

NOTE
On 1977 318 cid engines with high altitude package, reset curb idle speed to specification by adjusting the curb idle speed solenoid.

8. Reinstall all vacuum lines previously disconnected. Remove jumper wire used to ground carburetor idle stop switch.

9. Start engine and check for proper operation. Engine speed may increase, but do not readjust.

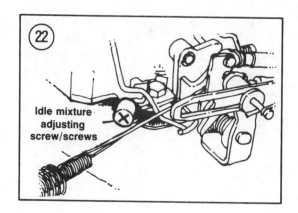

Idle mixture adjusting screw/screws

Fast Idle Adjustment
(All Models)

Curb idle speed and mixture adjustments must be made before setting the fast idle speed.

1. Set the parking brake and block the rear wheels.
2. Remove the air cleaner as described in this chapter.
3. Disconnect the EGR, heated air control and OSAC valve vacuum lines at the carburetor. If not equipped with an OSAC valve, disconnect the vacuum line leading directly to the distributor. Cap all carburetor vacuum ports.
4. On ELB or ESC engines, place the air cleaner to one side without disconnecting any wires or vacuum lines to the spark control computer. Connect a jumper wire between the carburetor idle stop switch terminals and a good engine ground (**Figure 17**).
5. Open the throttle and close the choke. Close the throttle to position the fast idle screw on the highest step of the fast idle cam, then move the cam until the screw drops to the second highest step. See **Figure 19**.
6. Start the engine and let the idle speed stabilize. Adjust the fast idle screw to obtain the fast idle rpm specified on the VECI decal.
7. Reconnect all vacuum lines and reinstall the air cleaner. Remove the jumper wire from ELB and ESC engines.

DASHPOT ADJUSTMENT

Some engines use a dashpot to reduce the rate of throttle closure during deceleration. To check and adjust:

1. Set the parking brake and block the rear wheels.
2. Connect a tachometer according to manufacturer's instructions.
3. Start the engine. Position the throttle lever so that its actuating tab touches but does not depress the dashpot stem.
4. Let the engine speed stabilize for 30 seconds. Note the tachometer reading. It should be 2,300 rpm for 6-cylinder and 2,500 rpm for V8 engines.
5. If the engine speed is not within the specifications in Step 4, loosen the dashpot locknut and turn the dashpot body in or out as required to obtain the specified rpm.
6. Retighten dashpot locknut and check that engine speed returns to the correct curb idle speed consistently.

Catalyst Protection Throttle
Positioner Adjustment

Some 1975-1976 engines are equipped with a catalyst protection system. This prevents the catalytic converter from overheating by holding the throttle open at the equivalent of the fast idle position when sudden deceleration takes place from above 2,000 rpm. To check and adjust:

1. Set the parking brake and block the rear wheels.
2. Connect a tachometer according to manufacturer's instructions.
3. Disconnect the wire at the throttle position solenoid and hold the throttle open.
4. Connect a jumper wire from the positive battery post to the solenoid. This should cause the solenoid plunger to fully extend.
5. Start the engine and increase rpm enough to make sure the solenoid is fully extended. Engine speed should be 1,450-1,550 when the solenoid is fully extended.
6. If the engine speed is not within the range specified in Step 5, adjust the solenoid.
7. Wait 30 seconds for the OSAC valve to provide vacuum spark advance and the engine speed to stabilize, then remove the jumper wire and reconnect the solenoid lead.
8. Slowly increase engine speed from idle and watch solenoid operation. As engine rpm exceeds 2,000 rpm, the solenoid plunger should fully extend and hold that position.

6

9. Slowly decrease engine speed. At or before 1,800 rpm, the solenoid plunger should retract. If it does not, the speed switch is defective and should be replaced.

CARBURETOR SERVICE

Removal/Installation

Flooding, stumbling on acceleration and general lack of performance may be caused by dirt, water or foreign matter in the carburetor. To verify the condition, the carburetor should be carefully removed from the engine without removing the fuel from the fuel bowl(s). Examine the fuel for contamination and disassemble the carburetor for cleaning.

Some brands of gasoline contain additives that can cause the fuel inlet needle to swell. This will affect fuel intake and float level, causing driveability problems. If a carburetor overhaul shows inlet needle swelling, change gasoline brands.

WARNING
Carburetor removal should be attempted only on a cold engine. Fuel spilled on a hot engine could be accidentally ignited.

1. Disconnect the negative battery cable.
2. Remove the air cleaner as described in this chapter.
3. Remove the fuel tank filler cap to relieve any pressure that might be present.
4. Place a suitable container under the carburetor fuel inlet fitting to catch fuel spillage. Disconnect the fuel line from the carburetor. Use two wrenches to avoid twisting the line. Plug the line to prevent leakage.
5. Disconnect the throttle linkage (**Figure 23**, typical).
6. Disconnect the choke linkage (**Figure 24**, typical).
7. Label and disconnect all vacuum lines from the carburetor.
8. Remove the carburetor attaching nuts. Remove the carburetor from the engine, holding it upright to prevent fuel spillage.
9. Stuff a clean cloth into the intake manifold opening to prevent small parts and contamination from falling inside.

10. Installation is the reverse of removal. Note the following:
    a. Use a new flange gasket and make sure it is properly oriented.
    b. For ease in starting, fill the carburetor bowl before installing the carburetor. Operate the throttle lever several times and make sure that fuel discharges from the pump jets prior to installation.
    c. Tighten the attaching nuts in an alternating pattern to prevent air leaks and/or warpage of the carburetor base. Tighten nuts to 17 ft.-lb. (6-cylinder) or 20 ft.-lb. (V8).
    d. Replace all worn or loose vacuum lines and reinstall lines in their original positions.
    e. Check linkage operation and set idle mixture and speed to specifications as described in this chapter.

Inspection and Overhaul

Dirt, varnish, water or carbon contamination in or on the carburetor are often the cause of unsatisfactory performance. Gaskets, accelerating pump diaphragms and power valves may leak, resulting in carburetion problems. Efficient carburetion depends upon careful cleaning, inspection and proper installation of new parts.

Each carburetor has an identification number stamped on the body or air horn. **Figure 10** shows a typical location. The identification number is necessary to obtain the proper carburetor overhaul kit.

The new gaskets and parts included in a carburetor overhaul kit should be installed when the carburetor is assembled and the old parts discarded.

When the carburetor is disassembled for cleaning, do not disassemble the linkage. The only internal adjustment that should be necessary is the float level. Follow the procedure specified on the instruction sheet provided with the carburetor overhaul kit.

Wash all parts except diaphragms, dashpots, solenoids and other vacuum or electrically operated assist devices in fresh commercial carburetor cleaning solvent. This can be obtained from any auto parts store; if not available, denatured alcohol may be used.

Rinse all parts in kerosene to remove traces of the cleaning solvent, then dry with compressed air. Wipe all parts which cannot be immersed in solvent with a clean, dry soft cloth.

Force compressed air through all passages of the carburetor.

CAUTION
Do not use a wire brush to clean any part. Do not use a drill or wire to clean out any opening or passage in the carburetor. A drill or wire may enlarge the hole or passage and change the calibration.

Check the choke shaft for grooves, wear or excessive looseness or binding. Inspect the choke plate for nicked edges and ease of operation.

Check the throttle shafts in their bores for excessive looseness or binding. Check the throttle plates for burrs which prevent proper closure.

Inspect the main body, air horn, nozzle bars and booster venturi assemblies (2-bbl. and 4-bbl. carburetors) for cracks or warpage.

Check brass floats for leaks by holding them under water which has been heated to 200° F. Bubbles will appear if there is a leak. Check composition floats for fuel absorption by gently squeezing and applying fingernail pressure.

Replace the float if the arm needle contact surface is grooved. If the floats are serviceable, gently polish the needle contact surface of the arm with crocus cloth or steel wool. Replace the float if the shaft is worn.

Replace all screws and nuts that have stripped threads. Replace all distorted or broken springs. Inspect all gasket mating surfaces for nicks and burrs.

Inspect the rubber boot of dashpots, if so equipped, for proper installation in the groove of the stem bushing. Check the stem movement for smooth operation. Do not lubricate the stem. Replace the assembly if defective.

Reassemble all parts carefully. It should not be necessary to apply force to any parts. If force seems to be required, you are doing something wrong. Stop and refer to the exploded drawing provided in this book or in the overhaul kit for your carburetor.

Holley 1920 Disassembly

Refer to **Figure 25** (typical) for this procedure. Not all Model 1920 carburetors will use all the parts shown in **Figure 25**.

1. Use carburetor legs to prevent throttle plate damage while working on the carburetor. If these are not available, thread a nut on each of two 2 1/4 in. bolts. Install each bolt in a flange hole and thread another nut to the bolt. This will hold the bolt securely to the carburetor and serve the same purpose as legs.

2. Remove the bowl vent rod bracket.

3. Disconnect the diaphragm link from the choke lever. Remove the bowl vent rod.

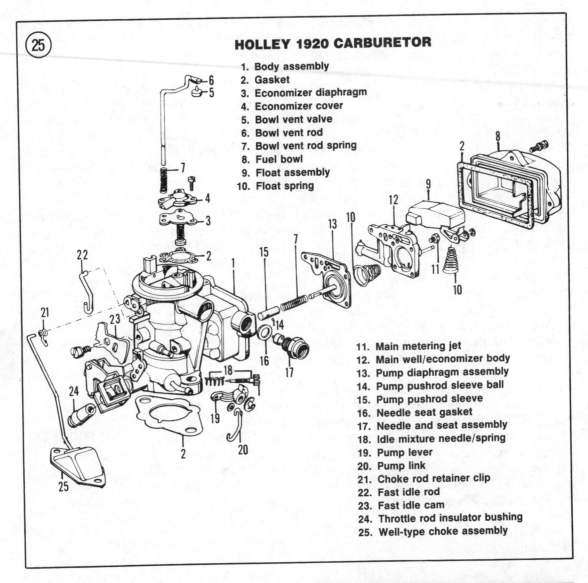

HOLLEY 1920 CARBURETOR

1. Body assembly
2. Gasket
3. Economizer diaphragm
4. Economizer cover
5. Bowl vent valve
6. Bowl vent rod
7. Bowl vent rod spring
8. Fuel bowl
9. Float assembly
10. Float spring

11. Main metering jet
12. Main well/economizer body
13. Pump diaphragm assembly
14. Pump pushrod sleeve ball
15. Pump pushrod sleeve
16. Needle seat gasket
17. Needle and seat assembly
18. Idle mixture needle/spring
19. Pump lever
20. Pump link
21. Choke rod retainer clip
22. Fast idle rod
23. Fast idle cam
24. Throttle rod insulator bushing
25. Well-type choke assembly

4. Remove the 3 screws holding the power valve (economizer) cover. Remove the cover, diaphragm, plunger and spring from the carburetor bowl. See **Figure 26**.

5. Separate the power valve diaphragm from the cover. Remove the gasket from the main body.

6. Loosen the fuel bowl cover screws. Remove the cover from the carburetor body. Remove and discard the gasket.

7. Remove fuel inlet fitting with needle valve and seat. See **Figure 27**. Separate needle valve from seat. Remove and discard the gasket.

8. Pull circlip from float hinge shaft, then slide float and spring from main body.

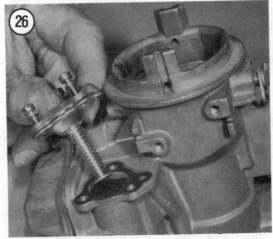

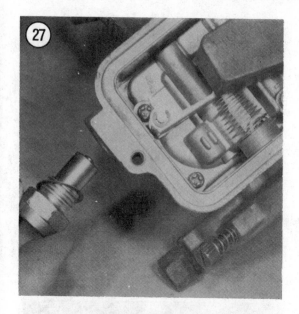

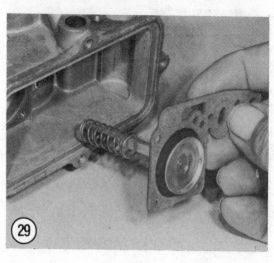

9. Remove metering body (**Figure 28**). Body contains 2 check balls and 2-stage power valve. Do not attempt to disassemble metering body. It is non-serviceable and must be replaced as an assembly if necessary.

10. Remove hairpin clip from accelerator pump rod. Separate pump rod from nylon pump lever.

11. Disconnect pump diaphragm stem and withdraw from carburetor (**Figure 29**). Diaphragm and gasket are an assembly and must be replaced as a unit if necessary.

12. Turn the idle mixture screw clockwise until it seats *lightly*, counting the number of turns required. Write this information down for reference during reassembly. Back out and remove screw and spring.

13. This completes carburetor disassembly. The main metering jet (in metering body) does not have to be removed for normal cleaning. Remove only if jet or metering body is to be replaced.

Holley 1920 Assembly

Refer to **Figure 25** (typical) for this procedure. Not all Model 1920 carburetors will use all the parts shown in **Figure 25**. Check replacement gaskets for proper punching by comparing them with old gaskets.

1. To reassemble, engage pump cam link in throttle shaft lever. Tilt lever up to align with nylon lever and hold in place.

2. Install pump diaphragm with spring. Connect diaphragm arm to nylon lever. Connect pump rod to lever and install hairpin clip.

3. Install idle mixture screw in throttle body. Turn screw clockwise until it seats *lightly*, then back it out the number of turns recorded during disassembly to provide a temporary idle adjustment setting.

4. Install metering body over pump diaphragm and tighten screws securely.

5. If main jet was removed from metering body (**Figure 30**), reinstall it securely.

6. Insert end of float spring in float hanger. Hook float hinge over metering body stud. Slide float and spring into carburetor body (**Figure 31**), then reinstall the circlip.

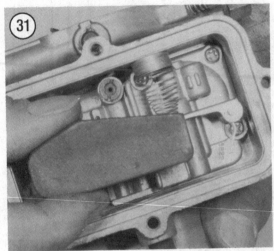

7. Install a new gasket over the fuel inlet valve fitting. Install inlet needle in valve seat (**Figure 32**), then install valve seat in fuel bowl and tighten securely.

8. Adjust float following the procedure and specifications provided in the overhaul kit.

9. Install power valve (economizer) diaphragm and cover (**Figure 33**). Make sure diaphragm stem rests on power valve lever, then install fuel bowl cover with a new gasket and tighten attaching screws securely.

10. Position tip of bowl vent rod over bowl vent. Center the rod in the casting cutouts with spring resting on carburetor body. Hold rod in this position.

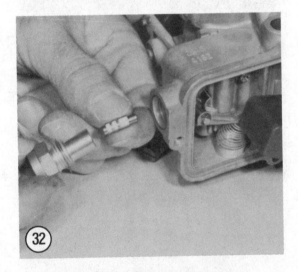

11. Connect vacuum diaphragm link to choke lever. Fit diaphram bracket over bowl vent rod and align screw holes.

12. Reinstall vacuum diaphragm bracket screws securely. Check operation of bowl vent rod and choke diaphragm to make sure they operate freely.

Holley 1945/6145 Disassembly

Refer to **Figure 34** (typical) for this procedure. Not all Model 1945/6145 carburetors will use all the parts shown in **Figure 34**.

1. Use carburetor legs to prevent throttle plate damage while working on the carburetor. If these are not available, thread a nut on each of four 2 1/4 in. bolts. Install each bolt in a flange hole and thread another nut to

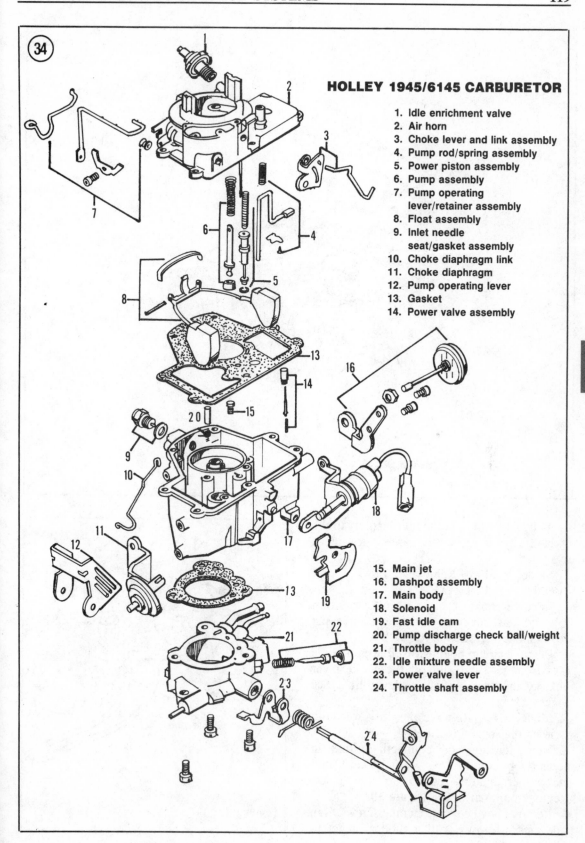

(34)

HOLLEY 1945/6145 CARBURETOR

1. Idle enrichment valve
2. Air horn
3. Choke lever and link assembly
4. Pump rod/spring assembly
5. Power piston assembly
6. Pump assembly
7. Pump operating lever/retainer assembly
8. Float assembly
9. Inlet needle seat/gasket assembly
10. Choke diaphragm link
11. Choke diaphragm
12. Pump operating lever
13. Gasket
14. Power valve assembly

15. Main jet
16. Dashpot assembly
17. Main body
18. Solenoid
19. Fast idle cam
20. Pump discharge check ball/weight
21. Throttle body
22. Idle mixture needle assembly
23. Power valve lever
24. Throttle shaft assembly

6

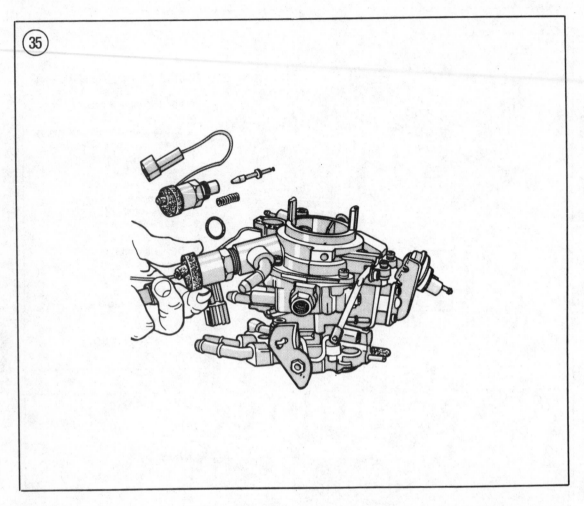

the bolt. This will hold the bolt securely to the carburetor and serve the same purpose as legs.

2. Model 6145—Remove bowl vent assembly. See **Figure 35**.

3. Remove choke actuator, throttle position solenoid, dashpot or any other external assist devices. See **Figure 36** (typical).

4. Remove circlip holding fast idle cam. Slide cam from its shaft and off the choke lever linkage, then remove choke lever link. See **Figure 37**.

5. Model 6145—Remove the duty solenoid. Discard the solenoid gasket.

6. Note location of connecting link in accelerator pump arm. Remove nut and lockwasher holding pump arm in place. Remove pump arm. See **Figure 38**.

7. Remove bowl cover attaching screws. Rap side of bowl cover with a rubber mallet to

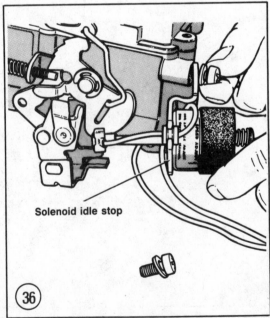

Solenoid idle stop

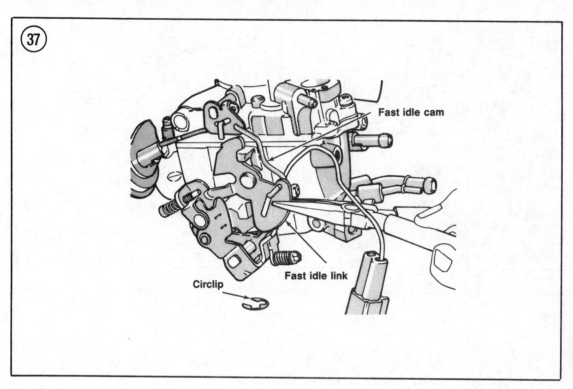

Fast idle cam

Circlip

Fast idle link

6

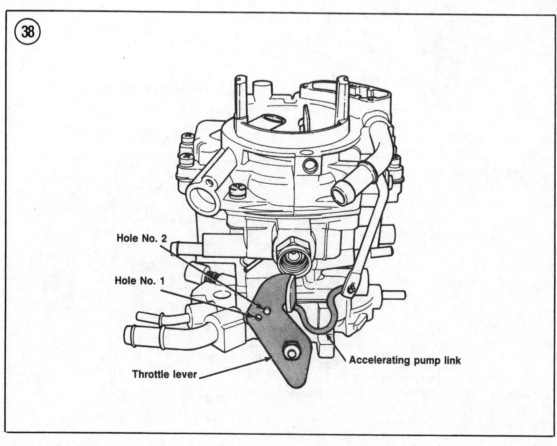

Hole No. 2

Hole No. 1

Throttle lever

Accelerating pump link

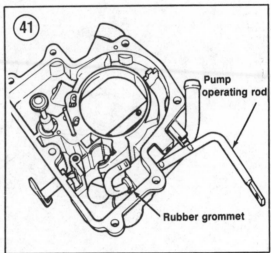

Pump
operating rod

Rubber grommet

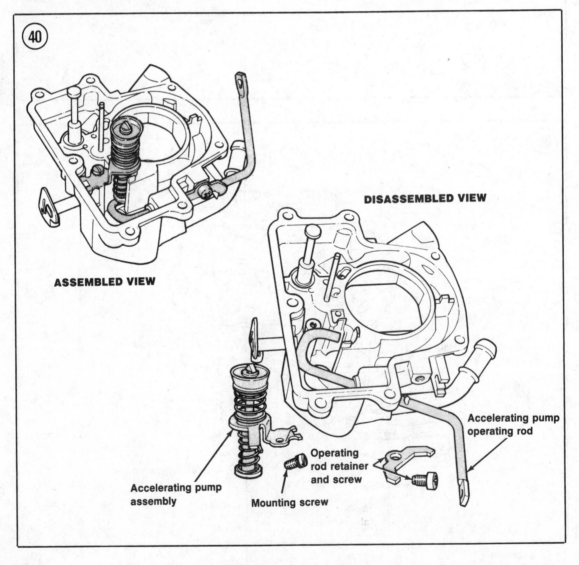

ASSEMBLED VIEW

DISASSEMBLED VIEW

Accelerating pump
assembly

Mounting screw

Operating
rod retainer
and screw

Accelerating pump
operating rod

break gasket seal. Lift bowl cover straight up and off main body to prevent damage to the main well tube, vacuum piston stem and accelerator pump assembly. See **Figure 39**.

8. Invert bowl cover. Remove and discard gasket. Remove pump operating rod retainer screw and retainer (**Figure 40**).

9. Pull up on pump drive spring, rotate pump rod slightly and remove pump assembly. See **Figure 40**.

10. Rotate pump operating rod to free rubber cover grommet, then remove rod. See **Figure 41**.

NOTE
The power piston assembly is staked in place and does not have to be removed for normal cleaning.

11. Model 1945—Turn cover right-side up and remove the bowl vent cap. Remove spring from vent adjusting screw. Loosen vent retaining screw and remove vent assembly.

12. Remove float shaft retainer, then lift float assembly up and out of main body. See **Figure 42**.

13. Unscrew and remove the fuel inlet fitting and needle valve assembly (**Figure 42**). Remove and discard the gasket.

14. Invert the main body and catch the pump discharge check ball and weight.

NOTE
Some Model 1945 carburetors use a one-piece power valve; others have a 3-piece assembly as shown in ***Figure 43***.

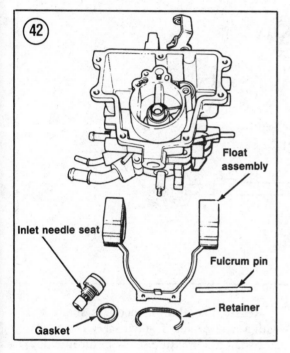

(42) Float assembly
Inlet needle seat
Fulcrum pin
Retainer
Gasket

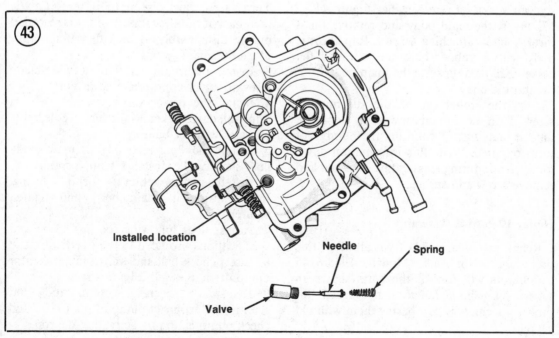

(43) Installed location
Needle
Spring
Valve

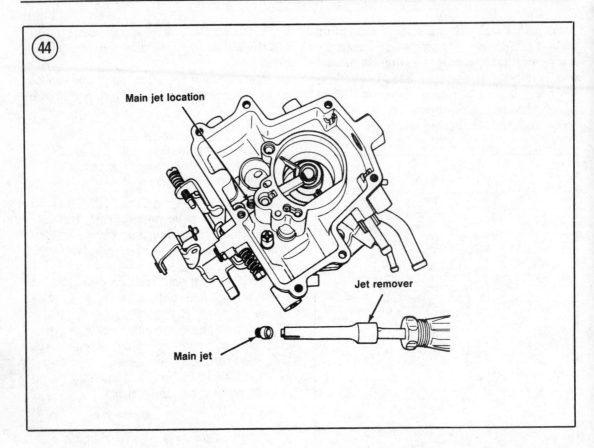

Figure 44

Main jet location

Jet remover

Main jet

15. Remove power valve assembly with an appropriate thin-wall deep socket.

16. Remove the main jet with a wide-blade screwdriver or jet remover. See **Figure 44**.

17. Invert the main body and remove the 3 throttle body attaching screws. Rap throttle body with a rubber hammer to break the gasket seal, then separate the main body from the throttle body.

18. Pry the limiter cap off the idle mixture screw. Turn the idle mixture screw clockwise until it seats *lightly*, counting the number of turns required. Write this information down for reference during reassembly. Back out and remove screw and spring.

Holley 1945/6145 Assembly

Refer to **Figure 34** (typical) for this procedure. Not all Model 1945/6145 carburetors will use all the parts shown in **Figure 34**. Check replacement gaskets for proper punching by comparing them with old gaskets.

1. Reassemble throttle body to main body with a new gasket. Tighten screws securely.

2. Install idle mixture screw in throttle body. Turn screw clockwise until it seats *lightly*, then back it out the number of turns recorded during disassembly to provide a temporary idle adjustment setting.

3. Install the main jet with a wide-blade screwdriver or appropriate jet installer.

4. Install the power valve assembly with a thin-wall deep socket. Make sure needle valve operates without binding.

5. Install the float assembly in main body float shaft cradle. Install retaining spring.

6. Install a new gasket on the fuel inlet fitting. Install fitting in main body and tighten securely.

7. Adjust float following the procedure and specifications provided in the overhaul kit.

8. Insert check ball and weight in accelerator pump discharge well (**Figure 45**).

9. Reinstall accelerator pump rod and grommet. Reconnect pump to pump rod and check pump action by activating the rod.

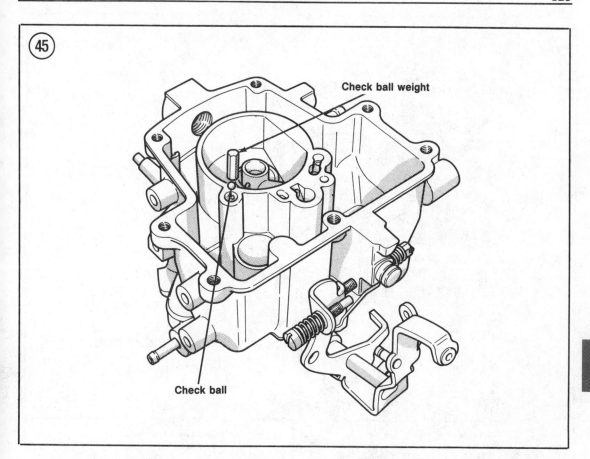

Check ball weight

Check ball

10. Model 1945—Drop vent valve and shaft in place in the bowl cover. Tighten the retaining screw and place spring on adjustment screw, then install vent cover.

11. Install a new gasket on the bowl cover. Carefully lower bowl cover onto main body. Make sure accelerator pump goes into pump well and vacuum piston rod rides under piston flange.

12. Install bowl cover screws. Tighten in an alternating pattern to 30 in.-lb.

13. Model 6145—Install a new feedback solenoid gasket on the bowl cover. Install a new O-ring on the duty solenoid. Lubricate O-ring with petroleum jelly and install solenoid. Tighten mounting screws securely.

14. Install pump arm, lockwasher and nut. Reinstall connecting link in accelerator pump arm. Link should fit into the same slot noted during removal.

15. Connect fast idle cam linkage to choke lever, then slip cam over shaft and install retaining circlip.

16. Install choke actuator, throttle position solenoid, dashpot or any other external assist devices removed from carburetor.

17. Model 6145—Install bowl vent assembly. See **Figure 35**.

Holley 2210/2245 Disassembly

Refer to **Figure 46** (typical) for this procedure. Not all Model 2210/2245 carburetors will use all the parts shown in **Figure 46**.

1. Use carburetor legs to prevent throttle plate damage while working on the carburetor. If these are not available, thread a nut on each of four 2 1/4 in. bolts. Install each bolt in a flange hole and thread another nut to the bolt. This will hold the bolt securely to the carburetor and serve the same purpose as legs.

2. Remove choke pulldown diaphragm, throttle position solenoid, dashpot or any other external assist devices.

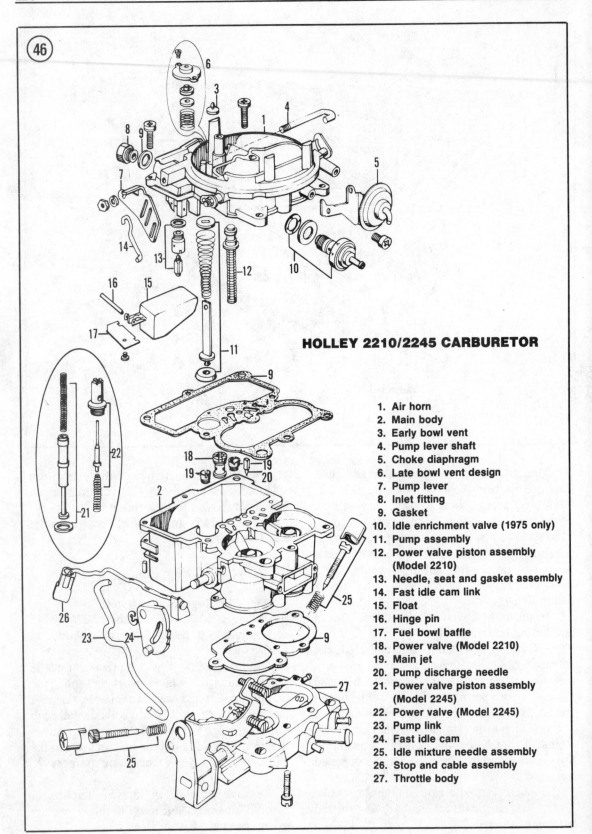

HOLLEY 2210/2245 CARBURETOR

1. Air horn
2. Main body
3. Early bowl vent
4. Pump lever shaft
5. Choke diaphragm
6. Late bowl vent design
7. Pump lever
8. Inlet fitting
9. Gasket
10. Idle enrichment valve (1975 only)
11. Pump assembly
12. Power valve piston assembly (Model 2210)
13. Needle, seat and gasket assembly
14. Fast idle cam link
15. Float
16. Hinge pin
17. Fuel bowl baffle
18. Power valve (Model 2210)
19. Main jet
20. Pump discharge needle
21. Power valve piston assembly (Model 2245)
22. Power valve (Model 2245)
23. Pump link
24. Fast idle cam
25. Idle mixture needle assembly
26. Stop and cable assembly
27. Throttle body

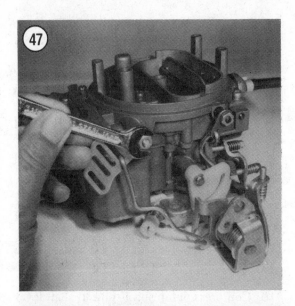

3. Remove nut and washer holding rocker arm, then pull arm from pump shaft. Note position of linkage in rocker arm, then disconnect linkage from rocker arm and throttle lever. See **Figure 47**.

4. Remove nut and washer holding choke lever to choke shaft. Disconnect fast idle rod from choke lever and fast idle cam. See **Figure 48**.

5. Note positioning of bowl vent lever spring ends, then remove circlip and carefully slide lever and spring off shaft. See **Figure 49**.

6. Remove the air horn screws. Rap air horn with a rubber mallet to break the gasket seal, then lift it straight up and off the main body to prevent damage to the main well tubes.

7. Invert air horn. Push up on accelerator pump and tilt to one side to disengage pump rod from shaft. Retrieve the washer.

8. Remove the bowl vent cover, plastic vent device, spring and seal. See **Figure 50**.

9. Remove the float retaining plate. Slide float hinge pin to one side and remove float assembly.

10. Remove inlet needle from needle valve, then remove valve with a wide-blade screwdriver. Remove and discard needle valve seat gasket.

11. If equipped with an idle enrichment circuit (1975 only), remove enrichment valve. See **Figure 51**.

6

12. Remove power valve assembly (**Figure 52**) with a wide-blade screwdriver.

13. It is not necessary to remove the main jets for cleaning purposes. If removed, however, be sure to note where each one goes, as the jet orifices may differ in size.

14. Invert the main body and catch the pump discharge check ball and weight (some models may use a weight without a check ball).

15. Invert the main body and remove the throttle body attaching screws. Rap throttle body with a rubber hammer to break the gasket seal, then separate the main body from the throttle body.

16. Pry the limiter caps off the idle mixture screws. Turn each idle mixture screw clockwise until it seats *lightly*, counting the number of turns required. Write this information down for reference during reassembly. Back out and remove each screw and spring.

Holley 2210/2245 Assembly

Refer to **Figure 46** (typical) for this procedure. Not all Model 2210/2245 carburetors will use all the parts shown in **Figure 46**. Check replacement gaskets for proper punching by comparing them with old gaskets.

1. Reassemble throttle body to main body with a new gasket. Tighten screws securely.

2. Install idle mixture screw in throttle body. Turn screw clockwise until it seats *lightly*, then back it out the number of turns recorded during disassembly to provide a temporary idle adjustment setting.

3. Install the main jets with a wide-blade screwdriver or appropriate jet installer, if removed.

4. Install inlet needle valve seat with a new gasket. Tighten seat securely, then install inlet needle.

5. Install power valve assembly and tighten

6. Install idle enrichment valve with a new O-ring, if so equipped.

7. Install check ball (if used) and weight in main body discharge well. See **Figure 53**.

8. Center float hinge pin in float assembly and seat in main body. Install float retaining plate.

9. Install vent valve seat, spring and valve in air horn. See **Figure 54**. Install vent valve cover and tighten screws securely.

10. Compress pump spring and fit shaft lever through air horn slot, tilting to one side to reconnect it to the pump (**Figure 55**). Be sure to reinstall the washer on the pump rod before connecting the pump shaft.

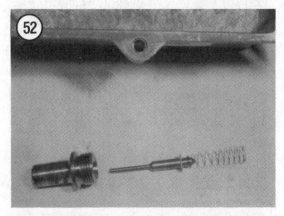

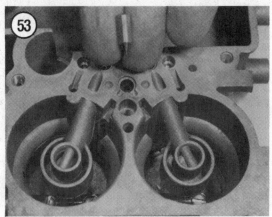

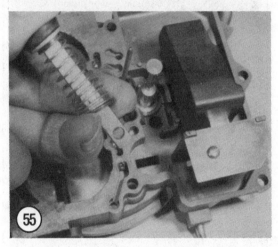

11. Invert the air horn and install a new gasket. Air horn has small locating pins which should engage holes in the gasket to keep it in place while reinstalling air horn to main body.

12. Lower air horn onto main body assembly. Make sure main well tubes and accelerator pump fit into their respective places in the main body. Reinstall and tighten air horn screws.

13. Position spring inside vent lever. Slip assembly onto shaft. Check lever action and then reinstall circlip.

14. Reconnect the choke lever and linkage. Install rocker arm and linkage.

15. Install choke pulldown diaphragm, throttle position solenoid, dashpot or any other external assist devices.

Holley 2280/6280 Disassembly

1. Use carburetor legs to prevent throttle plate damage while working on the carburetor. If these are not available, thread a nut on each of four 2 1/4 in. bolts. Install each bolt in a flange hole and thread another nut to the bolt. This will hold the bolt securely to the carburetor and serve the same purpose as legs.

2. Remove air cleaner stud and retainer assembly.

3. Remove cotter pin from accelerator pump arm link. Remove the pump arm link.

4. Remove the bowl vent solenoid (**Figure 56**).

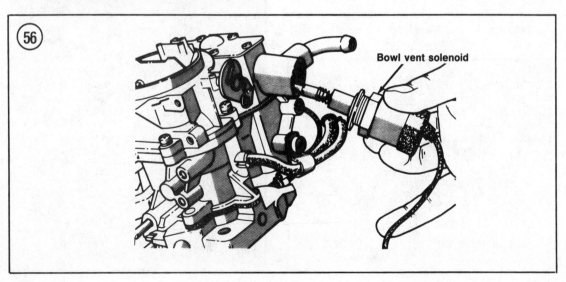

Bowl vent solenoid

5. Remove choke diaphragm, linkage and bracket as an assembly.

6. Remove nut and washer holding fast idle cam lever to choke shaft. Disengage fast idle connector link from lever and fast idle cam. Disconnect and remove accelerator pump operating link.

7. Remove the air horn screws. Lift air horn straight up and off main body to prevent damage to the main well tubes and accelerator pump. Remove and discard the gasket.

8. Remove the circlip holding the accelerator pump shaft. Pull shaft straight out, then remove pump arm and pump lever. See **Figure 57**.

9. Place an open-end wrench on the accelerator pump shaft flat and remove the cap nut. See **Figure 58**.

10. Gently pry upward on the retaining ring tangs and remove the vacuum power valve piston (**Figure 59**).

11. Gently pry plastic cap from mechanical power valve pushrod. Remove circlip and remove pushrod and spring. See **Figure 60**.

12. Model 6280—Remove the feedback solenoid (**Figure 61**).

13. Remove fuel inlet fitting from main body (**Figure 62**). Remove and discard the gasket.

14. Remove the float fulcrum pin, float baffle and float assembly (**Figure 62**).

15. Remove the main metering jets with a wide-blade screwdriver (**Figure 63**).

16. Use special tool part No. C-4231 to remove the mechanical and vacuum power valves. See **Figure 64**. Keep the needles with

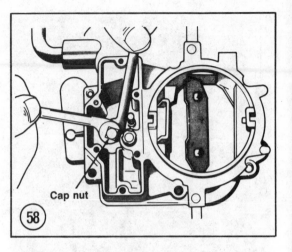

Cap nut

58

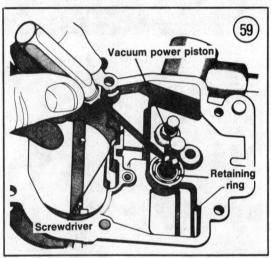

59

Vacuum power piston

Retaining ring

Screwdriver

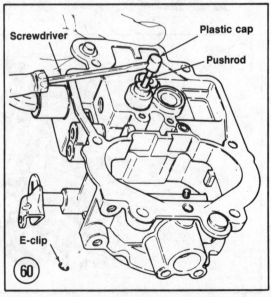

Screwdriver

Plastic cap

Pushrod

E-clip

60

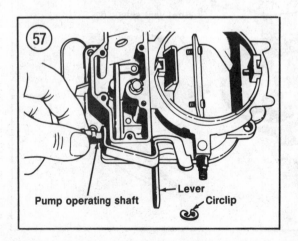

57

Pump operating shaft

Lever

Circlip

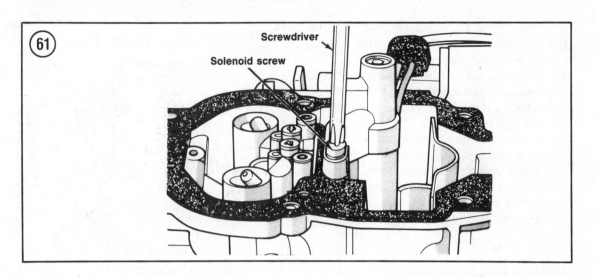

(61)

Screwdriver

Solenoid screw

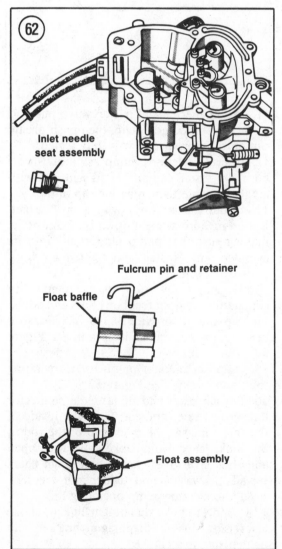

(62)

Inlet needle
seat assembly

Fulcrum pin and retainer

Float baffle

Float assembly

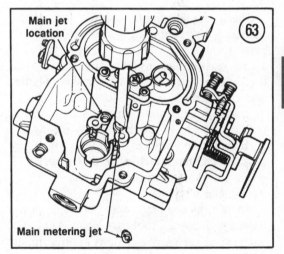

(63)

Main jet
location

Main metering jet

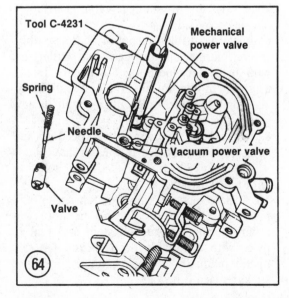

Tool C-4231

Mechanical
power valve

Spring

Needle

Vacuum power valve

Valve

(64)

6

their respective seats and properly identify each for reinstallation, as they must not be mixed up during reassembly.

17. Remove the venturi cluster screws. Remove the cluster and gasket (**Figure 65**). Discard the gasket. Do not attempt to remove the idle well tubes.

18. Invert the main body and catch the pump discharge check ball and weight.

19. Remove the 4 throttle body attaching screws. Rap the main body with a rubber hammer to break the gasket seal. Separate the throttle body and main body.

Holley 2280/6280 Assembly

Check replacement gaskets for proper punching by comparing them with old gaskets.

1. To reassemble, invert main body. Install the throttle body with a new gasket. Tighten attaching screws to 30 in.-lb.

2. Install accelerator pump discharge check ball and weight in the main body passage.

3. Install the venturi cluster with new gaskets. Tighten attaching screws securely.

4. Install main metering jets with a wide-blade screwdriver.

5. Install mechanical and vacuum power valves with special tool part No. C-4231. The vacuum power valve needle is approximately 0.050 in. longer and is installed on the throttle lever side; the mechanical valve is installed on the choke side.

6. Install float fulcrum pin in float assembly. Insert fulcrum pin through float baffle slot with baffle tabs pointing downward. Install assembly in fulcrum pin cradle of main body.

7. Install the fuel inlet fitting with a new gasket and tighten securely.

8. Adjust float following the procedure and specifications provided in the overhaul kit.

9. Model 6280—Install feedback solenoid with a new gasket.

10. Install vacuum power piston spring and piston in its cylinder in the air horn. Fit retaining ring over piston stem and seat in place with a suitable deep socket. Operate piston manually to make sure it does not stick; replace if it does.

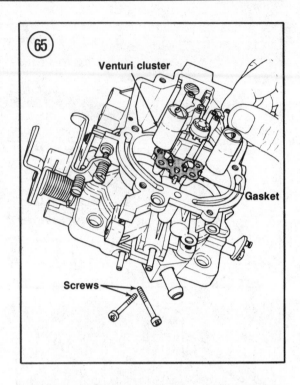

Venturi cluster

Gasket

Screws

11. Install mechanical power valve pushrod spring, pushrod and circlip, then push plastic cap onto pushrod until it is fully seated.

12. Insert accelerator pump assembly in air horn and install cap nut. Hold shaft flat with a wrench while tightening the cap nut.

13. Install the air horn with a new gasket. Lower air horn straight down on main body, making sure that pump plunger fits into its cylinder bore. Install and tighten air horn screws to 25 in.-lb.

14. Set pump override spring retainer to contact the air horn fuel bowl boss and adjust the cap nut to provide 0.310 in. clearance between the housing and cap nut. See **Figure 66**.

15. Install accelerator pump lever, operating shaft and circlip. See **Figure 57**.

16. Engage plain end of fast idle connector link in fast idle cam slot (from the inside of the cam). Engage the other end of the rod in the choke lever. Hold choke valve wide open and slide lever over choke shaft (align flats). Install lockwasher and tighten nut securely. Install accelerator pump operating link.

17. Connect choke diaphragm link in choke lever slot. Install diaphragm bracket and tighten screws securely.

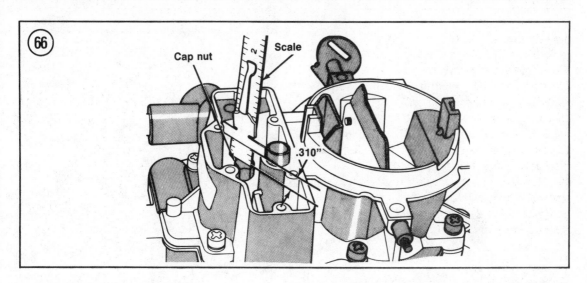

Cap nut · Scale · .310"

18. Install bowl vent solenoid.
19. Insert accelerator pump link in hole and install cotter pin.
20. Install air cleaner stud and retainer to air horn.

Holley 2300 Disassembly

Refer to **Figure 67** (typical) for this procedure. Not all Model 2300 carburetors will use all of the parts shown in **Figure 67**.
1. Use carburetor legs to prevent throttle plate damage while working on the carburetor. If these are not available, thread a nut on each of four 2 1/4 in. bolts. Install each bolt in a flange hole and thread another nut to the bolt. This will hold the bolt securely to the carburetor and serve the same purpose as legs.
2. Remove the fuel bowl and gasket and the metering block and gasket. Discard the gaskets.
3. Turn the idle adjusting needles clockwise until they seat *lightly*, counting the number of turns required. Write this information down for reference during reassembly. Back out and remove needles and gaskets. Discard gaskets.
4. Remove the main jets with a wide-blade screwdriver. See **Figure 68** for this location.
5. Loosen the power valve with a socket wrench. Remove the valve and discard the gasket. See **Figure 69**.

6. Remove the fuel level adjustment lockscrew and gasket.
7. Turn adjusting nut counterclockwise and remove locknut and gasket.
8. Remove but do *not* disassemble fuel inlet needle and seat (**Figure 70**). This is a matched assembly and is replaced as a set.
9. Remove float shaft circlip with needlenose pliers.
10. Slide float off shaft with attached spring (**Figure 71**).
11. Remove the fuel bowl baffle plate.
12. Remove the fuel level sight plug and gasket.
13. Remove the fuel inlet fitting and gasket.
14. Invert fuel bowl. Remove accelerating pump cover, diaphragm and spring. Pump check ball is *not* removable.
15. Invert carburetor. Remove throttle body attaching screws and lockwashers. Separate throttle body from main body and discard the gasket.
16. Remove the choke rod retainer from the choke housing shaft/lever assembly.
17. Remove the thermostat spring housing and gasket. Remove the choke housing from the main body. Remove and discard the tiny O-ring gaskets (**Figure 72**).
18. Remove choke housing shaft nut, lockwasher and spacer. Remove shaft and fast idle cam.
19. Remove choke piston/lever assembly. Remove choke rod and seal from main body. See **Figure 73**.

6

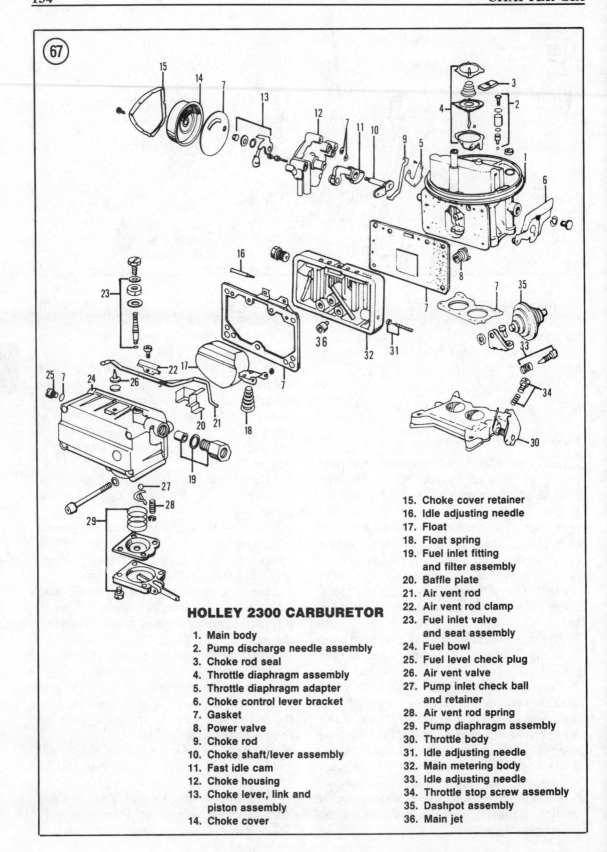

HOLLEY 2300 CARBURETOR

1. Main body
2. Pump discharge needle assembly
3. Choke rod seal
4. Throttle diaphragm assembly
5. Throttle diaphragm adapter
6. Choke control lever bracket
7. Gasket
8. Power valve
9. Choke rod
10. Choke shaft/lever assembly
11. Fast idle cam
12. Choke housing
13. Choke lever, link and piston assembly
14. Choke cover
15. Choke cover retainer
16. Idle adjusting needle
17. Float
18. Float spring
19. Fuel inlet fitting and filter assembly
20. Baffle plate
21. Air vent rod
22. Air vent rod clamp
23. Fuel inlet valve and seat assembly
24. Fuel bowl
25. Fuel level check plug
26. Air vent valve
27. Pump inlet check ball and retainer
28. Air vent rod spring
29. Pump diaphragm assembly
30. Throttle body
31. Idle adjusting needle
32. Main metering body
33. Idle adjusting needle
34. Throttle stop screw assembly
35. Dashpot assembly
36. Main jet

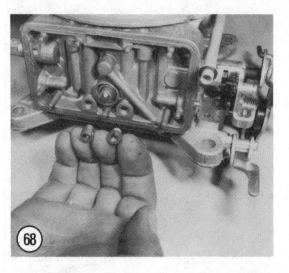

(68)

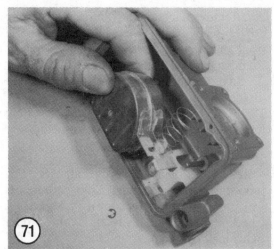

(71)

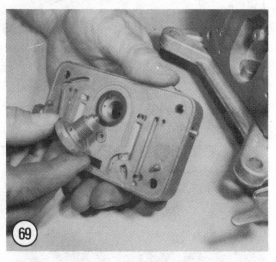

(69)

(72)

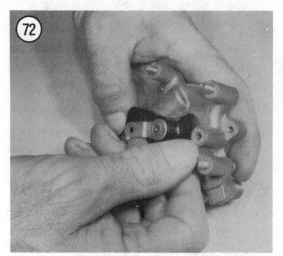

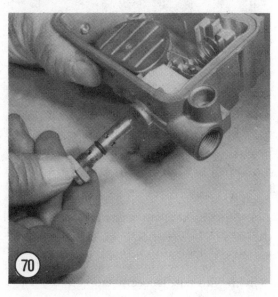

(70)

(73)

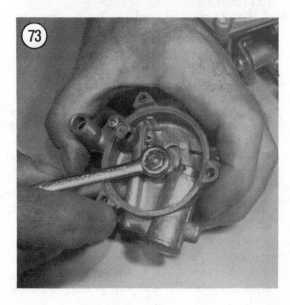

6

20. Remove accelerating pump discharge nozzle screw. Lift pump discharge nozzle from main body with needlenose pliers. Remove and discard gaskets. See **Figure 74**.

21. Invert main body and catch pump discharge needle as it falls out.

22. Remove accelerating pump operating lever from throttle body.

Holley 2300 Assembly

Refer to **Figure 67** (typical) for this procedure. Not all Model 2300 carburetors will use all of the parts shown in **Figure 67**. Check replacement gaskets for proper punching by comparing them with old gaskets.

1. Install accelerating pump operating lever to throttle body.

2. Drop pump discharge needle into pump well in main body. Lightly seat needle with appropriate size brass drift. Fit a new gasket on each end of discharge nozzle, insert discharge needle screw in nozzle and install assembly in discharge well. See **Figure 74**.

3. Install choke lever link/piston assembly in choke housing. Position on housing shaft and install spacer, lockwasher and nut.

4. Install new choke housing gaskets and position housing to main body, inserting choke rod in housing shaft lever. Projection on choke rod must be under fast idle cam to lift cam when choke is closed. Install choke rod cotter pin.

5. Fit thermostatic coil gasket to housing. Engage spring loop on spring lever, then install retainers and screws. Align index marks on housing/coil assembly to position specified in overhaul kit instructions and tighten screws.

6. Invert main body. Install throttle body to main body with a new gasket. Fuel inlet fitting must be on same side as pump operating lever. Install and tighten attaching screws and lockwashers securely.

7. Position accelerating pump diaphragm spring and diaphragm in pump chamber with large end of lever disc against operating lever. Install cover and finger-tighten retaining screws.

8. Check to see that diaphragm is centered, then compress it with the pump operating

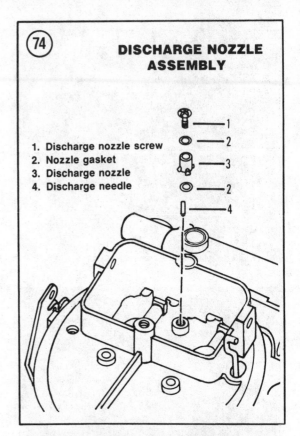

DISCHARGE NOZZLE ASSEMBLY

1. Discharge nozzle screw
2. Nozzle gasket
3. Discharge nozzle
4. Discharge needle

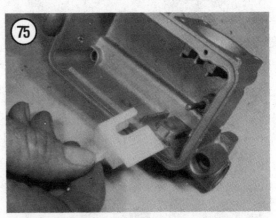

lever and tighten the retaining screws securely.

9. Install fuel inlet fitting with new gasket.

10. Install fuel level sight plug with new gasket.

11. Slide baffle plate over ridges in fuel bowl (**Figure 75**). Install spring on float and slide float over shaft with spring between ridges on boss of fuel bowl floor. Install float retainer circlip with needlenose pliers.

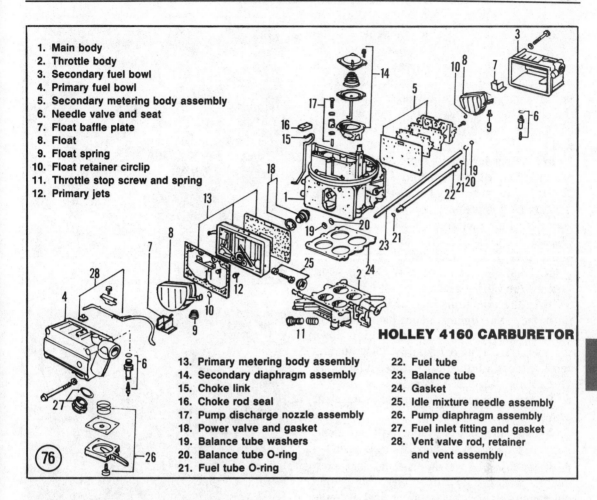

1. Main body
2. Throttle body
3. Secondary fuel bowl
4. Primary fuel bowl
5. Secondary metering body assembly
6. Needle valve and seat
7. Float baffle plate
8. Float
9. Float spring
10. Float retainer circlip
11. Throttle stop screw and spring
12. Primary jets

13. Primary metering body assembly
14. Secondary diaphragm assembly
15. Choke link
16. Choke rod seal
17. Pump discharge nozzle assembly
18. Power valve and gasket
19. Balance tube washers
20. Balance tube O-ring
21. Fuel tube O-ring

22. Fuel tube
23. Balance tube
24. Gasket
25. Idle mixture needle assembly
26. Pump diaphragm assembly
27. Fuel inlet fitting and gasket
28. Vent valve rod, retainer
   and vent assembly

HOLLEY 4160 CARBURETOR

12. Wipe new O-ring seal with petroleum jelly and install on fuel inlet needle/seat assembly.

13. Install needle/seat assembly in fuel bowl through top of bowl. Position adjusting nut gasket and nut of inlet needle/seat assembly, then align flat on ID of nut with flat on OD of inlet needle/seat assembly. Install fuel level adjustment lockscrew with new gasket.

14. Adjust dry float level to specifications provided with adjustment procedure in overhaul kit.

15. Install power valve in metering block with new gasket. Tighten snugly with socket wrench.

16. Install main jets in metering block with wide-blade screwdriver.

17. Install idle adjusting screws in metering block with new gaskets. Turn screws clockwise until they seat *lightly*, then back them out the number of turns recorded during

disassembly to provide a temporary idle adjustment setting.

18. Install a new gasket to the metering block using the dowels on the back of the block for alignment. Fit metering block and gasket to main body.

19. Position baffle plate and gasket on metering block.

20. Install retaining screws and new compression gaskets in fuel bowl.

21. Install fuel bowl to main body and tighten retaining screws securely.

22. Adjust accelerating pump to specifications provided with adjustment procedure in overhaul kit.

Holley 4160 Disassembly

Refer to **Figure 76** (typical) for this procedure. Not all Model 4160 carburetors will use all the parts shown in **Figure 76**.

1. Use carburetor legs to prevent throttle plate damage while working on the carburetor. If these are not available, thread a nut on each of four 2 1/4 in. bolts. Install each bolt in a flange hole and thread another nut to the bolt. This will hold the bolt securely to the carburetor and serve the same purpose as legs.

2. Invert fuel bowl and remove accelerating pump cover, diaphragm and spring (**Figure 77**). Inlet ball check is permanently installed.

3. Remove the primary fuel bowl and gasket. Remove the metering block and gasket (**Figure 78**). Discard the gaskets.

4. Remove the fuel line tube, fuel distribution tube, washer and O-ring seals. Discard the O-ring seals.

5. Turn the idle adjusting needles clockwise until they seat *lightly*, counting number of turns required. Write this information down for reference during reassembly. Back out and remove the idle adjusting needles and gaskets. Discard the gaskets.

6. Remove the main jets with a wide-blade screwdriver.

7. Loosen the power valve with a socket wrench. Unscrew valve and discard gasket.

8. Remove fuel level adjustment lockscrew and gasket. Turn adjusting nut counterclockwise and remove locknut and gasket.

9. Remove fuel inlet needle, seat and gasket (**Figure 79**). Do *not* disassemble needle/seat assembly. They are factory-matched; replace as a unit if necessary.

10. Remove circlip from float shaft with needlenose pliers. Slide float off shaft and remove spring.

11. Remove baffle plate from fuel bowl.

12. Remove fuel level sight plug and gasket. Remove inlet fitting and gasket.

13. Remove secondary fuel bowl and gasket. Remove metering body, plate and gasket with a clutch-type screwdriver (**Figure 80**).

14. Repeat Steps 8-12 to disassemble the secondary fuel bowl.

15. Invert carburetor. Remove throttle body retaining screws and lockwashers. Separate the throttle body from main body and discard the gasket.

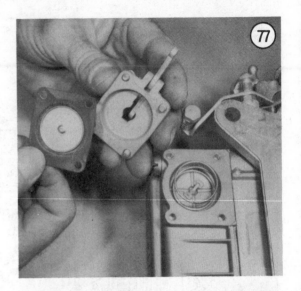

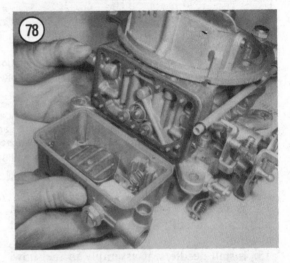

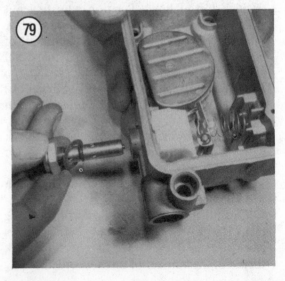

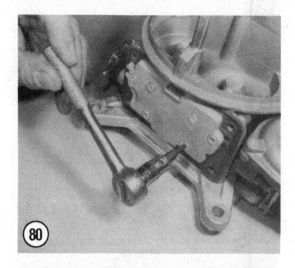

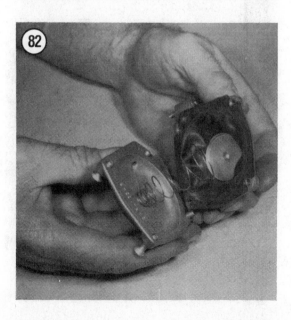

16. Remove choke rod retainer from choke housing shaft and lever assembly.

17. Remove choke cover screws, disengage thermostatic coil loop from choke lever and remove cover.

18. Remove choke housing and gaskets from main body. Discard gaskets.

19. Remove choke housing shaft nut, lockwasher and spacer. Lift out piston and choke link lever.

20. Remove choke rod and seal from main body.

21. Remove secondary diaphragm assembly and gasket from the main body (**Figure 81**).

22. Remove diaphragm housing cover and remove spring/diaphragm from housing (**Figure 82**).

23. Remove screw holding accelerating pump discharge nozzle in place. Remove nozzle and gaskets from main body. Discard gaskets.

24. Invert main body and catch pump discharge needle as it drops out.

Holley 4160 Assembly

Refer to **Figure 76** (typical) for this procedure. Not all Model 4160 carburetors will use all the parts shown in **Figure 76**. Check replacement gaskets for proper punching by comparing them with old gaskets.

1. Drop pump discharge needle into pump well in main body. Lightly seat needle with appropriate size brass drift. Fit a new gasket on each end of discharge nozzle, insert discharge needle screw in nozzle and install assembly in discharge well. See **Figure 83**.

2. Position secondary diaphragm in housing and put the spring in the cover. Install cover to housing and tighten retaining screws finger-tight. Pull diaphragm rod downward as far as it will go and tighten the retaining screws snugly.

3. Fit a new gasket on the secondary vacuum passage opening in the main body. Install the diaphragm housing to the main body.

4. Fit the seal on the choke rod and install the rod with the seal fitting into the retaining grooves underneath the air cleaner mounting flange.

5. Install choke piston, link and arm in choke housing. Install choke lever and washers on shaft. Screw retaining nut over fast idle shaft and tighten in place. Move choke lever back and forth to check operation of piston.

6. Install new choke housing gaskets to main body, then tilt housing to connect choke valve rod in hole on fast idle cam. Once rod and cam are connected, install housing screws and tighten securely. Install hairpin clip to choke valve rod.

7. Install a new gasket on the choke housing. Connect thermostatic coil loop to choke lever and install choke cover on housing. Set cover/housing index marks to position specified in overhaul kit instructions and install cover screws securely.

8. Invert main body and position a new gasket. Fit throttle body to main body with fuel inlet fitting on same side as accelerating pump lever, sliding the secondary diaphragm rod over the operating lever. Install throttle body attaching screws and lockwashers and tighten securely. Install retaining circlip on secondary diaphragm rod (**Figure 84**).

NOTE
*Refer to **Figure 85** and reassemble the primary fuel bowl first.*

9. Install fuel inlet fitting with a new gasket.

10. Install fuel level sight plug with a new gasket.

11. Slide the baffle plate over the fuel bowl ridges and install the float/spring assembly on the shaft. Float spring should fit between the ridges on the fuel bowl floor boss. Install circlip to hold float assembly on shaft.

12. Wipe new O-ring seal with petroleum jelly and install on fuel inlet needle/seat assembly.

13. Install needle/seat assembly in fuel bowl through top of bowl. Position adjusting nut gasket and nut of inlet needle/seat assembly, then align flat on ID of nut with flat on OD of inlet needle/seat assembly. Install fuel level adjustment lockscrew with new gasket.

14. Adjust dry float level to specifications provided with adjustment procedure in overhaul kit.

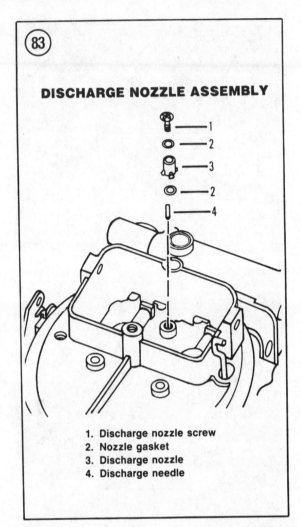

DISCHARGE NOZZLE ASSEMBLY

1. Discharge nozzle screw
2. Nozzle gasket
3. Discharge nozzle
4. Discharge needle

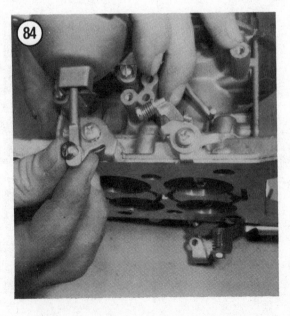

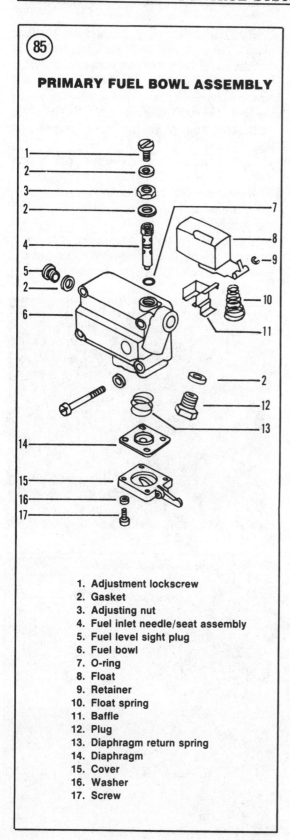

PRIMARY FUEL BOWL ASSEMBLY

1. Adjustment lockscrew
2. Gasket
3. Adjusting nut
4. Fuel inlet needle/seat assembly
5. Fuel level sight plug
6. Fuel bowl
7. O-ring
8. Float
9. Retainer
10. Float spring
11. Baffle
12. Plug
13. Diaphragm return spring
14. Diaphragm
15. Cover
16. Washer
17. Screw

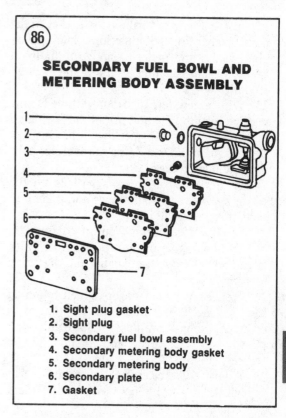

SECONDARY FUEL BOWL AND METERING BODY ASSEMBLY

1. Sight plug gasket
2. Sight plug
3. Secondary fuel bowl assembly
4. Secondary metering body gasket
5. Secondary metering body
6. Secondary plate
7. Gasket

6

15. Install power valve in metering block with new gasket. Tighten snugly with socket wrench.

16. Install main jets in metering block with wide-blade screwdriver.

17. Install idle adjusting needles in fuel bowl with new gaskets. Turn needles clockwise until they seat *lightly*, then back them out the number of turns recorded during disassembly to provide a temporary idle adjustment setting.

18. Install a new gasket on the back of the metering block. Fit metering block and gasket to main body. Install baffle plate and new gasket to metering block.

19. Install new compression gaskets on fuel bowl screws. Insert screws through fuel bowl, place bowl in position on metering block and tighten screws securely.

20. Wipe a new fuel distribution tube O-ring with petroleum jelly and install the O-ring on one end of the fuel line tube. Install this end of the tube in the primary fuel bowl recess.

21. Reassemble secondary fuel bowl by repeating Steps 10-14. See **Figure 86**.

22. Install a new metering body gasket to the main body. Fit the metering plate gasket, plate, gasket and metering body on the main body. Install retaining screws and tighten securely.

23. Wipe a new fuel distribution tube O-ring with petroleum jelly and install the O-ring on the other end of the fuel line tube. Fit fuel bowl to main body, guiding the fuel line tube into the bowl recess.

24. Install new compression gaskets on the retaining screws. Install screws and tighten in several stages to 50 in.-lb.

25. Install accelerating pump diaphragm spring/diaphragm in pump chamber with large end of lever disc against the operating lever.

26. Install cover and finger-tighten retaining screws. Check diaphragm to see that it is centered, then compress diaphragm with pump operating lever and tighten screws securely (**Figure 87**).

27. Adjust accelerating pump to specifications provided with adjustment procedures in overhaul kit.

Carter BBD Disassembly

Refer to **Figure 88** (typical) for this procedure. Not all BBD carburetors will use all the parts shown in **Figure 88**.

1. Use carburetor legs to prevent throttle plate damage while working on the carburetor. If these are not available, thread a nut on each of four 2 1/4 in. bolts. Install each bolt in a flange hole and thread another nut to the bolt. This will hold the bolt securely to the carburetor and serve the same purpose as legs.

2. Unclip and remove accelerating pump arm link.

3. Remove rollover check valve and gasket from top of air horn, if so equipped. Discard the gasket.

4. Remove step-up piston cover plate and gasket, if so equipped (**Figure 89**). Discard the gasket.

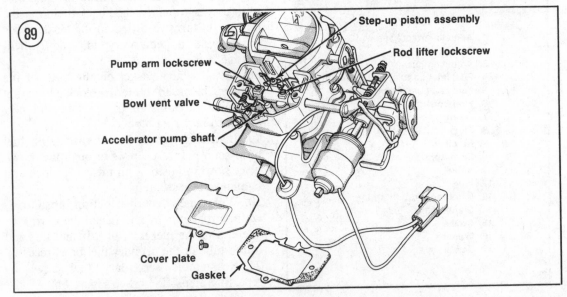

Step-up piston assembly

Rod lifter lockscrew

Pump arm lockscrew

Bowl vent valve

Accelerator pump shaft

Cover plate

Gasket

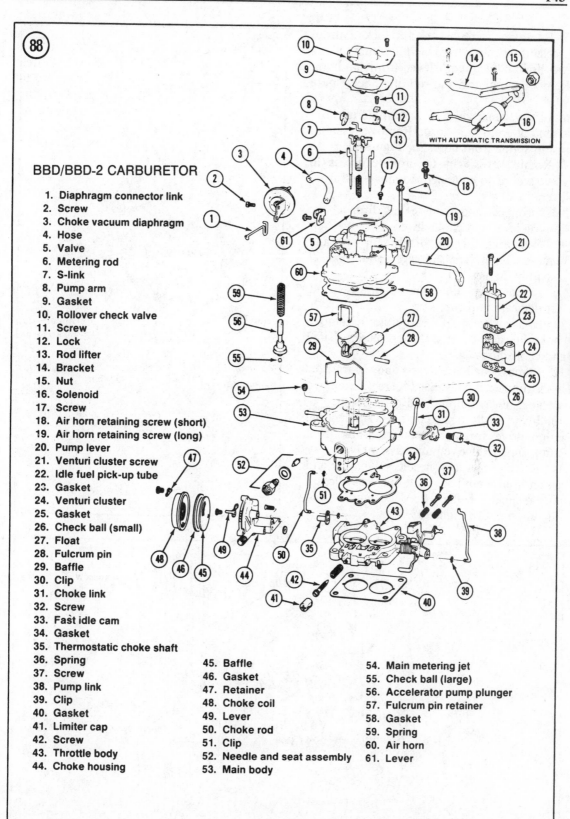

BBD/BBD-2 CARBURETOR

1. Diaphragm connector link
2. Screw
3. Choke vacuum diaphragm
4. Hose
5. Valve
6. Metering rod
7. S-link
8. Pump arm
9. Gasket
10. Rollover check valve
11. Screw
12. Lock
13. Rod lifter
14. Bracket
15. Nut
16. Solenoid
17. Screw
18. Air horn retaining screw (short)
19. Air horn retaining screw (long)
20. Pump lever
21. Venturi cluster screw
22. Idle fuel pick-up tube
23. Gasket
24. Venturi cluster
25. Gasket
26. Check ball (small)
27. Float
28. Fulcrum pin
29. Baffle
30. Clip
31. Choke link
32. Screw
33. Fast idle cam
34. Gasket
35. Thermostatic choke shaft
36. Spring
37. Screw
38. Pump link
39. Clip
40. Gasket
41. Limiter cap
42. Screw
43. Throttle body
44. Choke housing

45. Baffle
46. Gasket
47. Retainer
48. Choke coil
49. Lever
50. Choke rod
51. Clip
52. Needle and seat assembly
53. Main body

54. Main metering jet
55. Check ball (large)
56. Accelerator pump plunger
57. Fulcrum pin retainer
58. Gasket
59. Spring
60. Air horn
61. Lever

WITH AUTOMATIC TRANSMISSION

6

5. Remove screws and locks from accelerating pump arm and vacuum piston rod lifter. Slide pump lever from air horn. Remove pump arm and rod lifter. See **Figure 90**.

6. Lift vacuum piston and metering rod assembly from air horn. Remove vacuum piston spring from bore. See **Figure 91**.

7. Rotate bowl vent to provide access to valve seal, if so equipped. Remove seal from lever.

8. Disconnect and remove link from choke housing lever and choke lever.

9. Disconnect vacuum diaphragm line and remove diaphragm, linkage and bracket assembly (**Figure 92**).

10. Remove fast idle cam retaining screw, fast idle cam and clip.

11. Non-tamperproof carburetor—Remove choke housing cover, retainer, gasket, baffle and choke housing.

12. Remove air horn screws and separate air horn from main body. See **Figure 92**. Remove solenoid, if so equipped. Discard gasket.

13. Invert air horn and compress accelerating pump drive spring to remove S-link from pump shaft. Remove pump assembly.

14. Remove fuel inlet needle valve, seat and gasket from main body. Lift out float fulcrum pin retainer, baffle, float assembly and fulcrum pin. See **Figure 93**.

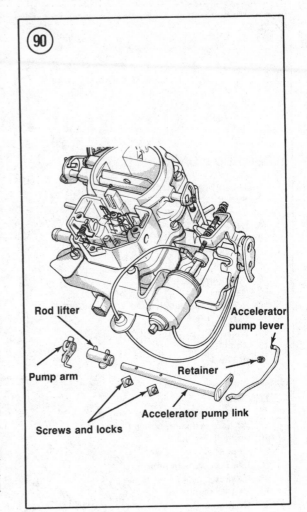

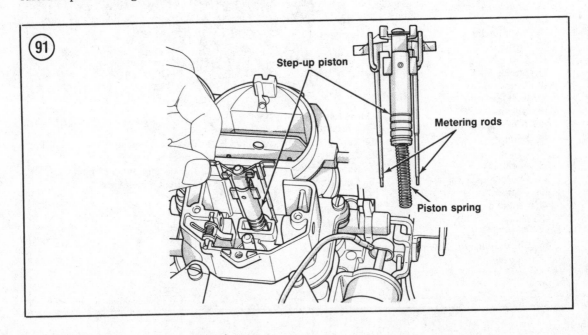

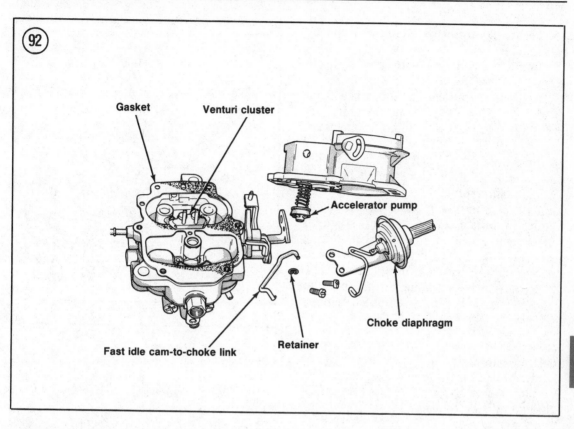

92

Gasket   Venturi cluster

Accelerator pump

Choke diaphragm

Fast idle cam-to-choke link   Retainer

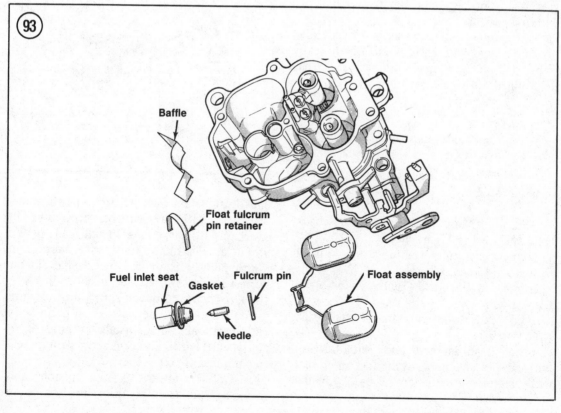

93

Baffle

Float fulcrum
pin retainer

Fuel inlet seat   Fulcrum pin   Float assembly

Gasket

Needle

15. Feedback carburetor—Remove feedback solenoid.

16. Remove main jets with a wide-blade screwdriver. See **Figure 94**.

17. Remove venturi cluster and gaskets from main body (**Figure 95**). Do not separate idle orifice tubes or main vent tubes from cluster. Discard gaskets.

18. Invert main body and catch accelerating pump discharge and intake check balls.

19. Non-tamperproof carburetor—Pry limiter caps from idle mixture screws. Count number of turns necessary to *lightly* seat each screw and note for reference during reassembly. Back out idle mixture screws and remove with springs from throttle body.

20. Remove screws holding throttle body to main body and separate assemblies. Remove and discard gasket.

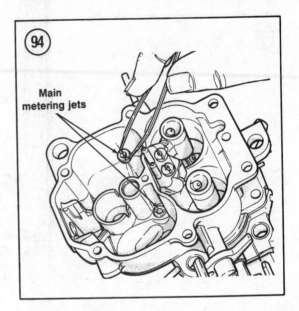

Main metering jets

BBD Assembly

Refer to **Figure 88** as required for this procedure. Not all BBD carburetors will use all the parts shown in **Figure 88**. Check gaskets for proper punching by comparing with old gaskets.

1. Non-tamperproof carburetors—Install idle mixture screws with springs and *lightly* seat. Back screws out same number of turns determined during disassembly.

> *NOTE*
> *Do not install limiter caps until carburetor has been installed on engine and adjusted.*

2. Invert main body, position new gasket and install throttle body. Tighten attaching screws snugly.

3. Turn main body upright and install check balls as shown in **Figure 96**.

4. Fit new gaskets to venturi cluster. Install cluster and tighten securely.

5. Install main jets with wide-blade screwdriver.

6. Feedback carburetor—Install feedback solenoid.

7. Install floats in main body with fulcrum pin and pin retainer. Install fuel inlet seat with gasket and tighten securely. Install needle in seat.

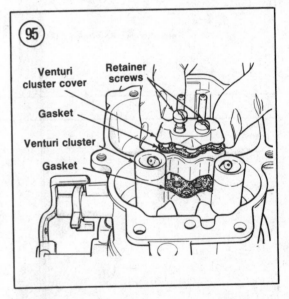

Venturi cluster cover
Retainer screws
Gasket
Venturi cluster
Gasket

8. Adjust float level to specifications provided with adjustment procedure in overhaul kit instructions. Install baffle plate.

9. Fit accelerating pump drive spring on pump plunger shaft and insert shaft in air horn. Compress spring and install S-link.

10. Drop vacuum piston spring into vacuum piston bore. Install new gasket on main body and install air horn. Install solenoid, if so equipped. Tighten air horns screws alternately to compress gasket properly.

11. Carefully lower vacuum piston and metering rod assembly into air horn bore

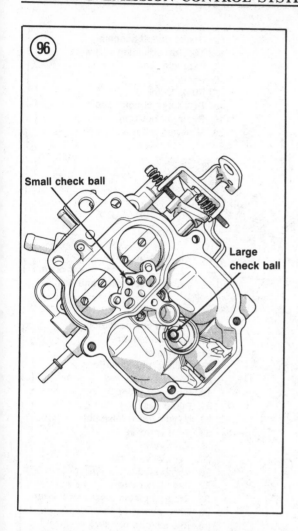

Small check ball

Large check ball

(Figure 91). Make sure metering rods fit into metering jets.

12. Rotate bowl vent assembly and install new vent seal, if so equipped.

13. Position lifting tangs of rod lifter under piston yoke. Slide accelerating pump lever shaft through rod lifter and pump arm. Install but do not tighten adjusting screws. Adjust step-up piston to specifications provided with adjustment procedure in overhaul kit instructions, then tighten adjusting screws.

14. Install fast idle cam and linkage.

15. Connect accelerating pump linkage to pump lever and throttle lever, then install retaining clip.

16. Install rollover check valve with new gasket, if so equipped.

17. Install vacuum diaphragm assembly and connect vacuum line to carburetor body.

18. Engage diaphragm link with choke lever slot. Install choke lever to choke shaft and tighten screw.

19. Non-tamperproof carburetor—Install choke housing to throttle body. Install baffle, gasket and cover to choke housing. Set cover 1/4 turn rich and tighten attaching screws.

20. Install link and retainer between choke lever and choke housing lever.

21. Install link and retainer to fast idle cam and choke lever.

22. Install step-up piston cover plate, if so equipped, to top of air horn with a new gasket.

Thermo-Quad Disassembly

Refer to **Figure 97** (typical) for this procedure. Not all Thermo-Quad carburetors will use all the parts shown in **Figure 97**.

1. Use carburetor legs to prevent throttle plate damage while working on the carburetor. If these are not available, thread a nut on each of four 2 1/4 in. bolts. Install each bolt in a flange hole and thread another nut to the bolt. This will hold the bolt securely to the carburetor and serve the same purpose as legs.

2. Remove altitude compensator and gasket, if so equipped. Discard the gasket.

3. Remove the idle stop carburetor switch and bracket assembly.

4. Remove rod retainers holding throttle connector rod to accelerator pump arm and throttle lever. Remove connector rod.

5. Remove accelerator pump arm screw. Disengage from pump rod S-link, leaving S-link connected to pump rod. Remove lever.

6. Remove rod retainers and washer holding choke diaphragm connector rod to choke vacuum diaphragm and air valve lever.

7. Remove rod retainer holding choke connector rod to choke countershaft.

8. Remove step-up piston cover plate. Remove metering rod cover plates, then remove step-up piston and link assembly with step-up rods attached. Remove step-up piston spring.

9. Remove discharge pump nozzle housing and gasket. Discard the gasket.

10. Invert carburetor and catch discharge check needle.

6

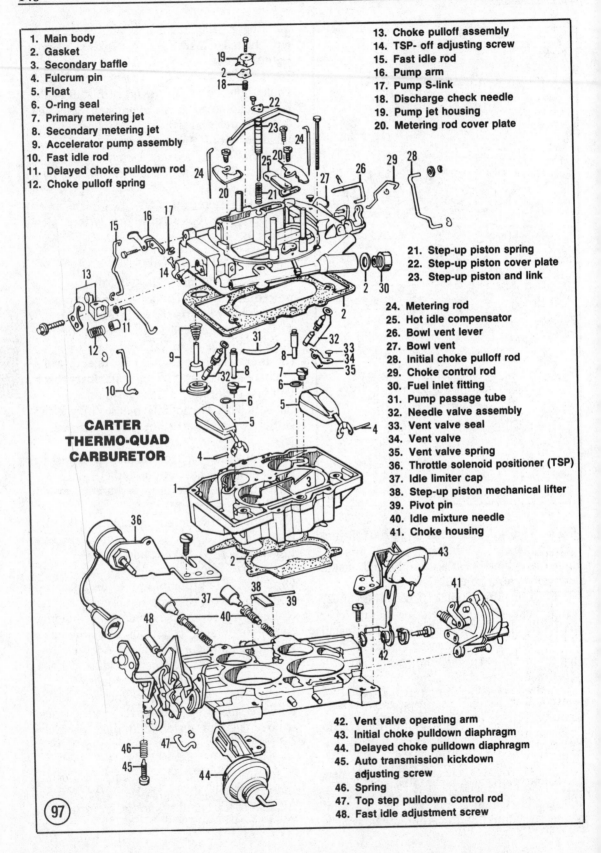

1. Main body
2. Gasket
3. Secondary baffle
4. Fulcrum pin
5. Float
6. O-ring seal
7. Primary metering jet
8. Secondary metering jet
9. Accelerator pump assembly
10. Fast idle rod
11. Delayed choke pulldown rod
12. Choke pulloff spring

13. Choke pulloff assembly
14. TSP- off adjusting screw
15. Fast idle rod
16. Pump arm
17. Pump S-link
18. Discharge check needle
19. Pump jet housing
20. Metering rod cover plate

21. Step-up piston spring
22. Step-up piston cover plate
23. Step-up piston and link

24. Metering rod
25. Hot idle compensator
26. Bowl vent lever
27. Bowl vent
28. Initial choke pulloff rod
29. Choke control rod
30. Fuel inlet fitting
31. Pump passage tube
32. Needle valve assembly
33. Vent valve seal
34. Vent valve
35. Vent valve spring
36. Throttle solenoid positioner (TSP)
37. Idle limiter cap
38. Step-up piston mechanical lifter
39. Pivot pin
40. Idle mixture needle
41. Choke housing

**CARTER
THERMO-QUAD
CARBURETOR**

42. Vent valve operating arm
43. Initial choke pulldown diaphragm
44. Delayed choke pulldown diaphragm
45. Auto transmission kickdown
    adjusting screw
46. Spring
47. Top step pulldown control rod
48. Fast idle adjustment screw

97

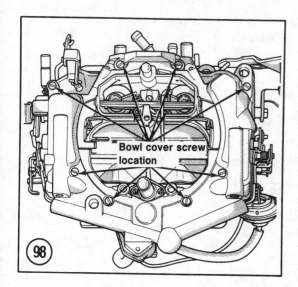

Bowl cover screw location

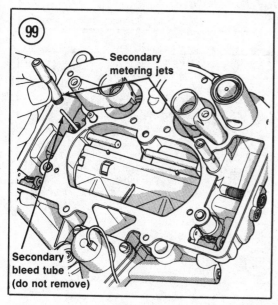

Secondary metering jets

Secondary bleed tube (do not remove)

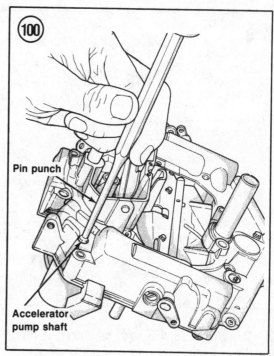

Pin punch

Accelerator pump shaft

17. Remove and discard the bowl cover gasket.

NOTE
To avoid damaging plunger shaft hole in bowl cover while performing Step 18, support the lower part of pump cylinder with your fingers.

18. Remove S-link from accelerator pump rod. Position a small rod on the upper end of the plunger shaft and tap lightly with a small hammer to remove the pump plunger assembly. See **Figure 100**.

19. Remove the L-shaped fuel inlet hose. Remove fuel inlet fitting and gasket. Discard the gasket.

20. Remove the solenoid bowl vent valve assembly.

21. Remove step-up actuating lever from throttle body.

22. Remove choke diaphragm and bracket assembly from throttle body.

23. Pry limiter caps from idle mixture screws. Count number of turns necessary to *lightly* seat each screw and note for reference during reassembly. Back out idle mixture screws and remove with springs from throttle body.

11. Remove bowl cover screws (**Figure 98**). Remove bowl cover and invert on workbench to protect float assembly.

12. Separate float bowl from throttle body.

13. Mark floats and air horn so they can be reinstalled in the same position as removed. Remove float lever hinge pins and lift out float assemblies.

14. Mark inlet needle valve seats. Remove needle seats with a wide-blade screwdriver.

15. Remove secondary metering jets (**Figure 99**).

16. Disconnect the plastic acceleration pump passage tube.

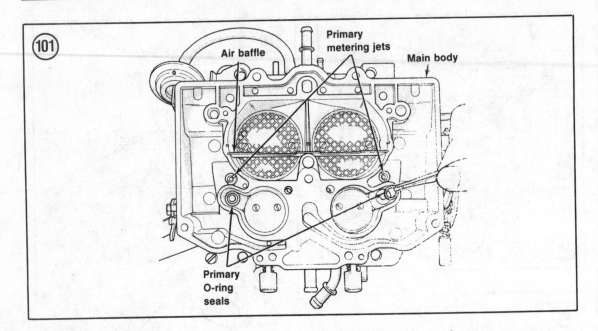

Air baffle — Primary metering jets — Main body — Primary O-ring seals

24. Remove and discard primary O-ring seals from main body.

25. Remove primary metering jets (**Figure 101**) from main body.

Thermo-Quad Assembly

Refer to **Figure 97** as required for this procedure. Not all Thermo-Quad carburetors will use all the parts shown in **Figure 97**. Check gaskets for proper punching by comparing with old gaskets.

1. Install idle mixture screws with springs and *lightly* seat. Back screws out same number of turns determined during disassembly.

> *NOTE*
> *Do not install limiter caps until carburetor has been installed on engine and adjusted.*

2. Install vacuum diaphram and bracket assembly on throttle body.

3. Install step-up actuating lever with its edges facing up. See **Figure 102**.

4. Install main body to throttle body with a new gasket.

5. Install primary metering jets in main body floor with a wide-blade screwdriver. Tighten securely.

6. Install new primary O-ring seals. They must be centered over the main body holes.

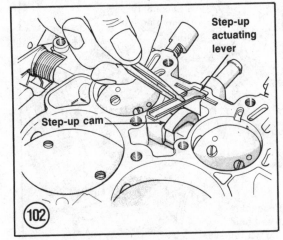

Step-up actuating lever — Step-up cam

7. Install secondary metering jets over bleed tubes (**Figure 99**). Tighten securely.

8. Install upper accelerator spring on pump plunger as shown in **Figure 103**. Install spring and plunger in cylinder. Compress spring until rod extends through the bowl cover, then install the S-link to hold the assembly in place.

9. Place check seat on a clean flat surface. Hold accelerator pump cylinder over check seat, then apply firm hand pressure to the bowl cover to press the check seat into the pump bore. See **Figure 104**.

10. Connect plastic accelerator pump passage tube.

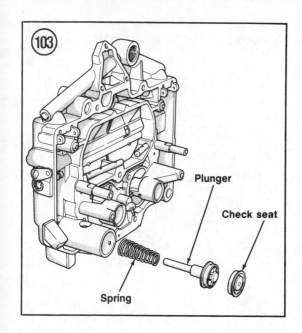

Plunger

Check seat

Spring

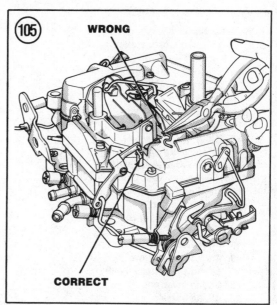

WRONG

CORRECT

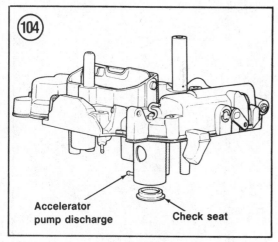

Accelerator
pump discharge

Check seat

11. Install pump discharge check needle in discharge passage.

12. If equipped with a bowl vent, install a new grommet on the vent arm, then install the solenoid vent valve assembly.

13. Install new gaskets on fuel inlet needle seats. Install seats in bowl cover with a wide-blade screwdriver and tighten securely.

14. Fit a new bowl cover-to-main body gasket on bowl cover, then install floats in same position as removed. Install float fulcrum pins.

15. Adjust float level to specifications provided with adjustment procedure in overhaul kit instructions. Install baffle plate.

16. Recheck to make sure the primary O-ring seals are centered over the holes in the main body, then lower bowl cover onto main body. Make sure vent operating lever engages vent actuating lever. Install bowl cover screws (**Figure 98**) and tighten to 35 in.-lb. in 2 stages.

17. Install fuel inlet fitting with a new gasket. Tighten fitting securely.

18. Install fuel line L-hose and clamp securely.

19. Engage pump rod S-link with accelerator pump arm, then position on air horn and install screw (**Figure 105**). Work lever to make sure it operates freely.

20. Fit one end of throttle connector rod in throttle lever hole and the other end in the specified step of the accelerator pump arm. Install rod retainers.

21. Install step-up piston spring in piston cylinder. Install piston assembly with step-up rods. Install cover plate and tighten securely.

22. Fit end of choke connector rod with hole into the choke lever shaft. Fit the other end of the rod to the choke countershaft, then install the rod retainer.

23. Hook one end of choke diaphragm connector rod to the air valve lever and install the washer and retainer. Fit other end of rod to diaphragm plunger and install retainer.

6

ROCHESTER QUADRAJET CARBURETOR ⑩⑥

1. Air horn
2. Air valve lockout lever
3. Lockout lever roll pin
4. Secondary metering rod hanger
5. Secondary metering rod
6-8. Screw
9. Pump actuating lever
10. Pump lever roll pin
11. Pump assembly
12. Pump return spring
13. Needle and seat assembly
14. Needle and seat gasket
15. Float needle pull clip
16. Air horn gasket
17. Primary metering rod
18. Primary jet
19. Choke shaft and lever
20. Choke lever screw
21. Choke lever lockwasher
22. Choke lever nut
23. Choke valve
24. Choke valve screw
25. Float assembly
26. Hinge pin
27. Intermediate choke lever
28. Float bowl baffle
29. Choke rod
30. Choke rod clip
31. Fast idle cam
32. Vacuum diaphragm rod
33. Vacuum diaphragm rod clip
34. Vacuum diaphragm bracket
35. Bracket screw
36. Vacuum diaphragm
37. Vacuum hose
38. Power piston
39. Primary metering rod spring
40. Power piston retainer
41. Pump discharge ball retainer
42. Pump discharge ball
43. Power piston spring
44. Float bowl insert
45. Float bowl assembly
46. Idle stop screw
47. Idle stop screw spring
48. Fuel filter spring
49. Fuel filter
50. Fuel inlet nut
51. Fuel inlet gasket
52. Throttle body gasket
53. Pump rod
54. Pump rod clip
55. Throttle body
56. Idle mixture needle
57. Idle needle spring
58. Throttle body screw
59. Cam lever
60. Fast idle cam
61. Lever/cam screw

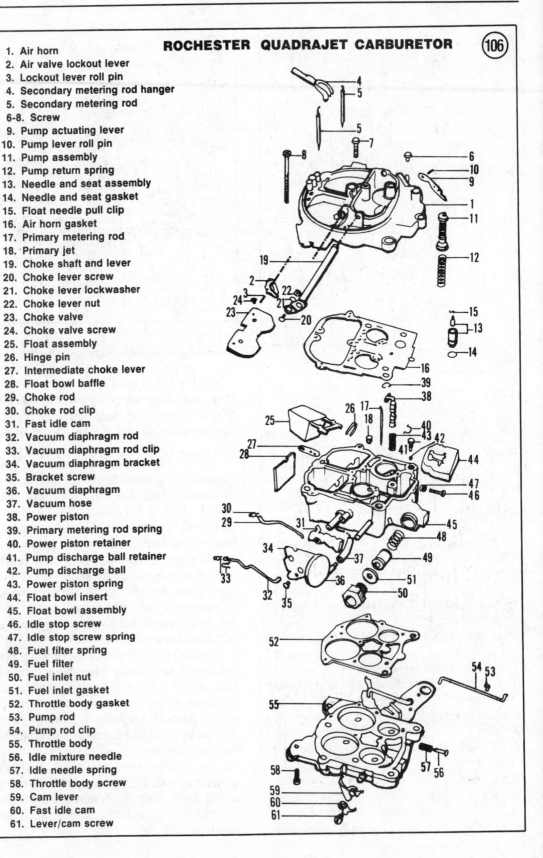

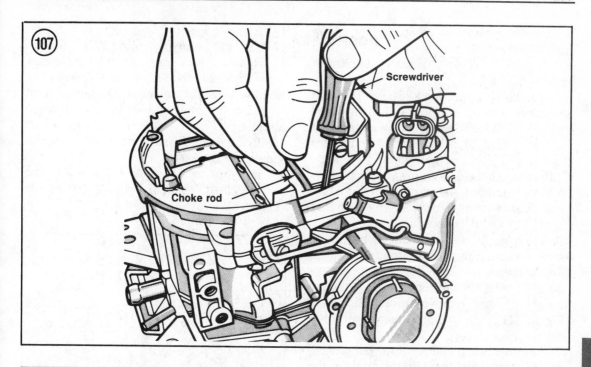

Screwdriver

Choke rod

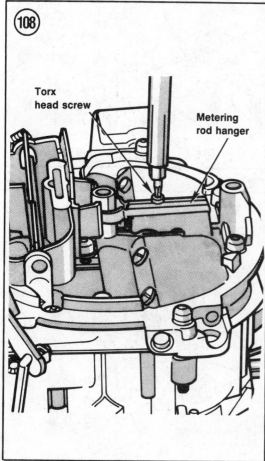

Torx head screw

Metering rod hanger

24. Install altitude compensator, if so equipped, with a new gasket. Tighten screws snugly.

25. Install idle stop switch and bracket.

Rochester Quadrajet Disassembly

Refer to **Figure 106** (typical) for this procedure. Not all Quadrajet carburetors will use all the parts shown in **Figure 106**. This carburetor should not be soaked in carburetor cleaner—use an aerosol cleaner and brush for cleaning purposes.

1. Use carburetor legs to prevent throttle plate damage while working on the carburetor. If these are not available, thread a nut on each of four 2 1/4 in. bolts. Install each bolt in a flange hole and thread another nut to the bolt. This will hold the bolt securely to the carburetor and serve the same purpose as legs.

2. Remove upper choke lever retaining screw. Remove choke lever.

3. Disconnect choke rod from lower lever inside float bowl by holding lever outward with a small screwdriver and twisting rod counterclockwise (**Figure 107**).

4. Remove Torx head screw from metering rod hanger (**Figure 108**). Remove hanger and metering rods.

5. Remove retainer from accelerator pump link. Remove link from lever.

6. Disconnect choke vacuum diaphragm hose at float bowl.

7. Remove air horn screws (**Figure 109**) and secondary air baffle deflector. Lift air horn straight up and off main body to prevent damage to the feedback connector or air horn bleed and accelerating well tubes.

8. Remove choke diaphragm and link.

9. Invert air horn and remove rich mixture stop screw with tool part No. C-4898. See **Figure 110** for screw location.

10. Drive out lean mixture and rich mixture screw plugs with an appropriate punch (**Figure 110**).

11. Lift solenoid metering rod plunger straight up and remove from main body (**Figure 111**). Remove and discard air horn gasket.

12. Remove pump plunger from pump well, then remove the plastic filler block from the fuel bowl (**Figure 112**).

13. Carefully remove each metering rod and spring assembly from metering jets (**Figure 113**). Handle carefully to prevent damage to assembly.

14. Remove feedback solenoid screw (**Figure 114**). Do not remove solenoid at this time.

15. Remove lean mixture solenoid screw with tool part No. C-4898 (**Figure 115**). Remove feedback solenoid. Do not attempt to disassemble solenoid—it is serviced as an assembly.

16. Remove the 2 solenoid tension springs shown in **Figure 116**.

17. Pull upward on float retainer pin and remove float assembly and inlet needle (**Figure 117**).

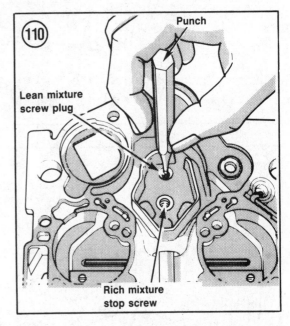

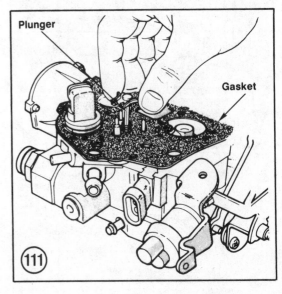

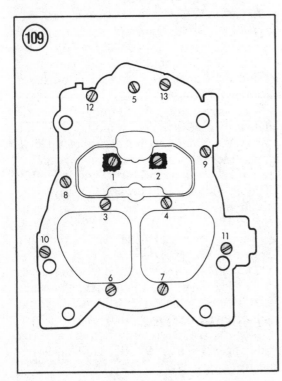

112

Plastic filler block

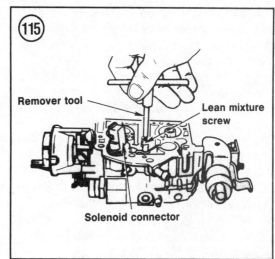

115

Remover tool

Lean mixture screw

Solenoid connector

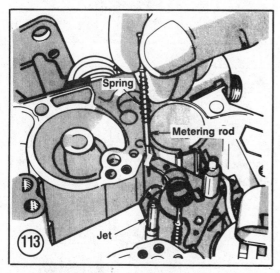

Spring

Metering rod

Jet

113

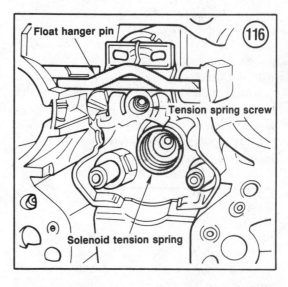

Float hanger pin

116

Tension spring screw

Solenoid tension spring

6

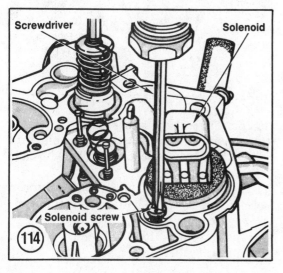

Screwdriver

Solenoid

Solenoid screw

114

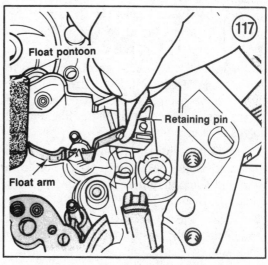

117

Float pontoon

Retaining pin

Float arm

18. Remove inlet needle seat and gasket from float bowl. Discard gasket.

19. Primary metering jets do not have to be removed for cleaning purposes. If removal is necessary, use tool part No. C-4898.

20. Remove pump discharge check ball retainer (**Figure 118**). Invert main body and catch check ball.

21. Remove fuel inlet fitting and filter assembly.

22. Remove the 3 screws and lockwashers holding throttle body to main body. Separate the components and discard the gasket.

Rochester Quadrajet Assembly

Refer to **Figure 106** as required for this procedure. Not all Quadrajet carburetors will use all the parts shown in **Figure 106**. Check gaskets for proper punching by comparing with old gaskets.

1. Install a new throttle body gasket on the bottom of the main body. Make sure gasket holes engage main body dowels. Install throttle body and tighten attaching screws securely.

2. Install a new filter assembly and the fuel inlet fitting. Tighten inlet fitting to 18 ft.-lb.

3. Install pump discharge ball and retainer screw. Tighten screw securely.

4. If main jets were removed, reinstall with tool part No. C-4898.

5. Install large mixture control solenoid tension spring over the boss on the bottom of the float bowl. See **Figure 116**.

6. Install the needle valve seat with a new gasket.

7. Slide float lever under needle pull clip to install inlet needle on float arm. Pull clip should hook over edge of float on float arm facing float pontoon. It should not be hooked in the float arm holes.

8. Install float fulcrum pin in float arm with loop end facing pump well. Align needle in seat and fulcrum pin in float bowl locating channels, then install float assembly.

9. Adjust float level to specifications provided with adjustment procedure in overhaul kit instructions.

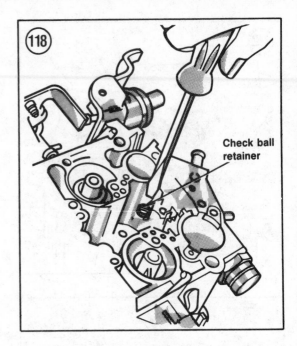

Check ball retainer

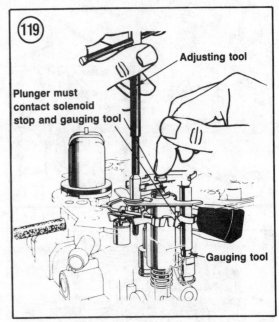

Adjusting tool

Plunger must contact solenoid stop and gauging tool

Gauging tool

10. Install feedback solenoid tension spring (**Figure 116**). Install feedback solenoid with pin on bottom of solenoid aligned with hole in bottom of bowl.

11. Install lean mixture screw through solenoid bracket hole until the first 6 threads are engaged.

12. Install gauging tool part No. C-4899 on left metering jet rod guide, then install

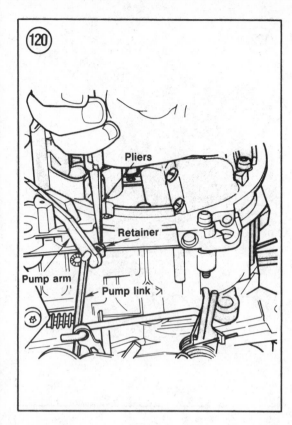

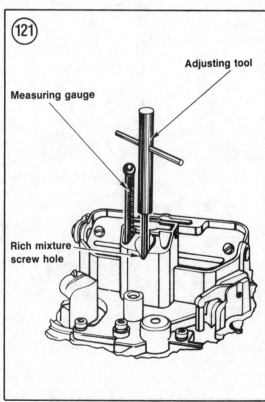

solenoid plunger. Hold plunger against solenoid and turn solenoid screw with tool part No. C-4898 until solenoid plunger touches gauging tool. See **Figure 119**. Remove plunger and gauging tool.

13. Install feedback solenoid screw (**Figure 114**). Install the plastic filler block.

NOTE
Each metering rod, jet and spring form a matched set. If any one is replaced, replace all.

14. Install metering rod and spring assemblies. Make sure rods fit into jet (**Figure 113**).

15. Install pump return spring in pump well, then install pump plunger assembly.

16. Depress pump plunger and install a new air horn gasket over main body locating dowels.

17. Hold gasket and pump plunger in position and install feedback solenoid plunger. Plunger arms must engage top of each metering rod.

18. Lower air horn onto main body. Make sure bleed tubes and accelerating well tubes fit into place.

19. Install secondary air baffle and air horn attaching screws (**Figure 109**). Tighten screws evenly in an alternating pattern to properly compress gasket.

20. Install air valve rod in lever slot. Install other end of rod in choke vacuum diaphragm. Install vacuum diaphragm.

21. Connect pump link to pump lever, then install retainer (**Figure 120**).

22. Install metering rod hanger with metering rods. Tighten screw securely. Work air valve up and down to check operation.

23. Fit choke rod into lower choke lever inside bowl cavity. Install rod in upper choke lever, then install choke lever.

24. Adjust rich mixture stop screw as follows:
   a. Install gauging tool part No. C-4900 in D-shaped air horn vent hole (**Figure 121**). It should float freely.
   b. Hold assembly at eye level. Read and record the gauge mark that aligns with top of air horn casting.
   c. Lightly depress gauging tool and repeat Step b.

6

d. Subtract the dimension recorded in Step b from that recorded in Step c. The difference is total solenoid plunger travel.

e. Insert tool part No. C-4898 in air horn access hole (**Figure 121**). Adjust rich mixture screw to obtain a total solenoid plunger travel of 1/8 in. Remove tools.

25. Install lean mixture screw plug, driving it into the air horn with a suitable punch until it is flush.

26. Install rich mixture screw plug, driving it into the air horn with a suitable punch until it is 1/16 in. below the air horn casting.

27. Install the solenoid idle stop, if so equipped.

Float Level
On-car Adjustment

Holley 1920, 2300 and 4160 carburetors must be removed from the engine to make float adjustments. The remaining carburetors used on Chrysler Corp. engines permit float adjustment without removing the carburetor from the engine. The following procedures are for float adjustments on the vehicle and do not require carburetor removal or disassembly.

Holley 1945, 6145 and 2280

Refer to **Figure 7**, **Figure 8** and **Figure 11** for this procedure.

1. Remove air cleaner as described in this chapter. On 2280 carburetors, remove the air cleaner attaching bolt from the carburetor.

2. On 1945 and 6145 carburetors, remove the bowl vent hose.

3. Disconnect choke linkage.

4A. On 1945 and 6145 carburetors, remove fast idle cam retaining clip. Remove fast idle cam and link.

4B. On 2280 carburetors, remove the nut and washer holding the fast idle cam lever to the choke shaft. Disconnect fast idle link from fast idle cam and lever.

5. Remove choke vacuum diaphragm, link and hose.

6. Remove dashpot, if so equipped.

7A. On 1945 and 2280 carburetors, remove cotter pin from accelerator pump link at throttle lever. Discard cotter pin.

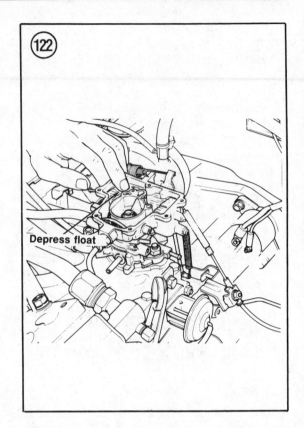

Depress float

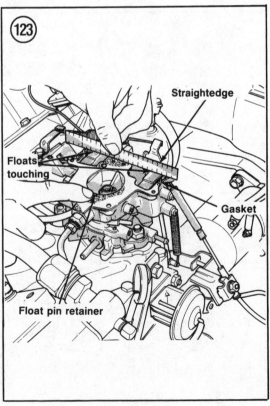

Straightedge

Floats touching

Gasket

Float pin retainer

7B. On 6145 carburetors, remove nut and washer at throttle shaft. Note the throttle lever hole position and remove the lever and link.

8. Remove carburetor air horn attaching screws. Lift air horn straight up and off carburetor to prevent damage to vacuum piston stem, accelerator pump and main well tubes.

9. Depress float until remaining fuel line pressure brings the fuel level to within 1/8-1/4 in. below the top of the fuel bowl (**Figure 122**).

10. Position air horn gasket on top of fuel bowl. Manually seat float pin retainer while measuring float height with a straightedge

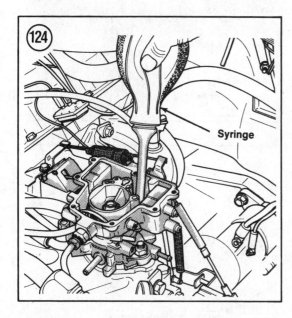

Syringe

across the gasket surface (**Figure 123**). That part of the floats that is farthest from the fuel inlet should barely touch the straightedge.

11. Compare to specifications furnished with the overhaul kit. If adjustment is necessary, bend the float tang.

12. Remove the gasket and use a clean syringe to drain the accelerator pump well of fuel. See **Figure 124**. This will keep the discharge check ball and weight in place when the air horn is reinstalled.

13. Install gasket to air horn. Lower air horn and gasket carefully onto carburetor bowl to prevent damage to the main well tubes. Make sure accelerator pump cup enters pump bore properly and that the discharge ball and weight remain in place.

14. Reverse Steps 1-8 to complete installation of air horn. Use a new accelerator pump link cotter pin. Check idle speed with a tachometer and adjust, if necessary, as described in this chapter.

6

Holley 2210 and 2245

Refer to **Figure 9** and **Figure 10** for this procedure.

1. Remove air cleaner as described in this chapter.

2. Remove air cleaner attaching bolt from carburetor.

3. Disconnect the bowl vent hose. Disconnect the choke vacuum diaphragm and idle enrichment valve hoses.

4. Disconnect the choke linkage.

5. Remove the nut and washer holding the accelerator pump rocker arm to the pump shaft. Set rocker arm aside.

6. Remove the nut and washer holding the choke lever to the choke shaft. Remove choke lever and fast idle connector link.

7. Remove air horn attaching screws. Lift air horn straight up and off to prevent damage to the main well tubes.

8. Invert air horn and measure the distance between the top of the float and the carburetor float stop (**Figure 125**). Compare to specifications included with carburetor overhaul kit.

9. If float requires adjustment, remove the baffle and bend the float adjusting tab with a

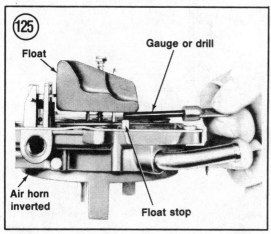

Gauge or drill

Float

Air horn inverted

Float stop

narrow blade screwdriver. Repeat Step 8 and Step 9 as required until specified clearance is obtained in Step 8.

10. Hold air horn in an upright position. If the bottom edge of the float is parallel to the underside of the air horn, the float drop is correct. See **Figure 126**. If not, bend the float arm tang until parallel surfaces are obtained.

11. Carefully install air horn on carburetor bowl, guiding accelerator pump plunger into its bore. Reverse Steps 1-7 to complete installation. Check idle speed and adjust, if necessary, as described in this chapter.

Carter BBD

Refer to **Figure 14** for this procedure. Float measurement requires the use of a float gauge designed for this carburetor. These are included in overhaul kits and should be saved for future use.

1. Remove air cleaner as described in this chapter.

2. Remove air cleaner attaching bolt from carburetor.

3. Disconnect choke assembly and vacuum diaphragm hose.

4. Remove clip holding accelerator pump arm link. Remove link.

5. Remove step-up piston cover plate and gasket from air horn.

6. Remove metering rod lifter lockscrew. Lift step-up piston and metering rod assembly

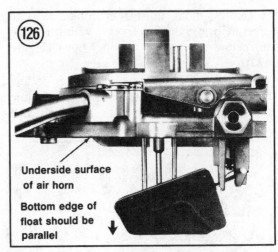

(126)

Underside surface of air horn

Bottom edge of float should be parallel

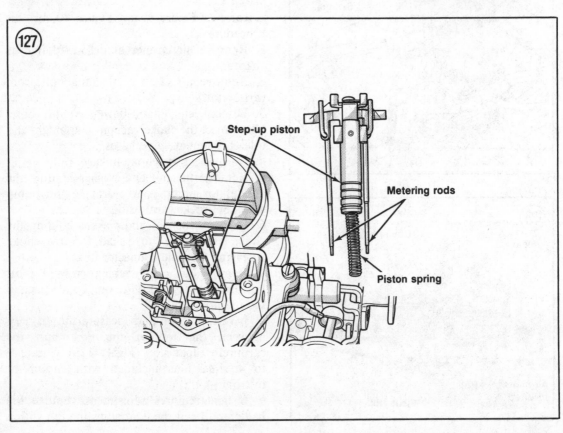

(127)

Step-up piston

Metering rods

Piston spring

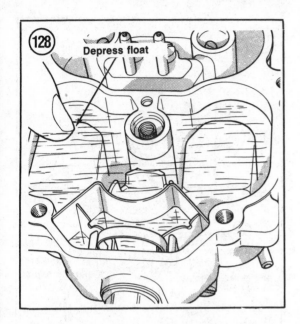

128 Depress float

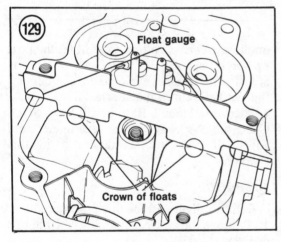

129 Float gauge

Crown of floats

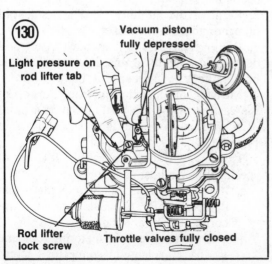

130 Vacuum piston fully depressed

Light pressure on rod lifter tab

Rod lifter lock screw

Throttle valves fully closed

straight up and remove from air horn. See **Figure 127**.

7. Remove air horn attaching screws. Lift air horn straight up and off main body. Remove float baffle.

8. Depress float assembly as shown in **Figure 128** until fuel in the bowl comes within 1/4-3/8 in. of the fuel bowl top.

9. Use 2 wrenches and back off flare nut, then tighten inlet fitting to 200 in.-lb. (23 N•m).

10. Seat float pin retainer by hand and measure from fuel bowl surface to the crown of each float as shown in **Figure 129**. Use the float gauge included with an overhaul kit for the carburetor. Compare reading to specifications.

11. If adjustment is required, hold the floats on the bottom of the fuel bowl and bend the float lip toward or away from the inlet needle as necessary. Do not let the float lip press against the needle during float adjustment, as the pressure may compress the synthetic rubber tip on the needle and give a false reading.

12. Install float baffle. Lower air horn onto carburetor body carefully, guiding accelerator pump cup into pump bore.

13. Install air horn attaching screws, step-up piston/metering rod assembly and metering rod lifter lockscrew.

14. Back off idle speed screw until throttle plates are completely closed. Be sure to count the turns necessary so the screw can be returned to its original position.

15. Depress the step-up piston fully while applying light pressure on the metering rod lifter tab and tighten the lockscrew. See **Figure 130**.

16. Install step-up piston cover gasket and plate.

17. Turn idle speed screw out the same number of turns used to back it off in Step 14.

18. Reverse Steps 1-4 to complete air horn installation. Check idle speed with a tachometer and adjust, if necessary, as described in this chapter.

Thermo-Quad

Refer to **Figure 15** for this procedure.

1. Remove the air cleaner as described in this chapter.

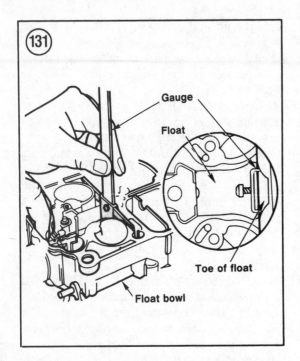

Gauge

Float

Toe of float

Float bowl

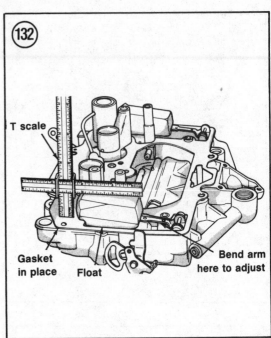

T scale

Gasket in place   Float

Bend arm here to adjust

2. Disconnect all vacuum lines from the bowl cover.

3. Remove the retaining clips holding the throttle connector rod to the accelerator pump arm and throttle lever. Remove rod from carburetor.

4. Remove accelerator pump arm screw. Disconnect pump arm from pump rod S-link (leaving link connected to pump rod) then remove lever.

5. Remove retainers holding connector rod to choke diaphragm and air valve lever.

6. Remove retainer holding connector rod to choke countershaft.

7. Remove step-up piston cover plate. Remove metering rod cover plates.

8. Remove step-up piston and link assembly with step-up rods. Remove step-up piston spring.

9. Remove discharge pump nozzle housing with gasket.

10. Remove bowl cover attaching screws. Remove bowl cover. Remove gasket.

11. Invert bowl and install gasket. Measure from the bottom side of each float to the bowl cover gasket surface with a T-scale as shown in **Figure 131** and compare to specifications.

12. If adjustment is required, bend the float arm at the point shown in **Figure 131** to

obtain the correct setting. Do not let the float lip press against the inlet needle during adjustment, as excessive pressure can damage the synthetic tip of the needle.

13. Reverse Steps 1-10 to install bowl cover. Check idle speed with a tachometer and adjust, if necessary, as described in this chapter.

Quadrajet

Refer to **Figure 16** for this procedure.

1. Remove the air cleaner as described in this chapter.

2. Remove the air horn, feedback solenoid plunger and air horn gasket.

3. Remove the plastic float bowl insert and depress float lightly against inlet needle while holding float bowl retainer in place.

4. Measure the float height from the top of the casting to the top of the float at a point 3/16 in. from the end of the float as shown in **Figure 132**.

5. If the float level is not within 1/16 in. of specifications, adjust as follows:

  a. If too high, hold retainer in place and depress center of float pontoon until correct height is obtained.

  b. If too low, remove metering rods and feedback solenoid connector screw.

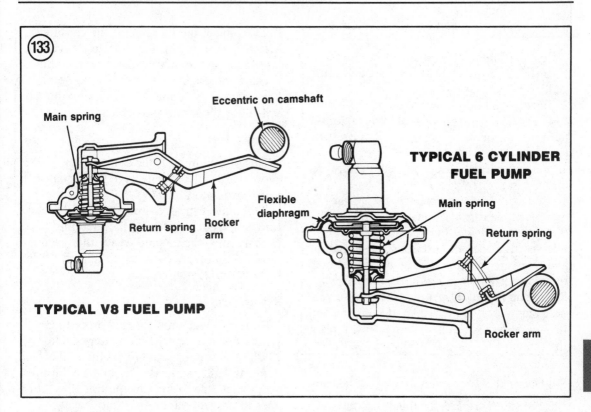

Main spring

Eccentric on camshaft

TYPICAL 6 CYLINDER FUEL PUMP

Main spring

Flexible diaphragm

Return spring

Return spring

Rocker arm

TYPICAL V8 FUEL PUMP

Rocker arm

6

Count and record the number of turns required to lightly seat the lean mixture screw. Remove the feedback solenoid and bend the float upward until correct height is obtained.

6. Recheck float level and reinstall solenoid. Lightly seat lean mixture screw and back out the number of turns recorded. Reinstall solenoid screw and metering rods.

7. Reverse Steps 1-3 to complete installation.

FUEL PUMP

All Chrysler Corp. passenger cars with carburetted fuel systems use a mechanical fuel pump bolted to the right side of the engine and mechanically operated by a camshaft eccentric. **Figure 133** shows typical V8 and 6-cylinder fuel pumps.

On all but the 400 and 440 cid V8, the pump rocker arm rides against the eccentric to provide the up and down motion of the diaphragm. The 400 and 440 cid V8 engines use a pushrod between the camshaft eccentric and the pump rocker arm.

The pump is non-repairable and must be replaced if defective. If replacement is

necessary, be sure to obtain a pump with the proper part number. Pumps that look alike may have different pumping pressures.

Chrysler Corp. passenger cars with electronic fuel injection use a rotary centrifugal type fuel pump mounted in the fuel tank as part of the filter/sending unit assembly. Testing by the amateur mechanic is limited to listening for the sound of the pump when the ignition is switched ON. If no sound is heard, check the 20 amp fuse in cavity 2 of the fuse block. Testing beyond this point should be referred to a dealer or qualified specialist.

The 2 most common fuel pump problems are incorrect pressure and low volume. Low pressure results in a too-lean mixture and too little fuel at high speeds. High pressure will cause carburetor flooding and result in poor mileage. Low volume also results in too little fuel at high speeds.

If a fuel system problem is suspected, check the fuel filter first. See Chapter Three. If the filter is not clogged or dirty, test the fuel pump.

Pressure Test

Refer to **Figure 134** for this procedure.
1. Install a T-fitting between the fuel pump and carburburetor.
2. Install a pressure gauge as shown in **Figure 134**. The connecting hose should be no longer than 6 in. or it may affect the pressure reading.
3. Vent the fuel pump to relieve any air trapped in the fuel chamber.
4. Connect a tachometer according to manufacturer's instructions.
5. Start the engine and run at the specified idle speed. Check the pressure gauge reading and compare to **Table 1**. The reading should remain constant or return to zero slowly when the engine is shut off. An instant drop to zero indicates a leaky outlet valve. If this occurs or if the pressure is too high or too low, replace the pump.

Volume Test

Refer to **Figure 135** for this procedure.

1. Disconnect the fuel line at the carburetor. Attach a hose to the fuel line to deliver the gasoline to a one quart (32 ounce) container.
2. Start the engine and run for 30 seconds. The container should be approximately half-full if the pump is satisfactory.

Vacuum Test

This procedure tests the ability of the pump to operate at full capacity as required to prime a dry carburetor.
1. Disconnect the fuel line at the carburetor. Attach a vacuum gauge to the fuel line.
2. Start the engine and read the vacuum gauge. It should show a minimum of 10 in. Hg vacuum. If not, replace the pump.

Replacement

Refer to **Figure 136** for this procedure.
1. Disconnect the negative battery cable.
2. Place a suitable container under the fuel pump to catch spillage. Disconnect the inlet and outlet lines from the pump. Plug both lines to prevent vapor and fluid leakage.

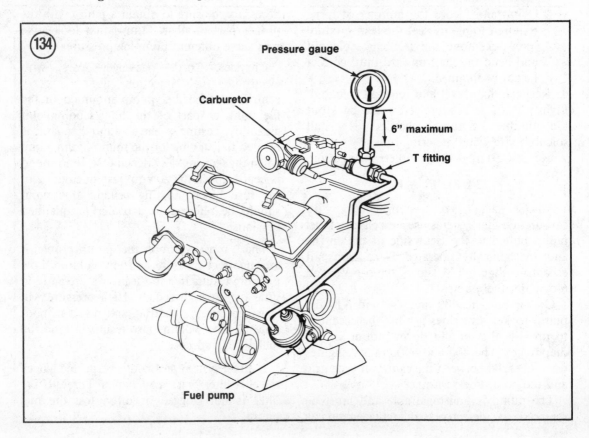

(134)

Pressure gauge

Carburetor

6" maximum

T fitting

Fuel pump

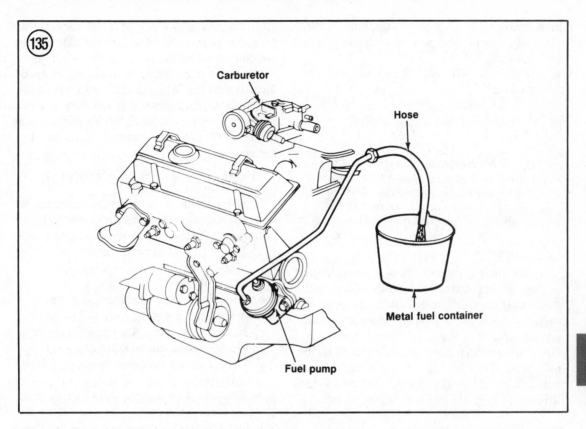

135

Carburetor

Hose

Metal fuel container

Fuel pump

6

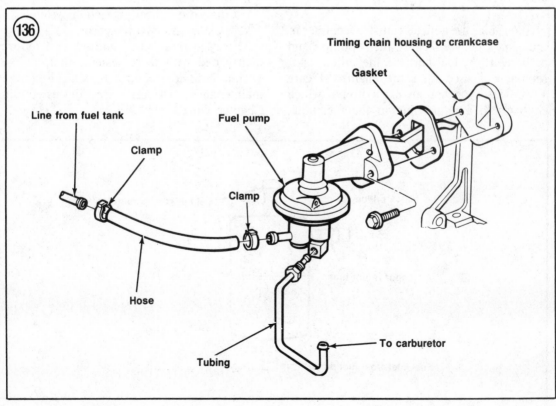

136

Timing chain housing or crankcase

Gasket

Line from fuel tank

Fuel pump

Clamp

Clamp

Hose

Tubing

To carburetor

3. Remove the 2 pump attaching bolts. Carefully remove the pump and gasket from the engine.

4. On 400 and 440 cid V8 engines, remove the pushrod.

5. Clean all gasket residue from the pump and the mounting pad on the engine.

> *NOTE*
> *Prior to pump installation, rotate engine until low point of pump cam lobe contacts the pump arm. This is done by holding the pump loosely in position and rotating the crankshaft until pressure on the pump lever arm is at a minimum.*

6. Installation is the reverse of removal. Use a new gasket coated on both sides with oil-resistant gasket sealer. If a pushrod is used, make sure it is properly installed in the engine and fits into the pump correctly. Alternately tighten attaching bolts to 30 ft.-lb. (40 N•m). Use new clamps on flexible hose connections. Start the engine and check for leaks.

FUEL FILTER

All engines use a metal canister fuel filter in the line between the fuel pump and carburetor. A dual-purpose fuel filter/vapor separator is used on some engines (**Figure 137**). This type has an extra nipple which connects to a return line to the fuel tank, allowing fuel vapors to be sent back to the tank. When replacing the fuel filter, be sure to use the correct type.

On some early engines, the filter may be located near the intake manifold (**Figure 138**). On most engines, however, the filter is close to the fuel pump on the right side of the block (**Figure 139**). Refer to Chapter Three for filter replacement.

EMISSION CONTROL SYSTEMS

Chrysler uses a number of interrelated systems to control emission of harmful pollutants. These include the following:

  a. Positive crankcase ventilation (PCV) system.
  b. Manifold heat control valve.
  c. Air injection or aspirator air system.
  d. Vapor saver system.
  e. Exhaust gas recirculation (EGR) system.
  f. Electric assist choke system.
  g. Orifice spark advance control (OSAC) system.
  h. Coolant controlled idle enrichment system.
  i. Catalytic converter.
  j. Catalyst overheat protection system.
  k. Exhaust gas oxygen sensor.

The carburetor and ignition system are interrelated with these systems to form the overall emission control system. Required maintenance services are discussed in Chapter Three.

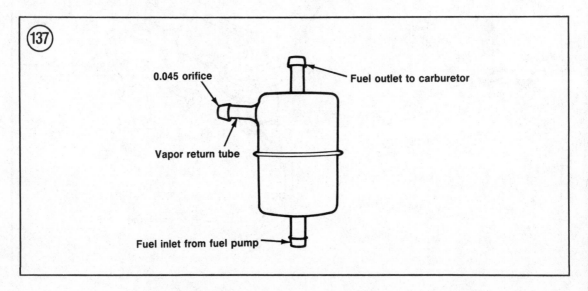

(137)

0.045 orifice

Fuel outlet to carburetor

Vapor return tube

Fuel inlet from fuel pump

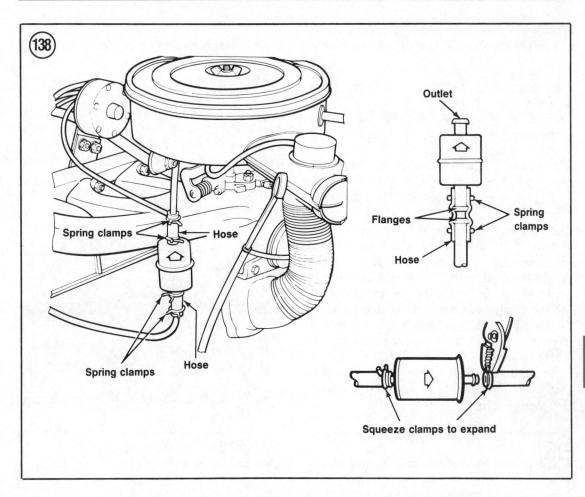

138

Outlet

Spring clamps — Hose

Flanges — Spring clamps

Hose

Spring clamps — Hose

Squeeze clamps to expand

6

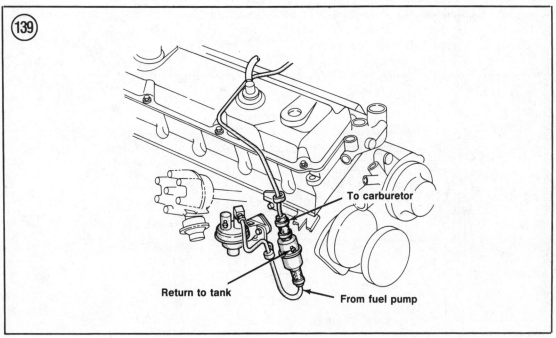

139

To carburetor

Return to tank

From fuel pump

POSITIVE CRANKCASE VENTILATION (PCV) SYSTEM

This system consists of a crankcase ventilation (PCV) valve mounted on a cylinder head cover (**Figure 140**) and connected by a hose to the base of the carburetor. Another hose connects the carburetor air cleaner to the crankcase inlet air cleaner. **Figure 141** shows the 6-cylinder and V8 PCV system.

The system is operated by manifold vacuum. Air drawn into the crankcase from the air cleaner through the inlet air cleaner circulates through the cylinder head cover(s) and crankcase, collecting fuel vapors. This vapor-laden air exits through the PCV valve and the passage into the carburetor body, where it is mixed with the air-fuel mixture being drawn into the cylinders. The vapors are thus burned and expelled though the exhaust system.

PCV system service consists of inspection and valve replacement at the intervals stated in Chapter Three.

NOTE
Do not attempt to clean a plugged PCV valve.

1. Start the engine and run at idle. Remove the PCV valve from the rocker cover. A hissing noise should be heard as air passes through the valve and a strong vacuum should be felt when a finger is placed over the end of the valve (**Figure 142**). If not, replace the valve.

2. Reinstall the PCV valve and remove the inlet air cleaner. Hold a piece of stiff paper,

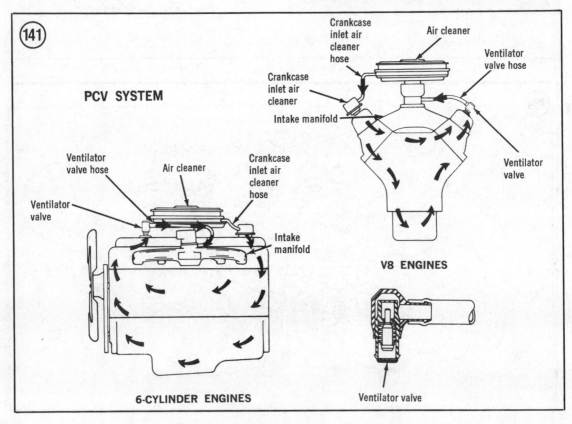

PCV SYSTEM

Ventilator valve hose

Air cleaner

Crankcase inlet air cleaner hose

Ventilator valve

Intake manifold

6-CYLINDER ENGINES

Crankcase inlet air cleaner hose

Air cleaner

Ventilator valve hose

Crankcase inlet air cleaner

Intake manifold

Ventilator valve

V8 ENGINES

Ventilator valve

such as a matchbook cover or parts tag, over the rocker cover opening (**Figure 143**). Wait approximately 60 seconds for crankcase pressure to be reduced. Shortly thereafter, the paper should be sucked to the rocker cover opening. If it is not, the PCV valve hose is probably plugged. Replace the hose.

MANIFOLD HEAT CONTROL VALVE

This butterfly valve located in the exhaust manifold system channels exhaust gases through a "heat chamber" adjacent to the fuel intake system (carburetor or intake manifold) during engine warm-up. This heat helps in the vaporization of the fuel mixture when the engine is cold. As the engine warms up, the valve directs the exhaust gases directly into the exhaust pipe.

Two types of control systems are used: a bimetallic thermostatic spring or a vacuum actuator. **Figure 144** shows the vacuum-operated version. Service to the heat control

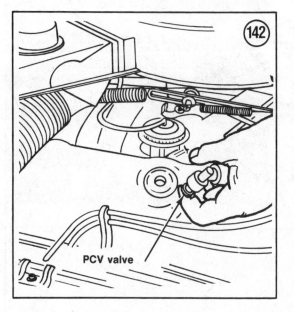

PCV valve

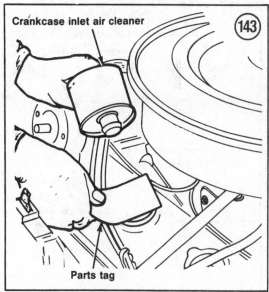

Crankcase inlet air cleaner

Parts tag

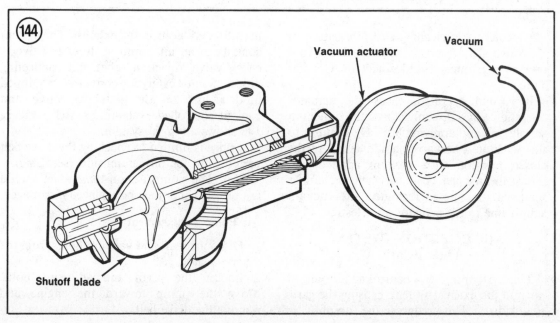

Vacuum actuator

Vacuum

Shutoff blade

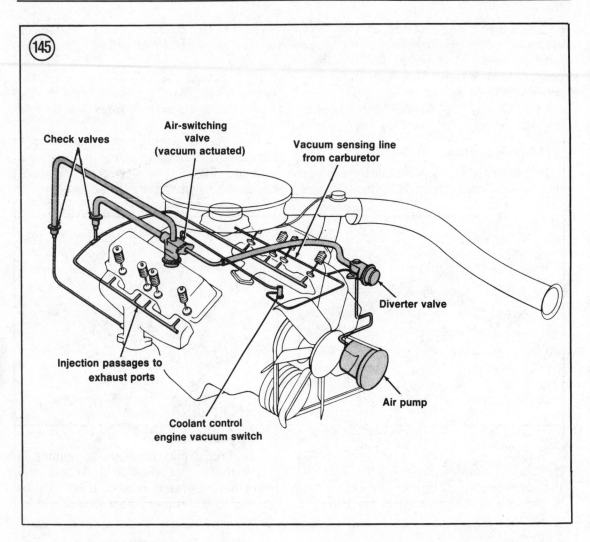

Check valves

Air-switching valve (vacuum actuated)

Vacuum sensing line from carburetor

Diverter valve

Air pump

Injection passages to exhaust ports

Coolant control engine vacuum switch

valve consists of cleaning and lubrication of the valve shaft bearings with a solvent (not oil) at the intervals specified in Chapter Three.

If vacuum-operated, check the actuator operation by disconnecting the vacuum supply line and applying 6 in. Hg vacuum to the actuator. The valve should move to the closed position with vacuum applied and return to an open position when vacuum is removed. Be sure to reconnect the vacuum supply line to the actuator after testing.

AIR INJECTION SYSTEM (AIR PUMP)

This system injects a controlled amount of air into the exhaust system, causing the gases to oxidize. This reduces the amount of harmful emissions in the exhaust. The system consists of an air pump, a diverter valve, a check valve, injection tubes and connecting hoses. Some catalytic converter equipped models use an air switching valve and coolant-controlled vacuum switch. **Figure 145** shows a typical system.

Service is limited to checking the drive belt periodically for proper tension (see Chapter Three). The pump is non-repairable, should not be oiled and must be replaced if damaged.

Air Pump Replacement

1. Disconnect air and vacuum hoses from the diverter valve.
2. Loosen the pivot and adjusting bolts. Move the pump toward the engine and remove the drive belt.

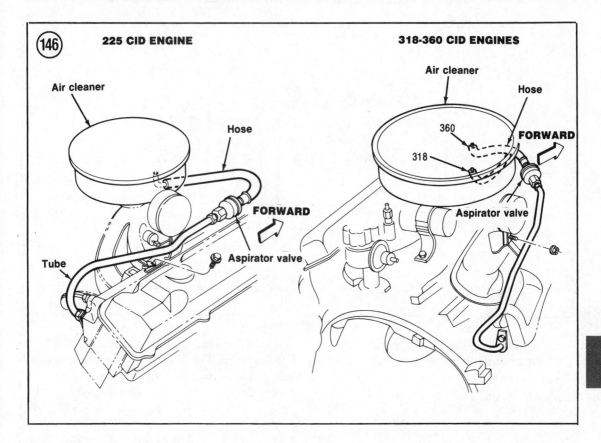

3. Remove the pivot and adjusting bolts. Remove the bracket attaching bolts. Remove the pump and bracket from the engine.

4. Remove the diverter valve, brackets and pulley from the pump.

5. Installation is the reverse of removal. Adjust drive belt as described in Chapter Eight.

ASPIRATOR AIR SYSTEM

This system is used on some 1978 and later models in place of an air pump system. It uses exhaust pressure pulsation to draw fresh air from the air cleaner into the exhaust system through a one-way aspirator valve. **Figure 146** shows typical aspirator systems.

The aspirator valve is located in a tube connected to the cylinder head on 6-cylinder engines and on the right-hand exhaust manifold of V8 engines. The valve is not repairable and should be replaced if not operating properly. Operation can be checked by removing the hose on the air cleaner side of the valve while the engine is running. If vacuum pulses can be felt at the aspirator valve inlet, the valve is good. If hot exhaust gas can be felt escaping from the valve inlet, replace the valve.

VAPOR SAVER SYSTEM

This system controls the emission of fuel vapors from the carburetor and fuel tank into the atmosphere. When fuel evaporates in the carburetor float chamber or fuel tank, the vapors are collected in the charcoal canister. Vapors are held in the canister until they can be drawn into the intake manifold when the engine is running.

Canisters on early models have a purge valve; later canisters are purged by an extra ported vacuum connection on the carburetor. Vehicles with a 25 gallon or larger fuel tank use dual canisters. The larger of the 2 receives vapors from the fuel tank while the smaller receives vapors from the carburetor.

The only service required for this system is a check of the condition and connection of

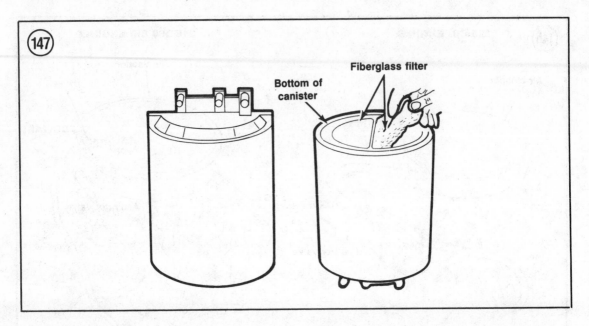

Bottom of
canister

Fiberglass filter

canister hoses, and replacement of the filter element if so equipped (**Figure 147**).

EXHAUST GAS RECIRCULATION (EGR) SYSTEM

This system controls the amount of oxides of nitrogen (NOx) in engine exhaust gases by allowing a predetermined amount of hot exhaust gas to recirculate and dilute the incoming air-fuel mixture. **Figure 148** shows a typical system.

Service consists of inspecting the system, replacing hardened or cracked hoses and faulty connectors and checking the operation of the EGR valve. Because of the complexity of the electrical and vacuum controls in a typical Chrysler Corp. EGR system, further service should be referred to your dealer.

System Check

1. Start the engine and warm to normal operating temperature (upper radiator hose hot). Let the engine idle with the throttle closed.
2. Watch the EGR valve stem while quickly accelerating to about 2,000 rpm (not over 3,000 rpm). If there is a change in the relative position of the groove on the EGR valve stem, the control system is operating

properly. If no change is observed, have a dealer check the control system operation.
3. If the control system operates properly in Step 2, disconnect the vacuum line at the EGR valve and connect a hand vacuum pump. Apply at least 10 in. Hg vacuum to the valve. There should be a noticeable change in engine idle speed (approximately 150 rpm). This indicates that exhaust gas recirculation is taking place. If there is little or no change in engine speed, the EGR valve or intake manifold passages are probably plugged by exhaust deposits.

Maintenance Reminder Light

An EGR maintenance reminder light on the instrument panel is used with 1975-1976 models. This light is designed to come on at 15,000 mile intervals to remind the driver that the EGR system should be serviced. It consists of an inline switch in the speedometer cable system. The switch must be reset with a screwdriver to turn off the light after EGR system service.

ELECTRIC ASSIST CHOKE SYSTEM

This system consists of an electric heating element to supplement engine heat during

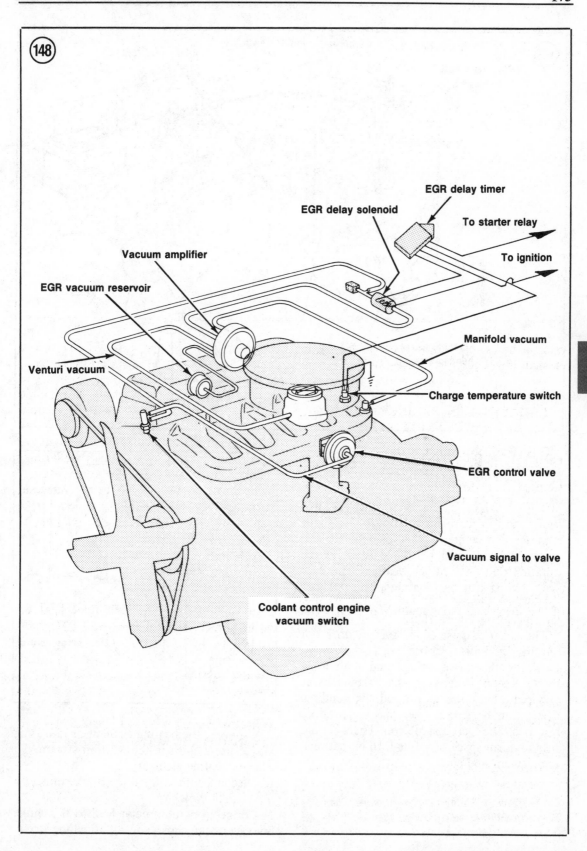

(148)

EGR delay timer

EGR delay solenoid

To starter relay

To ignition

Vacuum amplifier

EGR vacuum reservoir

Manifold vacuum

Venturi vacuum

Charge temperature switch

EGR control valve

Vacuum signal to valve

Coolant control engine
vacuum switch

6

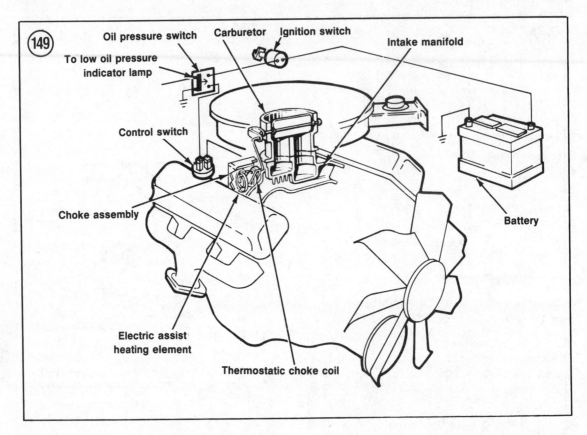

(149)

Oil pressure switch   Carburetor   Ignition switch

To low oil pressure
indicator lamp

Intake manifold

Control switch

Choke assembly

Battery

Electric assist
heating element

Thermostatic choke coil

engine warm-up to reduce the duration of choke operation. **Figure 149** shows a typical system.

Some engines use a dual stage control switch to shorten choke duration in both summer and winter. Other engines have a single control switch to shorten choke duration only in summer weather. The dual stage switch can be identified by a resistor connected across the 2 control switch terminals. See **Figure 150**.

The electric assist choke system does not require periodic service or adjustment. However, the choke linkage and shaft must move freely. Whenever the carburetor is serviced, check the choke rod for bending. Check to make sure the heating element does not touch the thermostatic coil. There should be a uniform space of about 1/16 in. between the element and coil.

CAUTION
When cleaning choke linkage, be careful not to spray cleaner on the heating element.

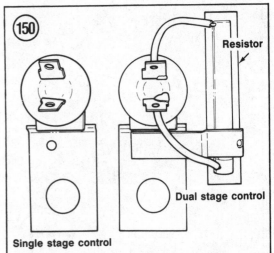

(150)

Resistor

Dual stage control

Single stage control

A short in the heating element or its wiring may cause a short in the ignition system. To test the heating element:
1. Disconnect the wire at the B+ terminal on the control switch.
2. Connect one ohmmeter lead to the choke housing or the choke control attaching screw.

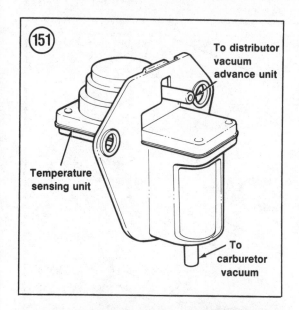

To distributor vacuum advance unit

Temperature sensing unit

To carburetor vacuum

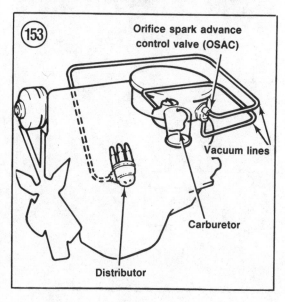

Orifice spark advance control valve (OSAC)

Vacuum lines

Carburetor

Distributor

3. Touch the other ohmmeter lead to any bare part of the choke wire connector at the switch *except* the B+ terminal.

4. A reading of 4-12 ohms indicates that the heating element is good. If the reading is outside this range, replace the choke and heating element assembly.

ORIFICE SPARK ADVANCE CONTROL SYSTEM (OSAC)

This temperature-operated vacuum control (**Figure 151**) contains an orifice which causes a delay in the ported vacuum to the distributor during acceleration from idle to part throttle when ambient temperature is above 60° F (15° C). During deceleration, the valve allows instantaneous application of vacuum to the distributor. This control of spark advance helps reduce oxides of nitrogen (NOx) in the exhaust.

The OSAC valve is firewall-mounted on 1973 models (**Figure 152**) and is on the side of the air cleaner housing on 1974 and later models (**Figure 153**). The non-repairable OSAC valve does not require periodic service, but the vacuum lines between the valve, carburetor and distributor should be checked for defects, damage or loose connections. Replace any lines that may allow air leakage.

To check valve operation, set the parking brake and warm the engine to normal operating temperature (upper radiator hose hot). Disconnect the OSAC valve vacuum line leading to the distributor and connect a vacuum gauge to the valve fitting. Increase engine speed to approximately 2,000 rpm. If a very gradual increase in vacuum over a period of 10-27 seconds is noted, the valve is operating properly (the time will vary with different engines). If vacuum pops up immediately or no vacuum is observed, replace the valve.

NOTE
This test should be conducted when outside temperature is above 68° F (20° C).

COOLANT CONTROLLED IDLE ENRICHMENT SYSTEM

This is a time delay mechanism in the EGR system which is dependent upon a

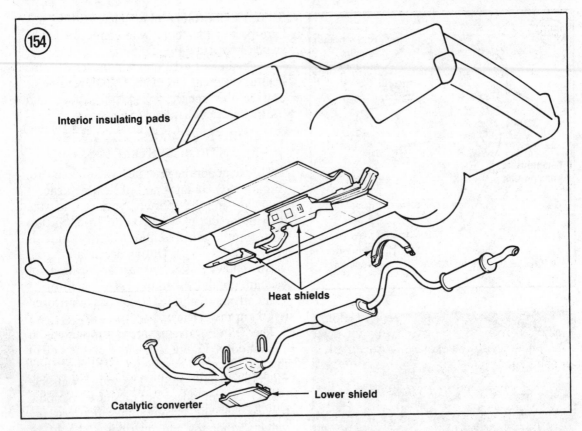

Interior insulating pads

Heat shields

Lower shield

Catalytic converter

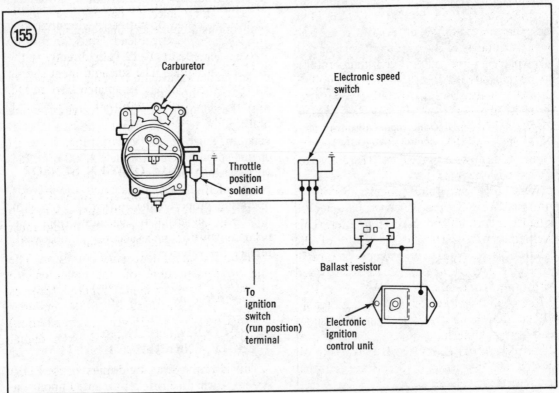

Carburetor

Electronic speed switch

Throttle position solenoid

Ballast resistor

To ignition switch (run position) terminal

Electronic ignition control unit

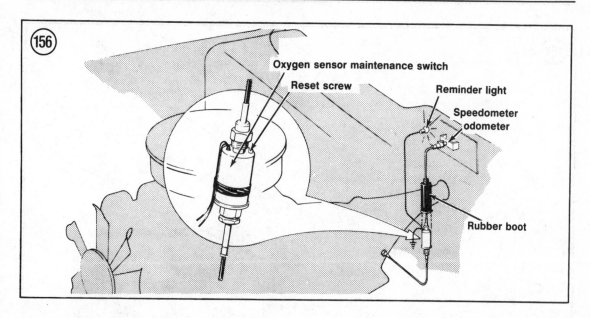

(156)

Oxygen sensor maintenance switch

Reset screw

Reminder light

Speedometer odometer

Rubber boot

thermostatic valve in the engine cooling system. It requires no periodic service other than maintaining the connecting vacuum line in good condition.

CATALYTIC CONVERTER

The catalytic converter promotes oxidation of hydrocarbons and carbon monoxide in the engine exhaust. The converter is located in the exhaust system. When exhaust gases pass over the catalyst in the converter, combustion takes place and normal internal temperatures inside the converter reach as high as $1,600°$ F. Outside temperature of the converter generally reaches $1,000°$ F. For this reason, special shields are used to prevent this heat from entering the passenger compartment. **Figure 154** shows a typical catalytic converter system with heat shields.

Some 1978 and later models also use a mini-oxidation converter located between the exhaust manifold and main converter. This mini-converter starts the oxidation of the exhaust gases before they reach the main converter. Special heat shields are also used with mini-converters.

The catalytic converter system requires no special maintenance other than the use of lead-free gasoline and a periodic check of heat shield condition. If removed, make sure all shields and insulating materials are returned to their proper places.

CATALYTIC CONVERTER OVERHEAT PROTECTION SYSTEM (1975-1976)

This system consists of a throttle position solenoid and electronic speed switch (**Figure 155**). It is used on 1975-1976 vehicles equipped with a catalytic converter to protect the catalyst from overheating in case of a system failure. With the engine off, check the throttle solenoid operation by disconnecting the solenoid electrical lead. Hold the throttle valve open and apply 12 volts directly to the solenoid terminal. The solenoid stem should extend when voltage is applied and retract fully when voltage is removed. If it does not, replace the solenoid.

EXHAUST GAS OXYGEN SENSOR

On 1979 and later engines equipped with a feedback carburetor, the exhaust gas oxygen sensor located in the exhaust manifold must be replaced when the maintenance reminder light on the instrument panel comes on. The mechanical portion of the maintenance reminder light system (**Figure 156**) is essentially the same as the EGR reminder light used on 1975-1976 vehicles. In addition, electronic control is provided by a digital switch module.

The digital switch module is housed in a green plastic case bracket-mounted under the

6

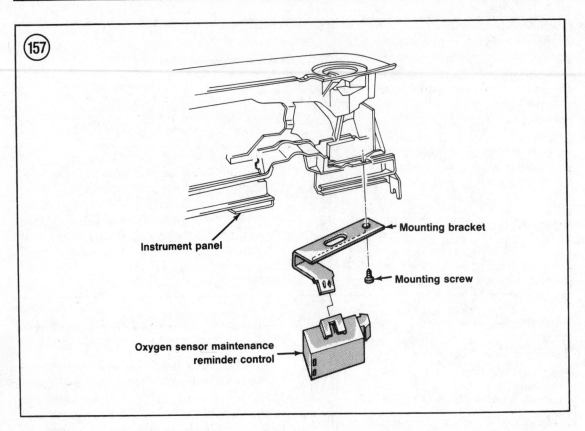

Instrument panel

Mounting bracket

Mounting screw

Oxygen sensor maintenance
reminder control

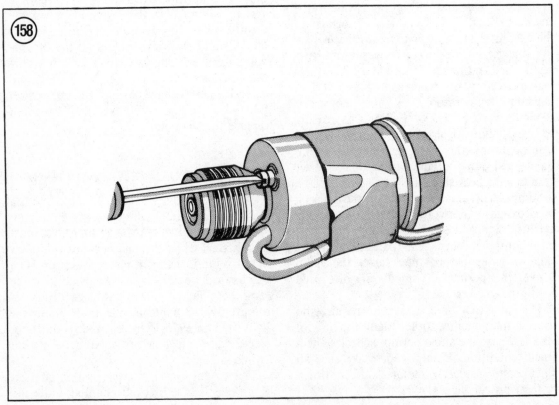

instrument panel (**Figure 157**, typical). This module contains a 9 volt alkaline battery to provide power whenever the vehicle battery is disconnected. After the sensor has been changed, remove the 9 volt battery from the module. Insert a screwdriver blade in the hole provided in the module. This will close the switch which controls the reminder lamp on the instrument panel. Install a new 9 volt alkaline battery in the module, then reset the maintenance switch with a screwdriver blade as shown in **Figure 158**.

Sensor Replacement

1. Disconnect the negative battery cable.
2. On 6-cylinder engines, remove the air cleaner as described in this chapter.

3. Disconnect the oxygen sensor connector.
4. Remove the sensor from the exhaust manifold with Chrysler tool part No. C-4589.

NOTE
Do not use a graphite-base anti-seize compound in Step 5, as it can electrically insulate the sensor from the exhaust manifold.

5. Coat the sensor threads with a nickel-base anti-seize compound such as Loctite LO-607.
6. Start the sensor into the exhaust manifold by hand, then tighten to 30-40 ft.-lb. (41-54 N•m) with Chrysler tool part No. C-4589.
7. Connect sensor electrical lead. Install air cleaner (if removed) and reconnect negative battery cable.

Table 1 FUEL PUMP PRESSURE SPECIFICATIONS

Engine Displacement	psi
198/225 cid	
1972-1980	3.5-5
1981-on	4-5.5
318 cid	
1972-1980	5-7
1981-on	5.75-7.25
340 cid	5-7
360 cid	5-7
400 cid	
1972-1974	3.5-5
1975	6-7.5[1]
1976-1978	5-7
440 cid	
1972-1974	3.5-5
1975	6-7.5[2]
1976-1978	5-7
440 cid HP	6.5-7
440 cid HP Police	5.5-6 .5

1. 2-bbl. Federal and 4-bbl. California only. For 4-bbl. Federal usage, 3.5-5 psi.
2. For California-sold vehicles only. For others, 4-5.5 psi.

6

CHAPTER SEVEN

ELECTRICAL SYSTEM

Chrysler Corp. passenger cars are equipped with a 12-volt, negative-ground electrical system. This chapter includes service procedures for the battery, charging system, starter, fuses and lighting system.

Use Chapter Two to help isolate any problem that develops in the electrical system. Many electrical problems can be traced to a simple cause such as a blown fuse, a loose or corroded connection, a loose alternator drive belt or a frayed wire. While these are easily corrected problems which may not appear important, they can quickly lead to serious difficulties if allowed to go uncorrected.

Repairing electrical components such as the alternator or starter motor is usually beyond the capability of the inexperienced mechanic and his tool box. Such repairs are best left to the specialized mechanic who is equipped with the necessary experience and tools.

It is often faster and more economical to replace defective parts instead of having them repaired. Make certain, however, that the new or rebuilt part to be installed is an exact replacement for the defective one removed. Also, make sure to isolate and correct the cause of the failure before installing a replacement. For example, an uncorrected short in an alternator circuit will most likely burn out a new alternator as quickly as it damaged the old one. If in doubt, always consult an expert.

BATTERY

The battery is perhaps the single most important component in the automotive electrical system. It is also the one most commonly neglected. In addition to checking and correcting the battery electrolyte level on a weekly basis (Chapter Three), the battery should be cleaned and inspected at periodic intervals.

An insulated battery shield is used on 1975 and later models to reduce battery temperature. Some heat shields also incorporate the windshield washer reservoir. See **Figure 1**.

Factory-supplied batteries on 1978 and later models incorporate a visual test indicator (**Figure 2**). The test indicator is a built-in hydrometer in one cell. It provides visual information for battery testing only and should not be used as a basis of determining whether the battery is charged or discharged.

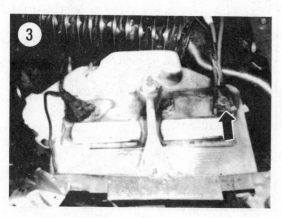

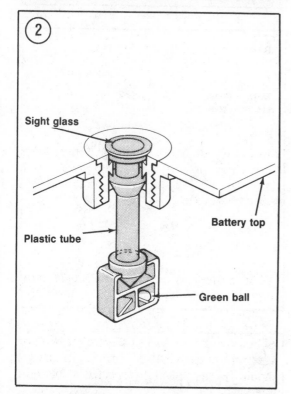

Sight glass

Plastic tube

Battery top

Green ball

Using the Test Indicator

Make sure the battery is level and the test indicator sight glass is clean. If necessary, wipe the sight glass with a paper towel moistened with water. A penlight is useful to determine the indicator color under dim lighting conditions. Look down into the sight glass. If it appears green in color, the battery has a charge sufficient for testing. If it appears red or black, the battery should be charged *before* testing. A light yellow appearence indicates that the battery should be replaced and the charging system checked. Do not charge, test or jump start the battery when the sight glass appears light yellow in color.

Care and Inspection

1. Loosen the nuts on the terminal clamp bolts (**Figure 3**) enough so the clamps can be spread slightly. Lift straight up on the negative clamp and remove it from the post, then remove the positive clamp.

> *NOTE*
> *If the cables will not come off the battery posts easily when the clamp bolt is loosened, use a battery terminal puller as shown in **Figure 4**. Hitting the terminal or trying to pry the clamp off the post can cause internal damage to the battery.*

2A. On 1972-1974 models, unscrew the nuts from the hold-down bolts and remove the hold-down frame.

2B. On 1975 and later models, remove the hold-down nut(s), then lift the heat shield up and off the battery. Retrieve the J-bolt(s).

7

3. Attach a battery carry strap to the terminal posts. Remove the battery from the engine compartment.

4. Check the entire battery case for cracks, chafing or other damage.

5. If the battery has individual removable filler caps, cover the vent holes in each cap with a small piece of masking tape.

NOTE
Keep cleaning solution out of the battery cells in Step 6 or the electrolyte will be seriously weakened.

6. Clean the top of the battery with a stiff bristle brush using a baking soda and water solution (**Figure 5**). Rinse the battery case with clear water and wipe dry with a clean cloth or paper towel.

7. Inspect the battery tray in the engine compartment for corrosion and clean, if necessary, with the baking soda/water solution. Rinse tray with clear water and wipe dry.

8. Remove the masking tape from the filler cap vent holes. Position the battery on the battery tray.

9A. On 1972-1974 models, install the hold-down clamp. Tighten the clamp bolt sufficiently to hold the battery from moving.

9B. On 1975 and later models, fit the heat shield over the battery, making sure the J-bolt(s) align with the hole(s) in the shield.

10. Clean the battery cable clamps with a stiff wire brush or one of the many tools made for this purpose (**Figure 6**). The same tool is used for cleaning the battery posts (**Figure 7**).

11. Reconnect the positive battery cable, then the negative cable.

CAUTION
Be sure the battery cables are connected to their proper terminals. Connecting the battery backwards will reverse the polarity and can damage the alternator.

12. Tighten the battery connections and coat with a petroleum jelly such as Vaseline or a light mineral grease.

13. If the battery has removable filler caps, check the electrolyte level. It should touch the

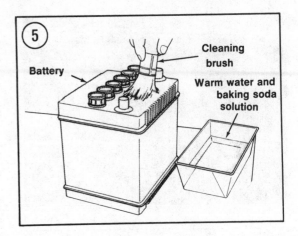

(5) Battery — Cleaning brush — Warm water and baking soda solution

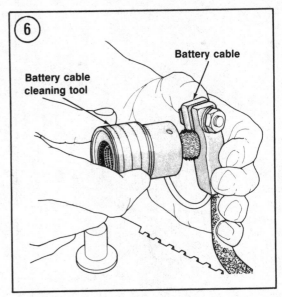

(6) Battery cable cleaning tool — Battery cable

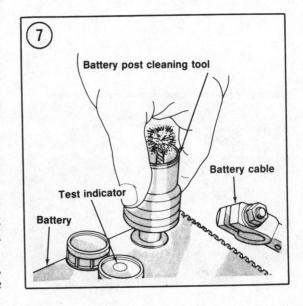

(7) Battery post cleaning tool — Test indicator — Battery cable — Battery

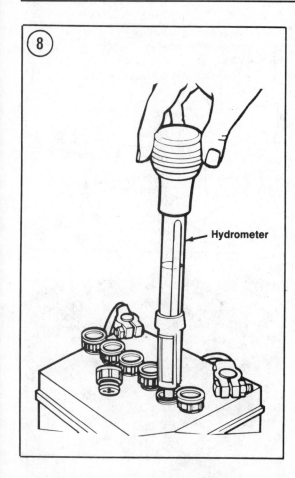

Hydrometer

of the electrolyte. This is the specific gravity for the cell. Return the electrolyte to the cell from which it came. The specific gravity of the electrolyte in each battery cell is an excellent indicator of that cell's condition. A fully charged cell will read 1.260 or more at 68° F (20° C). If the cells test below 1.200, the battery must be recharged. Charging is also necessary if the specific gravity of the battery varies more than 0.025 from cell to cell.

> *NOTE*
> *If a temperature-compensated hydro-meter is not used, add 0.004 to the specific gravity reading for every 10° above 80° F (25° C). For every 10° below 80° F (25° C), subtract 0.004.*

If the difference in specific gravity from one cell to another is greater than 0.025, one or more cells may be sulfated or otherwise poor. In such case, replace the battery before it causes trouble.

Charging

The battery does not have to be removed from the car for charging. Just make certain that the area is well-ventilated and that there is no chance of sparks or flames occuring near the battery.

> *WARNING*
> *Charging batteries give off highly explosive hydrogen gas. If this explodes, it may spray battery acid over a wide area.*

Disconnect the negative battery cable first, then the positive cable. On unsealed batteries, remove the vent caps and top up each cell with distilled water if necessary. Place a folded paper towel over the vent openings to catch any electrolyte that may spew as the battery charges.

Connect the charger to the battery (negative to negative, positive to positive). If the charger output is variable, select a low setting (5-10 amps), set the voltage regulator to 12 volts and plug the charger in. If the battery is severely discharged (below 1.125), allow it to charge for at least 8 hours. **Table 1** gives approximate charge rates.

bottom of the vent well in each cell. Top up with distilled water, if necessary.

Testing

> *NOTE*
> *This test procedure applies only to batteries with removable filler caps. A capacity and rate-of-charge test using special equipment is required in testing sealed maintenance-free batteries. These tests should be performed by your dealer or an automotive electrical shop.*

Hydrometer testing is the best way to check battery condition. Use a temperature-compensated hydrometer with numbered gradations from 1.100-1.300 rather than one with just color-coded bands. To use the hydrometer, squeeze the rubber ball, insert the tip in a cell and release the ball.

Draw enough electrolyte to float the weighted float inside the hydrometer (**Figure 8**). Note the number in line with the surface

On unsealed batteries, check charging progress with the hydrometer. After the battery has charged for a suitable period of time, unplug the charger and disconnect it from the battery. Be extremely careful about sparks. Test the condition of each cell with a hydrometer as described above.

If the specific gravity indicates that the battery is fully charged, and if the readings remain the same after one hour, the battery can be considered to be in good condition and fully charged. Check the electrolyte level and add distilled water, if necessary, then install the vent caps and reconnect the ground lead.

Jump Starting

If the battery becomes severely discharged on the road, it is possible to start and run a vehicle by jump starting it from another battery. If the proper procedure is not followed, however, jump starting can be dangerous. Check the electrolyte level before jump starting any vehicle. If it is not visible or if it appears to be frozen, *do not* attempt to jump start the battery, as the battery may explode or rupture. *Do not* jump start sealed batteries when the temperature is 32° F (0° C) or lower.

> *WARNING*
> *Use extreme caution when connecting a booster battery to one that is discharged to avoid personal injury or damage to the vehicle.*

1. Position the 2 cars so that the jumper cables will reach between the batteries, but the cars do not touch.
2. Connect the jumper cables in the order and sequence shown in **Figure 9**.

> *WARNING*
> *An electrical arc may occur when the final connection is made. This could cause an explosion if it occurs near the battery. For this reason, the final connection should be made to the alternator mounting bracket and not the battery itself.*

3. Check that all jumper cables are out of the way of moving parts on both engines.

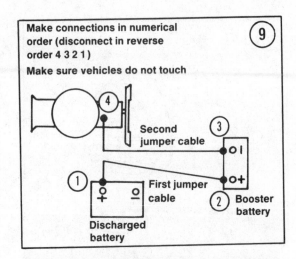

Make connections in numerical order (disconnect in reverse order 4 3 2 1)

Make sure vehicles do not touch

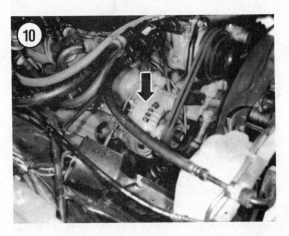

4. Start the car with the good battery and run the engine at a moderate speed.
5. Start the car with the discharged battery. Once the engine starts, run it at a moderate speed.

> *CAUTION*
> *Racing the engine may cause damage to the electrical system.*

6. Remove the jumper cables in the exact reverse order shown in **Figure 9**. Begin at point 4, then 3, 2 and 1.

CHARGING SYSTEM

The charging system consists of the battery, alternator, voltage regulator, ammeter and wiring. The various Chrysler alternators used on the vehicles covered in this manual differ primarily in output rating. All charging systems use an electronic voltage regulator.

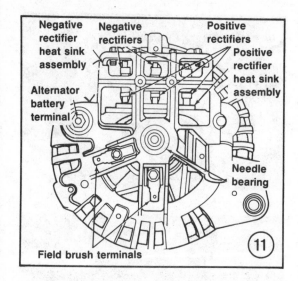

Negative rectifier heat sink assembly

Negative rectifiers

Positive rectifiers

Positive rectifier heat sink assembly

Alternator battery terminal

Needle bearing

Field brush terminals

⑪

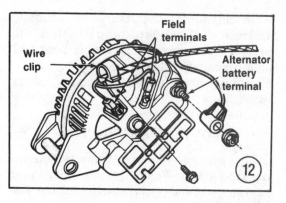

Wire clip

Field terminals

Alternator battery terminal

⑫

ALTERNATOR

The alternator is a self-rectifying, 3-phase current generator consisting of a stationary armature (stator), a rotating field (rotor) and a 3-phase rectifying bridge of silicone diodes. The alternator generates alternating current which is converted to direct current by the silicone diodes for use in the vehicle's electrical circuits. The alternator output is regulated by a voltage regulator to keep the battery charged. The alternator is mounted on the front of the engine and is belt-driven by the crankshaft pulley. **Figure 10** shows a typical alternator installation on a V8 engine.

Make sure the connections are not reversed when working on the alternator. Current flow in the wrong direction will damage the diodes and render the alternator unserviceable. The alternator output terminal must be connected to battery voltage (**Figure 11**). When charging the battery in the vehicle, disconnect the battery leads before connecting the charger. This is a precaution against incorrect current bias and heat reaching the alternator.

Preliminary Testing

The first indication of charging system trouble is usually a slow engine cranking speed during starting. This will often occur long before the charge warning light or ammeter indicates that there is a potential problem. When charging system trouble is first suspected, have it carefully tested, either

by a dealer or an automotive electrical shop. Before having the system tested, however, the following checks should be made to make sure something else is not the cause of what seems to be trouble in the charging system.
1. Check the alternator drive belt for correct tension (Chapter Eight).
2. Check the battery to make sure it is in satisfactory condition and fully charged and that the connections are clean and tight.
3. Check all connections at the alternator and voltage regulator to make sure they are clean and tight.

If there are still indications that the charging system is not performing as it should after each of the above points has been carefully checked and any unsatisfactory conditions corrected, have the system tested.

Removal/Installation

This procedure is generalized to cover all applications. On some vehicles, the alternator is mounted low on the engine under other accessory units and can only be reached from underneath the car. Access to the alternator is quite limited in some engine compartments and care should be taken to avoid personal injury during this procedure.
1. Disconnect the negative battery cable.
2. Unplug the connectors from the rear of the alternator (**Figure 12**, typical).
3. Loosen the belt tension adjuster at the alternator (A, **Figure 13**). Move the alternator toward the engine and remove the drive belt(s) from the pulley.
4. Unscrew the adjuster bolt. Remove the pivot bolt (B, **Figure 13**). Remove the alternator.

7

5. Installation is the reverse of removal. Make sure the alternator connectors are properly installed before connecting the negative battery cable.

6. Adjust the drive belt tension (Chapter Seven).

VOLTAGE REGULATOR

The electronic voltage regulator is mounted on the firewall (**Figure 14**). It contains no moving parts and cannot be adjusted. Ground is provided by the regulator case, mounting screws and mounting surface. If the regulator does not perform within factory specifications, it must be replaced.

Removal/Installation

1. Disconnect the negative battery cable.
2. Disconnect the connector plug at the regulator.
3. Remove the mounting screws.
4. Remove the regulator.
5. Installation is the reverse of removal.

AMMETER

To test ammeter operation, turn the headlights on but do not start the engine. At the same time, note the ammeter on the instrument panel. The needle should move toward the "D" or discharge scale. If there is no needle movement, check the terminals for loose wires. If the terminal connections are tight, the ammeter is defective. If the needle moves in the direction of "C" or charge, reverse the terminal wire positions.

The ammeter LED (light-emitting diode) on 1975 and later vehicles is mounted in the ammeter scale but works independently to monitor system voltage. It illuminates when system voltage drops to about 1.2 volts (ammeter needle in discharge area) to alert the driver to a discharge condition at idle due to a heavy electrical load. When engine rpm is increased or the electrical load reduced, the LED should turn off. If it does not, have the charging system tested for a malfunction.

If the LED illuminates when the ignition switch is turned to the ON position prior to moving the switch to START or if it blinks

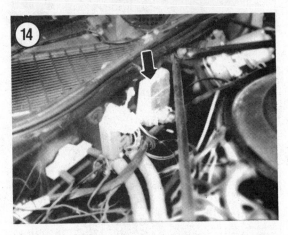

intermittently, check for a weak or defective battery.

STARTER

A direct drive starting motor with an externally mounted solenoid was used on 1972 6-cylinder engines. All other engines use either a 1.5 or 1.8 horsepower reduction gear starting motor with enclosed solenoid. The reduction gear starting motors are identical in appearance, but the field frame assembly on the 1.8 hp motor is 1/2 in. longer than the same assembly on the 1.5 hp motor. See **Figure 15**.

Starter service requires experience and special tools. The service procedure described below consists of removal and installation. Any repairs inside the unit itself should be done by a dealer or automotive electrical shop.

Removal/Installation

1. Disconnect the negative battery cable.

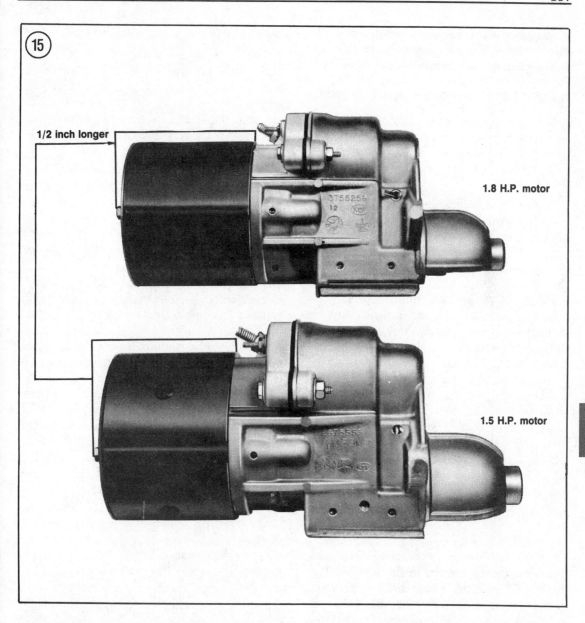

1/2 inch longer

1.8 H.P. motor

1.5 H.P. motor

7

2. Securely block both rear wheels so the vehicle will not roll in either direction.

3. Raise the front of the car with a jack and place it on jackstands.

4. If equipped with a heat shield, remove the bolt and nut holding it in place, then remove the heat shield.

5. Disconnect the cable at the starter, then disconnect the solenoid lead wires at their terminals.

6. On some models, it may be necessary to disconnect the Pitman arm from the steering linkage to provide sufficient access for starter motor removal.

7. If the transmission oil cooler lines interfere with starter removal, remove bracket, if bolted, or slide bracket off stud, if not bolted. On late models, it will be necessary to remove the stud nut holding the starter motor to the flywheel housing to free the bracket.

8. Remove the remaining starter mounting fasteners. Carefully remove the starter motor to prevent damage to the flywheel housing seal.

9. Installation is the reverse of removal. Hold starter motor in proper alignment and tighten fasteners securely.

ELECTRICAL CIRCUIT PROTECTION

Electrical circuits are protected by a variety of devices: fuses, circuit breakers and fusible links.

Fuses

A fuse is a safety valve installed in an electrical circuit which "blows" (opens the circuit) when excessive current flows in the circuit. This protects the circuit and electrical components such as the alternator from being damaged.

Fuses on 1972-1978 models are glass capsules with a thin metal link running through the center. It is this link that burns in half under a heavy electrical load. If this happens, the fuse may appear black or the break can be seen in the metal link.

Chrysler Corp. changed to the use of mini-fuses with the 1979 models. The mini-fuse is a flat design with 2 blades connected by a metal link and encapsulated in plastic. The plastic is color-coded according to amperage value. The mini-fuse functions in the same way as the older glass fuse, but is easier to replace.

Circuit Breakers

Some circuits are protected by circuit breakers mounted either in the fuse block or the circuit itself. A circuit breaker conducts current through an arm made of 2 different types of metal connected together. If too much current passes through this bimetal arm, it heats up and expands. One metal expands faster than the other, causing the arm to move and open the contacts to break the flow of current. As the arm cools down, the metal contracts and the arm closes the contacts, allowing current to pass. Cycling inline circuit breakers will repeat this sequence as long as power is applied or until the condition is corrected. Non-cycling circuit breakers use a coil around the bimetal arm to hold it in an open position until power is shut off or the condition corrected.

Fusible Links

Fusible links are different than fuses. A fusible link is a short length of insulated wire several gauges smaller than the circuit it protects. When heavy current flows through the circuit, the fusible link burns out, protecting the wiring and circuit components.

Correcting System Failures

Whenever a failure occurs in any part of the electrical system, always check the fuse to see if it is blown. Usually the trouble can be traced to a short circuit in the wiring connected to the blown fuse. This may be caused by worn insulation or by a wire which has worked loose and shorted to ground. Occasionally, the electrical overload which causes a fuse to blow may occur in a switch or motor.

A blown fuse should be treated as more than a minor annoyance; it should serve as a warning that something is wrong in the electrical system. Before replacing a fuse, determine what caused it to blow and correct the trouble. Never replace a fuse with one of higher amperage rating than that specified for use. With glass fuses, never use metallic material to bridge the fuse terminals. Failure to follow these basic rules could result in heat or fire damage to major parts or loss of the entire vehicle.

Fuse Replacement

To replace a glass fuse, carefully pry it out of its holder with the end of a pencil or similar non-metallic probe and snap a new one of the same amperage rating into place.

To replace a mini-fuse, pull the plastic covered fuse from the fuse box and insert a new one of the same amperage rating (color) in place.

Fusible Link Replacement

1. Obtain the proper service fusible link. Make sure the replacement link is a duplicate of the one removed regarding wire gauge, length and insulation. Do not substitute any other type of gauge or wire.
2. Disconnect the negative battery cable.

3. Cut damaged link from main harness wire.

4. Remove one inch of insulation from the main harness wire. Do the same with the new fusible link.

5. Wrap the stripped ends of the main harness wire and link together.

6. Solder the connection with a high temperature soldering gun and rosin type solder.

7. Let solder joint cool, then wrap splice with at least 3 layers of electrical tape.

8. Connect the negative battery cable.

LIGHTS

All lighting elements, with the exception of instrument illumination bulbs, are easily replaced. Individual replacement procedures vary slightly, but can be accomplished with the following procedures.

Headlight Replacement

The headlights are replaceable sealed-beam or halogen units. Do not install halogen units in a car not originally equipped with them. On single headlight installations, the high- and low-beam circuits and filaments are included in one unit. With dual headlight installations, one bulb on each side is a combination high- and low-beam unit marked 2 or 2A. The other bulb is a high-beam only unit marked 1 or 1A. Mounting tabs on this bulb permit its use only in the inboard or lower headlight support frame. Failure of one circuit in a combination lamp requires replacement of the entire lamp.

NOTE
If both filaments in a dual beam lamp fail at the same time, it is possible that there is a short in the wiring to that particular lamp. Check the fuse to make sure it is the correct amperage rating and replace if it is not. Carefully inspect the wiring and connector for chafing or damage and correct any breaks in the insulation.

1. Remove the screws holding the headlight door panel and/or trim ring in place. Remove the ring.

2. Loosen the headlight retaining screws, turn the light unit counterclockwise to align the large cutouts with the screws and remove the unit. Unplug the connector from the rear of the light.

NOTE
Do not turn the headlight beam adjusting screws. This will disturb the setting and the headlight beam will require adjustment.

3. Installation is the reverse of removal. Be sure the connector is firmly seated before installing the unit. Set the light in place; make sure the lugs on the light engage the recesses in the lamp holder. Set the retainer ring in place and turn it clockwise until the small end of each cutout engages a screw. Tighten the screws and install the outer trim ring and/or door panel.

Taillight/Parking/Turn Indicator Bulb Replacement

Proper operation requires a good ground. In most cases, this is provided through the lamp socket and housing to the vehicle. However, in some vehicles, the socket/housing assembly may be in a plastic component, requiring an extra ground wire. Where used, it is important that this ground wire be securely connected to a good ground.

1. Remove the lens with a screwdriver. Press inward on the bulb and turn it counterclockwise at the same time. Pull the bulb from the socket.

2. Wipe the inside of the lens and the lamp reflector clean.

3. Press a new bulb into the socket and turn it clockwise to lock it in place.

4. Install the lens. Do not overtighten the screws or the lens could crack.

7

Table 1 BATTERY CHARGE

	Normal Charge*	Rapid Charge
Charging current rate	2.0 ampere-hours	10.0 ampere-hours maximum
Checking for full charge	1. Specific gravity: 1.260-1.280 68°F (20°C) maintained constantly.	1. Specific gravity: 1.260-1.280 maintained at 68°F (20°C).
	2. 7.5-8.3 volts at terminals. Check with voltmeter.	2. Voltage: When a large volume of gas is emitted from the battery (in about 2-3 hours for fully discharged battery) reduce the charging rate to 2.0 amperes.
		3. Battery is fully charged when a voltage of 7.5 volts is maintained.
Charging duration	A battery with specific gravity of electrolyte below 1.220 at 68°F (20°C) will be fully charged in approximately 12-13 hours.	A battery with specific gravity of electrolyte below 1.220 at 68°F (20°C) will be fully charged in approximately 1-2 hours.

* When required, the quick charging method may be used; however, the recommended charging current rate should be under 2.0 amperes.

CHAPTER EIGHT

COOLING SYSTEM

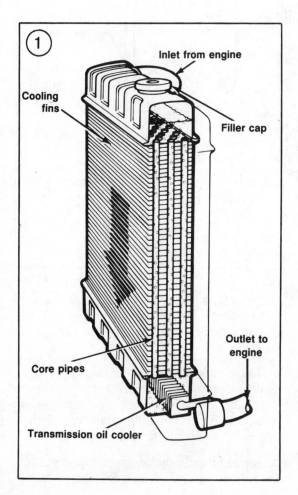

Figure 1 labels: Inlet from engine, Cooling fins, Filler cap, Core pipes, Outlet to engine, Transmission oil cooler

All models use a pressurized cooling system sealed with a 16 psi pressure-type radiator cap. The higher operating pressure of the system raises the boiling point of the coolant. This increases the efficiency of the radiator.

A downflow radiator design (**Figure 1**) is used on all vehicles. The radiator is constructed in a tube and slit-fin-core manner with the tubes arranged between upper and lower header tanks for vertical coolant flow. When used with an automatic transmission, the lower header tank contains an oil cooler for cooling the transmission fluid.

All 1973 and later vehicles are equipped with a coolant recovery system. This consists of a plastic overflow reservoir connected to the radiator filler neck by a hose (**Figure 2**, typical). When coolant in the radiator expands to the overflow point, it passes through the filler neck and into the plastic reservoir. Once the coolant remaining in the radiator cools down, it contracts. The vacuum created pulls coolant from the reservoir back into the radiator. This system prevents the radiator from boiling over. By remaining filled to capacity, cooling efficiency is maintained at all times.

Chrysler Corp. cooling systems consist of the radiator, coolant recovery reservoir (if so

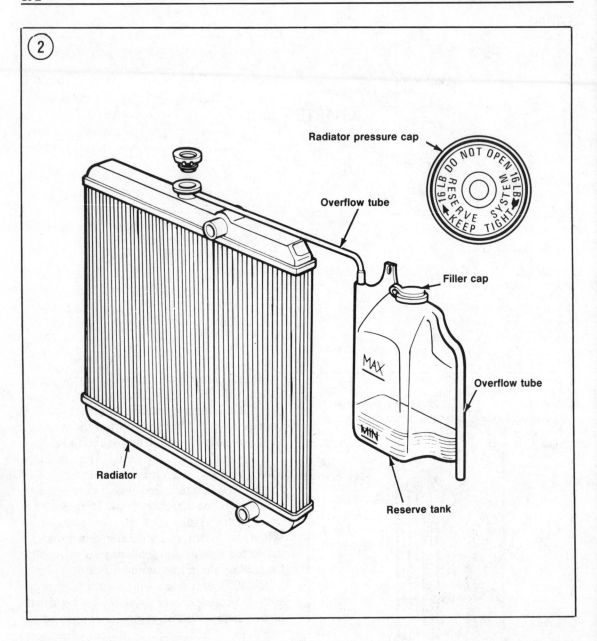

Radiator pressure cap

DO NOT OPEN 16 LB
RESERVE SYSTEM
16 LB
KEEP TIGHT

Overflow tube

Filler cap

MAX

Overflow tube

MIN

Radiator

Reserve tank

equipped), pressure cap, water pump, thermostat, fan or fan drive clutch, drive belt(s) and connecting hoses.

COOLING SYSTEM INSPECTION

1. Visually inspect the cooling system and heater hoses for signs of cracking, checking, excessive swelling or leakage.
2. Check that all supporting brackets for hoses are properly positioned (if used) and that the hoses are correctly installed in the brackets.

3. Inspect the front and rear of the radiator core and header tanks, all seams and the radiator drain valve for signs of seepage or leaks.

4. Make sure all hose connections are tight and in good condition. Check the hoses carefully at their clamps for damage or weakness. Overtightening strap-type clamps can cut the outer surface of a hose.

5. Remove the radiator pressure cap. Check the rubber cap seal surfaces for tears or cracks

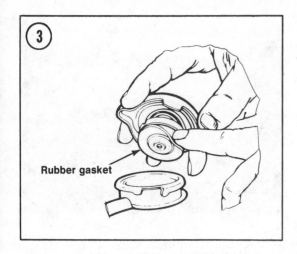

Rubber gasket

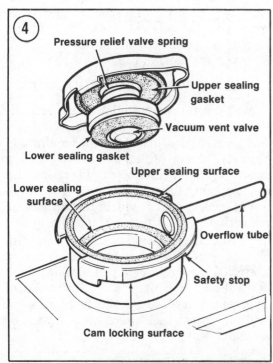

Pressure relief valve spring

Upper sealing gasket

Vacuum vent valve

Lower sealing gasket

Upper sealing surface

Lower sealing surface

Overflow tube

Safety stop

Cam locking surface

(**Figure 3**). Check for a bent or distorted cap. Raise the vacuum vent valve and rubber seal and rinse the cap under warm tap water to flush away any loose rust or dirt particles.

6. Inspect the filler neck seat and sealing surface (**Figure 4**) for nicks, dents, distortion or contamination. Wipe the sealing surface with a clean cloth to remove any rust or dirt. Install the cap properly.

7. Start the engine and warm to normal operating temperature. Shut the engine off and carefully feel the radiator. It should be hot at the top and warm at the bottom, with an even heat rise from bottom to top. Any cold spots indicate clogged areas.

8. Restart the engine and squeeze the upper radiator hose (**Figure 5**) to check water pump operation. If a pressure surge is felt, the water pump is functioning properly. If not, check for a plugged vent hole in the pump.

9. Visually check the area underneath the water pump for signs of leakage or corrosion. A defective water pump will usually leak through the vent hole at the bottom of the pump.

10. Check the crankcase oil dipstick for signs of coolant in the engine oil. On automatic transmission models, check the coolant for signs of transmission fluid leaking from the oil cooler.

PRESSURE CHECK

If the cooling system requires frequent topping up, it probably has a leak. Small leaks in a cooling system are not easy to locate, as the hot coolant evaporates as fast as it leaks out, preventing the formation of tell-tale rusty or grayish-white stains.

A pressure test of the cooling system will usually help to pinpoint the source of the leak. The cooling system and the pressure cap should both be tested by a dealer or qualified radiator repair shop.

If the cooling system passes a pressure test but continues to lose coolant, check for an exhaust leak into the cooling system. Drain the coolant until the level is just above the top of the cylinder head. Disconnect the upper radiator hose and remove the thermostat and water pump drive belt. Add sufficient coolant to bring the level to within 1/2 in. of the top of the thermostat housing. Start the engine and open the throttle several times while observing the coolant. If the level rises or if bubbles appear in the coolant, exhaust gases are probably leaking into the cooling system.

CAUTION
Do not run the engine with the water pump drive belt disconnected for more than 30 seconds or the engine may overheat.

COOLANT LEVEL CHECK

Always check coolant level with the engine and radiator cold. Coolant expands as it is heated and checking a hot or warm system will not give a true level reading.

CAUTION
Never remove the cap from a hot radiator while the engine is running. Severe scalding could result.

1. Check hose clamps for tightness. Be sure radiator drain valve is closed. **Figure 6** shows a typical drain valve location.
2A. On 1972 models, depress the radiator cap, rotate counterclockwise and remove from the filler neck. The radiator coolant level should be 3/4-1 1/2 in. below the pressure cap seat in the filler neck.
2B. On 1973 and later models, visually check the coolant recovery reservoir. The coolant level should be at the "COLD" mark embossed on the translucent tank.
3. If the coolant level is low, top up with a 50/50 mixture of ethylene glycol antifreeze and water. On 1973 and later models, add coolant to the recovery reservoir, not the radiator.

NOTE
To avoid the possibility of chemical damage to the cooling system, do not mix different brands of antifreeze.

5. Install the radiator or recovery reservoir cap.
6. Start the engine and warm to normal operating temperature (upper radiator hose hot).

7. Shut the engine off. Remove the radiator cap and recheck the coolant level. If necessary, add sufficient coolant to bring the level to the point specified in Step 2.
8. Install the radiator cap.

CHANGING ENGINE COOLANT

A 50 percent concentration of antifreeze in the coolant should be maintained even if you live in a climate that does not require this degree of freeze protection. Antifreeze is a good corrosion inhibitor and raises the boiling point of the coolant.

The cooling system should be inspected at regular intervals. If the coolant appears dirty or rusty, the system should be drained, flushed with clean water and refilled. Severe corrosion may require pressure flushing, a job for a dealer or radiator shop. Regardless of appearance, the coolant should be replaced and the system backflushed every 2 years or 24,000 miles.

Cylinder Block Flushing

1. Coolant can stain concrete and harm plants. Park the car over a gutter or similar area.
2. Open the drain valve at the bottom of the radiator (**Figure 6**). Remove the radiator cap and let the cooling system drain. Close the drain valve.
3. Remove the upper and lower radiator hoses at the radiator.
4. Remove the thermostat as described in this chapter. Temporarily reinstall the thermostat housing.

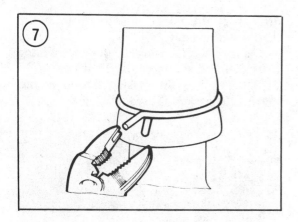

5. Connect a suitable adapter to the water inlet hose. Connect a drain hose to the water outlet hose.

6. Connect a pressurized water source or flushing gun (if available) to the adapter on the inlet hose.

NOTE
A flushing gun which utilizes both water and compressed air does the best flushing job. However, a garden hose attached to a pressurized water source may be used.

7A. If flushing gun is used, fill engine block with water, then apply short blasts of air (up to 20 psi). Allow engine to refill between air blasts. Repeat until water runs clear.

7B. If water only is used, allow water to run until it turns clear.

8. Reinstall thermostat with a new housing gasket or RTV sealant as described in this chapter.

9. Flush radiator as described in this chapter.

10. Remove flushing gun or hose and reconnect radiator hoses.

11. Fill cooling system to 1 1/4 in. below filler neck with a 50/50 mixture of ethylene glycol antifreeze and water.

12. Warm engine to normal operating temperature, then operate for another 5 minutes to remove any air trapped in the system. Check for leaks. Check coolant level and correct as necessary.

Radiator Flushing

1. With the radiator drained and hoses removed, connect a suitable adapter to the lower outlet. Connect a drain hose to upper outlet.

2. Connect a pressurized source of water or an air/water flushing gun (if available) to the outlet adapter.

CAUTION
If an air/water flushing gun is used, do not allow radiator internal pressure to exceed 20 psi, as radiator damage could result.

3A. If flushing gun is used, allow radiator to fill, then apply short bursts of air. Allow radiator to refill between bursts. Repeat until water runs clear.

3B. If water only is used, allow water to flush radiator until it runs clear.

4. Remove flushing apparatus and reconnect radiator hoses.

RADIATOR HOSES

Replace any hoses that are cracked, brittle, mildewed or very soft and spongy. If a hose is in doubtful condition, but not definitely bad, replace it to be on the safe side. This will avoid the inconvenience of a roadside repair.

Always replace a radiator hose with the same type removed. Plain or pleated rubber hoses do not have the same strength as reinforced molded hoses. Check the hose clamp condition and, if necessary, install new clamps with a new hose.

NOTE
The spring-type wire hose clamps installed at the factory gradually lose their tension and are not reuseable. It is a good idea to replace these clamps with a worm drive type at the first annual cooling system check to prevent cooling system leaks from developing.

Replacement

1. Place a clean container under the radiator drain valve. Remove the radiator cap and open the drain valve. Drain about one quart of coolant when replacing an upper hose. Completely drain it to replace a lower hose. If the coolant is clean, save it for reuse.

2. Loosen the clamp at each end of the hose to be removed (**Figure 7**). Grasp the hose and

8

twist it off the connection with a pulling motion.

3. If the hose is corroded to the fitting, cut it off with a sharp knife about one inch beyond the end of the fitting. Remove the clamp and slit the remaining piece of hose lengthwise, then peel it off the fitting.

4. Clean any corrosion from the fitting with sandpaper, then rinse the fitting to remove any particles.

5. Position the clamps at least 1/4 in. from each end of the new hose. Wipe the inside diameter of the hose and the outside of the fitting with dishwasher liquid. Install the hose end on the fitting with a twisting motion.

6. Position the clamps for easy access with a screwdriver or nut driver and tighten each clamp snugly. Recheck them for tightness after operating the car for a few days.

7. Fill the radiator with the coolant removed in Step 1. Start the engine and operate it for a few minutes, checking for signs of leakage around the connections.

THERMOSTAT

The thermostat is located in an elbow housing which connects to the upper radiator hose on 6-cylinder (**Figure 8**) and V8 engines (**Figure 9**).

The thermostat blocks coolant flow to the radiator when the engine is cold. As the engine warms up, the thermostat gradually opens, allowing coolant to circulate through the radiator. Check the thermostat when removed to determine its opening point; the heat range should be stamped on the thermostat flange. When replacing a thermostat, always use one with the same temperature rating.

Removal

1. Make sure the engine is cool. Disconnect the negative battery cable.

2. Place a clean container under the radiator drain valve. Remove the radiator cap and open the drain valve. Drain about one quart of coolant from the radiator. If the coolant is clean, save it for reuse.

3. Disconnect the bypass hose at the water pump, if necessary. If clearance is limited, disconnect the upper radiator hose at the thermostat housing.

4. Remove the thermostat housing retaining bolts. Remove the thermostat housing.

5. Remove the thermostat. Remove and discard the gasket, if used.

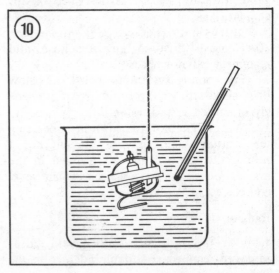

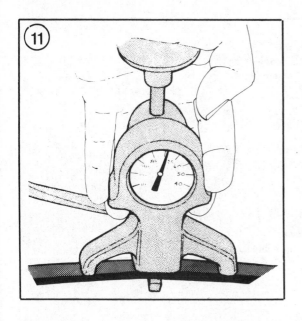

Testing

1. Pour some of the coolant removed from the cooling system in a container that can be heated. Suspend a thermometer as shown in **Figure 10**.

2. Heat the coolant to its boiling point, then suspend the thermostat in the coolant (**Figure 10**). Check coolant temperature when the thermostat opens sufficiently to permit insertion of a 0.001 in. feeler gauge in the valve opening. The feeler gauge should pass freely into the opening at a temperature of 182-189° F (185° F thermostat) or 192-200° F (195° F thermostat).

3. Continue heating the coolant to approximately 210° F (185° F thermostat) or 219° F (195° F thermostat). If the thermostat valve is not fully open at this temperature, replace it.

Installation

1. Clean all gasket or RTV sealant residue from the thermostat housing flange and cylinder head or manifold gasket surfaces with a putty knife.

2. Install a new gasket or run a thin bead of RTV sealant on the thermostat housing flange.

3. Install thermostat with pellet end toward engine. Vent hole should face upward on 6-cylinder thermostats.

4. Install thermostat housing with bolts. Tighten bolts to 30 ft.-lb. (40 N•m) on all 6-cylinder and 1972-1979 V8 engines. Tighten bolts to 200 in.-lb. (23 N•m) on all 1980 and later V8 engines.

5. Connect the bypass and/or upper radiator hose(s) if disconnected.

6. Fill the cooling system with the coolant removed in Step 2 of *Removal* procedure. Reconnect the negative battery cable. Start the engine and run for several minutes. Check for leaks and proper coolant level.

DRIVE BELTS

Inspection

Inspect all engine drive belts for wear and damage at each oil change period. Belts which show signs of wear, cracks, glazing or frayed/broken cords should be replaced.

Adjustment

Chrysler Corp. specifies the use of a belt tension gauge as the preferred means of setting belt tension accurately. All new belts should be tensioned to 120 lb. (530 N). Used belts (those run more than 15 minutes) should be tensioned to 70 lb. (310 N).

When limited access to the drive belt prevents the use of a tension gauge, the deflection method may be used to set tension.

Deflection method

This method should be used only when a belt tension gauge is not available or when limited access to the drive belt prevents the use of the tension gauge.

Depress the belt at a point midway between the pulleys. New belts should deflect 1/4-1/2 in.; used belts should deflect 1/4-5/16 in. If deflection is not in this range, loosen the accessory mounting bolts and use a lever between the accessory and its bracket to apply tension to the belt. Be careful not to damage the accessory when prying with the lever.

Tension gauge method

1. Install the belt tension gauge (**Figure 11**) at the points indicated in **Figure 12** and check

8

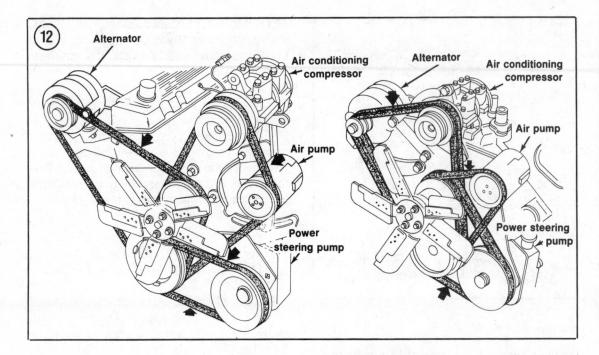

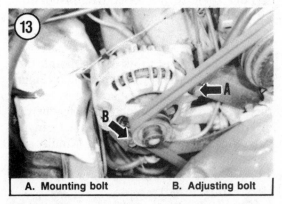

A. Mounting bolt   B. Adjusting bolt

tension according to the gauge manufacturer's instructions.

> *NOTE*
> *If dual belts are used to drive an accessory, check the tension on the front belt with the tension gauge. Trying to check tension on both belts with the gauge will result in an incorrect reading.*

2. If adjustment is required, loosen the accessory mounting and adjusting bracket bolts. Move accessory toward or away from engine until correct tension is obtained.

3. Tighten mounting and adjusting bolts, then recheck tension with the gauge.

Replacement

> *NOTE*
> *If dual belts are used to drive an accessory, they should be replaced in matched pairs.*

Cars equipped with power steering, air conditioning and/or an air pump require removal of these drive belts before the fan drive belt(s) can be removed.

1. On a car equipped with power steering, loosen the power steering pump at its mounting bracket. Move the pump toward the engine and remove the drive belt. Repeat

this step to remove the air pump drive belt, if so equipped.

2. Loosen the alternator mounting and adjusting arm bolts. **Figure 13** shows a typical V8 installation. Move the alternator toward the engine. Remove belt(s) from the alternator and crankshaft pulleys and lift them over the fan.

3. Place belt(s) over fan. Install belt(s) in water pump pulley, crankshaft pulley and alternator pulley grooves. Adjust belt tension as described in this chapter.

4. On cars equipped with an air pump, install and adjust the pump drive belt.

5. On cars equipped with power steering, install power steering pump drive belt.

Tighten pump at mounting bracket and adjust drive belt.

COOLING FAN

Some models are equipped with a fluid fan drive. This temperature-controlled fluid coupling permits use of a powerful fan without great power loss or noise. The fan speed is regulated according to the temperature of the air passing through the radiator core. The fan and fluid drive are removed as a unit.

Removal/Installation

1. Remove the fan shroud screws. Move shroud toward the engine to provide access to the fan.

2. Remove the attaching screws holding the fan to the water pump pulley hub.

3. Remove the fan and spacer, if so equipped.

NOTE
At this point, the water pump pulley on models equipped with a fan drive clutch will separate into two pieces, causing other drive belts to loose their tension. On such models, it is necessary to loosen the accessory units involved to remove tension from their drive belts before reinstalling the front half of the pulley and the fan drive clutch.

4. Installation is the reverse of removal. Tighten attaching screws to 200 in-lb. (23 N•m). Adjust accessory belts as described in this chapter.

8

CHAPTER NINE

BRAKE SYSTEM AND
WHEEL BEARINGS

Chrysler Corp. passenger cars use drum-type rear brakes on all models. Front brakes are either drum or disc type.

Three types of front disc brakes have been used since 1972: a fixed caliper (**Figure 1**), a sliding caliper (**Figure 2**) and a pin slider caliper (**Figure 3**). The fixed caliper design uses 2 pistons on each side of the disc; sliding and pin slider designs use a single piston and lateral pad movement to clamp onto the disc. The type used on a particular vehicle can be identified by comparing the caliper to **Figures 1-3**.

A self-energizing servo design (**Figure 4**) is used on all models with drum brakes. Drum brakes are self-adjusting and normally do not require adjustment. If brakes have been relined, however, initial adjustment is needed for safe operation.

A dual hydraulic system is used on all models, one for the front wheels and one for the rear wheels. Both are operated by a dual reservoir master cylinder (**Figure 5**). The reservoir nearest to the firewall provides brake fluid to the front brakes while the reservoir closest to the radiator supplies fluid to the rear brakes. Should one circuit fail, the other will bring the car safely to a stop.

The brake system of all Chrysler Corp. passenger cars use a hydraulic valve or switch of some type. Vehicles with front and rear drum brakes have a brake warning switch. Combination valves of differing types are used on disc/drum equipped models. Such valves (**Figure 6**, typical) may contain a metering or proportioning section (or both) in conjunction with the brake warning switch.

The combination valve contains a brake warning light switch. A failure in either the front or rear brake system causes a pressure loss differential which activates the warning switch to turn the brake warning light on. The light shuts off when the system is serviced, bled and the brake pedal depressed to center the piston. The proportioning section of the valve balances braking pressure between the front and rear brakes to minimize rear wheel skidding during hard braking. The metering or hold-off valve section delays front disc application momentarily until the rear drum brake shoes contact the brake drums.

An optional power brake booster utilizes engine intake manifold vacuum and atmospheric pressure for its power.

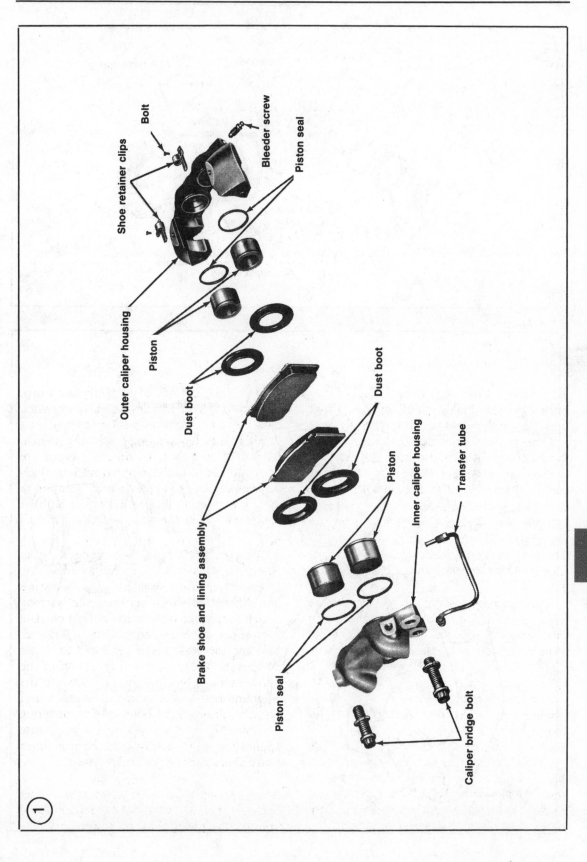

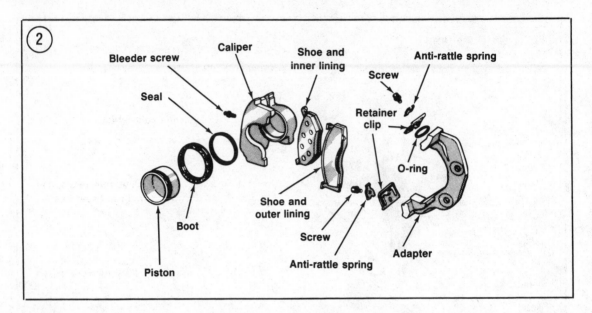

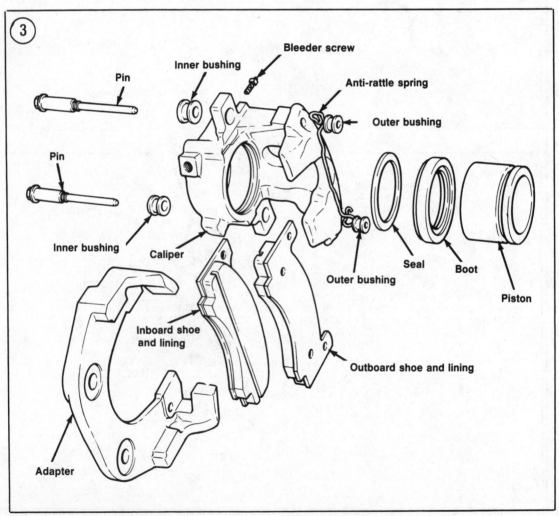

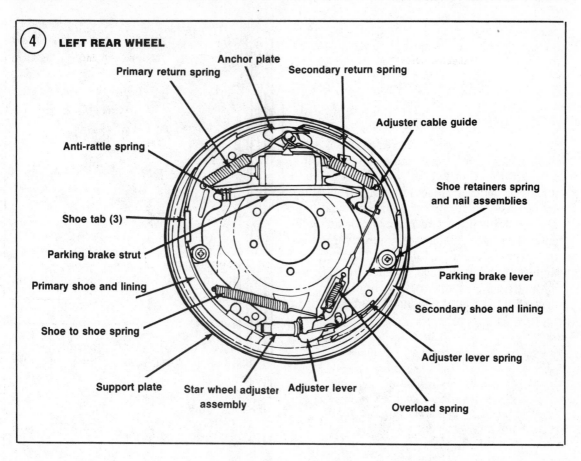

④ **LEFT REAR WHEEL**

Anchor plate

Primary return spring

Secondary return spring

Adjuster cable guide

Anti-rattle spring

Shoe retainers spring and nail assemblies

Shoe tab (3)

Parking brake strut

Parking brake lever

Primary shoe and lining

Secondary shoe and lining

Shoe to shoe spring

Adjuster lever spring

Support plate

Star wheel adjuster assembly

Adjuster lever

Overload spring

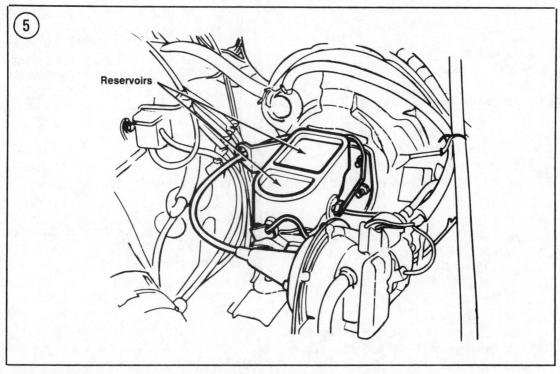

⑤

Reservoirs

9

The parking brake is a mechanical type, operating the rear brakes through a cable linkage.

DISC BRAKE PADS

Before removing the calipers for pad replacement, remove the master cylinder cover and use a large syringe to siphon about half of the fluid from the rear reservoir. Discard the fluid. This will prevent the master cylinder from overflowing when the caliper piston is compressed for reinstallation. *Do not* drain the entire reservoir or air will enter the system. Recheck the reservoir when the calipers are reinstalled and top up as required with fresh DOT 3 brake fluid. If no hydraulic line is opened, it should not be necessary to bleed the brake system after pad replacement.

> *NOTE*
> *If pads are to be reused, mark them so they can be reinstalled in the same position. Reused pads must always be installed in the same position from which they were removed.*

Removal

Fixed caliper

Refer to **Figure 1** for this procedure.
1. Set the parking brake. Block the rear wheels.
2. Remove the wheel covers and loosen the wheel lug nuts.
3. Raise the front of the vehicle with a jack and place it on jackstands.
4. Remove the wheel/tire assemblies.
5. Remove the pad retainer hold-down clips.

> *NOTE*
> *If pads cannot be easily removed in Step 6, it may be necessary to force the pistons into their bore slightly. Use a pair of water pump pliers to grasp the caliper housing and corner of the pad*

6. Use 2 pairs of pliers to grasp tabs on outer ends of brake pad and pull pad from caliper. Repeat this step to remove the other pad.

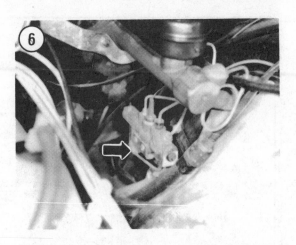

7. If caliper removal is necessary, remove bolts holding caliper to steering knuckle and slide caliper off brake disc.

Sliding caliper

Refer to **Figure 7** for this procedure.
1. Set the parking brake. Block the rear wheels.
2. Remove the wheel covers and loosen the wheel lug nuts.
3. Raise the front of the vehicle with a jack and place it on jackstands.
4. Remove the wheel/tire assemblies.
5. Unbolt and remove the retaining clips and anti-rattle springs, if so equipped.
6. Slide the caliper away from the disc, insert a screwdriver between the outer pad and caliper and pry the pad loose. See **Figure 8**. Remove the outer pad.
7. Support the caliper on the front linkage and remove the inner pad.

Pin slider

Refer to **Figure 3** for this procedure.
1. Set the parking brake. Block the rear wheels.
2. Remove the wheel covers and loosen the wheel lug nuts.
3. Raise the front of the vehicle with a jack and place it on jackstands.
4. Remove the wheel/tire assemblies.
5. Remove the caliper guide pins, caliper-to-adapter positioners and anti-rattle springs.
6. Slide the caliper off the brake disc and support it on the front linkage.

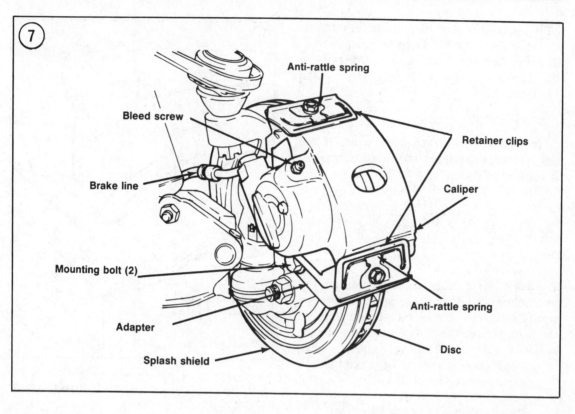

7

Anti-rattle spring

Bleed screw

Retainer clips

Brake line

Caliper

Mounting bolt (2)

Anti-rattle spring

Adapter

Splash shield

Disc

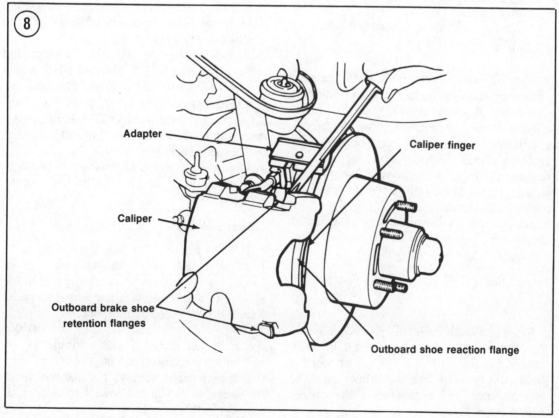

8

Adapter

Caliper finger

Caliper

Outboard brake shoe retention flanges

Outboard shoe reaction flange

9

7. Remove the outer pad from the caliper. Remove the inner pad from the adapter.

8. Press the inner and outer bushings from the caliper with a suitable tool. Discard the bushings.

Cleaning and Inspection

1. Inspect lining surfaces for wear. If the lining is worn to within 0.03 in. of either pad, replace all of the pads.

> *NOTE*
> *The inner pad may show more wear than the outer one. This is a normal condition and does not indicate a caliper problem.*

2. Check pads for damage caused by overheating. If lining surfaces have been overheated (indicated by blue-tinted areas on the pad), replace the pads. Pads must also be replaced if the linings have been contaminated by grease, oil or brake fluid.

> *WARNING*
> *If pads are replaced on one wheel, they must also be replaced on the other wheel to maintain equal braking action and avoid excessive brake pull.*

3. Carefully clean the outside of the caliper. Look for brake fluid leaks. Check condition of dust boots. If caliper is leaking or dust boots are deteriorated or damaged, have the caliper overhauled by a dealer or brake shop.

4. On sliding calipers, look for rust or corrosion. If present, remove the O-ring. Clean the surfaces with a wire brush and reinstall the O-ring.

5. Inspect the flexible brake hose attached to the caliper. Replace the brake hose if it is swollen, cracked or leaking.

Installation

Floating caliper

Refer to **Figure 1** for this procedure.

1. Depress both pistons into their bore as far as possible, using a flat metal bar or tool.

2. Insert new pads into the caliper until the ears on each pad seat against the caliper bridge.

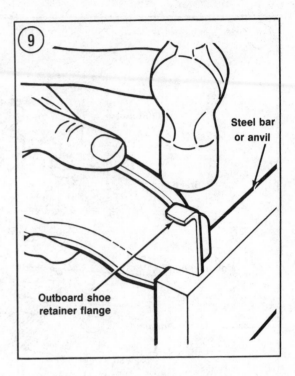

Steel bar or anvil

Outboard shoe retainer flange

3. Install retaining clips and tighten the bolts to 7-9 ft.-lb. (10-13 N•m).

4. Pump brake pedal several times until a firm pedal is obtained, indicating that the pads have seated properly.

5. Install wheel/tire assembly. Tighten lug nuts to 55 ft.-lb. (75 N•m). Install wheel covers and lower vehicle to the ground.

6. Check master cylinder fluid level and top up as needed with fresh DOT 3 fluid. Install reservoir cover and check for leaks around the caliper and hoses.

7. Check for firm pedal pressure. Road test the vehicle to make sure the brakes operate properly.

Sliding caliper

Refer to **Figure 2** for this procedure.

1. If new pads are to be installed, press caliper into its bore with a C-clamp and block of wood to provide clearance for the pads. Remove the C-clamp and block.

2. Slide a new outer pad into the caliper recess. When installed, there should be no free play between the pad flanges and caliper. If free play exists, remove the pad and bend the flanges as shown in **Figure 9**, then reinstall pad in the caliper.

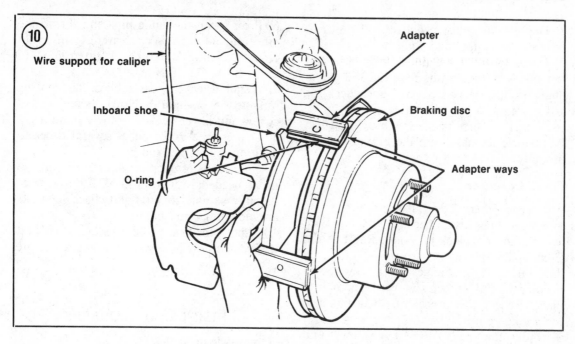

⑩

Wire support for caliper

Adapter

Inboard shoe

Braking disc

O-ring

Adapter ways

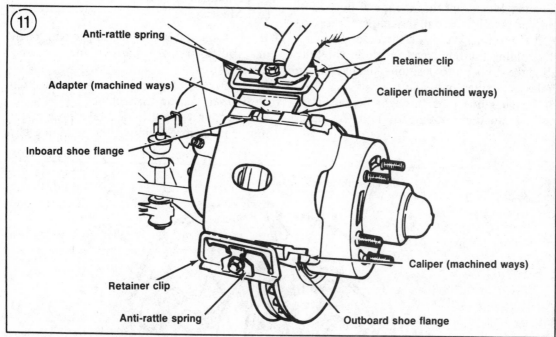

⑪

Anti-rattle spring

Retainer clip

Adapter (machined ways)

Caliper (machined ways)

Inboard shoe flange

Retainer clip

Caliper (machined ways)

Anti-rattle spring

Outboard shoe flange

9

3. Install the inner shoe on the adapter with its flange in the adapter's machined ways. See **Figure 10**.

4. Slide the adapter assembly in place in the adapter and over the disc.

5. Align the caliper on the adapter; don't pull the dust boot from its groove as the piston and boot slide over the inner shoe.

6. Install the anti-rattle springs (if so equipped) over the retainer plates. Install retainer plates and tighten bolts snugly to 170-260 in.-lb. (19-29 N•m). See **Figure 11**.

7. Install wheel/tire assemblies. Lower vehicle to the ground and tighten wheel lug nuts to 85 ft.-lb (115 N•m).

8. Depress the brake pedal several times to position the caliper and pads.

9. Check the master cylinder fluid level and top up as needed with fresh DOT 3 brake fluid. Install reservoir cover(s) and check for leaks around caliper and hoses.

10. Check for firm pedal pressure. Road test the vehicle to make sure the brakes operate properly.

Pin slider caliper

Refer to **Figure 3** for this procedure.

1. Press caliper piston back into its bore with a C-clamp and block of wood. Remove the C-clamp and block.

2. Compress the flanges of a new outer bushing in the caliper and work them into place. Repeat this procedure to install new inner guide pin bushings.

3. Slide new pads into the caliper and adapter. Make sure that the metal portion of the pad is fully seated in the caliper recess and that the thinner pad is on the outer side.

4. Holding the outer pad in place, carefully slide the caliper into position. Align guide pin holes in adapter and pads.

5. Install guide pins through the bushings, caliper, adapter, both pads and the outer bushings.

6. Press in on the guide pins and thread the pins into adapter. Work carefully to avoid cross-threading the pins. Tighten pins to 25-35 ft.-lb. (35-48 N•m).

7. Install wheel/tire assemblies. Tighten lug nuts to 65 ft.-lb. (88 N•m). Install wheel covers and lower vehicle to the ground.

8. Depress the brake pedal several times to position the caliper and pads.

9. Check master cylinder fluid level and top up as needed with fresh DOT 3 brake fluid. Install reservoir cover(s) and check for leaks around caliper and hoses.

10. Check for firm pedal pressure. Road test the vehicle to make sure the brakes operate properly.

DISC BRAKE CALIPERS

Removal/Installation (All Models)

1. Mark the left and right caliper with chalk or quick-drying paint for correct reinstallation.

2. Remove the caliper as described under *Disc Brake Pads* in this chapter.

3. Disconnect the flexible brake hose at the tube connection. Remove the retaining clip

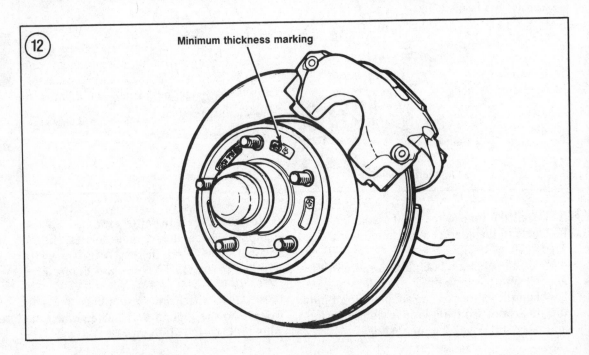

⑫ Minimum thickness marking

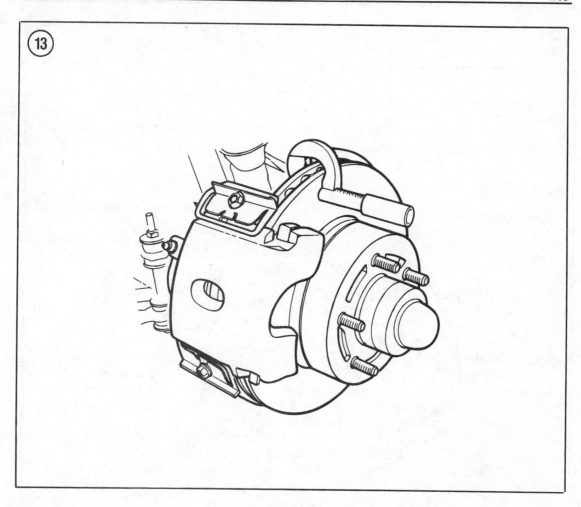

(13)

from the hose and bracket, then remove the hose from the bracket.

4. Unscrew the flexible hose at the caliper.

5. Installation is the reverse of removal. Bleed the brakes as described in this chapter.

BRAKE DISCS

Inspection

1. Remove the wheel covers and loosen the front wheel lug nuts.

2. Raise the front of the vehicle with a jack and place it on jackstands.

3. Remove the wheel/tire assemblies.

4. Check front wheel bearing adjustment as described in this chapter. Adjust if necessary.

5. Remove the caliper as described in this chapter, but do not disconnect the brake line. Suspend the caliper from the suspension with a length of wire to prevent stressing the line.

6. Inspect disc for deep scratches. Small marks are not important, but deep radial scratches reduce brake effectiveness and increase lining wear. If disc is deeply scratched, it can be turned on a lathe to smooth the surface.

NOTE
*Minimum disc thickness after refinishing must not be less than the number cast or stamped on the unmachined portion of the disc (**Figure 12**).*

7. Check thickness variation at 12 equally spaced points on the disc. Use a micrometer as shown in **Figure 13** and measure about one inch from the edge of the disc. If measurements vary by more than 0.0005 in., have the disc turned or replace it.

9

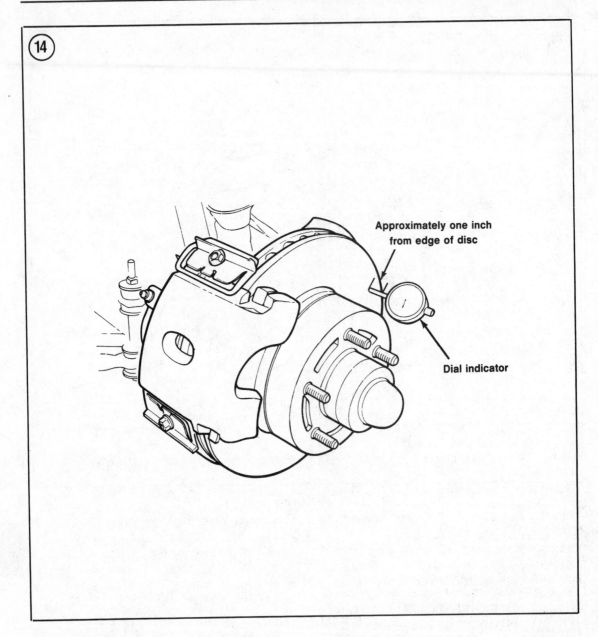

⑭

Approximately one inch from edge of disc

Dial indicator

8. Install a dial indicator to contact the disc's swept area (**Figure 14**). Rotate the disc one full turn and measure runout. Lateral runout must not exceed 0.025 in. for 1972 models or 0.004 in. for 1973 and later models. If runout exceeds this specification, have the disc turned or replace it.

Removal

1. Remove the wheel covers and loosen the front wheel lug nuts.

2. Raise the front of the car and place it on jackstands.

3. Remove the wheel/tire assemblies.

4. Remove the caliper as described in this chapter, but do not disconnect the brake line. Suspend the caliper from the suspension with a length of wire to prevent stressing the brake hose.

5. Remove the wheel bearing grease cap, cotter pin and nut lock.

6. Grasp the disc in both hands and pull it off the spindle far enough to loosen the wheel

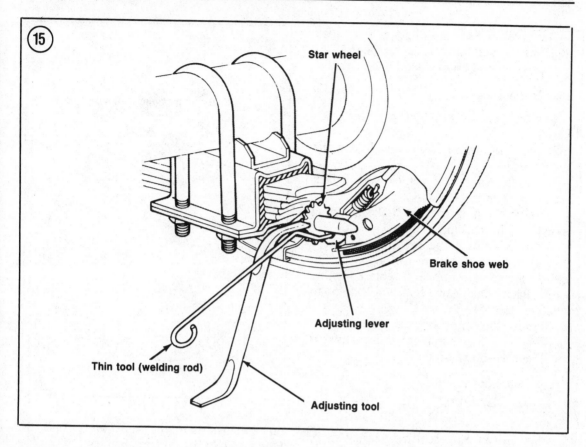

Star wheel

Brake shoe web

Adjusting lever

Thin tool (welding rod)

Adjusting tool

bearing thrust washer and outer wheel bearing.

7. Push disc back onto spindle. Remove thrust washer and outer wheel bearing.

8. Pull brake disc off spindle, together with inner wheel bearing and grease seal.

Installation

1. If a new disc is being installed, remove protective coating with carburetor degreaser. Install new wheel bearings as described in this chapter.

2. If original disc is being installed, pack wheel bearings with grease. The wheel bearing and grease seal must be in good condition. Keep braking surface of disc clean.

> *CAUTION*
> *Keep disc centered on spindle to prevent damage to grease seal or spindle threads.*

3. Install outer wheel bearing and washer. Install wheel bearing adjusting nut and tighten finger-tight. Make sure disc rotates freely.

4. Install caliper as described in this chapter.

5. Adjust wheel bearings as described in this chapter.

6. Install wheel/tire assemblies. Lower vehicle to the ground and tighten lug nuts. Install the wheel covers.

DRUM BRAKES

Front Drum Removal

1. Set the parking brake and block the rear wheels.

2. Remove the wheel covers and loosen the front wheel lug nuts.

3. Raise the front of the vehicle with a jack and place it on jackstands.

4. Remove the plug from the brake adjusting access hole in the support plate.

5. Insert a welding rod or other thin tool into the access hole and disengage adjusting lever from adjusting screw. Back off adjusting screw with a brake adjusting tool. See **Figure 15**.

9

6. Remove grease cap, cotter pin, lock adjusting nut and outer wheel bearing.
7. Pull wheel and drum assembly off spindle.

Rear Drum Removal

1. Set the parking brake. Block the front wheels.
2. Remove the wheel covers and loosen the rear wheel lug nuts.
3. Raise the rear of the vehicle with a jack and place it on jackstands.
4. Remove the plug from the brake adjusting access hole in the support plate.
5. Insert a welding rod or other thin tool through the access hole in the support plate and disengage adjusting lever from adjusting screw. Back off adjusting screws with a brake adjusting tool. See **Figure 15**.
6. Remove the wheel/tire assemblies.
7. Remove 3 Tinnerman retaining clips (if used) and the brake drum.

Drum Inspection

1. Clean drum with solvent before inspection.
2. Check drum for scoring, excessive or uneven wear, corrosion or glazed heat spots. Minor scratches can be removed with fine emery paper. If heat spots (blue-tinted areas) are visible, drum must be replaced.
3. Use a micrometer to measure drum for wear and out-of-roundness or have a dealer or machinist make the measurements. Maximum out-of-roundness is 0.002 in. If drum is out-of-round, scored or worn, have it turned on a lathe.

NOTE
If the maximum inside braking surface diameter shown on the brake drum is exceeded by wear or refinishing, replace the drum. See Figure 16.

Brake Shoe Removal

Brake linings worn to within 1/32 in. of a rivet (on a riveted lining) or the shoe (on a bonded lining) must be replaced. Brake linings contaminated by grease, oil or brake fluid must also be replaced. Replace linings

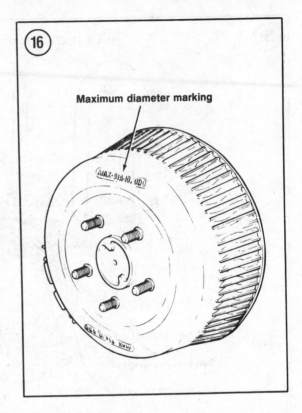

(16)

Maximum diameter marking

on both wheels at the same time. Refer to **Figures 17-20** for this procedure.

WARNING
Do not clean brake assembly with compressed air. Brake linings contain asbestos and the dust can be hazardous to your health. Clean assembly with a vacuum cleaner or use an old paint brush and wear a painter's mask over your nose and mouth.

1. Remove secondary brake shoe return spring, then remove primary return spring. Remove adjuster cable eye from anchor and detach from adjusting lever. See **Figure 21**.
2. Remove cable, overload spring, cable guide and anchor plate.
3. Remove adjusting lever from spring (slide forward to clear pivot and work from under spring), then remove spring from pivot. Remove adjuster spring from primary and secondary shoe webs (11-in. brake only).
4. Remove shoe retainers, springs and nails. See **Figure 22**.
5. On rear brakes, spread the anchor ends of the shoes and remove the parking brake lever

⑰   **NINE INCH BRAKE ASSEMBLIES**

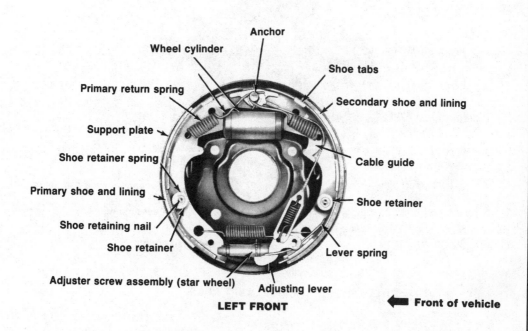

Anchor

Wheel cylinder

Shoe tabs

Primary return spring

Secondary shoe and lining

Support plate

Shoe retainer spring

Cable guide

Primary shoe and lining

Shoe retainer

Shoe retaining nail

Shoe retainer

Lever spring

Adjuster screw assembly (star wheel)

Adjusting lever

LEFT FRONT   ◄ **Front of vehicle**

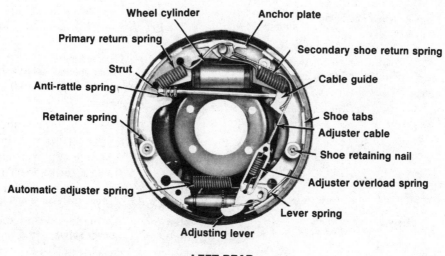

Wheel cylinder

Anchor plate

Primary return spring

Secondary shoe return spring

Strut

Anti-rattle spring

Cable guide

Retainer spring

Shoe tabs

Adjuster cable

Shoe retaining nail

Automatic adjuster spring

Adjuster overload spring

Lever spring

Adjusting lever

LEFT REAR

◄ **Front of vehicle**

9

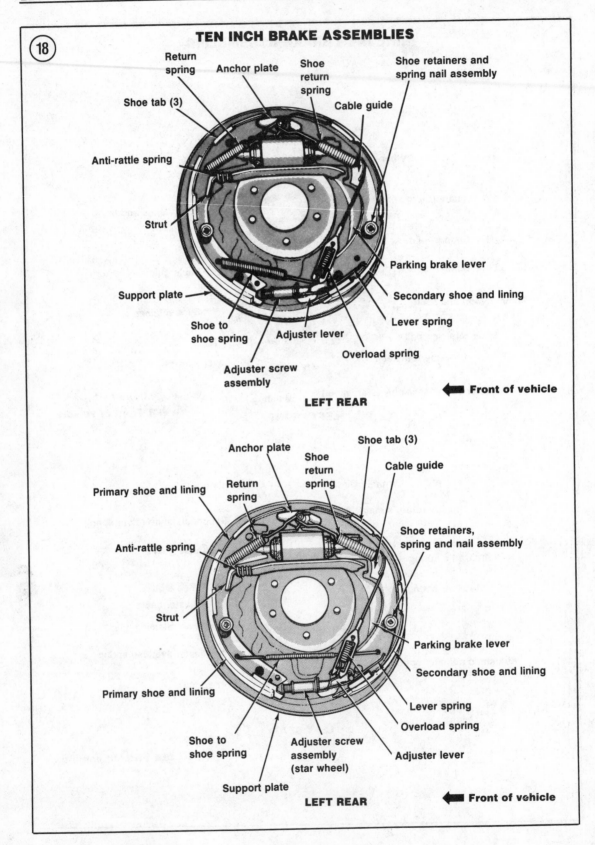

TEN INCH BRAKE ASSEMBLIES

⑱

Return spring

Anchor plate

Shoe return spring

Shoe retainers and spring nail assembly

Shoe tab (3)

Cable guide

Anti-rattle spring

Strut

Support plate

Shoe to shoe spring

Adjuster lever

Adjuster screw assembly

Overload spring

Parking brake lever

Secondary shoe and lining

Lever spring

◀ Front of vehicle

LEFT REAR

Anchor plate

Shoe return spring

Shoe tab (3)

Cable guide

Primary shoe and lining

Return spring

Anti-rattle spring

Strut

Shoe retainers, spring and nail assembly

Primary shoe and lining

Shoe to shoe spring

Adjuster screw assembly (star wheel)

Adjuster lever

Parking brake lever

Secondary shoe and lining

Lever spring

Overload spring

Support plate

◀ Front of vehicle

LEFT REAR

(19) ELEVEN INCH BRAKE ASSEMBLIES

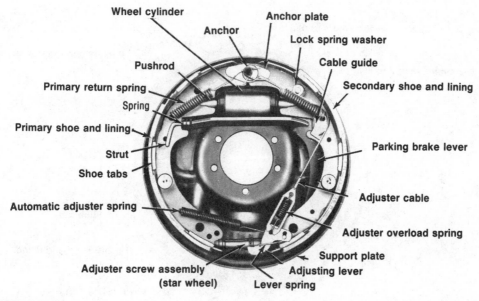

Wheel cylinder
Anchor
Anchor plate
Lock spring washer
Cable guide
Pushrod
Primary return spring
Spring
Secondary shoe and lining
Primary shoe and lining
Strut
Shoe tabs
Parking brake lever
Automatic adjuster spring
Adjuster cable
Adjuster overload spring
Support plate
Adjusting lever
Adjuster screw assembly (star wheel)
Lever spring

LEFT REAR

◀ **Front of vehicle**

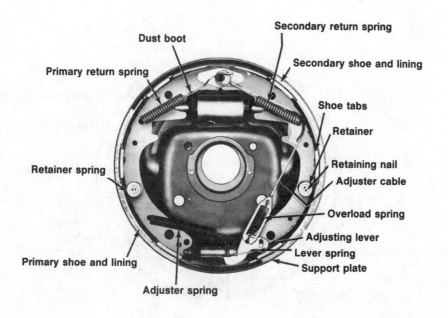

Dust boot
Secondary return spring
Secondary shoe and lining
Primary return spring
Shoe tabs
Retainer
Retaining nail
Retainer spring
Adjuster cable
Overload spring
Adjusting lever
Lever spring
Primary shoe and lining
Support plate
Adjuster spring

LEFT FRONT

◀ **Front of vehicle**

9

20 **ELEVEN INCH BRAKE ASSEMBLIES**
(WITHOUT AUTOMATIC ADJUSTERS)

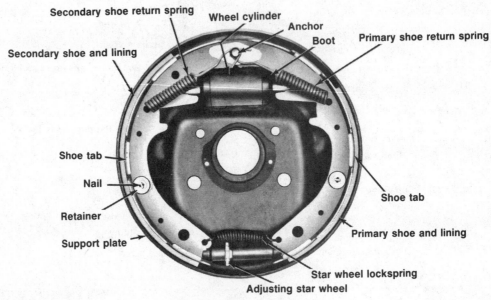

Secondary shoe return spring
Wheel cylinder
Anchor
Boot
Primary shoe return spring
Secondary shoe and lining
Shoe tab
Nail
Retainer
Support plate
Shoe tab
Primary shoe and lining
Star wheel lockspring
Adjusting star wheel

Right front ▶ **POLICE AND HEAVY DUTY**

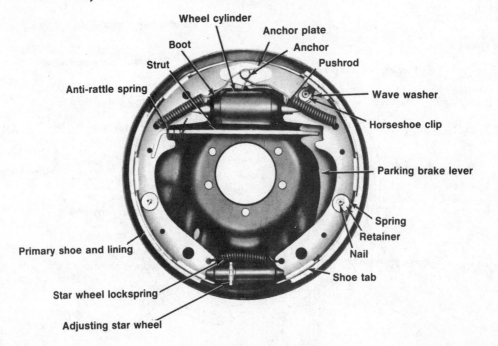

Wheel cylinder
Anchor plate
Boot
Anchor
Strut
Pushrod
Anti-rattle spring
Wave washer
Horseshoe clip
Parking brake lever
Spring
Retainer
Nail
Primary shoe and lining
Shoe tab
Star wheel lockspring
Adjusting star wheel

POLICE AND HEAVY DUTY **◀ Left rear**

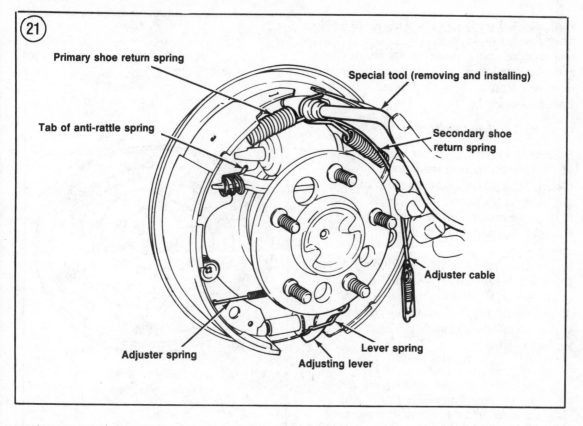

21

Primary shoe return spring

Special tool (removing and installing)

Tab of anti-rattle spring

Secondary shoe return spring

Adjuster cable

Adjuster spring

Lever spring

Adjusting lever

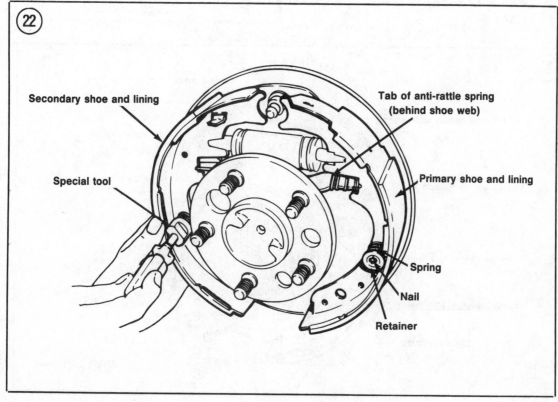

22

Secondary shoe and lining

Tab of anti-rattle spring (behind shoe web)

Special tool

Primary shoe and lining

Spring

Nail

Retainer

9

strut and anti-rattle spring. Disengage cable from parking brake lever.

6. Disengage both brake shoes from wheel cylinder pushrods (if so equipped) and remove from support plate. Remove starwheel assembly.

Front Brake Shoe Installation

Refer to **Figures 17-20** for this procedure.

1. Clean brake shoe contact areas on support plate (**Figure 23**) with crocus cloth to remove all rust. Lubricate these areas with a high-temperature brake grease such as Chrysler Support Plate Lubricant, part No. 2932524.

2. Position primary and secondary brake shoes in their relative positions on a clean work surface.

3. Install the adjuster assembly between the shoes with the starwheel next to the secondary shoe.

NOTE
The starwheel adjusting stud end for the left brake is stamped "L." The starwheel for the right side is stamped "R" on some models and not identified on others.

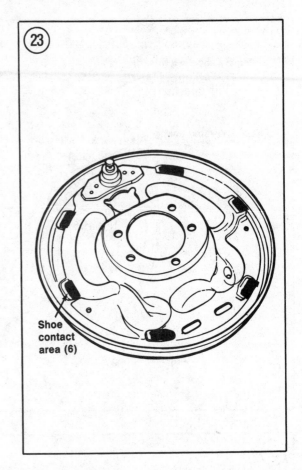

Shoe contact area (6)

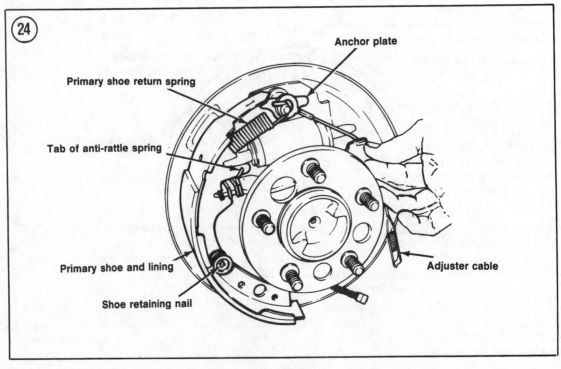

Primary shoe return spring

Anchor plate

Tab of anti-rattle spring

Primary shoe and lining

Shoe retaining nail

Adjuster cable

4. Install adjuster spring between primary and secondary shoes. Then install adjusting lever spring over pivot pin on secondary shoe web. Install adjusting lever under spring and over pivot pin, sliding it slightly to the rear to lock it in place.

5. Spread anchor ends of brake shoes to hold starwheel assembly in place and position assembly on support plate. At the same time, engage shoe webs with pushrods, if so equipped.

6. Install shoe retaining nails, springs and retainers.

7. Place eye of adjusting cable over anchor pin against anchor plate. Then install primary shoe return spring between shoe web and anchor.

8. Install cable guide in secondary shoe web. Hold guide in position and connect return spring between secondary shoe web and anchor.

NOTE

Make sure cable guide stays flat against secondary web and that secondary return spring overlaps primary return spring. Also make sure spring end loops around anchor are parallel. Squeeze with pliers, if necessary.

9. Install adjuster cable over guide. Hook end of overload spring in lever. Make sure cable eye is pulled tight against anchor and in a straight line with guide.

Rear Brake Shoe Installation

Refer to **Figures 17-20** for this procedure.

1. Before installing rear brake shoes, lubricate parking brake lever pivot point. Assemble lever to secondary shoe and secure with spring washer and retaining clip.

2. Apply a light coat of high-temperature grease at the shoe contact areas on the support plate shown in **Figure 23**.

3. Install cable in parking brake lever and slide secondary shoe against support plate. At the same time, engage shoe web with pushrod, if so equipped. Shoe web should rest against the anchor.

4. Insert the parking brake strut behind hub and in slot in parking brake lever. Place anti-rattle spring over other end of strut. See **Figure 24**.

NOTE

On 10-in. brakes, spring tab must point to upper rear on outside of shoe web on left brake. On right brake, it must point to lower front behind web. On 11-in. brakes, spring tab must point to lower front on outside of web on left side. On right side, it must point to lower front behind web.

5. Slide primary shoe into position. Engage with pushrod, if so equipped, and with free end of parking brake strut and spring.

6. Place anchor plate over anchor and install eye of adjuster cable over anchor.

7. Install primary shoe return spring between shoe web and anchor. Hold cable guide in position on secondary shoe web and install secondary return spring between shoe web and anchor, through cable guide.

NOTE

Make certain cable guide remains flat against web and that secondary return spring end loop overlaps primary return spring. If necessary, squeeze spring end loops with pliers (around anchor) to ensure that they are parallel.

8. Install adjuster assembly with starwheel next to secondary shoe.

NOTE

Left starwheel stud is stamped with an "L." The right one may or may not be stamped with an "R."

9. Install adjuster spring (11-in. brakes) between primary and secondary shoe webs.

10. Install adjusting lever spring over pivot pin on shoe web. Install adjusting lever under spring and over pivot pin. Lock in place by sliding lever slightly to the rear.

11. Install shoe retaining nails, springs and retainers.

12. Install adjuster cable over guide and hook end of overload spring in lever. Cable eye must be pulled tight against anchor and in a straight line with the guide.

9

Drum Installation (Front)

1. If a new drum is to be installed, remove protective coating with carburetor degreaser. Install new wheel bearings and grease retainer. Soak new grease retainer in light engine oil for at least 30 minutes before installation.

2. If original drum is used, be sure grease in its hub is clean and adequate. Pack the wheel bearings with grease. Install the inner bearing cone and roller assembly in the inner cup and install a new grease retainer.

3. Install the drum assembly, outer wheel bearing, washer and adjusting nut.

4. Adjust wheel bearing as described in this chapter. Install nut lock, cotter pin and grease cap.

5. Install wheel/tire assembly. Tighten lug nuts. Install wheel covers. Adjust brakes as described in this chapter.

Drum Installation (Rear)

1. If a new drum is to be installed, remove protective coating with carburetor degreaser.

2. Place drum over brake assembly and into place. Install Tinnerman retaining clips (if used).

3. Install wheel/tire assembly on axle shaft flange studs against drum. Tighten lug nuts. Install wheel covers.

4. Adjust brakes as described in this chapter.

WHEEL CYLINDERS

Whenever the brake drums are removed, inspect the cylinders for signs of leakage. Check boots for cuts, tears and heat damage (**Figure 25**). If any of these conditions are found, rebuild or replace the wheel cylinder as required.

Removal/Installation

1. Remove brake drums and shoes as described in this chapter.

CAUTION
In the following steps, do not bend rear brake line away from wheel cylinder after unscrewing the nut. Bending the brake line will make it difficult to reconnect and may cause it to crack. The wheel cylinder will separate from brake line when it is lifted out.

2A. On front wheel cylinders:
    a. Loosen tube fitting that connects brake hose to bracket on frame.
    b. Unscrew brake hose from wheel cylinder and lay hose aside.

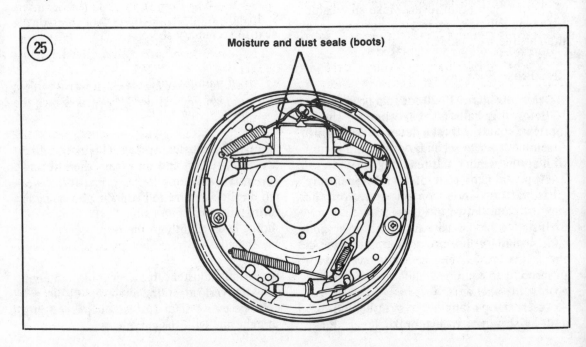

㉕ Moisture and dust seals (boots)

c. After detaching hose, remove 2 attaching bolts holding wheel cylinder to support plate.

d. Lift cylinder from support plate.

2B. On rear wheel cylinders:

a. Unscrew brake line nut from wheel cylinder.

b. Remove 2 bolts holding wheel cylinder to support plate.

c. Lift cylinder from support plate.

3. Installation is the reverse of removal. Wipe ends of brake lines and hoses clean before reconnecting. Tighten wheel cylinder installation bolts on 9 in. brakes to 110 in.-lb. (12 N•m); tighten all others to 220 in.-lb. (23 N•m). Bleed brakes and center the pressure differential valve as described in this chapter.

Overhaul

Wheel cylinders must be removed from the support plate for overhaul.

1. Remove rubber boot from each end of cylinder. Discard boots.

2. Remove pushrods, if so equipped.

3. Press inward on one piston. Remove the other piston/cup, cup expanders (if used), spring and the cup/piston you depressed.

4. Remove bleeder screw from cylinder.

5. Thoroughly clean all parts with clean brake fluid, then blow dry with compressed air.

6. Inspect pistons. Replace if scored, worn, corroded or otherwise damaged.

7. Check cylinder bore for scoring, corrosion, rust or wear. If any of these conditions are present and the bore cannot be cleaned with crocus cloth, replace the cylinder.

8. Make sure bleeder screw hole is clear. Install and tighten bleeder screw.

9. Coat cylinder bore, spring, pistons and new piston cups with clean brake fluid.

10. Insert spring (with expanders, if used) in cylinder. Install piston cups with their open end facing each other.

11. Install pistons in each end of cylinder with recessed ends facing open ends of cylinder.

12. Fit a boot over each end of the cylinder. Press down on the boot until it is fully seated against the cylinder shoulder.

13. Install pushrods, if usee.

BRAKE ADJUSTMENT

Disc Brakes

Disc brakes are automatically self-adjusting. No adjustment procedure is necessary or provided.

Drum Brakes

Drum brakes are self-adjusting during normal driving. Manual adjustment is only necessary after brakes have been serviced. This procedure is the same for front and rear brakes.

1. Raise the wheels off the floor and place the car on jackstands.

NOTE
Brake drums should be at normal room temperature when adjusting brake shoes. If shoes are adjusted when drums are hot and expanded, they may drag when the drums cool and contract.

CAUTION
Be careful not to damage adjusting screw notches in Step 2 and Step 3 or the self-adjusting mechanism will not function properly.

2. Remove adjusting hole plug from support plate. Working from support plate side, insert a welding rod or other thin tool through the adjusting hole (**Figure 26**). Push the self-adjuster lever away from the adjusting wheel.

3. Turn the adjusting wheel upward with a brake adjusting tool until the brakes lock the drum.

4. Back off the adjusting wheel until the brake drum can be turned with only a slight drag. Continue backing wheel off until brake drum turns freely.

5. Repeat the procedure on the opposite wheel.

Parking Brake

The parking brake should be adjusted after the service brake has been adjusted to prevent possible drag.

9

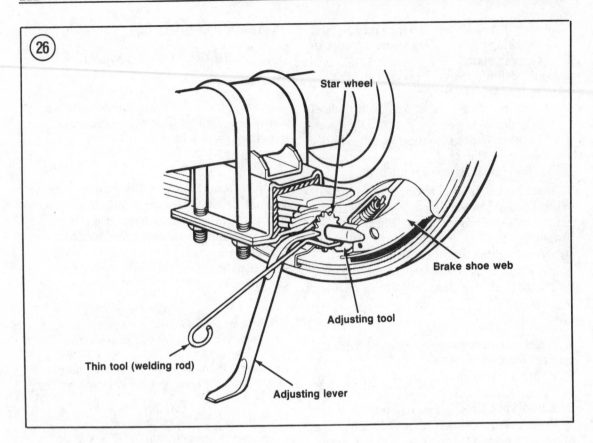

26

Star wheel

Brake shoe web

Adjusting tool

Thin tool (welding rod)

Adjusting lever

1. Fully release parking brake.

2. Block the front wheels and place transmission in NEUTRAL.

3. Raise the rear of the vehicle with a jack and place it on jackstands.

4. Locate the cable adjuster under the vehicle. Clean and lubricate the adjuster threads.

5. Back off the cable adjustment nut until there is slack in the cable. **Figure 27** shows a typical cable adjuster.

6. If service brakes have just been adjusted, proceed to Step 7. If they have not been adjusted, adjust them as described in this chapter.

7. Rotate rear wheels by hand while tightening cable adjustment nut until there is a slight drag on the wheels. Back off the nut another 2 full turns.

8. Apply and release the parking brake several times to make sure the rear wheels will turn freely without drag. If they do not, repeat Step 7.

9. Lower vehicle to the ground.

MASTER CYLINDER

Two master cylinder designs have been used on Chrysler Corp. passenger cars. The cast iron housing is used on 1972-1977 and some 1978 models. The aluminum housing was introduced on some 1978 models and is used on all 1979 and later vehicles.

Removal/Installation (Manual Brakes)

NOTE
Brake fluid will damage paint. Place rags beneath master cylinder. If any fluid spills onto a painted surface, wipe it off and wash with soapy water.

1. Disconnect the primary and secondary brake tubes from the outlets in the side of the master cylinder. **Figure 28** shows the aluminum housing; the cast iron type is similar. Plug the outlets.

2. Disconnect stoplight switch mounting bracket under the instrument panel and let it hang out of the way.

3. Pull the brake pedal backward with sufficient pressure to disengage the pushrod from the master cylinder piston.

NOTE
The pushrod retention grommet will be destroyed when the pushrod is disengaged. Install a new grommet when the master cylinder is reinstalled.

4. Remove the nuts holding the master cylinder to the cowl panel. Pull the assembly straight forward and remove it. Clean any retention grommet residue from the pushrod groove and piston socket.
5. Install a new retention grommet on the pushrod.
6. Fit the master cylinder to the cowl panel and install the attaching nuts. Tighten nuts to 170-230 in.-lb. (20-26 N•m).
7. Attach brake tubes to master cylinder and tighten to 150 in.-lb. (18 N•m).
8. Working under the instrument panel, moisten the pushrod grommet with water. Align the pushrod with the master cylinder

piston and apply sufficient pressure with the brake pedal to seat the pushrod in the piston. Install the master cylinder boot.
9. Fill the master cylinder to recommended level with clean DOT 3 brake fluid. Bleed brakes and center the pressure differential valve as described in this chapter. Depress brake pedal several times, then check master cylinder for brake fluid leaks.

Power Brakes

NOTE
Brake fluid will damage paint. Place rags beneath master cylinder. If any fluid spills onto a painted surface, wipe it off and wash with soapy water.

1. Disconnect primary and secondary brake tubes from the outlets in the side of the master cylinder (**Figure 28**). Plug the master cylinder outlets.
2. Remove nuts holding master cylinder to power brake booster.
3. Remove master cylinder.
4. Installation is the reverse of removal. Tighten master cylinder retaining nuts to 170-230 in.-lb. (20-26 N•m) and brake tube fittings to 150 in.-lb. (18 N•m). Fill master cylinder reservoirs to recommended level with clean DOT 3 brake fluid. Bleed brakes and center the pressure differential valve as described in this chapter. Depress brake pedal several times, then check master cylinder for brake fluid leaks.

Disassembly

Refer to **Figure 29** (cast iron cylinder) or **Figure 30** (aluminum cylinder) for this procedure.
1. Clean outside of master cylinder thoroughly.
2A. On cast iron cylinder, remove cover and gasket. Discard brake fluid. Clamp cylinder by a flange in a vise equipped with protective jaws.
2B. On aluminum cylinder, empty the fluid from the reservoir. Clamp cylinder in a vise equipped with protective jaws. Pull reservoir off while rocking it from side to side. See **Figure 31**. Remove the reservoir grommets.

9

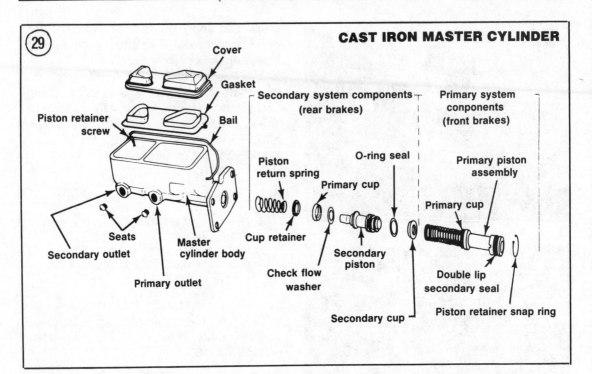

CAST IRON MASTER CYLINDER

(29)

Cover

Gasket

Bail

Piston retainer screw

Piston return spring

Primary cup

O-ring seal

Secondary system components (rear brakes)

Primary system conponents (front brakes)

Primary piston assembly

Primary cup

Cup retainer

Secondary piston

Check flow washer

Seats

Secondary outlet

Master cylinder body

Primary outlet

Secondary cup

Double lip secondary seal

Piston retainer snap ring

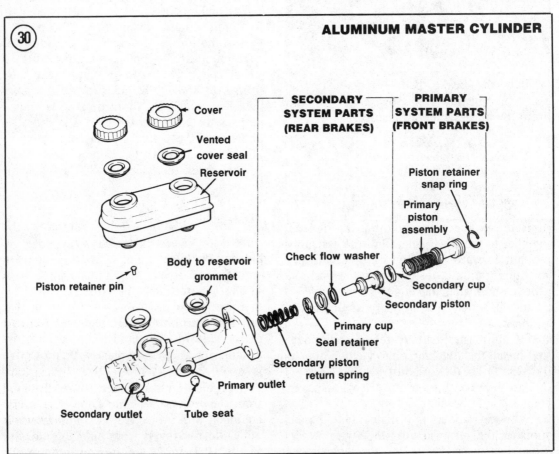

ALUMINUM MASTER CYLINDER

(30)

Cover

Vented cover seal

Reservoir

SECONDARY SYSTEM PARTS (REAR BRAKES)

PRIMARY SYSTEM PARTS (FRONT BRAKES)

Piston retainer snap ring

Primary piston assembly

Piston retainer pin

Body to reservoir grommet

Check flow washer

Secondary cup

Secondary piston

Primary cup

Seal retainer

Secondary piston return spring

Primary outlet

Secondary outlet

Tube seat

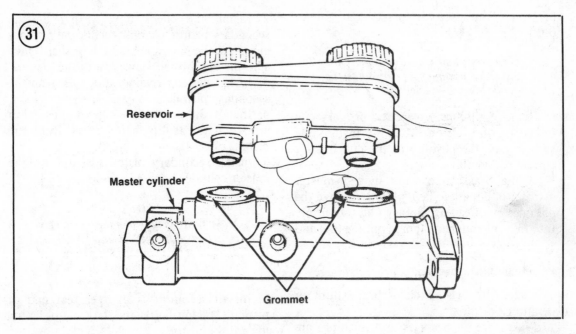

Reservoir →

Master cylinder

Grommet

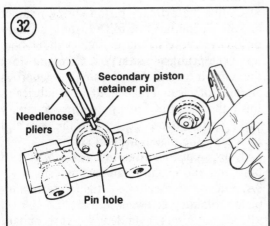

Secondary piston
retainer pin

Needlenose
pliers

Pin hole

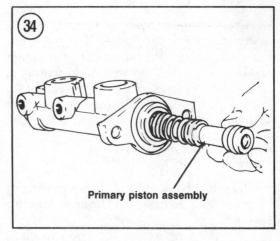

Primary piston assembly

9

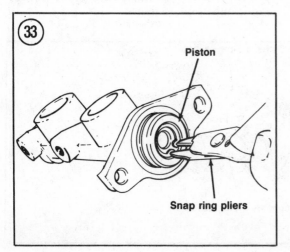

Piston

Snap ring pliers

3A. On cast iron cylinder, unscrew the secondary piston retaining screw.

3B. On aluminum cylinder, remove secondary piston retaining pin with needlenose pliers. See **Figure 32**.

4. Depress and hold primary piston in that position, then remove the snap ring from its groove (**Figure 33**).

5. Remove pushrod, if so equipped. Remove primary piston from master cylinder bore (**Figure 34**). Remove master cylinder from the vise and tap it on a bench to remove secondary piston. If secondary piston does not come out easily, cover end of master cylinder bore with a shop cloth and apply low

pressure compressed air to secondary outlet port.

NOTE
If compressed air is used to remove the secondary piston, new cups must be installed before reassembly.

6. Remove all cups, except the primary cup of the primary piston, from the pistons. Be sure to note the position of the cup lips for correct reassembly.

7. If the brass tube seats in the master cylinder outlet are to be replaced, remove the old ones by threading an Easy-Out tool firmly into the seat and then tapping out the tool and seat.

Cleaning and Inspection

1. Clean all parts in clean brake fluid or denatured alcohol.

2. Make sure all passages and openings are clear. Blow cylinder out with compressed air.

3. Check cylinder bore for scoring, pitting, corrosion or excessive wear. If any of these conditions are present in an aluminum cylinder, it must be replaced. Light scoring in a cast iron cylinder can be removed with a crocus cloth or by honing, provided the bore diameter is not increased by more than 0.002 in. (0.06 mm).

Assembly

Refer to **Figure 29** (cast iron cylinder) or **Figure 30** (aluminum cylinder) for this procedure.

1. Dip all parts except the body in clean brake fluid.

2. Install the check flow washer on the secondary piston. Carefully work the primary cup on to the piston behind the washer. Make sure the cup lip faces away from the piston.

3. Install the cup retainer and spring on the secondary piston.

4. Install the secondary cup in the piston groove with its lip facing away from the piston.

5. Install secondary piston assembly in the master cylinder bore (**Figure 35**).

NOTE
Make sure cup lips enter the bore evenly to avoid damage. Use a generous amount of clean brake fluid to lubricate the cups.

6. Install secondary cup over rear end of primary piston with the larger lip facing toward the piston.

7. Center the primary piston spring retainer on the secondary piston. Install primary piston assembly in the master cylinder bore up to the primary piston cup. Carefully work the cup into the bore, using a generous amount of clean brake fluid as a lubricant. Push the assembly in up to the secondary seal. Carefully work the lip into the bore and then push the piston in until seated.

8. Depress piston assembly with a wood or brass rod and install retaining snap ring.

9A. On cast iron cylinders, tighten secondary piston retaining screw.

9B. On aluminum cylinders, insert secondary piston retaining pin into housing and press or tap it until fully seated.

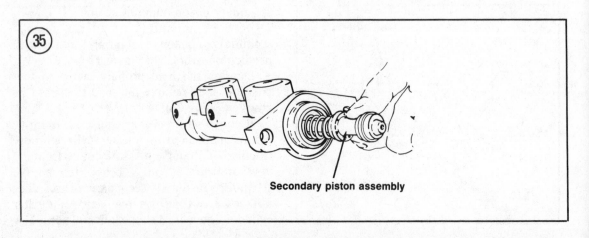

㉟

Secondary piston assembly

10. If tube seats were removed, install new ones by firmly pressing them into the master cylinder side outlets.

11. On aluminum cylinders, install new grommets as shown in **Figure 36**. Secure master cylinder in a vise equipped with protective jaws. Lubricate reservoir mating surfaces with clean brake fluid and press reservoir into grommets with a rocking motion until fully seated.

Bleeding

The master cylinder must be bled after an overhaul before reinstallation in the vehicle. Chrysler recommends the use of tool set part No. C-4029 for this procedure.

1. Mount the master cylinder in a vise equipped with protective jaws and install bleeding tubes. See **Figure 37**.

2. Fill both reservoirs with DOT 3 brake fluid. Use a wood or brass rod to slowly depress the primary cylinder. Allow the pistons to return under spring pressure. Repeat this step until all air bubbles have been expelled.

3. Remove bleeding tubes and plug master cylinder outlets to prevent further fluid spillage. Install reservoir caps and install the master cylinder in the vehicle.

BRAKE SYSTEM BLEEDING

The hydraulic system should be bled whenever air has had a chance to enter it or when braking effectiveness is reduced. If the pedal feels soft or if pedal travel increases considerably, bleeding is usually necessary. Bleeding is also necessary whenever a hydraulic line is disconnected.

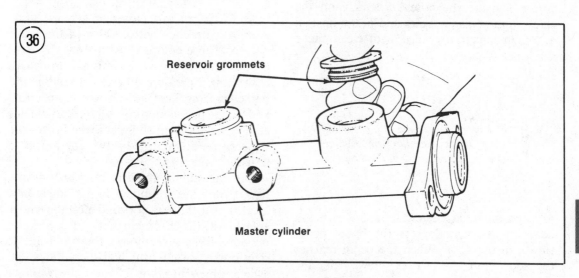

(36)

Reservoir grommets

Master cylinder

9

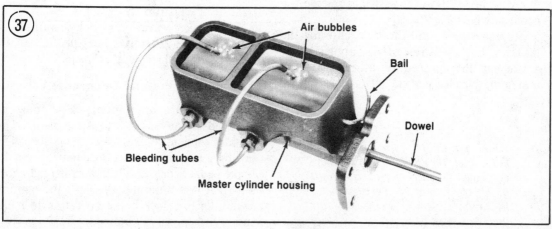

(37)

Air bubbles

Bail

Dowel

Bleeding tubes

Master cylinder housing

Because this procedure requires handling of brake fluid, be careful not to contaminate brake pads, shoes, discs or drums with fluid. Clean all dirt from bleeder screws before beginning. Two people are required to bleed the system—one to operate the brake pedal and the other to open and close the bleed valves.

Bleeding should be done in the following order: right rear, left rear, right front, left front.

1. Clean away all dirt around the master cylinder. Remove the cover(s) and top up reservoirs with clean DOT 3 brake fluid. Leave the top(s) off the reservoirs and cover with a clean shop cloth.

2. Fit an appropriate size box-end wrench over the bleeder screw at the right rear wheel.

3. Connect a rubber hose to the bleeder screw. Be sure the hose fits snugly on the screw. Submerge the other end of the hose in a container partially filled with clean brake fluid. See **Figure 38**.

> *CAUTION*
> *Do not allow the end of the hose to come out of the brake fluid during bleeding. This could allow air to enter the system and require that the bleeding procedure be done over.*

4. Open the bleeder screw about 3/4 turn and have an assistant depress the brake pedal slowly to the floor. When the pedal reaches the floor, close the bleeder screw. After the screw is closed, have the assistant release the pedal slowly.

5. Repeat Step 4 until the fluid entering the jar from the tube is free of air bubbles.

6. Repeat this procedure at each of the remaining bleeder screws.

> *NOTE*
> *Watch the master cylinder reservoir fluid level throughout the bleeding procedure. If either reservoir is allowed to empty, air will be sucked into the hydraulic system and the bleeding procedure must be repeated.*

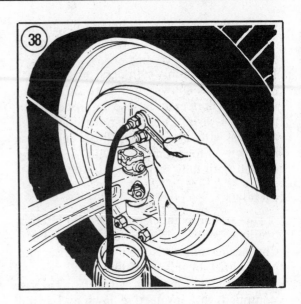

HYDRAULIC CONTROL VALVES

All Chrysler Corp. passenger cars use some type of hydraulic control valve in the brake system. Those equipped with front disc/rear drum brakes use a combination valve containing a pressure differential section and brake warning light switch with a metering and/or a proportioning section. Vehicles equipped with front and rear drum brakes use a pressure differential valve containing a brake warning light switch.

The pressure differential section/warning light switch are combined into a single unit located near the master cylinder on the fender splash shield or frame rail. If hydraulic pressure drops severely in either the front or rear brake system, the valve operates the switch which in turn activates the warning light on the instrument panel.

The brake warning switch assembly is replaceable if defective but the valves are serviced by replacement only.

Centering the Pressure Differential Valve

The pressure differential valve must be centered whenever the brakes are bled. To do so, turn the ignition switch to the ACC or ON position, but do not start the engine. Press the brake pedal firmly until the warning light goes out (if it was illuminated). Turn the ignition switch OFF. Check brake operation to make sure a firm pedal is obtained.

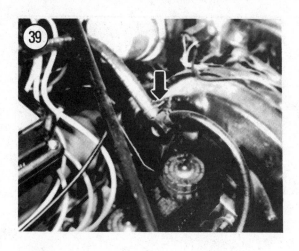

Testing

Brake warning switch

Turn the ignition key to the ON position but do not start the engine. Apply the parking brake. If the brake warning lamp on the instrument panel does not illuminate, check for a burned-out bulb, disconnected socket or a short/open circuit in the switch wiring. If none of these are found, replace the brake warning switch.

Metering valve

Have an assistant depress and release the brake pedal while you watch the metering valve stem. It should extend slightly when the pedal is depressed and retract when the pedal is released. If it does not, replace the combination valve.

Proportioning valve

A premature rear wheel slide when the brakes are applied indicates a malfunction in the proportion valve section of a combination valve. Have a dealer check brake line pressure at the valve and replace it if defective.

VACUUM BOOSTER

The vacuum booster uses intake manifold vacuum to reduce braking effort. It is serviced by replacement only.

Testing

1. Check the brake system for hydraulic leaks. Make sure the master cylinder reservoirs are filled to within 1/4 in. of the top.
2. Start the engine and let it idle for about 2 minutes, then shut it off. Place the transmission in NEUTRAL and set the parking brake.
3. Depress the brake pedal several times to exhaust any vacuum remaining in the system.
4. When the vacuum is exhausted, depress and hold the pedal with light foot pressure (15-25 lb.). Start the engine. If the pedal does not start to fall away under foot pressure (requiring less pressure to hold it in place), the vacuum booster unit is not working properly.
5. Disconnect the vacuum line at the booster. If vacuum can be felt at the line with the engine running, reconnect it and repeat Step 4. If the brake pedal does not move downward, perform Step 7.
6. Run the engine for at least 10 minutes at fast idle. Shut the engine off and let it stand for 10 minutes. Depress the brake pedal with about 20 lb. of force. If the pedal feel is not the same as it was with the engine running, perform Step 7.
7. If the booster is not working properly, check engine vacuum. Disconnect the vacuum hose from the booster check valve (**Figure 39**). Attach a vacuum gauge to the hose and run engine at idle speed. A reading of less than 14 in. Hg vacuum indicates engine problems. If the reading is greater than 14 in. Hg vacuum, the booster is defective.

Removal/Installation

Figure 40 shows a typical booster assembly installation with vacuum hose routing.
1. Disconnect the negative battery cable.
2. Remove the nuts holding the master cylinder to the vacuum booster. Carefully slide master cylinder off booster mounting studs and place to one side without disconnecting its hydraulic fittings.
3. Disconnect the manifold vacuum hose at the booster check valve.
4. Working underneath the instrument panel, place a small screwdriver between the center tang of the retaining clip and brake pedal pin. See **Figure 41**. Rotate screwdriver until center

9

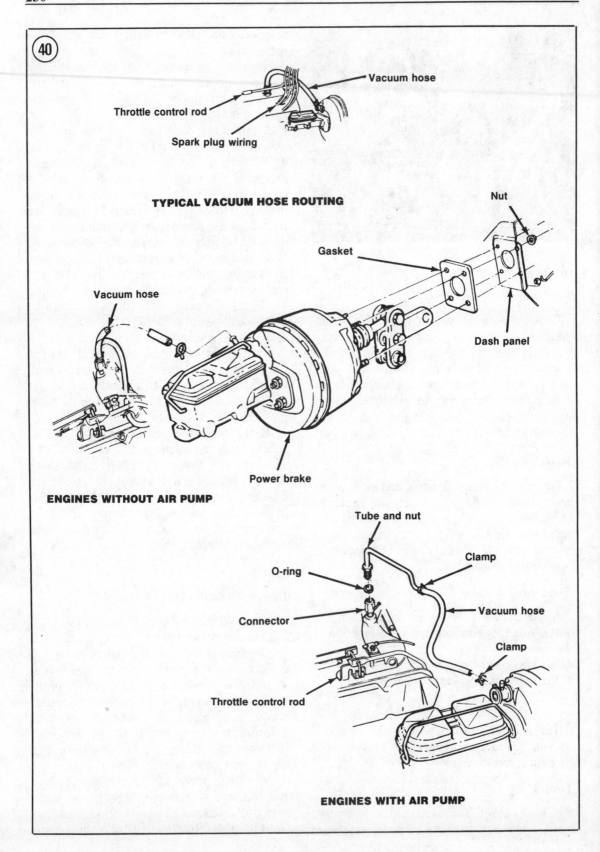

⁴⁰

Vacuum hose

Throttle control rod

Spark plug wiring

TYPICAL VACUUM HOSE ROUTING

Nut

Gasket

Vacuum hose

Dash panel

Power brake

ENGINES WITHOUT AIR PUMP

Tube and nut

O-ring

Clamp

Connector

Vacuum hose

Clamp

Throttle control rod

ENGINES WITH AIR PUMP

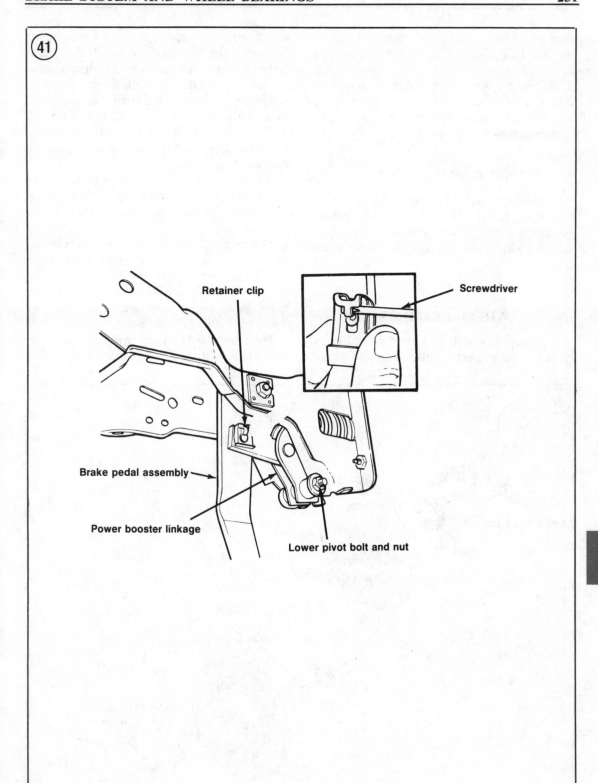

41

Retainer clip

Screwdriver

Brake pedal assembly

Power booster linkage

Lower pivot bolt and nut

9

tang of retaining clip passes over the end of the pin. Pull retainer clip off pin and discard it.

5. Remove lower pivot retaining bolt and nut. Remove the vacuum booster attaching nuts. Rotate linkage as required and remove vacuum booster from cowl panel.

NOTE
Save bushings and sleeve for reuse.

6. Installation is the reverse of removal. Lubricate pedal pin and bushings before installation. Use a new retainer clip. Road test the vehicle to make sure the brakes work properly.

WHEEL BEARINGS

Each front wheel and tire assembly is bolted to its respective front hub and brake drum (or disc brake rotor). Two opposed tapered roller bearings are installed in each hub. **Figure 42** shows a disc brake installation; drum brakes are similar. A grease retainer is installed at the inner end of the hub to prevent lubricant from leaking into the drum or onto the rotor. The entire assembly is retained on the spindle by the adjusting nut, nut lock and cotter pin.

Wheel bearings should be repacked with grease each time the brakes are relined. New wheel bearings must be installed when drums are replaced.

The rear brake drum assembly is retained to studs on the rear axle shaft flange by 3 Tinnerman retaining clips. The wheel and tire assembly mounts on the same rear axle shaft flange studs and is held against the hub and drum by the wheel lug nuts.

The rear wheel bearing is pressed onto the axle shaft just inside the shaft flange. The

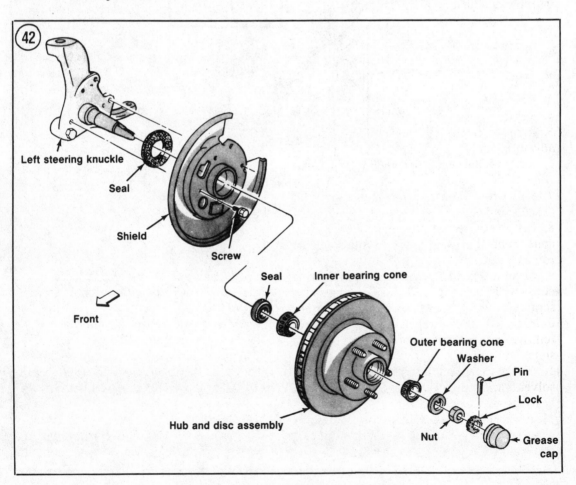

entire assembly is secured to the rear axle housing by the bearing retainer plate which is bolted to the housing flange. The inner end of each axle shaft is splined to the differential in the rear axle.

Bearing Service
(Drum Brake)

If bearing adjustment will not eliminate looseness or rough/noisy operation, the hub and bearings should be cleaned, inspected and repacked. If bearing cups or cone and roller assemblies are worn or damaged, they should be replaced.

1. Raise the vehicle with a jack and place it on jackstands.
2. Insert a narrow screwdriver through the brake adjusting hole at the inner side of the brake backing plate. Disengage adjusting lever from adjusting screw. Back off adjusting screw with brake adjusting tool.

CAUTION
Be careful not to damage adjusting screw notches or the self-adjusting mechanism will not function properly.

3. Remove wheel cover or hub cap.
4. Remove grease cap from hub.
5. Remove cotter pin, nut lock and bearing adjusting nut.
6. Remove thrust washer and outer bearing cone.
7. Pull wheel, hub and drum assembly off wheel spindle.
8. Remove inner oil seal and inner bearing cone from hub using a 3/4 in. non-metallic rod as a drift.
9. Clean lubricant off inner and outer bearing cups with solvent and inspect caps for scratches, pits, excessive wear and other damage. If cups are worn or damaged, remove with a drift positioned in the hub slots.
10. Clean inner and outer bearing cones with solvent and dry thoroughly. Do not spin bearings with compressed air.
11. Inspect cone and roller assemblies for wear or damage and replace if necessary. If cone and roller assemblies are replaced, new bearing cups should be installed.

12. Clean spindle and inside of hub with solvent. Cover spindle with a clean cloth and brush loose dust and dirt from brake assembly.
13. If inner and/or outer bearing cups were removed, install replacement cups in hub. Be sure to seat cups properly in hub.
14. Pack inside of hub with wheel bearing grease until grease is flush with inside diameter of both bearing cups.
15. Clean all old grease from bearings. Repack bearing cone and roller assemblies with wheel bearing grease. If a bearing packer is not available, work as much lubricant as possible between rollers and cages. Lubricate cone surfaces with grease.
16. Place inner bearing cone in the inner cup and install new oil seal with seal lip facing inward.
17. Install wheel, hub and drum assembly on wheel spindle. Keep hub centered on spindle to prevent damage to the grease retainer or spindle threads.
18. Install outer bearing cone and thrust washer on spindle, then install adjusting nut.
19. Adjust wheel bearings as described in this chapter and install a new cotter pin. Bend ends of cotter pin around the locknut to prevent interference with the radio static collector. Install grease cap.
20. If brake shoes were backed off to remove drum, adjust the brakes as described in this chapter.

Bearing Service
(Disc Brakes)

Refer to **Figure 42** for this procedure.
1. Raise the vehicle with a jack and place it on jackstands.
2. Remove wheel cover or hub cap.
3. Remove wheel/tire assembly.
4. Remove caliper as described in this chapter and suspend it from the suspension with a length of wire to prevent stressing the brake hose.
5. Remove grease cap from hub. Remove cotter pin, nut lock and adjusting nut from spindle. Remove thrust washer and outer bearing cone.

9

6. Pull hub and disc assembly off wheel spindle.

7. Remove inner oil seal and bearing cone from hub.

8. Clean lubricant from inner and outer bearing cups with solvent and inspect cups for scratches, pits, excessive wear and other damage. If cups are worn or damaged, remove with a drift.

9. Clean inner and outer bearing cones with solvent and dry thoroughly. Do not spin the bearings with compressed air.

10. Inspect cone and roller assemblies for wear or damage and replace if necessary. If cone and roller assemblies are replaced, new bearing cups should be installed.

11. Clean spindle and inside of brake disc with solvent. Cover spindle with a clean cloth and brush loose dust and dirt from brake assembly.

12. If inner and/or outer bearing cups were removed, install replacement cups in the brake disc. Be sure to seat cups properly in the disc.

13. Pack inside of the disc with wheel bearing grease until grease is flush with inside diameter of both bearing cups.

14. Clean old grease from bearings. Pack bearing cone and roller assemblies with clean wheel bearing grease. If a bearing packer is unavailable, work as much lubricant as possible between rollers and cages. Lubricate cone surfaces with grease.

15. Place inner bearing cone assembly in inner cup and install new oil seal. Make sure oil seal is properly seated.

16. Install hub and disc on wheel spindle. Keep disc centered on spindle to prevent damage to oil seal or spindle threads.

17. Install outer bearing cone and thrust washer on spindle, then install adjusting nut.

18. Adjust wheel bearing as described in this chapter and install a new cotter pin. Bend ends of cotter pin around locknut to prevent interference with radio static collector.

19. Install caliper as described in this chapter.

20. Install wheel/tire assembly. Install wheel cover or hub cap and lower vehicle to the ground. Pump the brake pedal several times to relocate the brake pads.

Bearing Adjustment

The front wheel bearing should be adjusted if the wheel is too loose on the spindle or if the wheel does not rotate freely.

1. Raise the vehicle with a jack and place it on jackstands.

2. Pry off wheel cover or hub cap and remove grease cap from hub.

3. Wipe excess grease from end of spindle. Remove cotter pin and nut lock. Discard cotter pin.

4. Loosen the adjusting nut 3 full turns. Rock the wheel, hub and disc/drum assembly back and forth several times to unseat the brake shoes.

5. Rotate the wheel, hub and disc/drum assembly while tightening the adjusting nut to 20-25 ft.-lb. (27-34 N•m) to seat the bearings.

6. Back off adjusting nut to completely release bearing preload.

7. Finger-tighten adjusting nut and then install the locknut with one pair of slots aligned with cotter pin hole. Install a new cotter pin and bend the ends around the nut lock castellations.

NOTE
This adjustment should result in no more than 0.003 in. of end play.

8. Check wheel rotation. If wheel rotates easily, install grease cap and hub cap or wheel cover. If wheel rotates roughly or noisily, clean or replace bearings and cups as necessary.

9. Pump the brake pedal several times to relocate the brake pads.

CHAPTER TEN

CLUTCH

Proper clutch adjustment on 1972-1980 models can add considerable length to the clutch's useful lifespan. No adjustment is provided for the clutch itself, but the clutch pedal linkage has an adjustable rod which is used to maintain clutch free play within specifications.

Models from 1981-on have a self-adjusting clutch linkage.

FREE PLAY ADJUSTMENT

Figures 1-9 show the various clutch pedal, torque shaft and linkage designs used on 1972-1980 Chrysler Corp. passenger cars. Refer to the appropriate illustration for your vehicle.

1. Set the parking brake and block the rear wheels.
2. Check the condition of the clutch pedal stop and install a new one if the old stop is worn or damaged.

3. Raise the front of the car with a jack and place it on jackstands.
4. Check the rubber insulator at the clutch fork. Replace it if damaged.

NOTE
If the adjusting nut is rusted or corroded, spray the nut and fork rod with a penetrating oil before attempting Step 5.

5. Position the insulator to rest lightly against the clutch fork. Turn self-locking adjusting nut until the washer is drawn up against the insulator. Linkage should now have about 5/32 in. of free play when the clutch pedal is depressed. This will provide about 1 in. of free play at the pedal.
6. If the adjusting nut does not turn freely, make sure the washer is not hanging up on the fork rod threads. Tap washer lightly to free it.

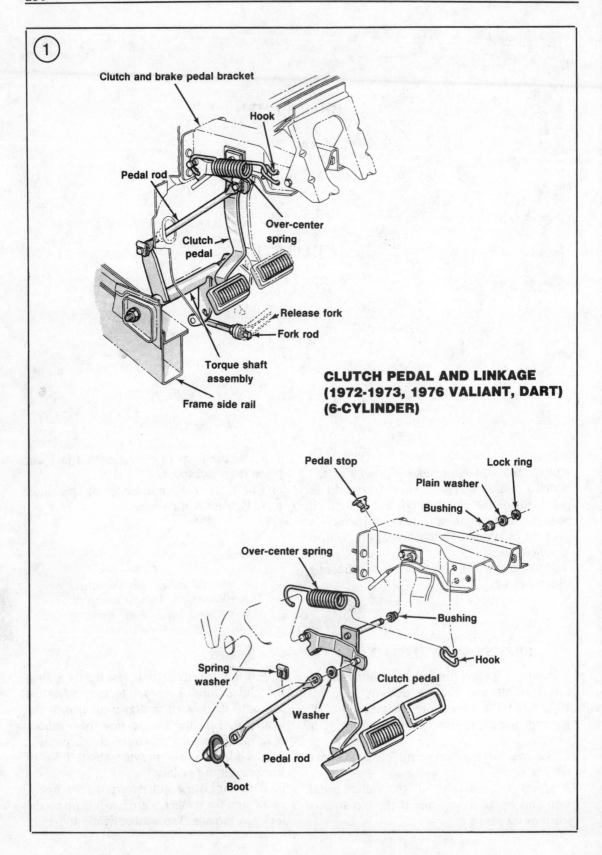

①

Clutch and brake pedal bracket

Hook

Pedal rod

Over-center spring

Clutch pedal

Release fork

Fork rod

Torque shaft assembly

Frame side rail

**CLUTCH PEDAL AND LINKAGE
(1972-1973, 1976 VALIANT, DART)
(6-CYLINDER)**

Pedal stop

Lock ring

Plain washer

Bushing

Over-center spring

Bushing

Spring washer

Hook

Clutch pedal

Washer

Pedal rod

Boot

(2)

CLUTCH PEDAL AND LINKAGE (1972-1975 VALIANT, DART) (V-8)

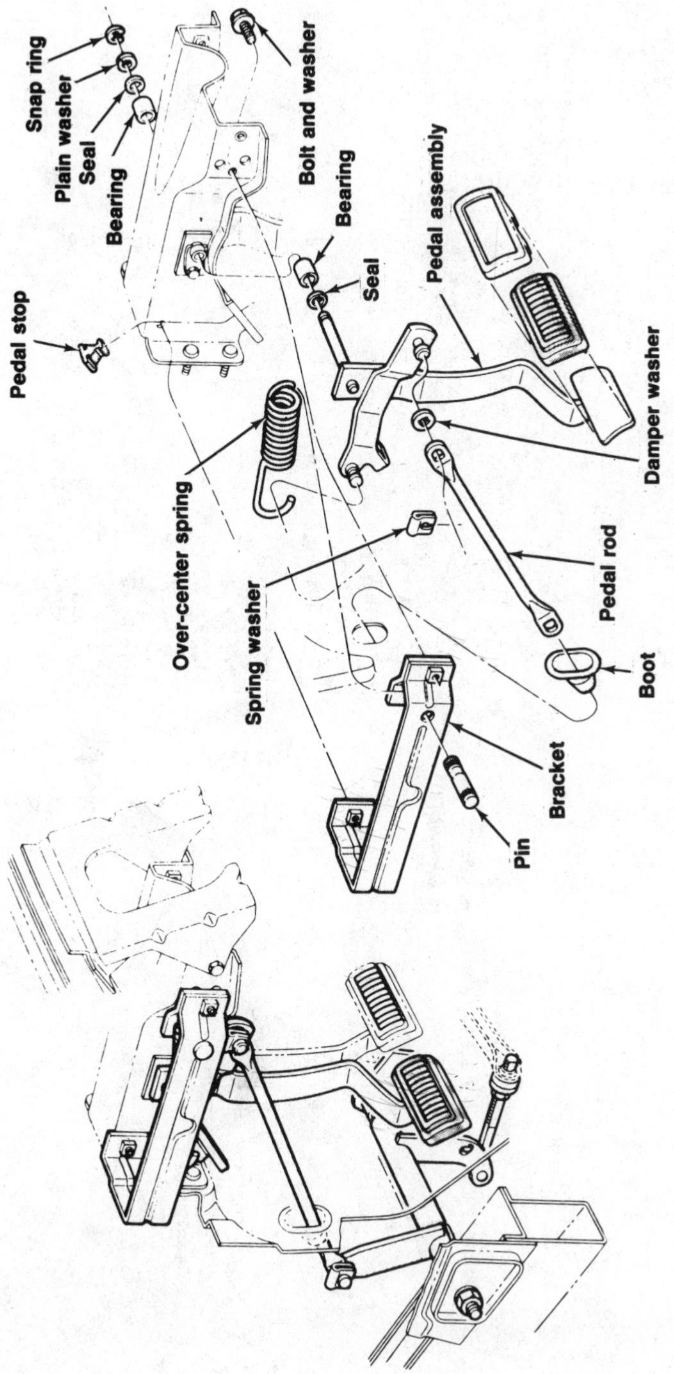

Snap ring

Plain washer

Seal

Bearing

Pedal stop

Bolt and washer

Bearing

Seal

Pedal assembly

Damper washer

Over-center spring

Spring washer

Pedal rod

Boot

Pin

Bracket

10

③

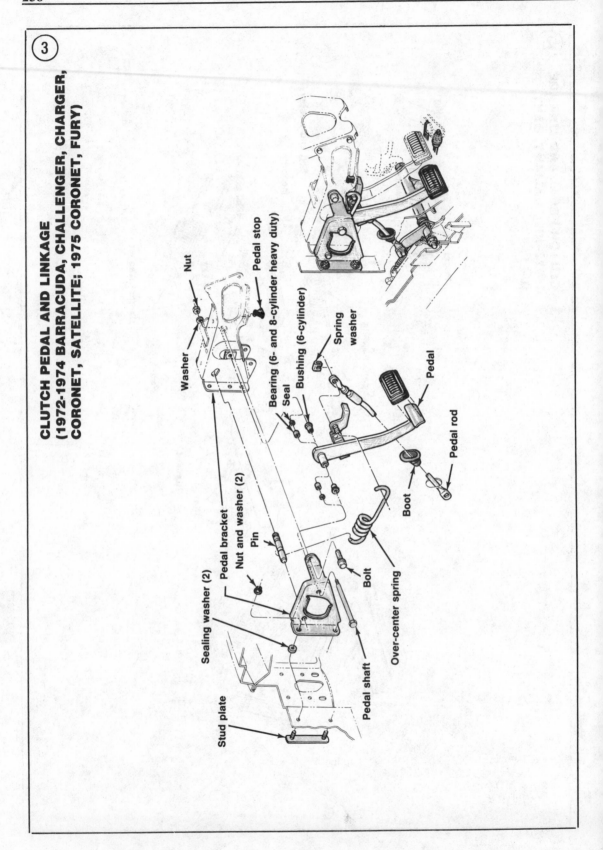

CLUTCH PEDAL AND LINKAGE
(1972-1974 BARRACUDA, CHALLENGER, CHARGER,
CORONET, SATELLITE; 1975 CORONET, FURY)

Nut

Washer

Pedal stop

Bearing (6- and 8-cylinder heavy duty)

Seal

Bushing (6-cylinder)

Spring washer

Pedal

Pedal rod

Boot

Over-center spring

Bolt

Pin

Nut and washer (2)

Pedal bracket

Sealing washer (2)

Pedal shaft

Stud plate

④ CLUTCH PEDAL AND LINKAGE (1976-1979 ASPEN, VOLARE)

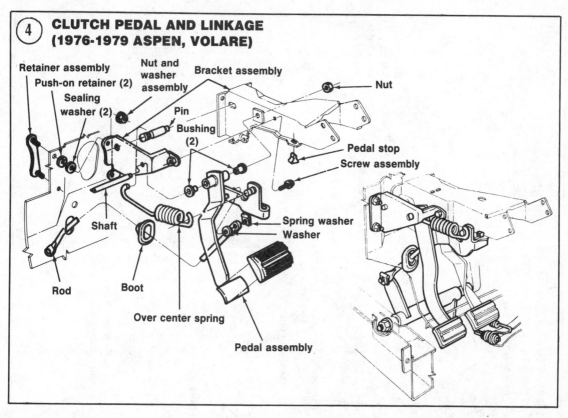

Retainer assembly
Push-on retainer (2)
Sealing washer (2)
Nut and washer assembly
Bracket assembly
Nut
Pin
Bushing (2)
Pedal stop
Screw assembly
Shaft
Spring washer
Washer
Rod
Boot
Over center spring
Pedal assembly

⑤ CLUTCH PEDAL AND LINKAGE (1976-1978 CORONET, FURY; 1977 DIPLOMAT, LEBARON)

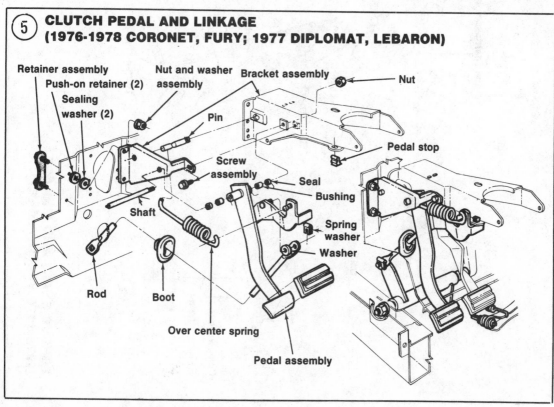

Retainer assembly
Push-on retainer (2)
Sealing washer (2)
Nut and washer assembly
Bracket assembly
Nut
Pin
Screw assembly
Pedal stop
Seal
Bushing
Shaft
Spring washer
Washer
Rod
Boot
Over center spring
Pedal assembly

10

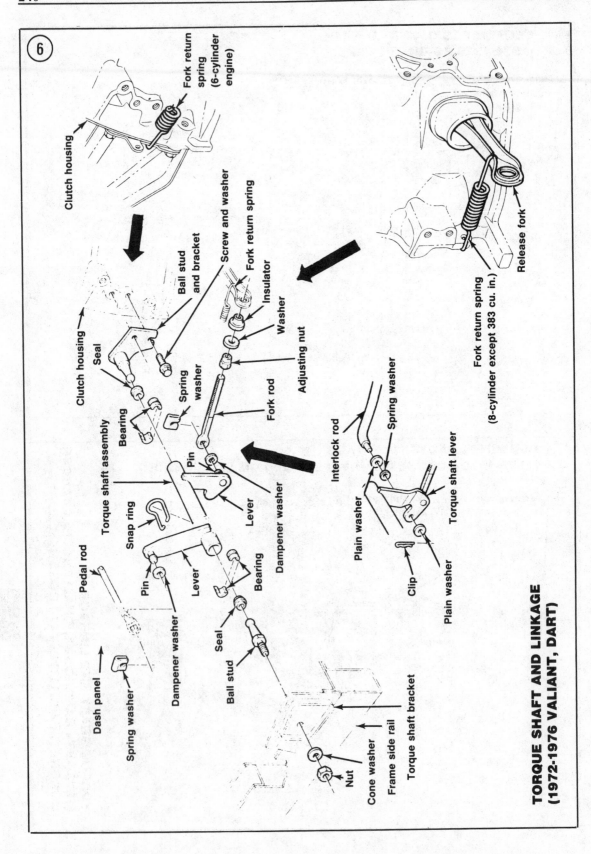

(6)

Fork return spring (6-cylinder engine)

Clutch housing

Clutch housing

Seal

Bearing

Clutch housing

Torque shaft assembly

Snap ring

Pedal rod

Pin

Lever

Dampener washer

Seal

Ball stud

Dash panel

Spring washer

Ball stud and bracket

Screw and washer

Fork return spring

Insulator

Washer

Adjusting nut

Spring washer

Fork rod

Pin

Lever

Dampener washer

Bearing

Interlock rod

Spring washer

Plain washer

Torque shaft lever

Clip

Plain washer

Release fork

Fork return spring (8-cylinder except 383 cu. in.)

Cone washer

Nut

Frame side rail

Torque shaft bracket

TORQUE SHAFT AND LINKAGE (1972-1976 VALIANT, DART)

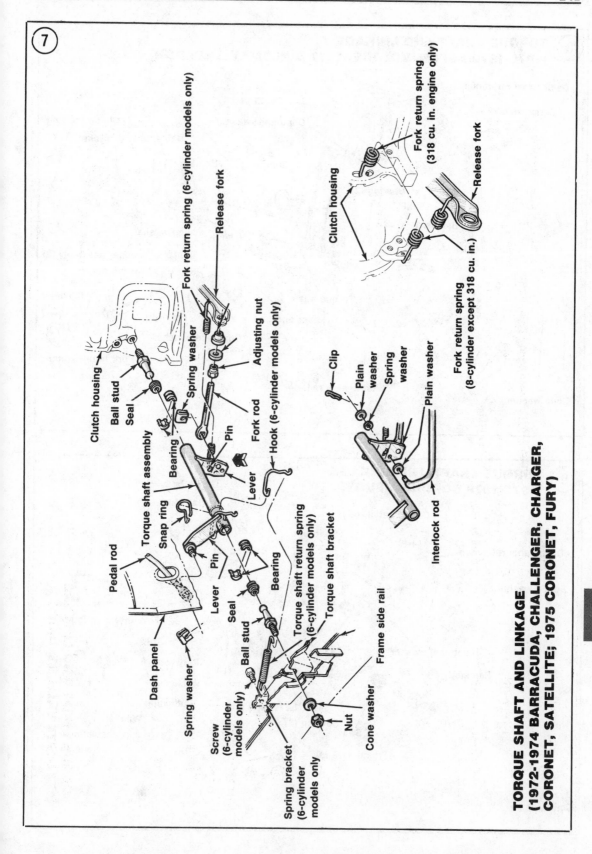

⑦

**TORQUE SHAFT AND LINKAGE
(1972-1974 BARRACUDA, CHALLENGER, CHARGER,
CORONET, SATELLITE; 1975 CORONET, FURY)**

10

⑧ TORQUE SHAFT AND LINKAGE
(1976-1979 ASPEN, VOLARE; 1977 DIPLOMAT, LEBARON)

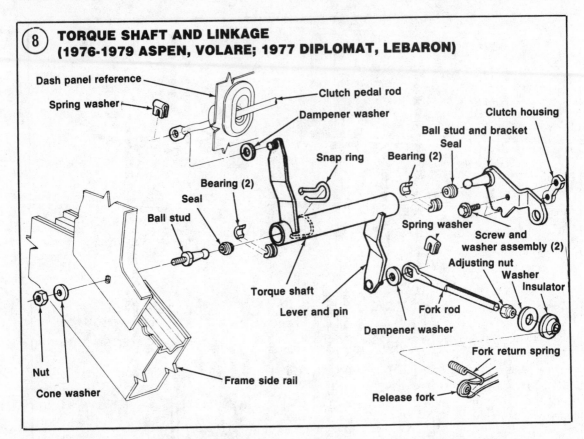

⑨ TORQUE SHAFT AND LINKAGE
(1976-1978 CORONET, FURY)

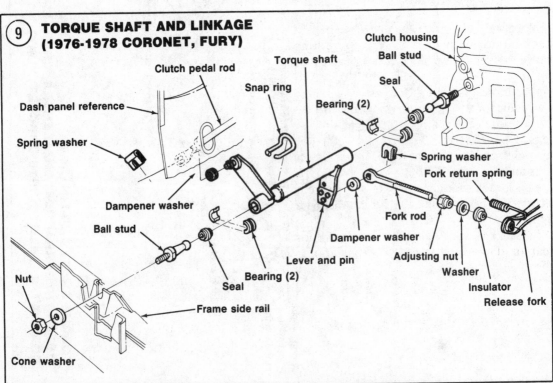

SHOCK ABSORBERS

Replacing shock absorbers is a relatively simple task. Although installation will vary slightly on different models, no special techniques or tools are required and the procedures in this chapter can be readily adapted to all models.

INSPECTION

1. To check the general condition of the shock absorbers, bounce the front, then the rear of the vehicle up and down several times and release. The car should not continue to bounce more than twice. Excessive bouncing is an indication of worn shock absorbers.
2. Raise the car on a hoist for the following steps if possible. If a hoist is not available, raise the car with a jack and place it on jackstands.
3. Check each shock absorber to make sure it is correctly installed and that all fasteners are tight.
4. Inspect the shock absorber insulators for wear or damage. Replace any that appear defective.

NOTE
If a defective insulator is an integral part of the shock absorber, replace the shock absorber.

5. Check the shock absorber for signs of fluid leakage. A light film of fluid is normal and does not mean the shock absorber should be replaced.
6. Disconnect the lower end of the shock absorber. Extend and compress the shock absorber as quickly as possible. Travel should be smooth on each stroke, with greater resistance on extension than on compression.
7. If the action of both front or rear shock absorbers is similar in Step 6, it is unlikely that either is defective. If one front or rear shock absorber is more erratic than the other, it is probably weak or defective.
8. Reconnect all shock absorbers.

FRONT SHOCK ABSORBERS

Refer to **Figures 1-5** for this procedure.

NOTE
On some models, you may have to remove the upper control arm bumper to provide enough clearance for shock absorber removal.

1. Loosen the front wheel lug nuts. Raise the front of the car with a jack and place it on jackstands. Remove the wheel/tire assembly.
2. Remove the nut, retainer or washer and bushing from the shock absorber upper end.
3. Remove nut from lower shock absorber attachment bolt. Remove bolt from shock

① FRONT SHOCK ABSORBER MOUNTING
   (ALL VALIANT, DART MODELS)

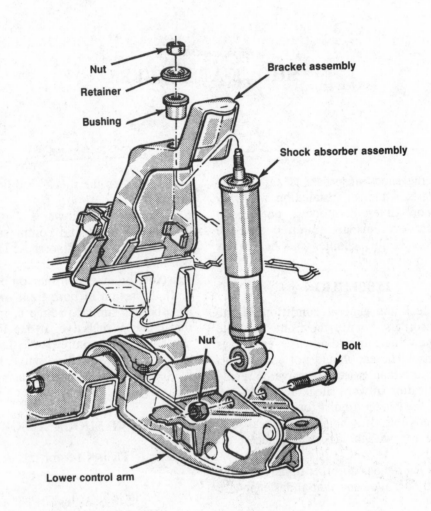

Nut

Retainer

Bushing

Bracket assembly

Shock absorber assembly

Nut

Bolt

Lower control arm

② FRONT SHOCK ABSORBER MOUNTING
(1976-ON ASPEN, VOLARE; 1977-1982 DIPLOMAT, LEBARON;
1979-ON MIRADA, CORDOBA, GRAN FURY, IMPERIAL; 1982-ON
FIFTH AVENUE)

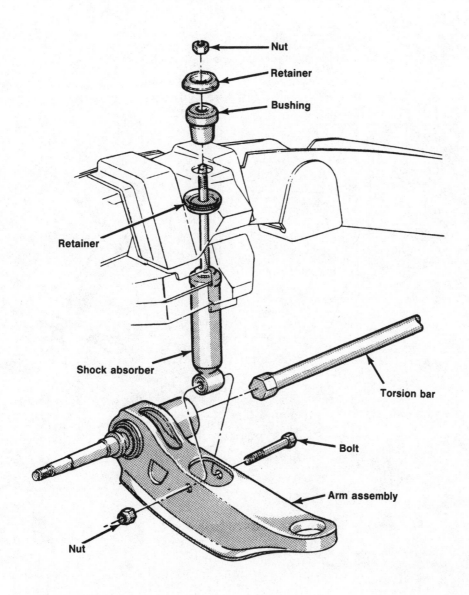

Nut

Retainer

Bushing

Retainer

Shock absorber

Torsion bar

Bolt

Arm assembly

Nut

11

③ FRONT SHOCK ABSORBER MOUNTING
(1972 SATELLITE, CHARGER, CORONET;
1972-1974 CHALLENGER, BARRACUDA)

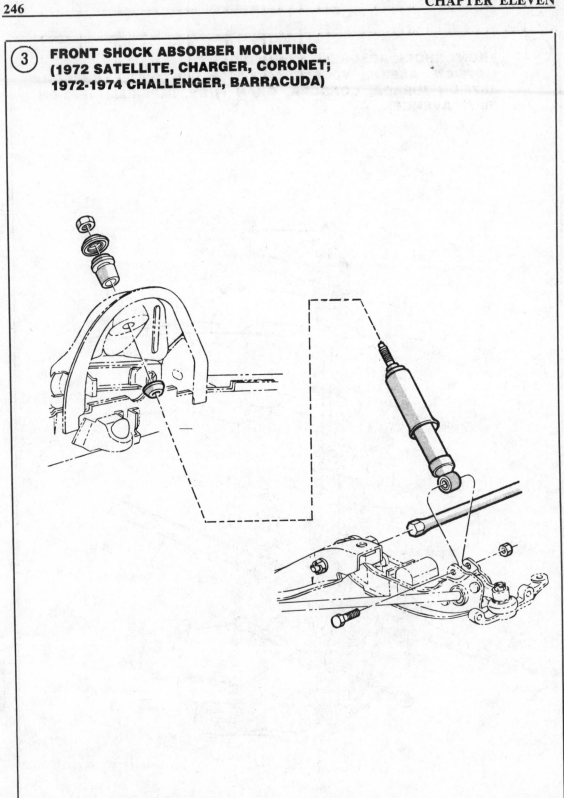

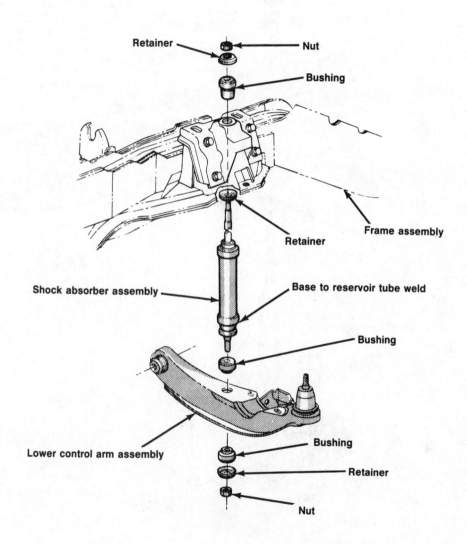

④ **FRONT SHOCK ABSORBER MOUNTING**
(1972 FURY; 1973 SATELLITE; 1973-1977 CORONET; 1973-1978
CHARGER; 1975-1978 CORDOBA, FURY; 1978-1979 MAGNUM; 1978
MONACO; 1980-1981 NEWPORT, ST. REGIS, NEW YORKER. 1983-ON
FIFTH AVENUE, DIPLOMAT, GRAN FURY)

Retainer — Nut
Bushing
Retainer
Frame assembly
Shock absorber assembly — Base to reservoir tube weld
Bushing
Lower control arm assembly
Bushing
Retainer
Nut

11

**⑤ FRONT SHOCK ABSORBER MOUNTING
(1972-1975 IMPERIAL; 1972-1978 CHRYSLER; 1974-1977
GRAN FURY; 1972-1977 POLARA, MONACO, ROYAL MONACO)**

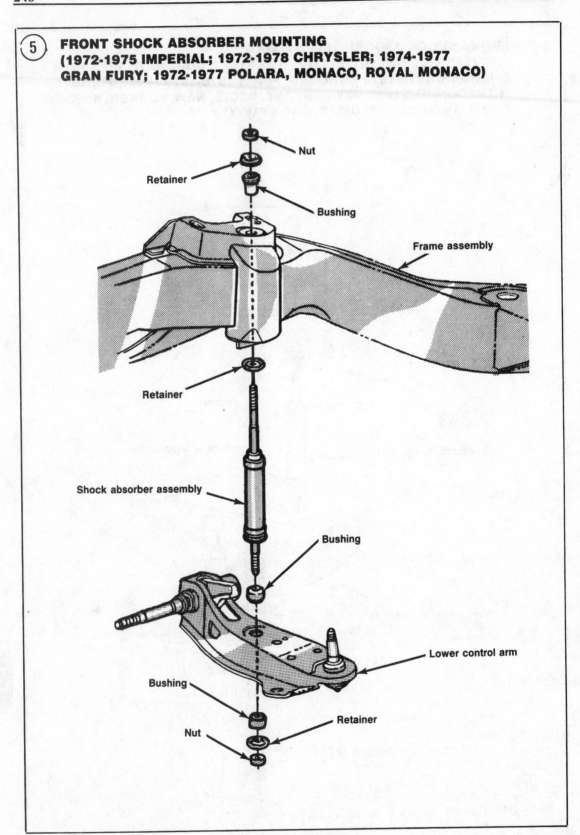

Nut

Retainer

Bushing

Frame assembly

Retainer

Shock absorber assembly

Bushing

Lower control arm

Bushing

Retainer

Nut

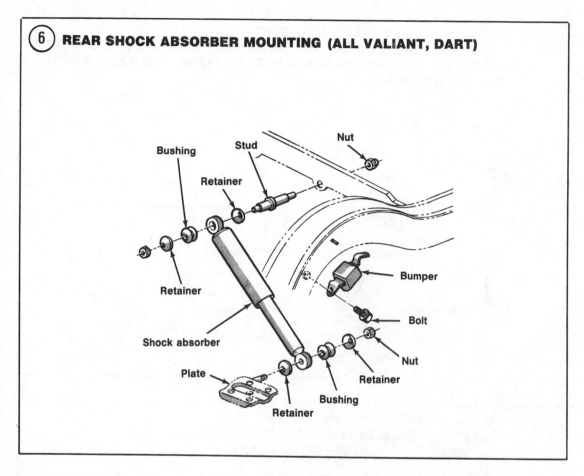

⑥ REAR SHOCK ABSORBER MOUNTING (ALL VALIANT, DART)

absorber eye and the lower control arm mounting bracket.

4. Push shock absorber upward to compress it completely, then pull it down and out of the upper mounting bushing to remove it from the vehicle.

NOTE
Before installing any shock absorber, hold in vertical position and fully extend it. Turn unit over and slowly compress it. Do not extend shock absorber while upside down. Repeat several times to expel all air trapped in the cylinder.

5. Remove steel sleeve from upper rubber bushing and dip bushing in water (not oil). Start bushing into hole of upper mounting bracket with a twisting motion. Tap bushing into position with a hammer and reinstall steel sleeve.

6. Expel air and compress shock absorber to its shortest length. Insert rod through upper bushing and install retainer and nut. Tighten to 25 ft.-lb. (34 N•m).

7. Align lower eye with mounting bracket holes, install shock absorber and tighten nut. Lower vehicle until its full weight rests on the wheels, then tighten nut to 35 ft.-lb. (48 N•m) for 1983-on vehicles or 50 ft.-lb. (69 N•m) on all others.

REAR SHOCK ABSORBERS

Removal/Installation

Refer to **Figures 6-9** for this procedure.
1. Raise the rear of the car with a jack and place it on jackstands. Position the jackstands under the axle assembly to remove the load from the shock absorber.
2. Remove the nut and retainer holding the shock absorber to the spring plate mounting stud. Remove shock absorber from stud.

11

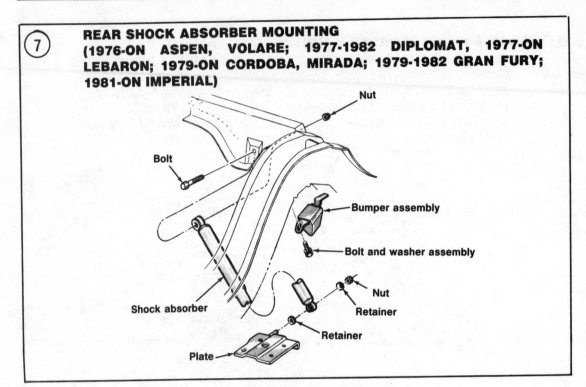

7 **REAR SHOCK ABSORBER MOUNTING
(1976-ON ASPEN, VOLARE; 1977-1982 DIPLOMAT, 1977-ON
LEBARON; 1979-ON CORDOBA, MIRADA; 1979-1982 GRAN FURY;
1981-ON IMPERIAL)**

Nut

Bolt

Bumper assembly

Bolt and washer assembly

Shock absorber

Nut

Retainer

Retainer

Plate

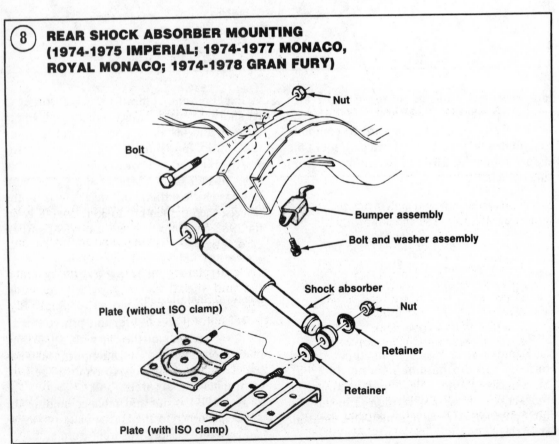

8 **REAR SHOCK ABSORBER MOUNTING
(1974-1975 IMPERIAL; 1974-1977 MONACO,
ROYAL MONACO; 1974-1978 GRAN FURY)**

Nut

Bolt

Bumper assembly

Bolt and washer assembly

Shock absorber

Plate (without ISO clamp)

Nut

Retainer

Retainer

Plate (with ISO clamp)

9 REAR SHOCK ABSORBER MOUNTING
(1972-1974 CHALLENGER; BARRACUDA; SATELLITE; 1972-1978 CHARGER; 1972-1977 CORONET; 1972-1978 POLARA/MONACO; 1975-1978 CORDOBA; 1972-1978 FURY; 1978-1979 MAGNUM; 1972-1973 CHRYSLER, IMPERIAL: 1982 NEWPORT, ST. REGIS, NEW YORKER; 1983-ON DIPLOMAT, FIFTH AVENUE, GRAN FURY)

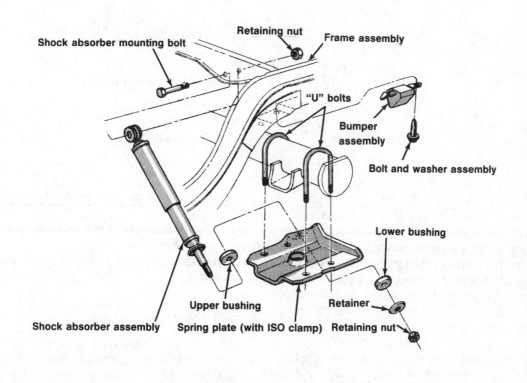

3. Remove the nut and bolt from the upper mounting. Remove the shock absorber.

NOTE
Before installing any shock absorber, hold in vertical position and fully extend it. Turn unit over and slowly compress it. Do not extend shock absorber while upside down. Repeat several times to expel all air trapped in the cylinder.

4A. In installation shown in **Figure 6**, position retainer on mounting stud and install shock absorber, then install cupped retainer and nut. Do not fully tighten nut at this time.

4B. In installations shown in **Figures 7-9**, align upper eye of shock absorber with mounting holes in crossmember. Install but do not fully tighten bolt and nut.

5. Place retainer on spring mounting plate stud and install shock absorber on stud. Install cupped retainer and nut. Do not fully tighten nut at this time.

6. Lower vehicle until its full weight rests on the wheels. In installation shown in **Figure 6**, tighten upper nut to 50 ft.-lb. (69 N•m). On all others, tighten upper nut to 70 ft.-lb. (97 N•m). Tighten lower nut to 35 ft.-lb. (48 N•m) for 1983-on vehicles or 50 ft.-lb. (69 N•m) for all others.

11

CHAPTER TWELVE

BODY

This chapter covers removal and installation of interior trim panels, door trim panels and weatherstrips. It also describes the tools, materials and techniques involved in repairing minor damage to automotive sheet metal. Repairing more substantial damage requires the use of expensive equipment and a skill level obtainable only through special training and practice.

Using the information provided, you should be able to select and use the necessary tools and materials to repair the type of dings and dents incurred in parking lots or other minor "fender-bender" accidents.

In addition, a section of the chapter deals with vinyl top restoration and repair. Installing a new vinyl top is expensive and also requires considerable skill and equipment. The information in this chapter will save you money while returning a damaged vinyl top to service.

Beyond the basic skills and knowledge described in this chapter, you will need patience and careful attention to detail. Don't try to hurry a repair.

INTERIOR TRIM PANELS

Removal of interior trim panels may be required to:

a. Repair damage to exterior sheet metal panels.
b. Locate and correct the cause of squeaks and other noise.
c. Locate and correct the cause of water leaks.

Panel Attachment Methods

Interior trim panels are generally held in place on the metal inner door panel by sheet metal screws. On many vehicles, the screw heads may be exposed and easily located. On others, they may be hidden under plastic caps or plugs which must be pried from the panel to gain access to the screw. This attachment method is generally used on kick panels as well as rear quarter lower and upper trim panels. On wagon and hatchback models, it is often used to secure the door or hatch trim panel.

In recent years, increasing use has been made of plastic trim panels held in place by attachment clips molded into the panel or by serrated plastic plugs with a molded decorative screw head. Clips are generally used for panels that are frequently removed, such as fuse block, storage compartment or steering column trim covers. Plugs are

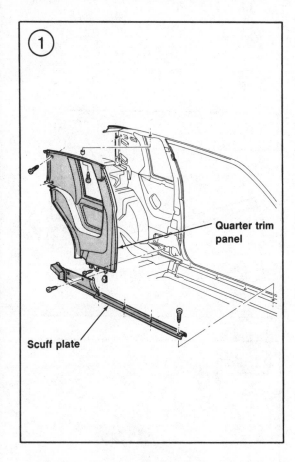

Quarter trim panel

Scuff plate

before the panel can be removed. See **Figure 1**.

Be sure to use the proper tools for removal of panel fasteners. When removing metal screws, use an appropriate size and type of screwdriver. Using the wrong size tool increases the chance of damage to the screw head or trim panel if the screwdriver should slip. Plastic plugs with a decorative screw head should be removed with a tool made by slotting a putty knife. This allows you to slide the putty knife blade under the panel edge on both sides of the plug. Pressure is applied evenly on the panel as you ease the plug from its hole in the inner door panel; this reduces the possibility of cracking or damaging the trim panel. Do *not* attempt to remove plastic plugs with a screwdriver or other pry tool.

Panel Removal
(Screw Fasteners)

1. Determine the location of all panel fasteners.
2. If plastic caps or plugs are used over the fastener heads, carefully pry each cap/plug from the panel with the tip of an appropriate size flat-blade screwdriver.
3. Fit the screwdriver head into the screw slot. Pressing downward on the screwdriver, slowly turn the screw counterclockwise to break the seal.
4. Repeat Step 3 to loosen all fasteners, then remove them from the panel. Place all screws in a suitable container to prevent them from being lost.
5. Grasping the panel on opposite sides, carefully lift it away from the inner panel frame. If the panel does not come off easily, there may be one or more hidden fasteners that have not been removed.
6. Installation is the reverse of removal. Do not overtighten the fasteners. Excessive pressure can crack or split the panel.

Panel Removal
(Plastic Plug Fasteners)

1. Determine the location of all panel fasteners.
2. If an appropriate removal tool is not available, fabricate one from a wide-blade

frequently used on the door or hatch trim panel on station wagon and hatchback models.

These attachment methods are generally satisfactory when the vehicle is new, but if the panel is removed frequently they can become the source of an annoying rattle or noise. Panel clips and plugs (like the panels themselves) tend to become brittle with age.

If a clip breaks off during panel removal, the panel will have to be replaced with a new one. Serrated plastic plugs can often be removed and reinstalled several times. However, since the plug's holding ability depends upon forcing its serrated diameter through a slightly smaller hole, it is generally more satisfactory to install new plugs. This assures a tight and noise-free fit.

One or two edges of some panels may be held in place by the edge of an adjacent panel or a sill/scuff plate. When this method is used, fasteners will have to be removed from the adjacent panel or the sill/scuff plate removed

12

putty knife or piece of strap iron as shown in **Figure 2.**

3. Carefully slip the slotted putty knife or tool under the panel edge so the plastic plug fits into the slot in the blade.

NOTE
If possible, do not remove the plastic plug from the trim panel in Step 4 or Step 5. Apply only enough pressure to free the plug from its hole in the inner panel frame.

4. Gently apply an increasing amount of outward pressure on the putty knife until the plug separates from the inner panel frame.

5. If the plug partially separates from the panel but cannot be easily popped from its hole, grasp it underneath the decorative head with a pair of needlenose pliers. Pad the area on the trim panel under the pliers to prevent possible damage and remove the plug from the inner panel frame hole with the pliers.

6. Before reinstalling the trim panel, check the condition of each plastic plug fastener. If bent, gouged or otherwise deformed or damaged, remove the plug from the panel with needlenose pliers as in Step 5.

7. To reinstall the trim panel, position it on the inner panel frame and align the panel plugs and frame holes. Gently tap the head of each plug with a rubber mallet until it is fully seated in its hole in the inner panel frame.

8. If any of the plugs were defective in Step 6 and removed from the panel, position a new plug in the panel hole after making sure it is aligned with the inner panel frame hole and repeat Step 7 to install the new plug.

Panel Removal (Plastic Clips)

1. Use a putty knife to carefully lift one edge of the panel. This should expose the snap-in clips on that side.

2. Repeat Step 2 on the opposite side of the panel, lifting it approximately the same amount.

3. Grasp the panel on each side and carefully remove it.

4. To reinstall the panel, position it in the opening. Holding the panel on each side so that finger pressure can be applied to the

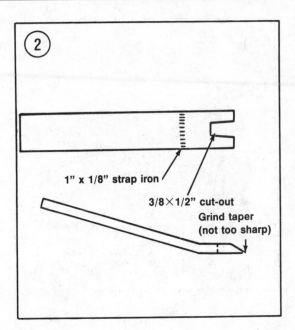

1" x 1/8" strap iron

3/8 × 1/2" cut-out
Grind taper
(not too sharp)

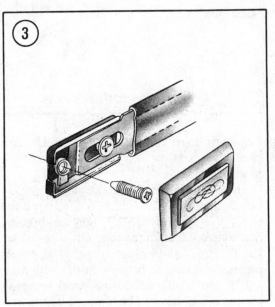

clips, depress the clips and carefully push the panel into place.

DOOR TRIM PANELS

Door trim panels are more complicated to properly remove and install than other interior trim panels. Their removal is required for the same reasons, as well as to service the window regulator and glass, outside door handle, door lock and any power components such as motors or solenoids.

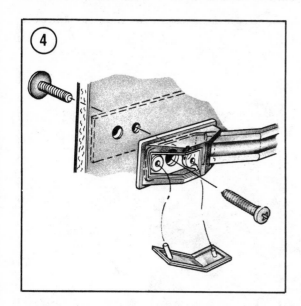

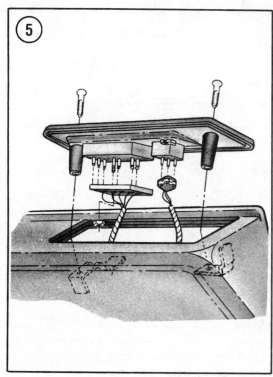

removed prior to door trim panel removal. On some trim levels, however, the armrest may be an integral part of the trim panel.

Independent assemblies are usually attached with sheet metal screws hidden from view. These may be located underneath or countersunk into the armrest. On some models, plastic pry caps or plugs must be removed to provide access to the screw head. Once all screws are located, it is simply a matter of removing them with the proper tools.

On older vehicles, the armrest retaining screws thread into a hole drilled in the inner door panel. Late-model vehicles generally use a snap-in nylon insert installed in the inner door frame to accept the screw. When this method of attachment is used, excessive pressure on the armrest can deform the nylon insert and cause the armrest to come off when using it to close a door. If this happens, the nylon insert should be discarded and a new one installed.

Pull Strap or Handle

A pull strap or handle is provided to assist in closing the door from the inside. On early models, this may be attached to the panel with screws after the panel is installed on the door. A second method used is to attach the strap or handle with screws prior to attaching the panel to the door frame (**Figure 3**). If this method is used, the trim panel can be removed with the pull strap or handle attached.

On later models, pull straps or handles are attached with sheet metal screws at each end after the panel is installed. The screws are hidden under snap-on trim caps or escutcheons held in place either by plastic pegs or snap-in clips. See **Figure 4**. The trim caps must be pried off carefully to prevent damage to the exterior finish or breaking of the peg or clip attaching device.

12

Power Accessory Switches

Power accessory switches may be installed in the trim panel or armrest with screws (**Figure 5**) or they may have molded plastic

Before a door trim panel can be removed, all attached accessories such as armrests, door pull straps and window regulator handles must be removed first.

Armrest

Trim panel armrests are generally independent assemblies which must be

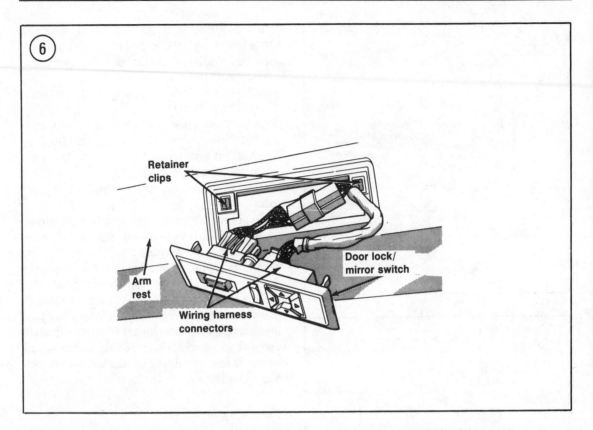

⑥

Retainer
clips

Door lock/
mirror switch

Arm
rest

Wiring harness
connectors

legs that snap into retainer clips in the panel
cutout (**Figure 6**).

If attached with screws, remove the screws
and lift the switch assembly from the trim
panel far enough to disconnect the electrical
connectors. If snap-in legs and retainer clips
are used, carefully pry the switch assembly
from the trim panel and disconnect the
electrical connectors.

Window Regulator Handle
Removal/Installation

Regulator handles are attached to the
serrated regulator shaft in 3 different ways:
   a. Allen-head screws.
   b. Wire lock rings.
   c. Roll pins.

Allen-head screw

Refer to **Figure 7** for this procedure.
1. Note the position of the handle for
reinstallation in the same position.
2. Remove the attaching screw with an
appropriate size Allen-head wrench.

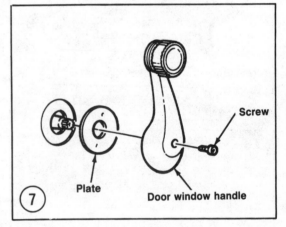

⑦

Screw

Plate

Door window handle

3. If the handle does not come off the
regulator shaft easily, carefully pry it free with
a padded screwdriver blade. Insert a piece of
wood between the screwdriver tip and the
trim panel to provide a pry point that will not
damage the panel.
4. Remove the plastic bearing plate, if so
equipped.
5. To reinstall the handle, clean the regulator
shaft serrations and lightly lubricate with

Tool

Retaining spring
disengaged

Push tool in
direction of arrow

Inside handle

grease. Slide the plastic bearing plate over the regulator shaft, if so equipped.

6. Position the handle as desired, align the shaft and handle serrations and press the handle onto the shaft.

7. If the handle does not slip onto the regulator shaft easily, gently tap it in place with a rubber mallet.

8. Install and tighten the attaching screw with an appropriate size Allen-head screwdriver.

Lock ring

Refer to **Figure 8** for this procedure.

1. Note the position of the handle for reinstallation in the same position.

CAUTION
Do not attempt to pry the lock ring off with a screwdriver. Pressure must be applied to each end of the lock ring at the same time to force it off the shaft. Attempts to pry the lock ring off with screwdrivers in Step 2 may result in damage to the trim panel.

2. Insert a lock ring removal tool between the handle trim ring and door trim panel. Align the tool with the ends of the lock ring, then push the lock ring off the handle shaft.

3. If the handle does not come off the regulator shaft easily, carefully pry it free with a padded screwdriver blade. Insert a piece of wood between the screwdriver tip and the trim panel to provide a pry point that will not damage the panel.

4. Remove the plastic bearing plate, if so equipped.

5. To reinstall the handle, clean the regulator shaft serrations and lightly lubricate with grease. Slide the plastic bearing plate on the regulator shaft, if so equipped.

6. Slip the lock ring over the handle shaft so it engages the shaft slots. Position the handle as desired, align the shaft and handle serrations and press the handle onto the shaft. When properly seated, the lock ring will fit behind the regulator shaft serrations.

7. If the handle does not slip onto the regulator shaft easily, gently tap it in place with a rubber mallet.

Roll pin

1. Note the position of the handle for reinstallation in the same position.

2. Insert a pin punch between the handle trim ring and door trim panel. Align the punch with the roll pin and gently tap the pin from the handle and regulator shafts.

3. If the handle does not come off the regulator shaft easily, carefully pry it free with a padded screwdriver blade. Insert a piece of wood between the screwdriver tip and the trim panel to provide a pry point that will not damage the panel.

4. To reinstall the handle, clean the regulator shaft serrations and lightly lubricate with grease.

5. Position the handle as desired, align the roll pin holes in the handle and regulator shafts, then press the handle onto the shaft.

6. If the handle does not slip onto the regulator shaft easily, gently tap it in place with a rubber mallet.

12

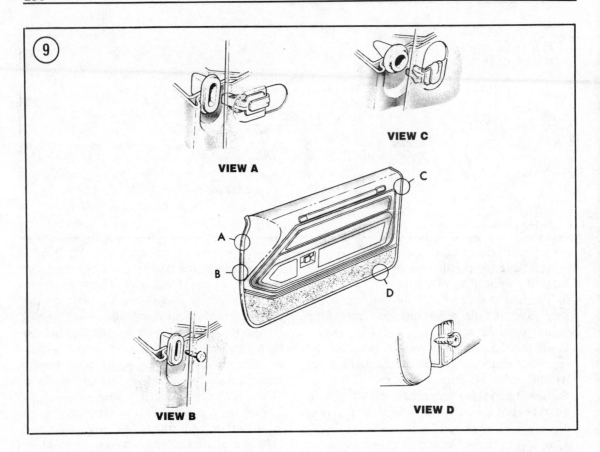

VIEW A

VIEW C

VIEW B

VIEW D

7. Insert the roll pin in the handle shaft hole and tap it in place with the pin punch and mallet.

Inside Door Handle

Inside door handles are attached with screws or lock clips similar to those used with window regulators and are removed using the same procedure. Recessed handles are contained within a cover plate or cup held in place by screws.

Door Trim Panel Removal/Installation

A door trim panel hangs across the inner door frame at the top and is tightly held to the frame by fasteners along the sides and bottom of the panel. The type of fasteners used to attach a door trim panel varies according to model year and trim level:

    a. Sheet metal screws.
    b. Pinched wire retaining clips.
    c. Serrated plastic push pins.

Figure 9 shows a variety of trim panel fasteners.

Door trim panel removal and installation requires the use of correct tools and patience to prevent damage to the panel. The majority of door trim panels are manufactured of a heavy pressed paperboard. Vinyl and/or other decorative trim is then stretched over the paperboard and stapled in place. Despite their solid appearance when properly installed on the door, such panels are quite fragile and can easily be damaged if improperly removed. The application of excessive pressure on the panel can result in its cracking or breaking. It can also cause the vinyl to pull away from the staples, which are often positioned close to the panel edge.

When wire or plastic retainers are used instead of screws, they are inserted in cutout areas along the side and bottom edges of the panel. If not removed very carefully with equal pressure on each side of the fastener, they tend to pull out of the trim panel instead of the inner door panel. Since there is no way to repair the trim panel where such damage is done, it cannot be reattached properly.

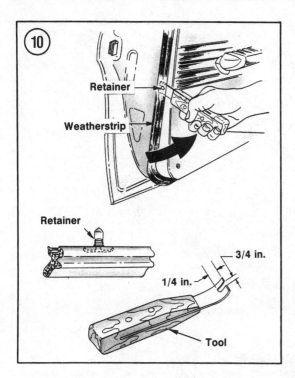

Some trim panels are made of fiberglass or other composite materials. These are generally attached with screws. Although such panels are not as fragile at those made of paperboard, they can be gouged or scratched if a screwdriver slips out of the screw head. They are also prone to cracking or splitting when excessive torque is applied to the screws.

This generalized procedure can be applied to the majority of door trim panels. Be sure to use the correct tools as specified and work slowly and carefully to avoid damage to the panel or fasteners. An inexpensive trim stick available at your local auto parts store should be used to disconnect trim panel fasteners from the inner door panel.

1. Remove the door inside handle and/or window regulator as described in this chapter.
2. Remove the pull strap or handle as described in this chapter.
3. If door is equipped with an inside locking rod knob, unscrew and remove the knob.
4. If equipped with power accessories, remove the switch assemblies as described in this chapter.
5. Remove the armrest as described in this chapter.

6. Remove the screw(s) from any escutcheons or cups enclosing handles or other activating devices on the door. Remove the escutcheon(s) or cup(s).
7. Remove any screws from each side and across the bottom of the door trim pad, if used.
8. Start at a lower corner on one side and carefully insert a trim stick between the trim panel and door inner panel. Apply pressure slowly and evenly until the trim panel fastener pops free of the inner door panel.
9. Repeat Step 8, working upward to disengage all fasteners on that side of the trim panel.
10. Repeat Step 8 and Step 9 to disengage all fasteners on the opposite side of the panel.
11. When all trim panel fasteners have been disengaged, lift the trim panel upward, slide it to the rear slightly and remove it from the inner door panel.
12. To reinstall the trim panel, hang it over the top of the inner door frame and seat into place. Make sure the panel fasteners align with their holes in the inner door frame. Sharply rap the outer face of the panel directly above one of the fasteners with the palm of your hand. This should seat the fastener in its hole. Repeat to install the remaining fasteners.
13. Reverse Steps 1-7 to complete panel installation.

WEATHERSTRIPS

A weatherstrip is used around the outer edges of a door or trunk lid and the inner edges of the door or trunk opening to provide a seal that is both air-tight and water-tight. The weatherstrip tends to deteriorate with age and should be replaced as required to maintain an effective seal against air, wind noise and entry of water.

A weatherstrip is attached in one of 3 ways:
a. A push-on fit over a metal weld flange. This type is generally held in place at various points by interior garnish moldings and can be removed and reinstalled as required.
b. Serrated nylon retainers (**Figure 10**) or clips. This type can be removed and

12

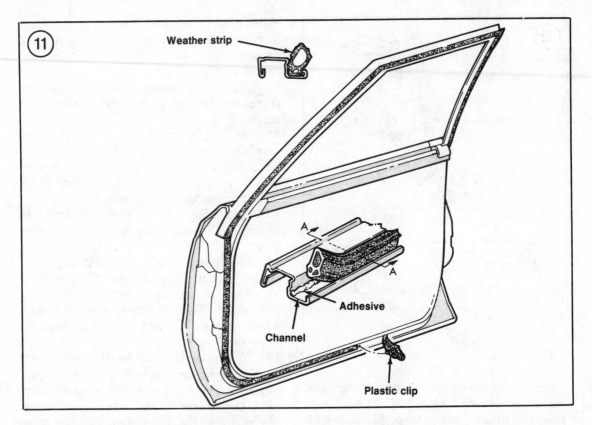

Weather strip

A

A

Adhesive

Channel

Plastic clip

reinstalled, with individual retainers available as a service part from your dealer if they are damaged.

c. Cemented into a channel with a special black adhesive. The weatherstrip cannot be reused, as removal generally damages or destroys it.

A combination of attachment methods may be used on a door or trunk lid and/or its opening. **Figure 11** shows the use of adhesive and plastic clips.

Removal/Installation (Push-on Fit)

1. Remove any interior garnish moldings that cover the weatherstrip.
2. Note the point at which the ends of the weatherstrip butt together.
3. Starting at the point noted in Step 2, carefully pinch the weatherstrip and pull it off the weld flange.
4. Check weld flange for distortion. If required, straighten weld flange by flattening with a pair of locking pliers or hammers.

5. Clean weld flange as required with solvent and wipe dry.
6. Starting at the point noted in Step 2, slip the weatherstrip over the weld flange and install it around the door or door opening without stretching it.
7. Cut the weatherstrip at a point about 1/4-1/2 in. longer than required to butt the ends.
8. If new weatherstrip includes a rubber sponge plug, insert the plug in one end.
9. Butt the ends of the weatherstrip together to form a compression joint.

Removal/Installation (Serrated Nylon Retainers or Clips)

1. Visually determine how weatherstrip is installed. On some vehicles, it may be necessary to remove the door trim panel as described in this chapter in order to properly remove the weatherstrip.
2. Using GM tool part No. J-21104 or a similar tool fabricated from a putty knife, disengage the weatherstrip at the retainer points. See **Figure 10**.

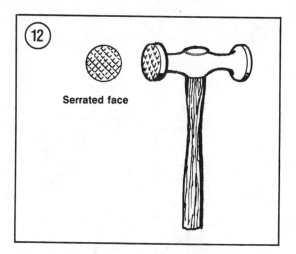

Serrated face

3. If part of the weatherstrip is cemented to the door or opening, remove it as described in this chapter.

4. Remove the weatherstrip.

5. To reinstall, check the nylon retainers and replace any that are damaged.

6. If adhesive was used to retain a part of the weatherstrip, clean the old adhesive from the door or opening with solvent and wipe dry.

7. Fit the weatherstrip to the door or opening and tap nylon fasteners in place with a hammer and blunt caulking tool.

8. If part of the weatherstrip was cemented to the door or opening, install it as described in this chapter.

Adhesive

1. Remove any fasteners holding the ends of the weatherstrip in place.

2. Apply a weatherstrip release agent (3M Improved Release Agent No. 08971, Kent Special Release Agent No. SR-A or equivalent) following the manufacturer's directions.

3. Break the adhesive bond between the door or opening and weatherstrip with a putty knife or other flat-bladed tool. Work carefully and slowly to avoid damage to painted surfaces.

4. Remove the weatherstrip.

5. Clean the old adhesive from the door or opening with solvent and wipe dry.

6. To reinstall, apply a continuous bead of weatherstrip adhesive to the door or opening surface.

7. Carefully press weatherstrip into position, then install any fasteners holding its ends in place.

BODYWORK TOOLS

In addition to the basic tools (wrenches and screwdrivers) needed to work on your vehicle, there are a few special tools required for body work. Hand tools such as hammers and dollies are relatively inexpensive and can be purchased at most auto supply stores. Power equipment such as grinders and polishers can be rented by the day or week. This section explains the basic tools required and how they are used.

Body Hammers

A shrinking hammer (**Figure 12**) will handle most body repair jobs. It has a rounded and beveled striking surface for general use and a squared striking surface for right-angle work. Some combination body hammers have a shrinking head on one end and a pick on the other. Shrinking hammers have a face similar to that of a file. When used with a dolly, the teeth on the hammer face make tiny indentations in the metal surface, causing it to shrink.

The ordinary claw or ball-peen hammer found in most home toolboxes is not recommended for body work, although in cases of minor damage where the intent is to fill the damage rather than work the metal back into shape, they can be used successfully.

Dolly Block

Best described as a small hand-held anvil, the dolly block is used as a pounding tool and as a back-up tool when a hammering force is applied to the opposite side of a panel. Although there are a wide variety of dollies available for specialized body work (**Figure 13**), the all-purpose dolly works well for most kinds of work. It serves as a hand-held hammer in limited under-panel space and conforms to almost any kind of panel contour. It has a flat surface for flat panel work, a sharp edge for bending and a rounded handle for concave dollying.

12

Body Grinder

A special heavy-duty body grinder (**Figure 14**) will make the job easier and faster. While expensive to buy, they can be rented at nearly any tool rental dealer. Adapter kits are also sold for most 3/8 in. power drills to convert them into a body grinder suitable for minor bodywork repairs.

The grinder used should rotate at least 4,000 rpm. Slower speeds can cause the sheet metal to overheat and distort, compounding the repair problem.

When grinding an edge with a body grinder, avoid using the top edge of the grinding disc, as the metal surface can cut the disc and pull the grinder out of your hands. To prevent this, use the bottom edge of the grinding disc. Work slowly into the metal surface with an even and firm pressure to maintain control of the tool at all times. See **Figure 15**. When you have finished using a body grinder, wait until the grinding surface has stopped rotating completely before you set it down.

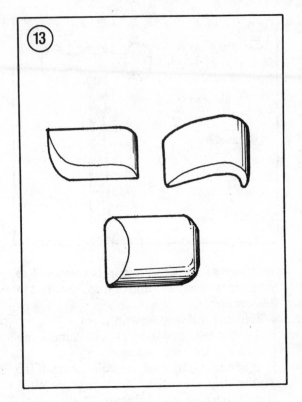

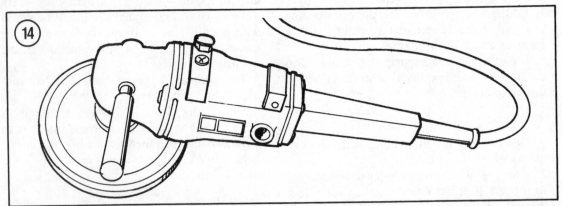

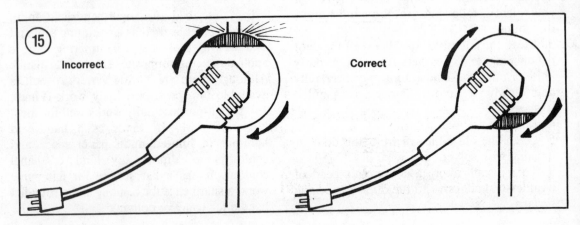

Grinding Discs

Grinding discs (**Figure 16**) are available from automotive supply stores. They come in various grits and can be cut to any size with an old pair of tin snips or scissors. Open-coat, coarse-grained (No. 16 grit) discs are used when paint must be ground off a surface. Close-coat discs are used for smoothing and working metal surfaces. A disc can also be cut as a "chopper" type to remove paint but should be used very carefully.

Pop-rivet Tool

The pop-rivet tool (**Figure 17**) is useful for panel replacement. This tool allows panel

edges to be riveted together from the outside surface. Some pop-rivet tools have interchangeable heads for rivet sizes from 1/8 to 5/16 inch. Riveted edges are much easier to weld, since the rivets keep the edges together and help reduce panel distortion from heat. Both aluminum and steel rivets are available; use steel rivets for body repair work.

Body Filler File

Commonly known as a "cheese-grater," this rounded file blade is used to rough-shape body filler when it has partially cured but not thoroughly hardened. See **Figure 18**. While handles are available for this tool, the body file is most effective when hand-held. To use it properly, hold the tool at a right angle to the panel and work diagonally across the filler surface.

16

No. 16 chopper

No. 24 Medium

No. 50 finish

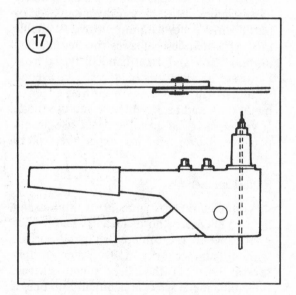

17

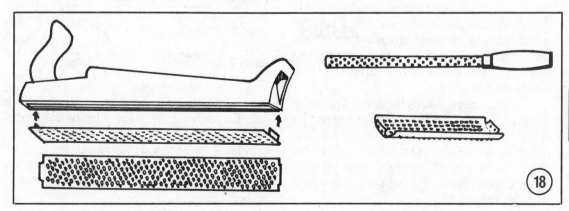

18

12

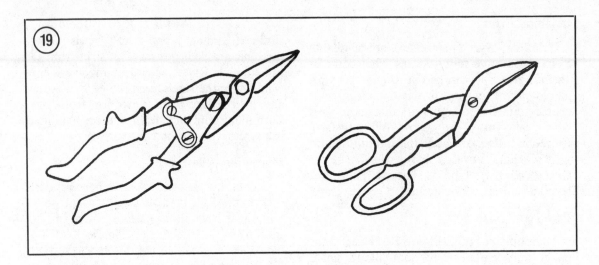

Metal Shears

Metal shears or tin snips (**Figure 19**) are necessary for sectioning or repaneling work. They can be used to clear away a damaged or rusted panel or for trimming edges. Available in several qualities, tin snips can be obtained in both left- and right-handed types from hardware or auto supply stores. Get a good pair that will hold a sharp cutting edge for metal work and be careful how you use them. If you wish to cut grinding discs, use an old pair of scissors or the less expensive type of tin snips.

Slide Hammer

A slide hammer (**Figure 20**) is often useful as a puller in those areas where it is impossible to get behind the metal surface with a hammer or a dolly. After drilling several holes in the sheet metal surface, thread the metal screw attachment into one of the holes. Move the slide weight backwards sharply against the striking plate and pull the metal out a small amount each time. Work slowly with this tool to avoid tearing the metal. It is best to pull at several places instead of just a few.

In some cases when the dent is really minor, you can achieve similar results by drilling holes in the sheet metal surface, threading a suitable sheet metal screw into one of the holes and pulling on the screw with a pair of pliers while tapping the panel with a hammer (**Figure 21**).

Welding Torch

Oxyacetylene welding equipment is used for heat shrinking of metal. The torch is adjusted for a neutral flame and used as in welding. The procedure is complicated but it offers the ideal solution to shrinking a large area. Done properly, it affords great control and minimizes the possibility of further damage to the metal. Done improperly, it will harden the metal. If you're not familiar with the proper use of welding equipment and a torch, avoid trying to heat shrink a panel this way. If you do use a torch, be sure to take the necessary safety and fire precautions.

Protective Clothing

Goggles should be worn during any grinding, filing, sanding or welding operation. Wear gloves when working with heat, during grinding operations or when cutting panels. A respirator or painter's mask should be worn when working with body filler or primer-surfacer.

Body Filler Tools

A discarded piece of hardboard or masonite will serve both as a mixing board and for carrying the body filler to the repair job.

Plastic spreaders or squeegees are used to apply the filler to the panel. These are made of a special material that will not bond easily to body filler.

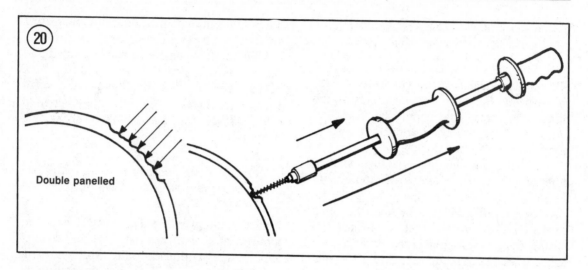

Double panelled

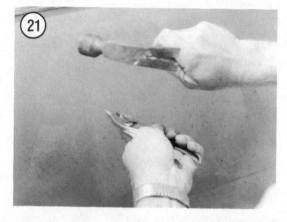

A 3-inch blade putty knife works well to mix the filler and hardener ingredients together.

Use an inexpensive grade of lacquer thinner as a solvent for cleaning body filler tools as soon as possible after their use before the filler has started to set up on them.

Miscellaneous Tools

A number of common tools can prove useful in some body repairs. A suction cup or rubber plunger of the type used to clear drains can be used to pull out larges areas of shallow damage on low-crowned panels such as doors. These are particularly useful when you want to avoid damage to the painted surfaces. Locking pliers can be used in various ways. One of their more important functions is to hold 2 pieces of metal in alignment.

BODYWORK MATERIALS

A good body repair job requires the use of various materials. This section explains the materials and how they are used.

Body Filler

There are several good brands of body filler available from automotive supply stores. Body fillers consist of 2 different materials which must be mixed together to start a catalyst action. Always mix the filler and hardener thoroughly, pressing them together on the mixing board. The 2 materials are generally different colors and are properly mixed when the colors are blended into one. Follow the manufacturer's instructions on the container as closely as possible; the amount of hardener to be used will depend upon the weather conditions.

A curing and hardening process starts when the filler and hardener are mixed together—similar to epoxy cement. The filler should be applied as soon as possible during the first stages of this hardening process.

NOTE
Application of filler in direct sunlight will reduce the curing time significantly and should be avoided.

NOTE
Do not apply filler thicker than 1/4 inch at a time. If a thicker application is required, let the first coat cure and sand

12

it, then apply subsequent coats as needed after each is cured and sanded.

You have about 10-15 minutes to apply the filler under ideal weather conditions. After this period, the filler becomes increasingly difficult to spread and should be discarded. Once the filler has been applied, clean the body filler tools immediately.

Generally, the filler material will start to cure within 10-15 minutes of application. This is the time to shape it with the cheese-grater file before the material fully hardens. It the material starts to peel off during filing, it has not cured long enough. Remove the excess filler and bring the high spots down by applying even pressure and smooth strokes from one side of the repair to the other. The cheese-grater shreds best when hand-held and pulled across the surface of the filler toward the user.

Spot and Glazing Putties

Spot putty is used to fill deep scratches and pits after they have been thoroughly sanded smooth and sprayed with primer-surfacer. Spot putty drys much faster than glazing putty and is used in very small amounts.

Glazing putty is generally used to wipe into a feather-edged line for filling purposes and dries slowly.

Always spray primer-surfacer before and after applying spot or glazing putty and avoid using the putty in excessive amounts.

Sandpaper

Sandpaper is available in a large variety of grit sizes for all sanding operations. It is available for wet or dry sanding applications. Keep sandpaper away from moisture and store it in a cool, dry area.

When wet sanding, provide the panel with a continuous flushing of water from a hose. This lubricates the sandpaper and helps to keep it sharp while flushing away the oxidized paint residues.

All sanding should be done in the same general direction. Do not sand in a crisscross pattern or with a circular motion. The use of a sanding block (block sanding) will help to keep uniform pressure on the sandpaper at all times and minimize the possibility of creating high/low spots with the sandpaper.

After the filler has been rough-shaped and has completely dried, block sand the area with a rubber-type sanding block and a rough grit sandpaper (No. 36 or No. 40 grit) to further level the surface after using the cheese-grater.

NOTE
Do not sand excessively or you may create a low spot which will have to be refilled.

Finish sanding with a No. 80 grit paper to remove any scratches left by the coarser paper. Areas within the filler which are still too low or rough will require an additional application of filler. Fill only those areas and again file off the filler before block sanding.

Once all imperfections have been removed and the filled area is satisfactory, finish the sanding (in preparation for primer-surfacer application) with progressively finer grits (No. 80 or No. 100 grit dry type) of sandpaper using the sanding block.

Block sanding is the final metal working phase and should not be hurried. You cannot spend too much time perfecting the area to be refinished with this operation.

Wax and Grease Remover

A good wax and grease remover must be used to remove all wax, asphalt and road tar from the panel. The solution will not remove dirt or oxidized paint layers. After use, clean away any residue with a strong detergent powder and grade No. 00 steel wool, rinsing well with plenty of cool water.

Primer-surfacer

Primer-surfacer contains a primer to cover old painted surfaces and a surfacer to fill in low spots. It is available in 3 colors: light grey, dark grey or red oxide. The color used is important only when dealing with transparent colors which require base coating. Otherwise, all 3 have identical characteristics.

Primer-surfacer must grip the metal surface tightly and provide a firm base for the paint coat. To do so, the surface must be prepared by sanding, masking and cleaning. Several coats may be applied to do the filling but a coat should not be applied too thickly or it will not dry properly. The material must be allowed to flash-off between coatings or pin-holes may develop. "Flashing" is the time required for the lacquer thinner to evaporate from the freshly sprayed primer-surfacer.

Never load up a panel with primer-surfacer in direct sunlight. This can trap escaping thinners and cause problems. If a large amount of primer-surfacer is required on the repair panel, load up the panel gradually, allowing each coat to flash-off properly, and then expose it to heat or direct sunlight for curing.

Primer-sealers

The primer-sealer seals off the old finish and makes sure that it bonds well to the new one. It is used as an undercoat and does not require sanding. It dries rapidly and lays down in a smooth layer to reflect all the surface preparation. It will require tacking with a tack-rag and a final cleaning with compressed air in preparation for the top or finish coats.

Primer-sealers are available in a transparent form or in a variety of colors. Colored sealers are used when base-coating for a deeper, transparent color. Sealer will stretch the life expectancy of the paint by at least a year and provides a good bond between the undercoat and finish coats.

Thinners

Fast-, medium- or slow-drying thinners are available for use with primer-surfacers, depending upon the weather conditions. In very cold weather, use a fast-drying thinner. A medium-drying thinner works well in mild temperatures but in hot weather, use a slow-drying thinner.

BASIC BODYWORK

There are 2 approaches to bodywork—replace or repair. Which one you select depends on the economics of the damage. In some cases, it may be less expensive and time-consuming to simply replace the damaged panel. This is particularly true with late-model vehicles, where the sheet metal used in a panel is too thin to permit extensive repair.

Replacing Damaged Panels

Replacing a fender, for example, is a relatively straight-forward job. Most fenders are attached with screws or bolts and some form of body caulking. Fender replacement amounts to removing the headlight or taillight (and marker lights) and removing the screws or bolts. See **Figure 22**. Replacing a door is even easier. Simply remove the hinges or hinge pins and remove the door. Other panels may be spot-welded in place, presenting more of a challenge to the beginner.

Replacement panels are available from 3 sources:

a. Your dealer.
b. A wrecking yard.
c. Independent sources.

A panel obtained from your dealer guarantees that it will fit your car as perfectly as possible. It is also the most expensive source.

A used panel from a wrecking yard can be a good buy, provided it is not extremely rare or extremely popular at the time you need it. Both factors tend to drive the price up. Carefully select a replacement panel from a wrecking yard to make sure it is not damaged or rusted.

Independent sources such as auto repair stores and some automotive chains offer replacement parts for many popular vehicles (especially older ones) at reasonable prices. However, these parts are often fiberglass instead of metal and, while they are supposed to be a bolt-on fit, may require considerable rework to align properly with adjacent panels.

If the panel is bolted or screwed in place, remove all fasteners. Keep all nuts, bolts and washers together in a cardboard box or coffee can. You might find it easier to keep track of where the fasteners belong by rethreading them back into the mating nuts after the panels have been removed. Replace any fasteners that are badly rusted. If fasteners are coated with dirt or undercoating, clean them in solvent and lightly oil the threads before reuse.

12

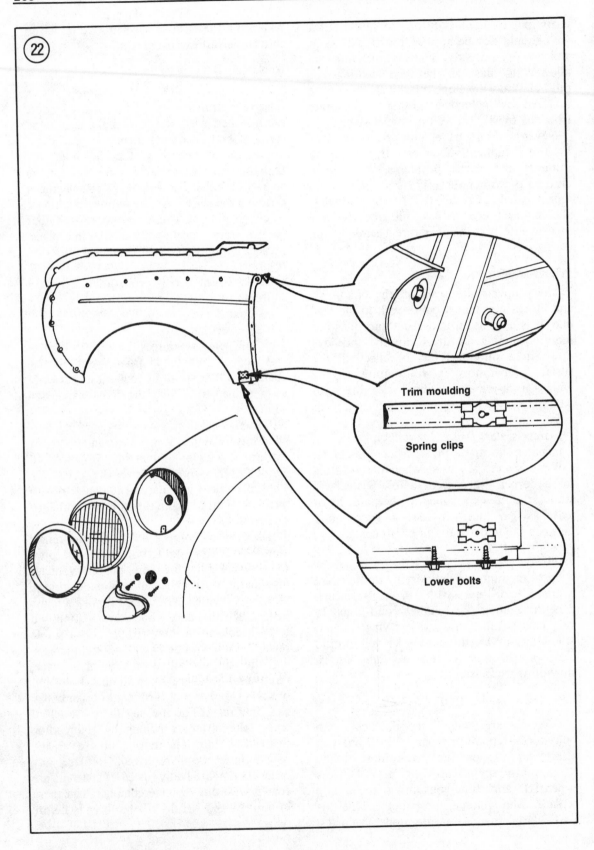

The following procedure can be used to replace the majority of spot-welded panels.

1. Look for a slight depression in the metal surface where the panels join together. This is the point where the panels can be separated and the damaged panel removed.

2. Use a stone grinding bit in a small electric drill to drill out the spot welds. A 3/8 in. drill bit can also be used, utilizing only the tip of the bit to drill out the spot welds. Do not drill completely through the panels.

WARNING
Wear gloves to protect your hands from sharp metal edges while cutting the damaged panel or working around the sharp panel edges in the following steps.

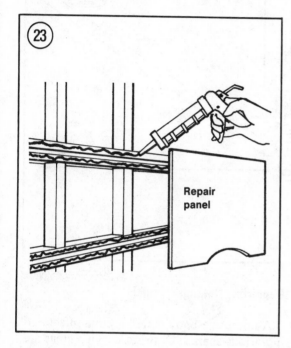

Repair panel

3. Once drilled, the panels should separate and their overlapping edges should pull apart. You can then cut away the panel surface with metal shears.

4. Work any small remaining strip of panel loose with pliers to fatigue the metal where spot welds remain stuck together.

5. Once the damaged panel has been removed, check the inner structure for damage.

6. Straighten all spot welds and grind them off smoothly. A small grinding disc mounted to a hand drill will do the job.

7. Straighten all connecting panel edges and inner panel connecting edges to restore correct alignment. Use the small grinding disc for metal finishing.

8. Some recaulking may be required between the inner and outer panels or at braces in the inner structure. Apply caulking to the areas which need it before setting the repair panel in place (**Figure 23**). This works better than trying to squeeze it into the panels after they have been joined together.

9. Clamp the replacement panel in place with locking pliers (**Figure 24**), fitting it to the surrounding panel edges (small C-clamps can also be used in some cases). Try to position the clamping tools at the flattest place on the panel. Excessive pressure at the clamping tool will bend and damage the panels.

10. Align the replacement panel at all sides and double-check to make sure the panel surface aligns with adjoining panel surfaces.

11. Once aligned, use a 3/16 in. drill bit (for installing 1/8 in. rivets) and drill holes at a right-angle to the panel on each side of the clamping tool. Space the rivet holes 2-3 inches apart, repositioning the clamping tool each time and drilling on each side of the tool. Use steel-type rivets for body repanelling

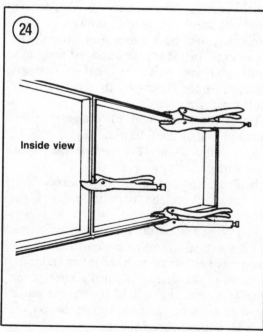

Inside view

12

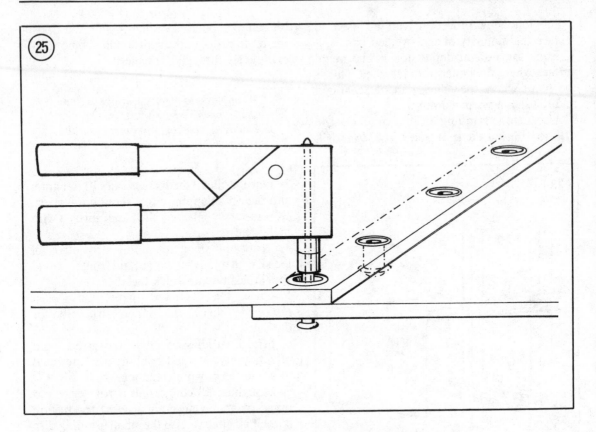

work. Install the rivets (**Figure 25**) with the finish side exposed. Where panel edges are more than 2 thicknesses, use a larger diameter rivet.

12. Drill and rivet each corner of the panel first, then drill and install rivets along each side of the panel.

13. When panel replacement is completed, the seams should be spot-welded or brazed together for a more permanent repair before the trim panels and mouldings are reinstalled. Low temperature welding must be maintained throughout the welding operation, whether it is done by gas or electrically. Small electric welders or welding tanks can be rented if you want to do the job yourself. Use a low temperature brazing rod.

14. Regrind all areas where the welding has burned off paint and finish the welds where they are exposed to the surface.

15. Treat all bare metal with a solution of Metal-prep and wipe it dry.

16. Apply a primer-surfacer coat as soon as possible; bare metal will surface rust within hours.

Repairing Damaged Panels

Automotive body panels are manufactured in various shapes. Outward-curving areas are called crowns; inward-curving or concave areas are known as reverse crowns. A body panel may also have ridges and flanges. The crowns and ridges are the strongest areas of a panel and are most resistant to damage. However, once damaged, they are also the most difficult to repair.

Hand tools are used to straighten sheet metal in one of the following ways:

a. Striking a direct blow on the metal surface.

b. Providing resistance to a direct blow applied on the opposite side of the metal.

c. Prying against the metal surface.

To successfully repair a dented area, you must have access to both the outer and inner surfaces of the damaged panel. Outer panels usually receive the bulk of the impact but in most cases, inner and connecting panels will also be pushed out of shape.

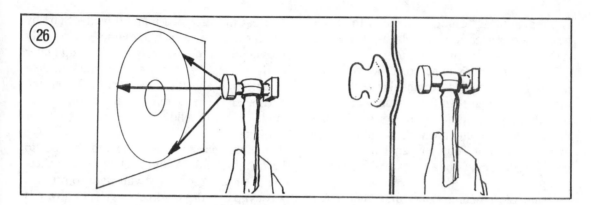

Close examination may reveal additional (indirect) damage not noted on first inspection. Look for creases or bulges directly associated with and in the vicinity of the point of impact. Any inner structure distortion should be repaired or replaced before replacing outer panel sections. If frame damage has been done, refer the job to a frame shop.

Metalworking Hints

To gain sufficient working space to effectively swing the body hammer and to position the dolly, remove all trim panels that will provide space behind the damaged panel surfaces. For example, removing the wheels will provide working space beneath fenders. Fenders and doors are actually easier to work on while mounted to the main body section. Occasionally, you may want to remove a panel to repair it. If so, be sure to realign the edges to the adjacent body panels when it is reinstalled.

Plan on utilizing an area about twice the size of the damaged area to repair the surface. It may be necessary to remove door handles, outside mirrors, mouldings or even the fender, hood or trunk lid to provide sufficient room to make the repair without having to work around obstacles.

If a quarter panel is damaged in an area close to the door edge, simply open the door to avoid accidentally grinding the door panel. Roll windows up tightly to prevent dust from entering the interior. Cover the windows with a tarp or canvas to prevent grinding slag from

damaging the glass. Never set body tools on the hood panel or fenders; this can scratch and damage the paint surface.

If the vehicle is to be placed on jackstands, be sure to position the stands at all 4 corners of the chassis to distribute the weight evenly. This will prevent any stresses which can lead to misalignment of the panel openings.

Repairing a damaged panel involves working with the points of stress (**Figure 26**). Grind the damaged area with a coarse grinding or "chopper" type disc. Once the paint has been removed, the high points of the damaged area can be easily seen. Use the hammer and dolly combination to unlock the stress. Move around both the outer and inner surfaces, starting at the perimeter and working inward to remove a small amount of the damage each time you strike it.

Bring the low spots up with a hammer while supporting the surface from behind with the dolly. Strike the high points down against the dolly's mass, but don't hold the dolly too close to the dent or you'll stretch the metal. If the hammer rings when you strike at the surface, back up the dolly a little. Supporting the metal surface allows you to shape its surface exactly as required. Settle for slightly less than a perfectly restored surface; finish off the repair using body filler material. Follow up with block sanding and primer-surfacer undercoating to complete the repair job. With practice, you can soon learn to do it well.

Sectioning

Sectioning or shorting a panel may be done to replace only a part of the panel. Sectioning

12

is often an ideal technique to use with panels which are rusted out in places, since the rusted area is the only damage.

Use a carpenter's pencil or other soft lead pencil to mark off a rectangular section an inch or two larger than the damaged or rusted area in the panel. Drill at one corner and use metal shears to cut away the damage. Any discarded hood or quarter panel which has a flat surface may be used as sectioning material.

Grind the patching panel first, then cut a section 1-2 inches larger in length and width than the hole it is to cover. Mount this repair section behind the rectangular opening and drill holes for rivets (**Figure 27**). Be careful not to drill your hand; use a block of wood to back up the panel while drilling it. Install one rivet at a time and be sure the panels are positioned tightly together when drilling.

To join the edges of 2 panel sections, use a ribbon section of sheet metal (at least 3 inches wide) and fit the ribbon up and behind the joining edges. Drill and rivet systematically. This method of joining panel edges will minimize warpage of the panels during the welding operation and is superior to a butt-welded edge.

Once the edges have been welded, grind the rivets away. Braze the holes closed or countersink the rivet holes and fill them with body filler.

Heat Shrinking

This is a technique used to repair a stretched metal surface. Heat makes the sheet metal malleable so it can be hammered back into its original shape.

> *WARNING*
> *Panel undercoatings can ignite or melt and run off. They can burn your hands severely. Always wear a glove on the hand used to work the dolly. Be sure to use only a clean shop rag which is free of any chemical residue. Have a fire extinguisher within reach. When possible, have a helper watch for fire when the torch is in use.*

1. Grind away all paint or body filler material.

2. Heat the stretched metal directly. Start by heating a circle an inch in diameter, gradually moving the torch inward toward the diameter of the circle. The metal will become red, then brighter red and then turn yellow. When the perimeter is cherry-red and the center of the circle is bright yellow, the metal is ready for working.

3. Quickly place the dolly behind the spot to be metal shrunk. Avoid backing up the sheet metal surface too firmly; you want to provide a backup in order to force a high spot down. If you hold the dolly too firmly against the sheet metal surface, it could further stretch the metal instead of shrinking it.

4. Use the shrinking hammer and work around the perimeter of the spot, tapping the stretched metal inward toward the center of the circle. Eight or ten light but firm strikes at the surface should accomplish this shrinking procedure.

5. Cool the spot slowly with a clean, water-saturated shop rag. Pass the wet rag across the surface slowly a number of times, cooling it gradually rather than all at once. You can see the metal shrink as it slowly cools.

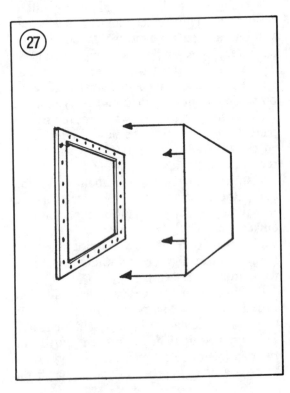

Feather-edging

Once the repair area has been completed, surrounding paint edges must be smoothed off and tapered back. This process is called "feather-edging." To feather-edge, sand the paint end-line with a sanding block held flat against the repair panel. You can feel the

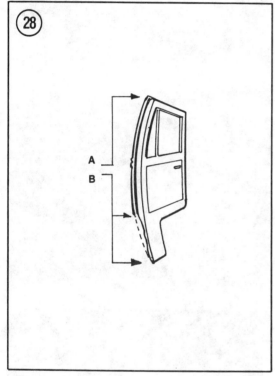

uneven edge with your hand, so taper the paint edge back until it is smooth to the touch.

Coarse sandpaper such as No. 180 or No. 220 may be used to accomplish the largest part of the feather-edging, but a good finish sanding should follow with No. 280 or No. 320 grit paper. Feather-edging must be done properly or the finish paint will magnify the defect.

Avoid dishing out the plastic body filler material in the process of feather-edging; use only moderate and even pressure at the paint end-line. Excessive pressure on the sanding paper will clog and dull its cutting ability. Keep the sandpaper cutting edges sharp by using plenty of water in the area being sanded.

Door Repair

Use the following procedure to repair the edge of a dented door. Lines A and B, **Figure 28** show the extent to which the damaged area differs from the original contour. To repair surface dents, also see *Quarter Panel Repair* in this chapter.

1. Hammer the damaged door edge back into the correct contour as indicated in **Figure 29**. Hold the dolly's surface hard against the outside sheet metal just below the spot you will strike with the hammer.

2. Continue hammering until the door edge assumes the correct contour above and below

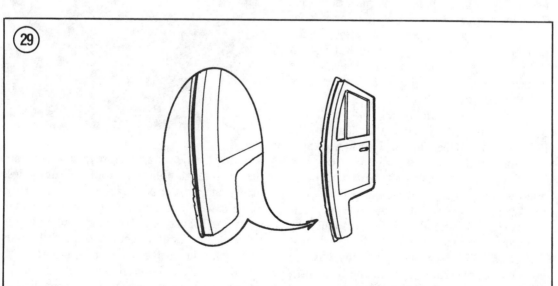

12

the damaged panel. Close the door periodically and check it for alignment with the pillar.

3. Move the dolly to the inside edge and again hold it firmly against the edge. The sheet metal may be doubled and even tripled at this point and difficult to move. Hammer solidly against the dolly's mass, driving high spots in (**Figure 30**).

4. Switch back and forth with the hammer and dolly combination from the inside to the outside surfaces of the door. Strike the metal only hard enough to move it a small amount each time.

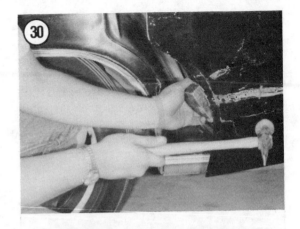

> ### NOTE
> *The door edge must be hammered as straight as possible. Using body filler on edges and surfaces of panels which open and close (hoods, doors, trunk lids) is not a good idea. The impact of closing these panels can jar the filler loose or crack it over a period of time.*

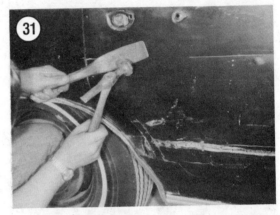

5. Use a spoon and hammer as required to contour the door panel and take out most of the high spots (**Figure 31**).

6. Grind the edge as required. If the grinding disc is too large to reach the really close or difficult areas of the inner door edge, cut a smaller grinding disc and mount it to the grinder. Once the contour line has been restored, you can repair the surface damage.

7. Grind the panel surface with an open-coat No. 16 disc or a "chopper" disc to remove the paint (**Figure 32**). Grind over to but not on the panel edge. Grind 2-3 inches beyond the damaged area. This will give a better picture of the extent of the damage.

8. Remove the trim panel and hold the combination dolly behind the dent at the lowest point of the damaged surface. Apply firm and steady pressure to the outside, then use the shrinking hammer with the other hand to strike soft blows at the perimeter of the dented surface. Unless the dent is extensive, the metal should respond by gradually moving outward. If the dented surface is tightly stressed, you may have to push harder with the dolly on the back side, but be careful to avoid stretching it.

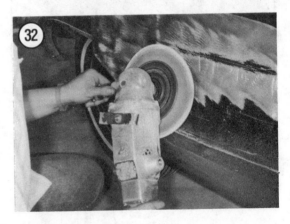

9. Once the dent has been reversed, even out the surface as follows. Hold the dolly less firmly against the back side and work on the outside with the hammer to drive the high spots in (**Figure 33**). Move around with the hammer and dolly to get all of the high spots and make the surface as even as possible.

10. Regrind the damaged area with a No. 36 or No. 50 grit (closed-coat) grinding disc to

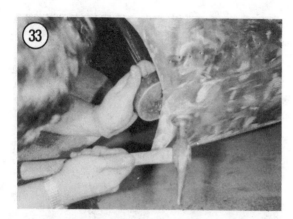

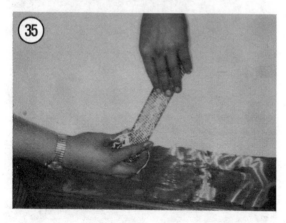

the area to be treated with body filler. The lowest area in the repair should not exceed 3/8 in. in depth.

14. Mix and apply sufficient body filler to completely fill the depressions and provide the surrounding metal with a light coating. Spread the filler in all directions, passing across the panel left to right, then wiping upward and downward. Apply enough pressure with the body filler spreader to work out any bubbles that might be trapped in the lowest area of the dent. Finish off with smooth light strokes across the entire damage area. See **Figure 34**.

15. Allow the filler to cure enough so it will grate away cleanly and not clog the cutting edge of the cheese-grater file. Grate the area evenly, moving left to right and diagonally. See **Figure 35**.

16. Let the body filler finish curing, then block sand the entire surface with No. 36 dry-type sandpaper. Let the sanding block lap over onto the bare metal surface to smooth out any grinding disc marks. Sand the body filler until the surface is even and smooth.

17. Repeat Step 16 with No. 80 dry-type sandpaper and apply enough pressure to remove the No. 36 sandpaper marks.

18. Feather-edge as necessary before applying any primer-surfacer. If you have ground off the entire side panel, feather-edging will be minimal. However, if the repair area is small, you may have to feather-edge all 4 sides of the repair.

19. Mask off the area to be primer-surfaced from the nearest panel edge or moulding line. Mask the inner panels also, as primer-surfacer will blow through the moulding holes and into the spaces between the panel openings. Sand the area around the repair surface with a No. 220 grit sandpaper to ensure a good bond between paint and primer-surfacer. Wipe and blow the area clean with compressed air.

20. Spray a coat of thinned primer-surfacer (follow manufacturer's instructions for thinning). Apply a double wet coat and let it flash, allowing the thinner time to evaporate out of the primer-surfacer. The panel can be sanded in about 2 hours.

remove the grinding marks and continue evening out the surface. Do not press too hard with the grinder, as overheating the surface will distort the sheet metal.

11. Check the panel for low and high spots. If any are found, repeat Step 10.

12. Repeat Step 11, then give the surface a final grinding with a No. 50 grit disc.

13. Make sure the panel is completely clean and that all paint has been ground away from

12

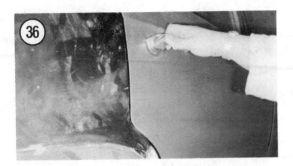

21. Check door alignment to make sure the crown line matches that of the quarter panel (**Figure 36**).

22. Sand the primer-surfacer with a No. 280 grit wet or dry sandpaper. Use water and a sponge to keep the panel wet while sanding. Sand only enough to get a clear picture of the surface condition.

23. Check the surface for low spots. If there are spots that additional coatings will not sufficiently fill in, use spot putty. Wipe small amounts of the putty directly into the scratches. Small amounts will dry hard in an hour or less. Large amounts applied all at once will not dry, but will shrink and crack instead. Spot putty must be applied a little at a time, in separate applications, and must always be sanded between applications.

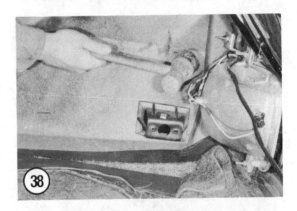

24. Once the deep scratches and other imperfections have been filled with spot putty, allowed to dry and block sanded, spray the area with another double wet coat of primer-surfacer. Let this flash, then spray another coating in the same manner. You can apply up to 6-8 coats of primer-surfacer, letting each one flash off between coatings.

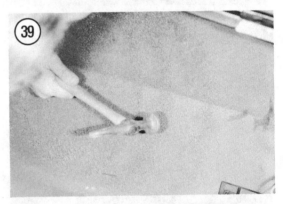

25. Once the final coat of primer-surfacer has been applied, let the surface stand for about 2 hours, then sand it with a No. 280 or No. 320 grit paper. Use the sponge and water to wet the panel while sanding.

26. Allow the sanded surface to dry 2-3 hours and then spray 2 additional double wet coats of primer-surfacer.

27. Let the surface dry for at least 8 hours. When thoroughly dry, sand with No. 400 grit wet or dry sandpaper and use plenty of water to flush the panel.

28. Allow the area to dry, then apply a primer-sealer undercoating.

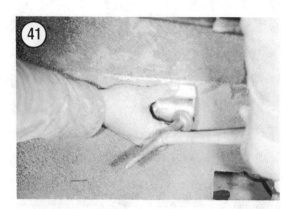

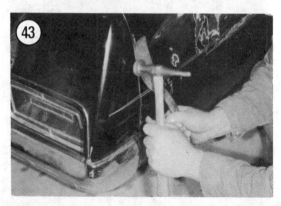

Quarter Panel Repair

Use the following procedure to remove scrapes and creases from quarter panels. See **Figure 37** (typical).

1. Remove any panel trim mouldings and clips that will interfere with the repair, if so equipped.

2. Remove the marker light, if so equipped.

3. Start working the dent from the inside with a hard rubber hammer to bring the panel closer to its original shape (**Figure 38**).

4. Place the dolly on the outside of the panel and work the dent from the inside with a shrinking hammer (**Figure 39**).

5. If there are tight spots close to the panel corners that are difficult to reach with the head of the shrinking hammer, use a pick hammer as shown in **Figure 40**. Do not back up the panel with a dolly when using the pick hammer.

6. Once the panel is fairly smooth, work the entire area slowly and evenly from the inside with the hammer and dolly to bring the damaged area back to its original shape. See **Figure 41**.

7. Carefully remove any high spots with a body file (**Figure 42**).

8. Use a spoon and hammer as shown in **Figure 43** to match the end of the panel with the fender cap.

9. If the panel has a sculpture line, it must be redefined. A contour file used above and below the line will help to restore it (**Figure 44**).

10. After the panel has been straightened and contoured as best you can, grind the panel with a No. 24 disc to remove all paint in and around the damaged area (**Figure 45**).

12

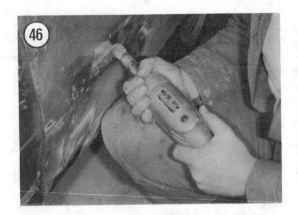

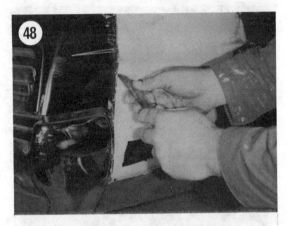

11. Remove any paint from low spots with a rotary brush (**Figure 46**) or body filler will not adhere properly.

12. Wipe on enough body filler to completely fill the depressions and to provide the surrounding metal with a light coating. Spread the filler in all directions, passing across the panel from left to right, then wiping upward and downward. Apply sufficient pressure to work out any bubbles that might be trapped in the lowest areas of the dent. Finish off with smooth light strokes across the entire damage area (**Figure 47**).

13. Remove any excess filler from between adjacent panels with a sharp instrument while the filler is still wet (**Figure 48**).

14. Grate off the area evenly, moving left to right and diagonally (**Figure 49**). The filler should be cured enough that it grates away cleanly and does not clog the cutting edge of the cheese-grater file.

15. Perform Steps 16-28 of *Door Repair* in this chapter.

Fender Wheelwell Repair

Use the following procedure to remove scrapes, dents and creases from fender wheelwells. **Figure 50** shows typical damage of this type.

1. Remove any panel trim mouldings and clips that will interfere with the repair, if so equipped.

2. Remove the headlight, tail light or marker light as required.

3. Grind the damaged area to re-establish the wheelwell opening line (**Figure 51**). Use a No. 24 grit open-coat disc and work both the

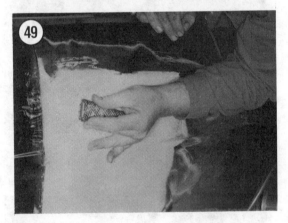

dented area and 2-3 inches outside the perimeter of the dent.

4. For larger wheelwell dents, dolly out the wheelwell opening or hammer it from behind. Don't stretch the metal with strong hammer blows; work on points of stress.

5. Once the wheelwell line has been re-established as well as possible, switch the dolly to the backside of the dent and start

metal moves. Try to move it a small amount with each blow. This will return the metal to form without stretching it.

7. When the wheelwell has been straighted and the line re-established as best you can, regrind the damaged area with a No. 36 or No. 50 closed-coat disc. Avoid overheating the surface area with the grinder as this can distort the surface contour.

8. Wipe on enough body filler to completely fill the depressions and to provide the surrounding metal with a light coating. Spread the filler in all directions, passing across the panel from left to right, then wiping upward and downward. Apply sufficient pressure to work out any bubbles that might be trapped in the lowest areas of the dent. Finish off with smooth light strokes across the entire damage area.

9. Grate off the area evenly, moving left to right and diagonally (**Figure 52**). The filler should be cured enough that it grates away cleanly and does not clog the cutting edge of the cheese-grater file.

10. Perform Steps 16-28 of *Door Repair* in this chapter.

REFINISHING

Once you have completed the repair, it must be masked and painted. The best approach, of course, is to have the job done by a professional. If you're experienced with spraying paint, you might consider renting a spray gun and compressor to do the job.

However, advances in spray can technology have made it possible for many home mechanics to apply the paint themselves without special equipment, provided the area to be sprayed is not too large. You can buy the necessary primer-sealer and top coat at your local auto supply store; most stock a variety of automotive paint supplies in spray can form. You'll also need a supply of tack clothes and masking paper/tape. If it's just a small job, you can often get by using old newspapers as a substitute for regular masking paper.

If paint is to be applied over part of the older painted surface, rough it up with sandpaper to provide a good tooth for the new coat. Use a sanding block, No. 400 grit

working to relieve the points of stress. These are usually at the perimeter of the dented surface.

6. Position the dolly to provide backup for the hammering operation. Drive the high spots down and bring the low spots up from behind with the dolly. Work to even out the surface. Watch closely while you strike with the hammer and check how much the sheet

12

wet-or-dry sandpaper and water. Be sure to sand horizontally from left to right; a circular motion leaves sand scratches that will show through the finish coat.

Remove the sanding dust with compressed air, if available. Avoid cleaning the surface with water, as some may remain between body panels, door jambs or the like. Absolutely no moisture should be present when you start spraying. Once all sanding dust has been removed, wash the surface down with a solvent-type cleaner like Prep-Sol or Pre-Kleano.

Mask off the area to be painted. If you're painting an entire panel, masking is a simple matter. Masking is more difficult when you're painting a small portion of a panel such as a door crease or wheelwell dent. The idea is to paint small repairs in such a way that they do not look as if they have just been painted. This usually involves painting a somewhat larger area than that repaired, in order to take advantage of body contour lines that will help blend the fresh paint into the old. Masking should be done carefully to prevent the possibility of overspray on adjacent panels, glass or trim.

When masking is completed and you are ready to spray the primer-surfacer, run a clean tack rag over the entire surface to remove any contamination. Primer-surfacer should be sprayed in very light coats so it will dry uniformly. If sprayed in a single heavy coat, it will dry with pinholes which will affect the adhesion and appearance of the color coats.

To apply the primer-surfacer (and subsequent color coats), hold the spray can parallel with one end of the panel and about 14-18 inches away. Depress the finger spray valve tip and draw the can across the surface, keeping the two parallel. Do not release the spray valve until you've reached the masking paper on the other side of the panel. Make as many passes from side-to-side as necessary to cover the area to be painted. Each spray pass should slightly overlap the previous one. Don't worry if they don't blend together perfectly—it's better to spray two light coats than a heavy one that may run or sag.

Let the primer-surfacer flash off, then give the surface a light sanding (left-to-right) with No. 400 grit dry sandpaper. Blow off the sanding dust and repeat the tack cloth/Prep-Sol or Pre-Kleano treatment. If the first coat did not completely cover the panel area, repeat the procedure a second time.

Most painters recommend at least 24 hours between applying the primer-surface and the first color coat. When you're ready to apply the color coat, it's done in the same manner as applying the primer-surfacer; spray a light coat with overlapping passes. Let the paint flash off and spray a second coat, if necessary.

Be sure to choose your paint area carefully. If you must spray outdoors, pick a day with a moderate temperature (75° F), no wind and keep the surface to be painted out of direct sunlight. If you work indoors, make sure there is adequate ventilation and good lighting available.

When you've finished spraying, resist the temptation to remove the masking paper. Let the finished job stand 2-4 hours. This will give the paint sufficient time to dry completely. Removing the masking paper too soon can result in ragged paint edges or other defects.

VINYL TOP REPAIR

Properly cared for, a vinyl top will often last the life of the vehicle. Unfortunately, the vinyl top is generally the most neglected part of the vehicle's exterior surface. Replacing a damaged vinyl top can cost several hundred dollars.

Two types of vinyl tops are installed: those with pads and those without pads. The padded top is more difficult and expensive to install and less can be done to repair it once deterioration sets in. The unpadded top is cemented directly to the metal roof of the vehicle but it can be repaired fairly easily if necessary.

A vinyl top should be treated periodically with wax or other solution designed to keep the vinyl supple. This will reduce the possibility of cracking or splitting. Vinyl sprays are also available from auto supply

stores. This material is used just as spray paint and is ideal to restore or change the color of a faded top. Like spray paint, it should be applied in light, thin coats and allowed to flash-off before a second coat is applied. Depending upon the color involved, it may require several coats to obtain the desired appearance.

A vinyl top should be periodically inspected for cracks, splits or signs that it is buckling or coming loose. Any cracks or splits should be sealed as soon as possible to prevent moisture from entering and further loosening the cement. An ideal way to do this is to apply a small quantity of a silicone rubber sealer used to install windshields. This will fill up the crack or split and make it watertight. Once the sealer has dried thoroughly (usually 48 hours), touch up the repaired area with a can of vinyl spray. If the top is sufficiently faded, this is a good time to restore the color with the vinyl spray while hiding the repaired spots.

If the condition of the top is allowed to deteriorate sufficiently, loose spots will develop where the cement no longer holds the vinyl to the metal surface. In such cases, the force of the wind while driving may be enough to lift and rip a weakened section of the top. See **Figure 53**.

If this occurs, an unpadded vinyl top can be repaired at home. Most vinyl top shops will turn down a repair job, preferring instead to install a new top. To do it yourself, start by studying the top and the damage. You do not want to install a patch, as there is no way to hide the fact. The best plan of action is to remove a portion of the top and install a new section to cover that removed. The size of the piece removed and replaced will depend upon the top itself and the amount of damage.

The greatest difficulty encountered is in matching the new top section to the old one. Vinyl used for automotive tops usually have a pebble-grained finish and like all consumer items, the style and color of the finish changes periodically. If the top is several years old, it may be difficult to locate repair material with the same style or color of finish.

Most shops that install vinyl tops buy their tops precut and sewn from a manufacturer. While it may be possible to locate a scrap of material large enough to do the job at a vinyl top shop, you should also check out upholstery shops and stores which sell cloth. They can generally offer advice and help in locating a suitable replacement vinyl.

Once you have located a piece of replacement vinyl, you'll need a quart of contact cement, a metal straightedge and cutting knife, scissors and a brush that can be used to remove bubbles when the material is applied.

The job is far easier when the metal trim strips are removed, but this can also pose problems. Most trim strips are held in place by plastic snap clips, which tend to become brittle with age. Trim strips and their retainers, like the vinyl top itself, are changed periodically by the industry and it may prove difficult to obtain new snap clips if the old ones break when the trim strip is removed. Work carefully and pry the trim strips free, saving the snap clips.

Use the straightedge and knife to cut away the section to be replaced. You'll want a perfectly straight line to match, so work carefully. Any crooked lines will stand out and ruin the appearance of your repair. If some areas of that part of the vinyl top to be removed still adhere to the metal, use a hair drier to heat the surface. This will generally loosen the adhesive enough to allow the vinyl to be pulled free.

Square up one end of the replacement material with the straightedge and knife to assure a perfectly straight replacement line. With the replacement material upside down, run a length of the double-adhesive tape used to install mirror tile along the end just squared up and carefully fold this over. The result will be a double thick strip of vinyl material where it will match the remainder of the top.

Position the replacement material on the top of the vehicle and overlap the replacement line on the old top with the new material. Carefully trim for an approximate fit along the sides and front, remembering that the vinyl will stretch when it is installed. At this stage, however, it is better to cut too little than too much. Once the replacement section has been semi-fitted to the old top, remove and carefully roll it up to prevent any damage.

Any adhesive remaining on the metal, as well as any rust spots that may have developed, must be sanded off. The replacement section must have a clean, smooth surface for proper adhesion when the new cement is applied. A reciprocating or rotary sander will generally do the job (**Figure 54**). Change grit paper frequently, as the dried contact cement tends to clog the grit quickly.

Once all dried cement and/or rust has been removed from the metal surface, wipe the surface with a cloth moistened in paint thinner to remove all dust and residue. When the thinner has flashed-off, you're ready to begin spreading a coat of contact cement on the metal and the underside of the replacement vinyl. Follow the manufacturer's instructions carefully and work quickly at this point, as the cement on one will be drying while you are applying it to the other.

Start by spreading enough newpapers to provide a working surface for the vinyl. Unroll the vinyl and apply the cement with a paint brush. You should start with the vinyl, since its surface is quite porous and the cement will take longer to set up. When this is finished, apply a coat to the metal top of the vehicle (**Figure 55**). Make sure the cement is applied uniformly and thinly. If the application is too thick, it will not set up properly.

While waiting for the cement to set up, run another strip of double-adhesive mirror tile tape along the front edge of the remaining

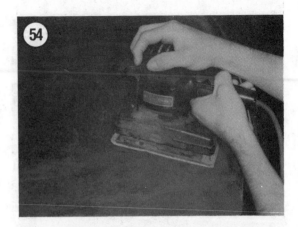

vinyl top on the vehicle. When the replacement vinyl is installed, you will place its double-thick edge on this strip. This not only helps to prevent the entry of water under the seam, it further raises the seam line and creates the illusion of a manufactured seam.

This is more satisfactory than a butt seam, as it protects the old top seam line from inclement weather and prevents further deterioration of the cement under the top. Depending upon the top and vehicle on which you're working, you may want to futher emphasize this line when the replacement portion has been installed by screwing a thin metal strip about one inch wide across the double-thick edge. While strictly cosmetic, this can make the seam more acceptable visually.

When the contact cement has lost its tackiness, you should have the help of an assistant to install the replacement material. Carefully climb onto the trunk lid (be careful

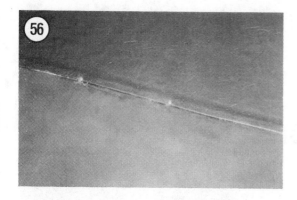

strokes, just as you'd apply wallpaper. Work quickly and carefully to remove all bubbles while your assistant pulls forward on the replacment material to stretch it properly.

Once all bubbles or wrinkles have been brushed out, reinstall the trim strip snap clips and fit the trim strips into place. This should satisfactorily hold the sides and front of the replacement material in position. If you have broken one or more of the snap clips during removal and could not obtain additional new ones, it may be necessary to secure the trim with sheet metal screws.

Drill holes through the trim strip and into the roof metal with a 3/16 in. bit and install suitable length sheet metal screws as required. If done properly, the head of the screw can be painted the same color as the trim strip and will not be noticeable, especially if evenly spaced instead of randomly installed.

The rear seam of the repair may be further strengthened by installing the metal strip mentioned earlier, or by installing several sheet metal screws (**Figure 56**). When finished, run a thin bead of the rubber silicone windshield sealer along the seam edge as a further precaution against the entry of water.

The end result will be a vinyl top that appears to have been professionally installed, restoring its serviceability as well as its good looks (**Figure 57**). This will enhance the appearance of your vehicle, as well as saving you the cost of a new top.

not to dent it) and have him hand you the material. He should then position himself on the hood. Have him hold the front end of the material above the cemented surface while you align the rear seam.

When the seam is properly aligned on the mirror tape, brush the replacement section onto the top of the vehicle with wide curving

INDEX

13